Praise for The Yugas

"This book may change your view of history and your understanding of the future. *The Yugas* by Selbie and Steinmetz reveals the little known teachings of Sri Yukteswar and Paramhansa Yogananda regarding the cycles of humankind's cultural, social, and spiritual evolution—which differs greatly from the history of civilization to be found in our present textbook dogmas. The cycles of enlightenment that Sri Yukteswar began teaching nearly 120 years ago—and many of the discoveries that he predicted—are now being verified by modern science. The coming of the great Energy Age taught by the master teacher Sri Yukteswar and his most famous disciple Paramhansa Yogananda promises an enlightened future for all who recognize the coming of a raising of consciousness for the human species. Selbie and Steinmetz have produced a text that is both well-researched and an exciting, informative read."

—Brad Steiger, author of *Worlds Before Our Own* and Sherry Steiger, author of *Indian Wisdom and Its Guiding Power*

"The book casts an important new light on the history and evolution of the human race and the mysteries of the great cycles of time that we must all honor. All those who want to understand our species and the hidden cosmic influences that govern our lives will benefit from its detailed examination. Those who study the book carefully will come away with a transformed vision of our world and its spiritual potentials."

—David Frawley (Pandit Vamadeva Shastri), author of *Astrology of the Seers* and *Yoga and Ayurveda*

"*The Yugas* by Selbie and Steinmetz is an excellent and easy read that challenges the notion that ancient man was simplistic and unaccomplished, within the framework first put forth by Swami Sri Yukteswar in *The Holy Science*."

—Michael Kane, host of Distopian Times

"*The Yugas* presents us with a glimpse into the future. Not only mankind's future, but also our own personal future, as we journey through our way to enlightenment. An understanding of these cycles of *Yugas* as a natural process of growth and development, and not of wars and perpetual suffering, un-blurs our vision of our inner potential. Taken from the teachings of Sri Yukteswar and his student, Paramhansa Yogananda, The Yugas is a profound gift from a great master and his beloved disciple."

—Robert R. Hieronimus, PhD, host of 21st Century Radio,
author of *United Symbolism of America*

"Steinmetz and Selbie are to be congratulated in their brilliant attempt to change the course of our stereotyped thinking about cosmology, ancient history, and modern science.... All over the ancient world we find quantum leaps of the intellect far beyond the concepts we have about that age. How and why do these occur? The authors of this book have delved deep into the esoteric secrets of many ancient traditions and come up with their own unique contribution to the nature of these strange occurrences."

—Mata Devi Vanamali, Vanamali Ashram, Rishikesh,
author of *The Play of God*

"This consciousness-raising study, which presents a profound and necessary challenge to conventional science, is a vital addition to the growing recognition among independent researchers that ancient civilizations were often far more technologically or spiritually advanced than we are today.... In an indispensable work, both intellectually and emotionally satisfying, Selbie and Steinmetz bring us a stirring new paradigm which reveals how our power to transform ourselves is the measure of our power to transform the world in accordance with the cosmic pattern."

—Geoff Ward, host of Mysterious Planet, author of
Spirals: the Pattern of Existence

"Selbie and Steinmetz have given us a thesis that is uncompromisingly accurate in its chronicle of significant events and their correspondence to the yugas—cycles of human consciousness—in which they occurred. What emerges is an astonishing, compelling, and altogether enlightened view of evolution itself."

—James Surendra Conti, East-West Bookstore

"This potentially transformational book... contains the most incisive and useful information on these cosmic epochs that I have ever seen.... Information is power, and in this case, interpretation and explanation is power—power toward personal transformation. The great wisdom of Yukteswar and Yogananda, which has been revered and uplifted by Yogananda's disciple Kriyananda, is thus passed down through the ages."

—Katherine Diehl, journalist

"After years of intensive research, Selbie and Steinmetz have turned their findings into a complete and comprehensive whole with some amazing and revolutionary looks on human history—and have brought to light long-forgotten wisdom of ancient civilizations far more advanced than previously thought in spirituality, philosophy, and maybe even science. If you are interested in the history of humanity and the anticipations and possible enrichments that their teachings might bring us, both now and in the future, then this book is definitely a must-read."

—A. G. M. Pietrow, Founder of Parascientifica.com

"*The Yugas* presents the optimistic view that the rapid changes that we see in our times are inexorably leading us to a better day for humanity; we are at just the beginning of a journey through a series of ascending epochs, during which the expression of mankind will only improve."

—Alexandra Bruce, author of *2012: Science or Superstition* and *Beyond the Bleep*

"*The Yugas* is a brilliantly written text based on extensive historical research validating the theory of the ages of human development proposed by Swami Sri Yukteswar in *The Holy Science*. This book provides us with an optimistic view of our future as we leave the remnants of *Kali Yuga* or the dark age in our past. *The Yugas* explores the current electrical age of *Dwapara Yuga*. This enlightening age brings the opportunity of illumination and peace on our planet as we navigate toward the divine light of the central Sun."

— Dennis M. Harness, PhD, Vedic Astrologer, writer, and author of
The Nakshatras: The Lunar Mansions of Vedic Astrology

"*The Yugas* gave me a glimpse of the sweeping panorama of the ages. My mind shifted. My consciousness was transformed. If you are at all interested in where humanity has been and where we are headed, I highly recommend that you read this book."

— Richard Salva, author of *The Reincarnation of Abraham Lincoln* and *Walking with William of Normandy*

"*The Yugas* [is] an extraordinary source of detailed information about the little known concept of the Cosmic Cycles of time. The details given in *The Yugas* can be used as a source of knowledge and inspiration for understanding the natural movements occurring in our earthly existence."

— Patricia Morris Cardona, Cosmic Mysteries School

THE YUGAS

THE YUGAS

Keys to Understanding Man's Hidden Past,
Emerging Present and Future Enlightenment

From the Teachings of Sri Yukteswar
& Paramhansa Yogananda

Joseph Selbie and David Steinmetz
Foreword by Swami Kriyananda

CRYSTAL CLARITY PUBLISHERS   Commerce, California

CRYSTAL CLARITY PUBLISHERS
1123 Goodrich Blvd. | Commerce, California
crystalclarity.com | 800.424.1055
clarity@crystalclarity.com

ISBN   978-1-56589-253-8 (print)
ISBN   978-1-56589-634-5 (e-book)
Library of Congress Cataloging-in-Publication Data 2010000978

Cover design and layout by Renée Glenn Designs
Interior design and layout by Michele Madhavi Molloy

Dedication

We dedicate this book to the notion that

understanding enables change,

and to the observation that

a new paradigm must be established

before an old paradigm can fade away.

Contents

THE YUGAS

Satya

Satya

Treta

Treta

Dwapara

Dwapara

Kali

Kali

Present

Foreword

By Swami Kriyananda

I am sincerely pleased to be able to recommend this book, with enthusiastic applause. The subject has long interested me — indeed, from my youth. But I am deeply impressed by the depth of research and the astuteness with which the authors have approached their subject. I have written several books myself that included some of the points contained here, but this book goes far beyond my own minor contribution to the subject.

It was Swami Sri Yukteswar, in his book *The Holy Science*, who first propounded this revolutionary explanation for changes that have occurred in human consciousness over the centuries. I had already written a "source theme" in high school for my English class, when I was sixteen, which showed my fascination even then with ancient civilizations. Not to belabor what may seem a purely personal point of view, what interested me then, and what interests me as much today nearly seventy years later, is that I found the traditional explanation for ancient civilizations wholly unsatisfactory. It made (and makes) no sense to me for mankind to have spent many thousands of years as a "hunter and gatherer," and then suddenly to appear in a mere instant, so to speak, as the founder of great civilizations, complete with cities, industries, literature, education, and sophisticated cosmologies.

The name I chose for my source theme went something like this: "Ancient civilizations and their view of the universe." (I had wanted to study, further, what it was in those civilizations that had influenced people to develop those views, but here I was forced to admit failure; I could discover no such subjective influences.)

Mankind must, from the start, have had all the intelligence he needed to build cities and, with them, the appurtenances of a sophisticated civilization. Indeed, I'd read that the brain capacity of Cro-Magnon Man was larger than our own. And I wondered, on reading Egyptian history, how it happened that such a mighty civilization, after building the great pyramids, had descended to the level of mediocrity that has been evident in historic times. I simply wasn't convinced by the conclusions reached by the historians, developed from the data they had gathered. In fact, the more I read their conclusions, the more I inclined to agree with Napoleon's statement, "History is a lie agreed upon."

One thing that bothered me about the insights of so many historians, antiquarians, and other "specialists" was that they allowed facts to assume a separate reality of their own, seeming quite inadequate in their understanding of human nature. It was as if their approach to history had been only to gather those facts, but to make no attempt to place themselves actually in the shoes of the people they wrote about.

One wonderful thing about Sri Yukteswar's revelations (and to me they did in fact seem revelatory) was that he wrote at a time when a descending cycle of enlightenment—as described in this book—could be observed merging historically into an ascending cycle, and bringing radical change in human awareness with the birth of our present era, or *yuga*, of energy. Many facts of history over the last three thousand years are more or less known. Sri Yukteswar's explanation of those facts was, for me, deeply satisfying. This book presents his thesis with crystal clarity.

Selbie and Steinmetz have, in my opinion, produced a work of genius. They have gone, I think, as deeply into this subject as present-day knowledge permits. I am convinced that, living as we do in a cosmic environment, and one infinitely greater, therefore, than our environment on this little Earth, we are influenced also by that larger environment. We cannot but be affected: not only in our weather, but even in our consciousness. I am persuaded that many changes in human awareness take place not only because of the accretion of knowledge, but also in response to waves of conscious energy flowing into our planet from outside. For I believe that cosmic energy affects even human intelligence and awareness.

I am so enthusiastic on these points, indeed, that my very interest might induce me to repeat some of the points so excellently covered in this book! Let me therefore bow off the stage at this point, with only this comment: If you aren't satisfied with what you've read, or been taught, about the linear development of civilization, you will find in this book an alternate picture of our Earth's history that will, I think, thrill you.

Acknowledgements

This book could not have been written were it not for Sri Yukteswar and Paramhansa Yogananda. Their twentieth century writings and teachings led the way in making the ancient teachings of India understandable to the Western mind. The significance of the yugas, in particular, had become lost in Indian tradition, but these two great souls presented the yugas anew, in simple clarity, giving them fresh relevance to our modern energy age.

This book also owes a great debt to the many talks and articles of Swami Kriyananda (J. Donald Walters) on the impact and qualities of the yugas. He has added rich dimension and depth of detail to our understanding of the yugas.

We would also like to acknowledge the legions of scientists and researchers willing to explore beyond orthodoxy — be they archeologists, professionals, and gifted amateurs alike, who are not satisfied with the standard linear theory of human development, or doctors and biologists, who are not satisfied with the standard material theory of human consciousness. Their dedicated work, and their thousands of books, articles, and lectures, present for all to see an astonishing number of unsolved mysteries of the ancient past, and fundamental gaps in our modern understanding of man.

We would like to thank the many people, too numerous to name, whose kind words and encouragement helped keep this book moving forward. We want to thank several people who have helped directly with the writing and publishing of this book: Prakash Van Cleave, Anandi Cornell, Richard Salva, Latika Parojinog, Leah Kirk, Timothy Hickey, Madhavi Molloy, Renée Glenn, Skip Barrett, and Naidhruva Rush.

Finally we want to thank both of our wives, Janakidevi Steinmetz and Lakshmi Selbie for their many, many hours of editing, and for their unfailing patience and support.

Introduction

In 1905 Albert Einstein turned the world of physics upside down—for the first time the world saw the now famous equation, $E=mc^2$. Einstein fundamentally altered our understanding of the physical universe by proving that all matter was essentially condensed energy.

The nineteenth century view of the physical world was primarily mechanical; all matter was considered solid and fundamentally immutable. Although matter was considered to be made up of infinitesimally small objects, these were seen as solid objects nonetheless, and were believed to obey the same basic laws as did the sun and the planets. Time, too, was thought to be an unyielding constant throughout the universe, unaffected by changing conditions. In the nineteenth century the universe was seen as a very large machine, a clockwork of infinite size, functioning precisely and inexorably in its slow grandeur.

Today we hold a very different view of the physical world. All matter is understood to be energy in a condensed form. Not only do we consider matter mutable, we know that the tiniest atom is capable of being transmuted into vast amounts of energy. Both the incredibly destructive force of nuclear weapons, and the prodigious energy of nuclear power, testify to the profound implications of the deceptively simple equation $E=mc^2$.

Our view of the larger universe has also undergone a revolution. We now know that objects in space do not move in straight lines—because there *are* no straight lines. Space itself is curved and the universe is finite. No physical object can go faster than the speed of light. The speed of light is, in fact, the only constant in the universe—all else is measurable only in relation to that constant. Even time is understood to be relative to light.

The atom, previously conceived of as a constellation of tiny objects, like a miniature solar system with the nucleus taking the place of the sun (you probably made a model of one in sixth grade), has given way to a concept that cannot even be visualized. Physicists now conceive of the atom as a tiny area of space in which objects wink into and out of the quantum, subatomic world—a world where the very act of trying to observe the atom actually changes what is observed. Niels Bohr, the eminent early twentieth-century physicist and Nobel Prize winner, called the quantum world Potentia. Others have referred to it as quantum flux or quantum foam, an energetic maelstrom just below the threshold of measurable perception.

String theory, the latest "theory of everything," goes even further. String theory posits that there are no actual physical structures at all, that even the unimaginably small sub-atomic structures that physicists try to study, such as quarks, are, in reality, made up of even smaller vibrating strings and rings of energy.

Just a little more than a hundred years ago we understood our world to be made up of matter, interacted with by energy. Now we understand our world to be made up of energy, assuming the form of matter.

Today we are on the brink of another major conceptual change — this time, not in the field of physics, but in the field of history and the development of civilization. Just as Einstein overturned conventional thinking due to the anomalous, but undeniable fact that the speed of light is constant, history and archeology are similarly confronted with undeniable anomalies that are beginning to overturn conventional thinking about the course of man's development.

The current theory of the development of mankind is linear, much as was the nineteenth century's view of the universe. According to current theory, prior to roughly 8000 BC, mankind existed in wandering tribes of hunter-gatherers on the edge of survival. Sometime between 8000 and 3000 BC, mankind learned to cultivate crops and domesticate livestock. These agricultural skills are believed to have allowed groups of people to settle in one place permanently, and because they had adequate food supplies, to have significantly increased their chances of survival. Once populations were permanently settled, large structures were built for the first time, trading and commerce began, language developed, government became necessary, tools and implements became more complex and useful — and this development continued in a more or less straight line culminating in today's modern civilization.

However, there are many facts that simply do not fit into the theory of mankind's development as described above. Some of these anomalous facts that don't fit into conventional theories have come to light recently as the result of applying modern scientific disciplines, such as DNA mapping and radiometric dating, to artifacts from the past. Other anomalous facts have been around so long that their very familiarity blurs their significance—but they are staring us right in the face!

The most famous structures in the world are the Pyramids of Giza, sited together with the enigmatic Sphinx. To this day, after thousands of years of conjecture, we still don't know two of the most basic things about the pyramids: how they were built and why they were built.

Mainstream historians and archeologists maintain that the pyramids were built over the course of two or three decades by thousands of workers, using simple tools. Even if we grant that a primitive culture could figure out how to transport the vast amounts of stone to the building site, we are still left with the mystery of how they cut, dressed, and placed 2.5 million blocks at an average rate of one block every four minutes for twenty years. Some of these blocks weigh as much as 70 tons and were taken to a height nearly half that of the Empire State Building. Further, if conventional thinking is to be accepted, all this was accomplished using only wood, stone, or copper tools, and plaited ropes.

Even if a "primitive culture" can plausibly be shown capable of dealing with such major construction challenges, no one has been able to explain the degree of accuracy and skill achieved in the construction. Nor has anyone been able to explain how a "primitive culture" could have *designed* such complex structures (which needed to be designed *in detail* before they were begun), or how such a culture could have maintained the organizational commitment, for two or three decades, that was required to build the pyramids.

The accuracy and skill demonstrated by the construction of the pyramids is remarkable even by today's standards. The base of the Great Pyramid, the largest of the three central pyramids, covers an area of thirteen acres, *yet the level of its base does not vary more than five-eighths of an inch*. The joints between the stone blocks facing the pyramid are not mortared, and are cut so accurately that one cannot put something even as thin as a credit card between the stones.

Of the "Seven Wonders of the Ancient World" the Great Pyramid of Giza is the only one still standing—and it may still be standing long after the skyscrapers of today fall down. It was built with amazing foresight: the site has been able to support the weight of the heaviest structure on earth for thousands of years, without the pyramid shifting or tipping.

Mainstream archeologists and historians date the construction of the Sphinx and the Pyramids of Giza to approximately 2500 to 2900 BC, but there is intriguing evidence that the Great Sphinx may be far older than the Pyramids. The age of ancient structures is often determined by carbon dating any wood or organic material found in the structure, but the Sphinx is made entirely of stone, offering nothing to carbon date. However, the long-term weathering effects of wind and water on stone do give us a rough estimate. Geologist Dr. Robert Schoch, a well-respected scientist and a tenured member of Boston University's faculty, makes a convincing argument that the results of water erosion found on the Sphinx indicate that it was carved *at least* 7,000 years ago, far, far earlier than accepted by conventional theory.

We might be excused for ignoring the significance of the Sphinx and the Pyramids, if they were the only anomalies that didn't fit into a linear view of history and man's development of civilization.

But there are many more anomalies.

Mainstream thinking has it that man learned to cultivate crops and domesticate animals in a period of a few thousand years (8000 to 3000 BC), more or less haphazardly, in isolated areas such as the Fertile Crescent, the Indus River Valley in Pakistan, or the Yellow River Valley in China. New scientific methods applied to artifacts unearthed in recently excavated archeological sites around the world, however, indicate that domesticated animals and cultivated grains existed far earlier than 8000 BC. Evidence of domesticated goats and sheep has been found in Afghanistan dating back to 13,000 BC, and recent research indicates that cultivated spelt grains found in Israel date to 21,000 BC.

Mainstream thinking has it that mankind learned to build structures gradually, by trial and error, learning from mistakes and often building on top of the older, cruder structures. This pattern of development holds true back to about 500 BC. Archeologists working under modern Rome have found, for example, that the more recent, upper layers of their excavations employ more sophisticated building techniques, and that the older, lower layers employ more primitive building techniques.

There are even older archeological finds, however, that reveal the pattern of development in reverse. In the ancient ruins of Mohenjo-daro, near the Indus River in Pakistan, the oldest layers (from approximately 3000 BC) revealed the most sophisticated buildings. City streets were laid out in straight lines with cross streets and formed a grid similar to that found in modern cities. Houses had running water, radiant heat, and systems for sanitation. There were public baths and plazas. And perhaps most intriguing, there were standard-sized bricks and standard weights used consistently in the construction of buildings in an area of 100,000 square miles. By contrast, later development in the same area became increasingly less sophisticated over the succeeding centuries, until by 1500 BC the building standards were significantly poorer.

Mainstream historical and archeological thinking has it that language developed in isolated areas around the world, and that, through time, languages mixed and borrowed from one another until we have what we know today. Yet there is solid linguistic evidence that all Western languages from Finnish to English, from Hebrew to French can trace their origins back to Sanskrit, the most ancient language of India. Furthermore, Sanskrit, one of the most complex and sophisticated written languages in the world, can be traced back to at least 7000 BC; *even then*, it possessed a greater degree of structural and grammatical sophistication than it has today. It would be more true to say that the Western languages of today *devolved* from Sanskrit rather than that they *evolved* from Sanskrit.

These and other anomalous facts and discoveries simply do not fit with the current linear theory of the development of civilization. Not only do we need to push the dates of man's development farther and farther into the past, but we have to find a way to understand how mankind knew many things in the distant past that are now considered modern knowledge. How is it possible that the Sphinx was carved perhaps as long as 7,000 years ago? How was it possible for the pyramids, some of the most well-constructed structures in the world, ancient or modern, to be built with such accuracy and skill at the supposed *dawn* of civilization? How was it possible for ancient man to already be using cultivated grains 23,000 years ago? How can the earliest construction of an ancient city, such as Mohenjo-daro, be the best? How could Sanskrit have started out as one of the most complete and well-structured languages in the world over 9,000 years ago?

The picture that emerges from these and myriad other mysteries is that mankind had highly sophisticated knowledge in the past, much earlier, than is commonly thought—and that mankind lost much of that knowledge for several thousand years between then and now.

What could explain this?

~~~~~~~~~~~~~

In 1894, near Calcutta, a small work was written — *The Holy Science*, by Swami Sri Yukteswar. In the introduction to this slim volume, Sri Yukteswar not only explained the knowledge and sophistication of the past, but also predicted the explosion of knowledge in the twentieth century. He further predicted that the keynote discovery for the twentieth century would be that all matter is made up of "fine matters and electricities." Sri Yukteswar's prediction was made over twenty years before, and a world away from, the publication in 1905 of Einstein's theory of relativity, including $E=mc^2$, that energy and matter are equivalent. Sri Yukteswar did not write as a scientist, but as a seer and sage, and as a modern exponent of the wisdom long held in India's ancient tradition of teachers and texts.

In *The Holy Science*, Sri Yukteswar describes a recurring cycle of human development, called the cycle of the yugas, or ages. The complete cycle is made up of an ascending half, or arc, and a descending half, or arc, each lasting 12,000 years. In the ascending arc of 12,000 years, mankind evolves through four distinct ages, or yugas, reaches the peak of development, and then devolves through the four ages, in reverse order, in another 12,000 years of the descending arc. Thus, in the course of 24,000 years, mankind as a whole rises in knowledge and awareness, and again falls, in a cycle that occurs again and again.

Sri Yukteswar tells us we are currently in the ascending half of the cycle, in the second age, or *Dwapara Yuga*. Sri Yukteswar goes on to describe higher ages beyond our own when mankind will communicate telepathically; will understand the subtle laws of thought that underlie energy; will overcome the limitations of time; and will perceive the subtlest law of all — that Divine consciousness underlies all reality.

Sri Yukteswar explains that the cycle of the yugas is caused by influences from outside our solar system that affect the *consciousness* of all mankind. As mankind's consciousness changes as a result of this influence, so also does mankind's perception, awareness, and intellect. In the higher ages that Sri Yukteswar describes, mankind not only *knows* more but is able to *perceive* more than we do today; mankind as a whole not only has more advanced *capabilities* but becomes *motivated* profoundly differently as the ages unfold. In the higher ages described by Sri Yukteswar, perceptions and abilities considered highly unusual today, will be as normal to everyone alive at that time, as cars, planes, and telephones are to us today.

Where, you might be asking, is the evidence for the yugas? Much of it is right under our noses.

For centuries, during what Sri Yukteswar describes as mankind's lowest age, or *Kali Yuga*, most Europeans believed that the world was *flat*. Intelligent, educated men and women held it to be self-evident that the world was flat. Today a child knows that the world is round—and can tell you how one can deduce it for oneself. Watch a ship come into view far out to sea. You will see that the top of the ship appears first, and gradually the rest of the ship comes into view from top to bottom.

Today we hold it just as self-evident that the world is *round*, and we chuckle over the thought that people could have imagined it to be flat. In 1900 AD, scientists thought the earth and universe to be an enormous machine, running with clocklike precision from the beginning of time. We may perhaps chuckle over how wrong they were. Yet that was barely more than a hundred years ago, and now we take the Einsteinian view of the universe for granted.

Much of what is today considered self-evident support for a linear theory of mankind's development may soon make us chuckle again. There are children's puzzles that ask the child to try to find other objects cleverly "hidden" in a picture—perhaps the shape of a swan in a cloud, a trumpet in tree branches, or a wagon in a porch railing. These objects, initially hard to find, seem to jump out at us once we've identified them. So too, as we take a fresh look at our past with a cyclic view of human development in mind, evidence that has been hiding in plain sight "jumps out at us."

Museums have thousands of artifacts that are not on display, stored in basements and vaults. These artifacts are usually considered to be of less interest—or, as is often the case, have not, for lack of time, expert resources, or money, been thoroughly examined. Some of these artifacts may well be unappreciated evidence of higher knowledge in the past.

For example, the Antikythera Device, considered to be at least 2,000 years old, was found underwater off the Greek island of Antikythera in

1901. It was only recently examined thoroughly enough, using modern imaging techniques, to discover that it contained over 120 highly precise clockwork gears—evidence of technology that *shouldn't* have existed so long ago. Who knows how many other objects, some in dusty storerooms, some on public display, will suddenly "jump out at" researchers and scientists as their new implications become obvious in the light of new understanding.

What's more, there are thousands of ancient structures, such as the pyramids in Central America, that have not even been excavated or that, like the Pyramids of Giza, remain unexplained. As another example, the Nazca plains in Peru have stylized depictions of animals, such as a hummingbird and a monkey, "drawn" on the ground on such a large scale that they are recognizable as a hummingbird or a monkey only when one is hundreds of feet in the air—such as one would be in an airplane or helicopter. It remains unexplained why a society would invest years of toil in creating things they couldn't see—unless they did have a way to see them!

Puzzling over both old and new finds is a new generation of scientists, archeologists, paleontologists, paleo-geneticists, paleo-astronomers, underwater archeologists, linguists, and practitioners of myriad other disciplines, taking a closer look at current assumptions, dogmas, and unsolved mysteries of history and prehistory. Many of these scientists are applying never-before-used techniques and state-of-the-art technology to re-examine ancient artifacts and sites. While often considered crackpots by mainstream historians and archeologists, these scientists are presenting findings that are increasingly hard to ignore—and their findings are often at variance with mainstream thinking.

In this book we highlight some of the most interesting discoveries of the new generation of archeologists and other scientists that shine a fresh light on our distant, often hidden, past. It is now known, for example, that science, astronomy, and mathematics were far more advanced in the India of the *fifth and sixth millennia BC* than in Europe during the *first millennium* AD. Indian thinkers then knew that the earth and other planets orbited the sun. They used the concept of the zero within a sophisticated system of mathematics, and they had a concept of the atom not so different from ours of today.

We also explore the implications of Sri Yukteswar's yuga cycle for our emerging present. Sri Yukteswar explains that we fully emerged from the lowest age, or *Kali Yuga*, into our present energy age, or *Dwapara Yuga*, in 1900 AD. The subsequent twentieth century discoveries and knowledge have changed not only our understanding of the physical sciences, but have also profoundly changed our culture and society. Business, government, popular culture, religion — everything — is currently undergoing rapid change, and, according to Sri Yukteswar, will do so for some time to come.

We also explore the future. According to Sri Yukteswar, mankind as a whole will become telepathic, and in the highest age, or *Satya Yuga,* will be aware of the Divine consciousness underlying all reality. According to Sri Yukteswar, mankind is just emerging from the darkest of ages, and the future holds the promise of much greater things to come — not just in the realm of technology and invention — but in expansion of knowledge, awareness, and perception, that will usher in an enlightened future.

We hope you will find this book both intriguing and inspiring. Many people lament the pace, and results, of the kaleidoscopic changes taking place in the world. Though our times show rapid changes, the cycle of the yugas shows us, reassuringly, that these changes are not random, but rather are the unfolding of man's innate potentials. And though mankind's future will bring lessons, some of them hard ones, we are moving forward into expanding awareness and undreamed-of potential.

PART ONE

The Yugas

Chapter 1

The Cycle of the Yugas

A n understanding of the cycle of the yugas gives us unparalleled insight into the past, present, and future development of mankind. Sri Yukteswar, a modern exponent of the yugas, and on whose insights this book is based, explains that mankind goes through clearly discernible ages, or yugas. Each yuga changes the consciousness of mankind. As mankind's consciousness changes, so do civilization and human development.

An understanding of the cycle of the yugas reveals that, like two sides of the same coin, the development of mankind is inextricably bound together with the development of every man's consciousness. The yugas are a unique contribution to the world's knowledge because they unite the study of the inner and outer man. Historians have long sought a key with which to unlock the secrets of the past. But the key has eluded them because they have looked only to the outer man. Only when we make the correlation of inner consciousness to outward behavior does the seeming chaos of history fall into a discernible pattern.

It is not, however, the pattern most modern historians and archeologists expect to find.

The yugas describe a cycle of human development that not only predicts highly advanced ages in the *future*, but indicates that they have occurred in the *past* as well. The yuga cycle includes ages less advanced than our own, ages full of ignorance and darkness, and ages so much more advanced than our own present age that we cannot fully comprehend them. And, as is implicit in the meaning of the word "cycle," we learn that once mankind's peak is reached, there is inevitable decline; and once mankind's darkest point is reached, there is inevitable advancement.

The yugas are a tradition in India that goes back thousands of years. Sri Yukteswar does not base his understanding of the yugas on tradition alone, however. Sri Yukteswar's insights spring from self-realization. His understanding of the yugas is born of deep intuition. Yet his explanation is clear and succinct, and, as he intended, approachable by the Western scientific mind.

Sri Yukteswar outlines the yugas in the introduction to his book, *The Holy Science*. Writing in 1894, Sri Yukteswar predicted several developments that have since come to pass—the rapid development of knowledge in the twentieth century, and the discovery that energy underlies all matter. Sri Yukteswar's explanation predates Einstein's $E=mc^2$ by over ten years. These were not predictions in the usual sense of the intuitive perception of singular events; rather Sri Yukteswar's predictions arose from an understanding of the consequence of the change in mankind's consciousness from one yuga to the next. The most recent transition from one yuga to the next was fully completed in the year 1900 AD, just five years before Einstein's conceptions fundamentally changed our worldview.

Sri Yukteswar's prediction, however, was not about Einstein *as an individual*. Had it not been Einstein who perceived and formulated the relationship between energy and matter, it would have been someone else. What Sri Yukteswar predicted was the *inevitability* that this knowledge would come to light, due to the fundamental change in the consciousness of mankind taking place at that time.

Sri Yukteswar is known to the world primarily through the writings of Paramhansa Yogananda, his foremost disciple and author of *Autobiography of a Yogi*. Sri Yukteswar and Yogananda shared a mission to present the teachings of India in such a way that Western minds could appreciate and understand them within the context of Western thinking and modern science. Yogananda lived in the United States from 1920 until his death in 1952. He was a tireless and inspiring exponent of the teachings of yoga, and was able to present the ancient teachings of India in a fresh, clear, and thoroughly modern way.

This book continues their tradition by presenting the concept of the yugas in the context of Western thinking, science, and scholarship.

We believe you will find that the simple concept of the cycle of the yugas—Sri Yukteswar needed only twelve brief pages to describe it—has profound implications for both the inner and outer man. For, as you will learn as you journey through this book, the inner and outer man are inextricably linked.

The basic concept is simple. As explained by Sri Yukteswar, in 1900 AD mankind fully entered Dwapara Yuga, the second of four ages. In Dwapara Yuga mankind as a whole can comprehend, as he put it, the "fine matters and electricities"[1] that comprise all matter. Dwapara Yuga can be called the Energy Age, and it lasts for 2,000 years. The age preceding Dwapara Yuga is called Kali Yuga, and is the darkest of all the ages, in which mankind can comprehend only gross matter. Kali Yuga can be called the Material Age and lasts 1,000 years. The age that succeeds Dwapara Yuga is called Treta Yuga; in this age mankind can comprehend the "divine magnetism"[2] that underlies all energy, and man's mental capabilities are highly advanced. Treta Yuga can be called the Mental Age and lasts 3,000 years. The last and most advanced of the ages is called Satya Yuga, in which mankind can "comprehend all, even the spirit beyond this visible world."[3] Satya Yuga can be called the Spiritual Age and lasts 4,000 years.

Each yuga has transition periods (sandhis) from and to the next yuga. Referred to as the dawn and twilight of the yugas, the transitions are 1/10 of each yuga's length. Thus the transition into and out of Kali Yuga is 100 years for a combined duration of 1,200 years (100+1,000+100=1,200). Dwapara Yuga's transitions are 200 years before and after Dwapara for a combined duration of 2,400 years (200+2,000+200=2,400). And similarly, Treta Yuga's combined duration is 3,600 years, and Satya Yuga's combined duration is 4,800 years.

The order of the four yugas, progressing toward greater advancement, is Kali, Dwapara, Treta, and Satya Yuga. Adding together the duration of each yuga and its sandhis (1,200+2,400+3,600+4,800), we see that the ascending arc of the yuga cycle requires 12,000 years to reach the peak of mankind's development. Then mankind's consciousness begins to decline, and the yugas pass through the descending arc in reverse order, Satya, Treta, Dwapara to Kali Yuga, in another span of 12,000 years. Together, the ascending arc and the descending arc, which form one complete cycle of the yugas, takes 24,000 years to complete (see Figure 1).

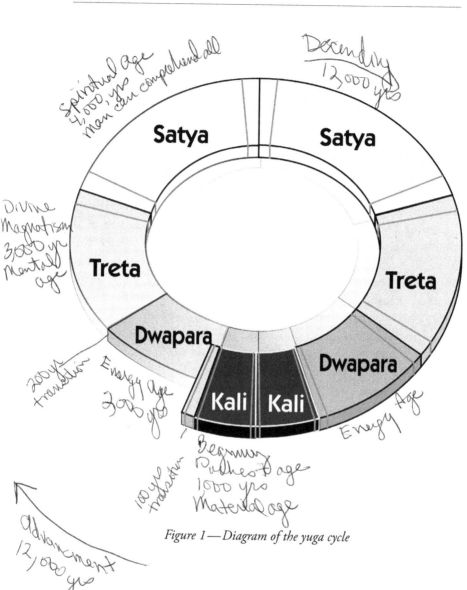

Figure 1 — Diagram of the yuga cycle

[handwritten annotations: Spiritual age 4,000 yrs man can comprehend all; Descending 12,000 yrs; Divine Magnetism 3,000 yr Mental age; 200 yr transition Energy age 3000 yrs; 100 yr transition Beginning Darkest age 1000 yrs Material age; Energy Age; Advancement 12,000 yrs; Holy Sci.]

In *The Holy Science*, Sri Yukteswar describes the astronomically calculated dating of the yugas with elegant efficiency:

> We learn from the Oriental astronomy that moons revolve
> round their planets and planets turning on their axes revolve
> with their moons round the sun, and the sun again with
> its planets and moons taking some star for its dual revolve

round each other in about 24000 years of our earth which causes the backward movement of the equinoxal points round the Zodiac.[4]

In the appendix we explore in greater detail the nature of the dual and how it and our solar system "revolve around each other." Briefly expressed, Sri Yukteswar indicates that there is a star, referred to as a dual, with which our solar system revolves, a movement that can be deduced from the backward movement of the equinoctial points round the zodiac.

The backward movement of the equinoctial points round the zodiac is a well-accepted astronomical phenomenon. The equinox, whether vernal (spring) or autumnal (fall), is the day when the length of the day exactly equals the length of the night all over the world. Every year, at each equinox, we are in precisely the same position relative to our sun, and yet we consistently observe that we are not in precisely the same position relative to the zodiac. We are very slightly short of a full revolution around the zodiac. This phenomenon is called the "precession of the equinoxes." According to modern astronomy, it will take approximately 26,000 years to come full circle again. Some current astronomical theories suggest that the rate of the precession may not be constant. This inconstant rate may explain the discrepancy between the current estimate for the precession, which is 26,000 years, and Sri Yukteswar's phrase that it takes "about 24,000 years"[5] to complete a cycle of the yugas.

Sri Yukteswar attributes the precession of the equinoxes to the revolution around our dual, and most importantly, he indicates that it is the revolution around our dual that changes human consciousness through the yugas:

The sun also has another motion by which it revolves round a grand centre called *Bishnunavi* which is the seat of the creative power *Brahma* the universal magnetism. It informs us further that this *Brahma* the universal magnetism regulates *Dharma* the mental virtues of the internal world. When the sun during its revolution round its dual comes to the place nearest to this grand centre the seat of *Brahma*—this takes place when the autumnal equinox comes to the first point

of Aries—this *Dharma* the mental virtue becomes so much
developed that man can easily comprehend all even the spirit beyond this visible world.[6]

The last time the autumnal equinox occurred at the first point of
Aries was 11,500 BC. At this time, our solar system was at the point
nearest to Brahma, and mankind was at the peak of development.
Twelve thousand years later, or 500 AD, our solar system had moved
to the point farthest from Brahma, and mankind was at its lowest
point of development.

In India, *Brahma* is understood to be the creative force that brings
the universe into being. In this instance, *Brahma* has shades of meaning. From the perspective of physics, we now know that the center of
our galaxy, and indeed of most galaxies, contains a supermassive black
hole. More pertinently, it is now also believed that the black hole in the
center of our galaxy is not the *result* of our galaxy forming, but rather a
significant *cause* of our galaxy forming. Thus, even on a physical level,
the creative force that brought our galaxy into being lies in the "grand
center" of the galaxy.

On a more subtle level, Sri Yukteswar explains that our solar system
and all its inhabitants are profoundly affected by subtle vibrations, or
the "universal magnetism"[7] emanating from the "grand center" (which
may well be the center of our galaxy). It is this influence that elevates
mankind as we come nearer to the source, and which causes mankind
to decline as we go farther from the source. Thus, as Sri Yukteswar
phrases it, the universal magnetism or *Brahma* "regulates *Dharma* the
mental virtues of the internal world."[8]

Dharma, like *Brahma*, has many shades of meaning. It is often
translated as "righteousness," but this has too religious and judgmental
a connotation than is helpful to capture the proper meaning. "Virtue"
comes closer to the meaning without the unfortunate connotations of
righteousness; especially if we think of virtue's secondary meaning as
not just moral strength, but goodness. But even goodness doesn't fully
capture the subtlety of *dharma*.

Nowadays, goodness is often associated with dullness. A common
theme in science fiction is to depict a future from which war, poverty,
and disease have been eliminated, but apparently all that remains for
people to do is stand around spouting platitudes and being insufferably

1) Dharma—virtue
   righteousness,
   goodness

and boringly "good." Not an inviting future. Or goodness is associated with narrow-mindedness. Not long ago, a fictional radio skit (done by a well-known radio personality) portrayed a woman, a pillar of society, who decided to "organize" her community's Halloween celebration, i.e., take all the fun out of it. She was described, amusingly, as a "good woman, in the worst possible sense of the word." Not the kind of person we want to become.

Dharma, as we need to understand it in this context, is more than goodness and righteousness. Sri Yukteswar employs the phrase "the mental virtues of the internal world." The "internal world" refers to our inner consciousness, which implies more than outer behavior. People in whom dharma is elevated are alive, aware, creative, intuitive—far from dull and boring. They possess a lively and keen intelligence; deep, calm feeling; intuitive perception; the desire to enrich the world in which they live; a joyful, humorous, and warm embrace of life; and a continuous and conscious awareness of the Spirit within and without. To fully express dharma therefore, is to fully express our highest potential.

As we develop as individuals, we increasingly manifest our higher potentials. We express dharma more and more completely. So too does mankind as a whole. In any age there are those whose degree of development is greater than the norm. And there are also those whose degree of development is less than the norm. Today we have wise men and sages among us, as well as those who are considerably less aware. In describing the yugas, Sri Yukteswar makes the distinction that, although "mankind as a whole" shares a level of awareness, a degree of development of *dharma* or mental virtue, during each age or yuga, yet there will always be men and women who rise above the general awareness of mankind, who find their connection to Brahma, the universal magnetism, by other means.

An understanding of the cycle of the yugas is profoundly reassuring in our tense and troubling times. Sri Yukteswar offers a vision of our times as a natural process of growth and development—not an apocalyptic powder keg. Our age may be likened to the teenage years before one settles into a mature adulthood. The cycle of the yugas also offers a very high vision of our own inner potential—far greater than one finds in the average history textbook!

Higher "Ages" in Other Cultures

One might think that Sri Yukteswar's concept of the yugas is unique. It *is* unique in its clarity, but not in concept. Many other cultures express similar ideas through their traditions and myths. Giorgio de Santillana, a former professor of history at MIT, and co-author of *Hamlet's Mill*, explores myth after myth about higher ages in the past, drawn from ancient culture after ancient culture. The idea of higher ages existing in the past appears to be woven into most cultural traditions, giving credence to their reality.

In the West, we are most familiar with the ancient Greek tradition of the Golden, Silver, Bronze, and Iron Ages, which we know through the writings of Hesiod and Plato. During Hesiod and Plato's time, roughly the beginning of what Sri Yukteswar tells us is the descending Kali Yuga, which began in 700 BC, the tradition was that mankind was then in the Iron, or lowest age, and that mankind had descended from the Golden Age, through the Silver and Bronze Ages.

The historian of philosophy, W. K. C. Guthrie, in his book *In the Beginning: Some Greek Views on the Origins of Life and the Early State of Man*, gives this description of the Greek Golden Age (also called the Age of Kronos) as:

> not wealth and luxury, but a sufficiency of natural food in conjunction with high moral character and a complete absence of wars and dissension. Ease and happiness are linked to simplicity and innocence of mind.... Kronos in his wisdom appointed gods or spirits to take care of men.[9]

People lived very simply in the Golden Age. There were no wars and discord because they had no possessions over which to fight. There was no agriculture but the land produced food of itself, the climate being agreeable.

The clear similarity of Guthrie's description of the Golden Age and Sri Yukteswar's of Satya Yuga is striking. If this were one isolated example, we could easily assume it was coincidence, but there are many more examples from other cultures, including Norse, Celtic, Hopi, Lakota, Persian, and ancient Egyptian.

In ancient Persia, the Zoroastrian tradition, which existed about 500 BC in the area of present-day Iran, spoke of Zurvan daregho-chvadhata, or the time of the long dominion, a cosmic year that spanned 12,000 years, divided into four periods of 3,000 years. The four ages were symbolized by a tree with four branches of gold, silver, steel, and iron.

Norse myths describe a succession of ages: an age of peace, an age of the development of social orders, an age of increasing violence, and a degraded age of cruel winters and moral chaos, ending in an annihilation called the Ragnarok after which the world is restored.

The tradition of four ages appears also in the Celtic mythology of Ireland. The first Celtic age, Partholon, is associated with the white color of silver. The second age, Nemed's, is associated with the red color of bronze and is followed by the Tuatna de Denann, the Golden (yellow) age. The fourth age, Milesians, is black. Interestingly, the *Mahabharata*, India's great epic scripture, identifies the same colors, in the same order, as the "colors of god" during the corresponding yugas.

Manetho, an Egyptian priest of circa 300 BC, wrote a history of Egypt in the Greek language, of which only fragments, mostly lists of kings, have survived. But Manetho also tells of an age when gods ruled humanity, followed by a period of rule by demigods and heroes, then an age of rule by ordinary men. The sequence once again clearly reflects a progression of descending ages.

The Hopi of the American Southwest speak of four worlds. Author Frank Waters, himself a Hopi, describes them in *Book of the Hopi*. In the first world the people were pure, happy, and healthy. The people felt one with one another and with nature. By the third world, people lived in big cities and there was corruption and war, and in the fourth world people lived in a hard world marked by duality, "heat and cold, beauty and barrenness."

Ancient Indian traditions speak of the Bull of Dharma. The tradition involves a Sanskrit play on words: the term "*Vrisha*" means both "bull" and "virtue," or "dharma" in Sanskrit. As we mentioned earlier in this chapter, dharma increases and then decreases as the yugas go through the cycle of 24,000 years. In Satya Yuga, the highest age, Indian tradition records that the Bull of Dharma stood on four legs, while in the next age, Treta Yuga, the Bull stood on only three legs, in Dwapara Yuga, two legs, and in Kali Yuga, one leg.

Sri Yukteswar writes that dharma is only one-quarter developed in Kali Yuga, one-half developed in Dwapara Yuga, three-quarters developed in Treta Yuga, and fully developed in Satya Yuga.

Since both the myth of the Bull of Dharma and the tradition of the yugas come from India, this clear conformance between Sri Yukteswar and the myth of the Bull of Dharma is not too surprising. But an extraordinarily similar myth can be found in North America—the myth of the White Buffalo.

The Native American Lakota (Sioux) have a traditional story of a visit by a celestial white buffalo woman who arrived from the West, clad in white and carrying a pack that held a sheaf of sage. Buffalo Woman gave the Lakota their ceremonies and religion. She taught them how to pray and sing, and how to use the sacred pipe, which she also carried in her pack. She taught that there were four ages, and that in the highest age, the sacred White Buffalo, which figures prominently in Lakota myths, stands on all four legs. During the second age, White Buffalo stands on three legs, and in the third and fourth ages, it stands on two and then one leg. After giving her teachings, Buffalo Woman departed toward the West, the same way she had come.

Of the many parallels found in the myths described above, several stand out especially:

1. All reached their current form sometime in Kali Yuga (700 BC to 1700 AD). Kali is the lowest yuga in the cycle.

2. All express the belief that the myth-tellers lived in the lowest of the ages they describe.

3. All describe a process in which mankind has *descended* from higher ages, in a succession from a highest age, through less evolved ages, and finally into the lowest age.

4. All describe the highest age as a time of spiritual harmony, physical plenty, and greatly expanded awareness.

These parallels, we are told by mainstream historians, anthropologists, and archeologists, are only unremarkable coincidences, the result of shared archetypes in the human psyche. Many of these myths are considered by scholars to be origin myths, stories that primitive people told to explain how the world came to be. Yet the recurring theme of higher ages, and the remarkable similarities in their descriptions, suggests more than just a coincidence of archetypal imagination.

If, in fact, higher ages existed in the past, as Sri Yukteswar describes, knowledge of the higher ages would have passed down to increasingly less aware generations, resulting in an increasingly inexact understanding, expressed through the language and symbols of their subsequent time and culture. The description of the higher age, as told from the perspective of the lowest age, would naturally suggest only a primitive understanding.

It is perhaps more remarkable than not that these age myths survived at all, given the opportunity for disintegration over time. That they have survived for thousands of years, across many diverse cultures, on different continents, is a likely indication of their importance to ancient man — and of their shared core of truth.

Chapter 2

The Kali Yugas

Timeline

700 BC   Beginning of most recent descending Kali Yuga

600 BC   End of 100-year transition period (*sandhi*) from descending Dwapara Yuga

500 AD   End of descending and beginning of ascending Kali Yuga

1600 AD   Beginning of 100-year transition period (*sandhi*) to ascending Dwapara Yuga

1700 AD   End of most recent ascending Kali Yuga

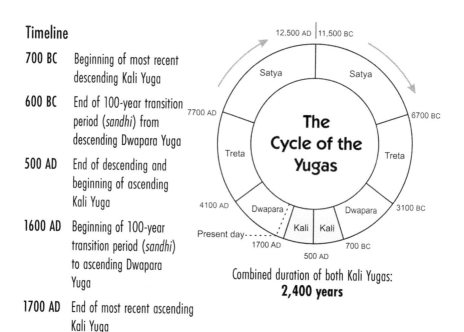

Combined duration of both Kali Yugas:
2,400 years

The part of our past we know best is generally referred to as *recorded history* — approximately from the beginning of the classical Greek civilization to the present. The beginning of recorded history also coincides almost exactly with the beginning of the age Sri Yukteswar tells us is the lowest and darkest age of man — Kali Yuga.

According to Sri Yukteswar, Kali Yuga man was able to comprehend only *gross matter*; and the age of Kali Yuga was distinctively shaped by this limited awareness. While it is true that during Kali

Yuga there were men and women of keen intellect and strong moral disposition, and who accomplished works of great beauty and enduring value—exquisite sculpture, soaring architecture and insightful philosophy—these were the exceptions. Mankind as a whole existed in a low state. The average man or woman, from our modern perspective, lived a life of ignorance and passivity.

Because the very process of recording history tends to distort it, most people today are not aware of what life was like for the average man and woman in Kali Yuga. Historians emphasize events and accomplishments that stand out and have interest for us today. Historians also tend to glorify things that would be considered unacceptable today—simply because they were accomplishments—however dark the deeds were that brought them to prominence. The "Glory that was Rome" would ignite a worldwide protest and a United Nations intervention if it were happening today—but, because it was prominent in its time, it has been elevated to the status of greatness by historians.

To truly understand Kali Yuga we need to look below the surface of history. Historians do not dwell on the common man—he is just not as interesting! Yet if we are to understand the yugas, we must focus on the awareness, capabilities, motivations, and activities of the common man—mankind as a whole, as Sri Yukteswar phrases it—not on the ruling elite, the highly educated, or those whose accomplishments in art, philosophy, and literature give them lasting fame.

What one discovers, after filtering out the prominent people and events, so to speak, is that the vast majority of people who lived during Kali Yuga were farmers, herdsmen, laborers, artisans, conscripted soldiers, servants, or slaves. Pleasures were simple, sensory, and earthy—eating, drinking, sex. Good fortune was rudimentary and tangible—food, clothing, few possessions. Activity was basic—laboring long and hard to stay alive, enjoying the pleasures that came, enduring hardships. Life expectancy was low—disease, misfortune, and famine were commonplace.

Average people were passively accepting of their lot. Their passivity expressed itself as fatalistic acceptance of circumstances, lack of will to change, or even the belief that they could change circumstances. There was very little social mobility. Chances were that the circumstances you were born into, whether as a carpenter, farmer, or artisan, were the circumstances you would likely die in. India's caste system hardened into a hereditary straightjacket during Kali Yuga. Emperors, Caesars, and kings passed on their thrones to their heirs. Farmers were farmers for generation upon generation.

Almost no one could read or write. Education, or even access to written thought, was limited to a tiny percentage of the population. From China to Rome, the written word was preserved, if it was preserved at all, by the wealthy and by religious communities such as monasteries. Even the knowledge that *was* preserved was done so very selectively. Intolerance for other viewpoints was the norm. During Kali Yuga, ignorance was all but willful; nearly all prior knowledge was deliberately destroyed during Kali Yuga.

Two examples stand out. In the third century AD, the Library at Alexandria was destroyed along with hundreds of thousands of volumes of ancient writings; and approximately 500 years earlier, the Emperor Chin Shi Huang-ti of China had *all the books in China* burned. The following list of dates and destruction gives us a glimpse of the profound level of intolerance and ignorance that characterized Kali Yuga:

527 BC   The Persians burn Egyptian temples and papyri

490 BC   The Persians destroy literary works of Athens

330 BC   Alexander the Great, in Persepolis, destroys 12,000 volumes of the Magi

214 BC   Chinese Emperor Chin Shi Huang-ti has all books in China burned

146 BC   The Romans destroy 500,000 Phoenician scrolls at Carthage

52 BC   Julius Caesar destroys library at Druid College

250 AD   Library at Pergamum destroyed by zealous Christians

272 AD   The main Library of Alexandria destroyed by Romans

391 AD   Theophilus levels the "daughter library" at Alexandria1

What might we know of the past had this destruction not occurred?

Not only profoundly ignorant, more often than not the people of Kali Yuga were considered property, either as outright slaves, or virtual slaves, such as serfs, who were tied to the land and subject to the lord of the land. Women were subject to their husbands and fathers. Human rights as we understand them today did not exist.

Nowhere is this more apparent than in the Roman Empire. Rome was built on the backs and lives of slaves, usually drawn from peoples conquered by Roman armies. Though slavery still exists today hidden in dark corners of society, in Kali Yuga it was commonplace. It was also brutal. Owners had the power of life and death over their slaves. Perhaps most shocking to our sensibilities today, is the killing of slaves *for entertainment* in the Coliseum of Rome—a practice that continued for five centuries. The Emperor Trajan, in the second century AD, provided a *spectacle* during which 10,000 slaves were killed before the cheering crowd—*in one day*.

Although slavery to this degree did not exist in China and India during Kali Yuga, historians generally agree that these regions had no need to bring in slaves from elsewhere. Both India and China had sufficiently large populations and well-established feudal systems. The virtual slavery of serfdom was already in place. Slavery was well established among the Aztecs. Slavery was rife in Africa. It is perhaps ironic that Africans would be the last victims of slavery in the eighteenth and nineteenth centuries AD, since they had been maintaining a culture of slavery for over two thousand years. In fact, initially, it was the dominant African tribes who sold their fellow Africans to the Europeans and Americans.

The slavery of Kali Yuga, during which time owners and rulers had the power of life and death over the enslaved, has no antecedent in the ancient cultures that came before Kali Yuga. This comes as a surprise to most people. Hollywood movies showing thousands of slaves building the pyramids in Egypt are movie myths—long since discredited. It is now understood that the workers who built the pyramids were not only well housed and fed, but paid as well. Egyptians did have a form of indentured servitude—but nothing like the slavery of the Romans. Egyptians who chose indentured servitude were free to own property, maintain their own homes, raise families; while they devoted their efforts to the affairs of their master, their children were not automatically born into slavery. Egyptian indentured servitude has the feel of a career choice more than what we commonly think of as slavery.

Kali Yuga brutality wasn't confined to the treatment of slaves. Kali Yuga was also a time of conquest and subjugation by force. Kali Yuga was the time of Alexander the Great, Emperor Chin of China, Julius Caesar, Genghis Khan, and Tamerlane, just to name a few of the better known men who ruthlessly conquered and subjugated vast territories. In the process conquering armies burned cities to the ground, put the inhabitants to the sword, killed for sport, tortured for example, enslaved, or raped. Tamerlane is said to have built a mountain of 60,000 human heads during the sacking of a city. If a Roman general felt that his troops were getting out of line and needing to be reined in, he could "decimate" them — have every tenth man beaten to death by his comrades as an object lesson to them all.

Conquest and defense may be the most defining forces in Kali Yuga. Civilization was organized around walled cities, castles, citadels, and fortifications, and the armies needed to defend them, or the armies needed to crush them. Throughout the world, from Japan to Europe to Central America to Africa, one was either the conqueror or the conquered. In the early part of the descending Kali Yuga this at least resulted in order — the Pax Romana of the Roman Empire, or Emperor Chin's uniting of the seven Chinese provinces, for example. But by the lowest point of Kali Yuga (approximately 200 to 800 AD) conquest became merely plunder and destruction. The very names, Vandal and Hun, free-ranging invaders who swept through Europe, Central Asia, and India during this time, are synonymous with wanton destruction.

Religious understanding during Kali Yuga was largely materially-oriented and propitiatory. People sacrificed things of value — animals, food, possessions — in order to bargain with the gods for good fortune. This reached its lowest manifestation with human sacrifice. Propitiating, bargaining, and bartering with the gods were a natural extension of how the common man thought about his world. He offered objects of earthy, *material* value to get things of earthy, *material* value in return. The more important the need, the greater the sacrifice required. It is not surprising, against the background of such belief, that one of the central tenets of the Catholic Church, formed in the heart of Kali Yuga, was that Christ died as a sacrifice for the sins of mankind.

Kali Yuga is the only era in history during which human sacrifice is known to have been practiced. There is no record, or evidence, of it having happened in ancient cultures prior to 700 BC. The Aztecs, especially, are infamously known for their practice of human sacrifice. During the re-consecration of the Great Pyramid of Tenochtitlan in 1487, historians believe that over *80,000 prisoners* were sacrificed. Estimates of the number of people sacrificed by the Aztecs, in the 1400s, run as high as *250,000 annually.*

Slavery, subjugation, and ritual sacrifice of such brutality are inconceivable to us today. Yet during Kali Yuga these practices were widespread.

Most of the world religions existed during Kali Yuga—Hinduism, Buddhism, Islam, Christianity. Though exalted in their origins, the common man's practice of them was ritualistic; daily prayer, daily offerings, daily sacrifice. Religion, during Kali Yuga, was rigid, like the stone used as the primary building material. Each religion demanded exclusive adherence. Priests insured obedience. Rival religions were abhorred; their books burned, their adherents forcibly converted—or slain.

Side by side with the major religions existed hundreds of other religious practices. Considered pagan by orthodox religionists, most were bound up with worshipping physical representations of nature, nature spirits, and the gods of the land. Higher spiritual knowledge existed, but was hidden away and protected in convents and monasteries, temples and ashrams. Kali Yuga was a time when only a few were able to understand and use spiritual practices that were inwardly directed.

The average person neither knew, nor embraced, what we today might call moral behavior. He simply took what gains and pleasures he could while taking the path of least resistance. Knowing nothing beyond the senses, he sought sensual pleasure. The educated and ruling classes lived the same sense-directed life as the common man—the elite simply did so on a grander scale. From Kali Yuga we get the *orgy* and the *bacchanalia.* These examples of excess were not the practices of Bohemian subcultures of the day, but were the pride of the elite. Concubines, harems, mistresses, sexual excess can be found during Kali Yuga in the courts of all the rulers from China to India and from Persia to Rome to Central America. Practices considered depraved today were sought after. Comprehending only sensory pleasure, more sensory pleasure must have seemed an obvious felicity.

Engineering (science and technology were not even concepts in Kali Yuga) was grounded in the application of known forces, such as man power, animal power, and water power, to simple materials such as wood, stone, and crude metals. Within these limits, builders and craftsmen showed significant ingenuity and skill, ingenuity that resulted in the roads and aqueducts of Rome, the cathedrals of Europe, and the thousands of palaces and temples built throughout the world, many of which still exist today. At the same time, we see the same basic limits to engineering skill throughout the world. Even civilizations completely isolated from one another employed the same basic methods and engineering techniques.

Though Kali Yuga did produce its high-minded poets, philosophers, noble statesmen, and did erect beautiful churches, temples, and monuments, the experience of the average man was that of *passive and ignorant acceptance* of simple, hard, and basic lives. The material consciousness of Kali Yuga, as Sri Yukteswar describes, meant man himself was regarded as little more than another object, an attitude that fostered brutality and inhumanity. Many, no doubt, were not directly touched by such brutality, but nonetheless lived their lives within the oppressive and materialistic mores of their age, each person seeking primarily to survive physically and maximize the pleasures of the senses.

The "Footprint" of the Yuga Cycle

Every yuga evolves, or devolves (as is the case in a descending yuga), through the span of its years. Gradually, but inexorably, descending Kali Yuga, beginning in 700 BC, devolved to its low point in 500 AD, over its span of 1200 years. Then, just as gradually, but inexorably, ascending Kali Yuga, beginning in 500 AD, evolved back to its high point in 1700 AD, over the span of 1,200 years.

Modern historians, well settled into their current shared convictions, see only a straight line of upward development from the time of the ancient Greeks (approximately 500 BC) up to today. However, if we view the past with a fresh perspective, *drawing on the same historical facts as are modern historians*, we can clearly see the pattern of devolution and evolution suggested by the yugas—we can see a descent followed by an ascent rather than a straight upward line of progress.

Much of recorded history is political. That is to say it records the rise, fall, consolidation, and disintegration of empires, countries, cities, and cultures. What most of us learned in school is that empires came and went more or less randomly as a result of ever shifting circumstances—leadership, trade, climate, and the technology of war among the most prominent.

Yet if we stand back from the detail of political history, we can see a pattern in the seemingly random rise and fall of kingdoms and empires (see *Figure 2*): consolidation of political empires through the middle years of descending Kali Yuga, followed by their disintegration through the ending years of descending Kali Yuga and the beginning years of ascending Kali Yuga, and then another period of consolidation of political empires through the middle years of ascending Kali Yuga.

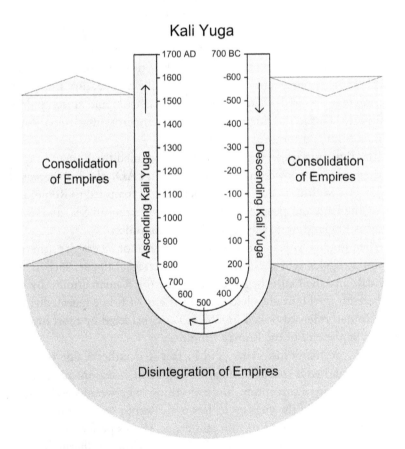

Figure 2—Disintegration and consolidation of empires in the Kali Yugas

The Roman Empire serves as a good example of the pattern of consolidation followed by disintegration in descending Kali Yuga (see *Figure 3*). Rome's fortunes began near the beginning of the descending Kali Yuga and ended almost exactly at Kali Yuga's lowest point, 500 AD.

Rome began as a republic, with a semi-democratic system of government. Historians usually cite the founding of the Republic of Rome around 500 BC as the beginning of the Roman Empire. The political center of the Republic was the Senate, a ruling body made up of two representative groups—the Plebians, or commoners, and the Patricians, or wealthy class. The Senate ably managed the affairs of the Roman state for many years.

In the early centuries of Kali Yuga (approximately 500 to 100 BC) various *dictators*, as they were known (because they could dictate to the Senate), were appointed by the Senate to help the republic weather a crisis or a war; when the crisis ended, the normal rule by the Senate was subsequently completely restored. Over time, however, the dictators became stronger and stronger until by the first century BC, Julius Caesar was declared Dictator for Life. His heirs, and unscrupulous usurpers, became the line of Caesars and emperors that ruled Rome with absolute power until its ruin.

The Emperor Trajan is considered to have ruled the Roman Empire at the peak of its power in the second century AD. The empire was at its largest, wealthiest, and most influential. All roads led to Rome, and all of the land and peoples around the Mediterranean Sea, and as far away as England, were subject to Rome's dominion.

Then gradually, Rome began to lose control of its empire. Internal power struggles split the Empire in two. External threats such as the Vandals and the Goths began to beat back the Roman armies. By the fifth century AD invaders had sacked the city of Rome repeatedly; the last Roman ruler was killed in 476 AD—considered by most historians to be the end of the Roman Empire.

There are many historians (and in fact it is rather a side industry in academia) who speculate on why Rome fell—reasons range from lead poisoning to corruption, and everything in between. Viewed from the perspective of the yuga cycle, however, Rome's devolution from its semi-democratic origins to ruin and chaos, makes perfect sense when understood as the inevitable result of the decline of dharma during descending Kali Yuga.

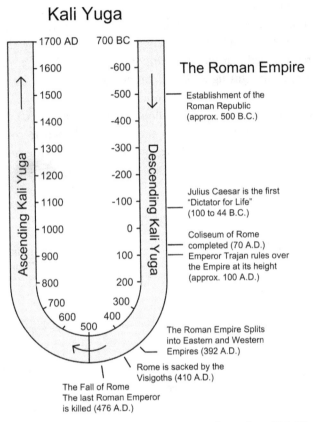

Figure 3 — Decline of the Roman Empire in descending Kali Yuga

The Roman Empire began in service to the people of Rome, creating an orderly world in which its citizens could flourish, and defending them ably against outside foes. Then, as the age darkened, Rome became focused on expansion, conquest, and wealth; it built its cities and engineering triumphs on slave labor. As the age darkened further, Rome could not maintain even order; forces outside and inside tore at the Roman Empire like wolves at a carcass. Then, all order gone, Europe plunged into centuries of petty warring and ignorance—a time aptly called the Dark Ages.

The Dark Ages were a period of extreme isolation, ignorance, and splintered political units throughout what is now Europe. Charlemagne's rise in the late eighth century AD brought the beginning of the end of this period of disintegration, a movement of reconsolidation that the hegemony of the Catholic Church continued through the fifteenth century AD. Though clearly a religious institution today, the Catholic Church wielded considerable temporal power during the Middle Ages in Europe, appointing kings, encouraging the Crusades, and exerting control over a still fractious Europe.

Rome and Europe were not alone in experiencing such an arc from consolidation to disintegration and chaos and then re-consolidation into new political empires. One can find the same pattern all over the world (see *Figure 4*).

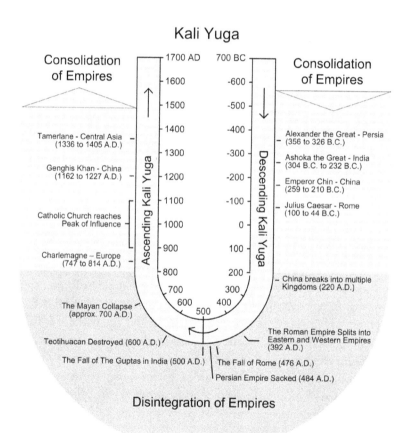

Figure 4—Disintegration and consolidation of empires worldwide

In China, the Emperor Chin (from whose name comes "China") ruthlessly united the seven warring provinces of China in the third century BC. Centuries of rule under one emperor finally collapsed in the third century AD with the fall of the Han Dynasty. The Chinese refer to the three centuries of fragmentation and turmoil that followed as the *Period of Utter Darkness*. Amidst near-total absence of law and order, the country was ravished by bandits, former farmers who had lost their crops and villages; and starving soldiers learned to survive by violence. From the time the Han fell in 220 AD, it would be another thousand years before China would once again be united under one ruler—Genghis Khan's grandson, Kublai Khan, who ruthlessly crushed all resistance to Mongol rule of China.

In the fourth century BC, Alexander the Great overthrew the Persian Empire and then reorganized it into a larger empire. However, by the fifth century AD, the Empire had fragmented and weakened so much that the Hephthalites were able repeatedly to invade; in 484 AD the invaders succeeded in slaying King Firuz, seizing the royal treasures and devastating the country. Persia was never fully united again until the conquest by Tamerlane (also known as Timur) in the late fourteenth century AD.

In India, Ashoka the Great united India through conquest, and by approximately 250 BC extended the Mauryan Empire to its largest size. The Mauryans ruled all of the Indian subcontinent. Subsequent dynasties, however, ruled less and less effectively until the Gupta Dynasty, greatly weakened by war and by internal causes, at last fell in 500 AD, whereupon the Hunas (known as the Huns in the West) destroyed the great North Indian cities and trading centers and the Buddhist monasteries in the northwest. The Huna rule in India was oppressive, but brief. All of India became politically fragmented and would remain so for 700 years as dozens of dynasties came and went, often at war with each other. It wasn't until the oppressive Moslem invaders began ruling large parts of India, beginning with the Delhi Sultanate in 1206 AD and continuing with the Moghul Empire in 1526 AD, that India was again reunited as a single political entity.

In Central America, the Teotihuacan Civilization reached its peak of influence and size in approximately 500 BC. However, by the end of the sixth century AD, the Teotihuacan Empire, named after what at the time was one of the world's largest cities, was burned and plundered.

The facts surrounding the destruction of Teotihuacan remain a mystery. A long interval of food shortage appears to have preceded the disintegration and collapse of Teotihuacan society. Teotihuacan civilization never recovered.

The Mayan Civilization, which existed contemporaneously with the Teotihuacan and began in approximately 200 AD, experienced two centuries, known as the Mayan collapse, from approximately 700 to 900 AD, during which the Mayans nearly died out. Their culture survived and revived and was at its peak when the Europeans arrived in the fifteenth century AD.

Around the world we can see the same pattern revealed during the descending and ascending Kali Yuga periods—consolidation, disintegration, and re-consolidation. The political entities and empires that re-formed in ascending Kali Yuga were never specifically the same as those that disintegrated, but they ruled the same geographies and cultures. As Mark Twain wryly put it, "History doesn't repeat itself, but it rhymes."

Unlike the consolidation period in descending Kali Yuga, which ends in disintegration, the consolidation period in ascending Kali Yuga continues to gain momentum, and ends with the consolidation of world empires by the Europeans. The European conquest of the world resulted in several vast empires. By approximately 1700 AD, the end of ascending Kali Yuga, the British, French, Spanish, Portuguese, and Dutch held sway over nearly the entire world.

Also, unlike the disintegration that followed the period of consolidation in descending Kali Yuga, what followed the consolidation of empires in ascending Kali Yuga was the moderating influence of Dwapara Yuga and entry into what is known as the Colonial Period. The Colonial Period is marked by the awakening in the conquering powers of a sense of humanistic responsibility to those conquered; it ends by the middle of the twentieth century in the gradual granting of freedom to all the colonies, for reasons primarily of conscience.

A Symmetrical Pattern of Ideas

Many parallels exist between the Golden Age of Greece and the Renaissance (see *Figure 5*). The flowering of art, literature, and philosophy that occurred in Greece from 650 to 350 BC was at the beginning

of the descending arc of Kali Yuga; the Renaissance occurs near the end
of the ascending arc of Kali Yuga. In fact, many Renaissance thinkers saw the catalyst for the Renaissance in the rediscovery of classical
Greek philosophy, which had been guarded in Christian monasteries,
notably the Irish monasteries, and also husbanded by the emerging
Muslim civilization.

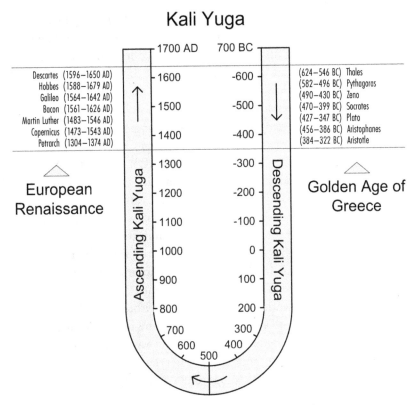

Kali Yuga

Figure 5—Flowering of philosophy in the Kali Yugas

The philosophy of the Greeks during the Golden Age was character-
istically rational, logical, and empirical. Socrates' most famous dictum
is "Know thyself." There was much speculation and philosophic conjecture as to man's nature, and man's relationship to higher reality, the
gods, or God—but without religious dogma, doctrine, or organized
religious preconceptions. The assumption was that man could reason
and experience his way to an understanding of Truth.

Similarly, European Renaissance thinkers dared to put man, and man's ability to reason and perceive, at the empirical center of the debate—which put many at odds with the Church. From Petrarch (1304 to 1374 AD), considered to be the "father of humanism," to René Descartes (1596 to 1650 AD), who penned "cogito ergo sum," "I think, therefore I am," the Renaissance resonated with classical Greek philosophy and ideas.

Nor was the emergence of humanist ideas unique to ancient Greece and renaissance Europe. In China, a philosopher of great influence, Wang Yangming (1472–1529 AD), a Neo-Confucianist, held as his central belief that man was inherently capable of *intuition and reason* regardless of his station in life, a philosophy that pitted him against orthodox Confucianists who believed only scholars and rulers were capable of such heavenly qualities. Wang Yangming had many students who spread humanistic ideals throughout China.

In India, Akbar the Great (1556–1605 AD), one of the Moghul Emperors, was himself a "renaissance man." He was known to be an architect, artisan, artist, armorer, blacksmith, carpenter, construction worker, engineer, general, inventor, animal trainer, lacemaker, linguist, technologist, and theologian. Akbar promulgated a new religion, "Din-i-llahi," or Divine Faith, in an attempt to bridge the many religions present in India. The Divine Faith had no priestly class or orthodoxy and focused entirely on self-improvement.

Throughout the world, as Sri Yukteswar wrote, "people began to have respect for themselves"[2] as Kali Yuga came to an end. Rigid and oppressive religious dogmas gradually gave way to reason, and the possibility that man was more than the servile creation of a fearsome Divinity. Mankind was awakening from a dark dream.

Knowledge of Mechanics and Astronomy
Lost and then Rediscovered

Modern historians, due to their "straight-line-development" approach to understanding the past, maintain that each event, invention, or new bit of knowledge, is built on inventions and knowledge that came before it. But there is a clear record of mechanical and astronomical knowledge that was known in descending Kali Yuga, which became lost and forgotten for more than a thousand years before the knowledge was "rediscovered" in ascending Kali Yuga (see *Figure 6*).

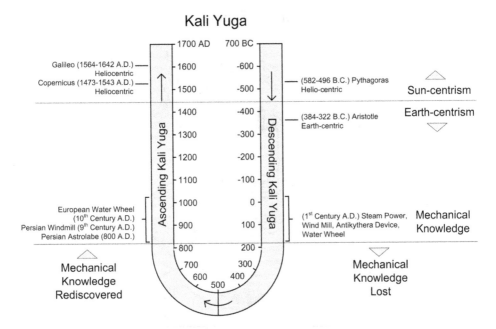

Figure 6 — The decline and resurgence of physical and mechanical knowledge in the Kali Yugas

It is amazing to see how much technology was available to the Greco-Roman world. By the end of the first century AD, near the middle of the descending Kali Yuga, the Romans knew how to construct efficient water mills, although they were little used.

Heron (or Hero) of Alexandria, a notable Greek inventor and mathematician of the first century AD, is the author of two extraordinary treatises, "Air Pressure Devices" and "Self-Moving Devices," in which he describes nearly a hundred diverse inventions, including devices powered by steam and wind, such as a vertical windmill.

Heron's most intriguing creation may be the *aeolipile*, or "wind ball," which employed a steam jet to create spinning motion (see *Figure 7*). By itself, it probably could not have been adapted to perform useful work, but combined with the piston and cylinder that Heron employed in his design for a fire-fighting pump, and the valves he devised for a water fountain powered by compressed air, we have the ingredients for the invention of the steam engine.

Heron's Engine

Figure 7—Heron's aeolipile steam-jet device drawn from his written description. (NASA/courtesy of nasaimages.org.)

A first century AD device, known as the "Antikythera Device" (because it was found underwater near the island of Antikythera in Greece), has recently been re-examined to reveal that it has extraordinarily sophisticated gears, over 120 in all, that would have allowed the user to predict many astronomical events, such as the motion of the sun and planets, the cycles of Venus, and eclipses. Called the first mechanical calculator, the device is the most complex precision instrument ever found in the ancient world.

Yet despite known uses of these mechanical principles during or before the first century AD, despite surviving detailed written descriptions of how they could be constructed and used, the knowledge and use of these particular mechanical principles died out for 600 years or longer.

A much more simple device than the Antikythera Device, the astrolabe, which was used to calculate the motion of the sun and planets, was not constructed again until the eighth century AD in Persia. And even then, the sophistication of the astrolabe did not come close to that of the Antikythera Device. The complexity and precision of the gearing in the Antikythera Device was not rivaled until mechanical clocks were developed in the late thirteenth century AD.

The windmill and watermill did not return to use until the ninth and tenth centuries AD, respectively. Records show that in 1086, only a century after their re-introduction, 5,624 water mills were in operation in Great Britain. Perhaps even more surprising, the steam engine did not see another working model until 1551 when a Turkish inventor, Taqi al-Din, developed a device that would rotate a spit.

The knowledge that our solar system is sun-centered (heliocentric) rather than earth-centered (geocentric) is considered to be a breakthrough discovery championed by Copernicus near the end of the fifteenth century AD. But Pythagoras, the Greek philosopher and mathematician, who lived approximately 2,000 years before Copernicus, had already formulated the same idea.

According to his students, Pythagoras (582–496 BC) seems to have understood the scale and arrangement of the solar system. There is some evidence to indicate that Pythagoras gained his astronomical knowledge from the Egyptians. He taught that the earth is a sphere suspended in space, that it rotates, causing night and day, and that the spherical sun is more than 100 times as large as Earth. (In fact, the diameter of the sun by modern measure is 109 times that of Earth.) He taught that the evening star and the morning star are the same planet, Venus, at a time when it was commonly thought that they were separate bodies.

In 250 BC, the Greek astronomer Aristarchus of Samos, himself a student of the Pythagorean School, proposed that the stars and sun are fixed, and that Earth revolves around the sun. But the religious orthodoxy of his day was deeply opposed, and the concept died out.

From the time of Aristotle (384–322 BC) onwards, the explanations of planetary systems adhere to strictly geocentric principles.

Eighteen centuries later, Copernicus would acknowledge Aristarchus as the inspiration for his theory of a heliocentric solar system. Aristarchus is sometimes called the Copernicus of Antiquity, or the Ancient Copernicus. Galileo's persecution for supporting Copernicus echoes the reaction of religious leaders to Aristarchus, the difference being that, in the ascending Kali Yuga, the heliocentric model eventually won out in spite of the objections of the Church. Not so in the descending Kali Yuga, when the rigid views of Aristotle and the prevailing religious dogma of an earth-centric universe closed the door firmly on what we consider today as the truth.

If it were true that history is a straight line of upward development, then surely the obviously more logical heliocentric view of our solar system would have prevailed in descending Kali Yuga. Yet the simpler and more orthodox earth-centric view prevailed.

If it were true that history is a straight line of upward development, then surely these mechanical inventions would have continued to be developed during descending Kali Yuga. Their advantages are obvious to us today, compared to the use of animal and human power that prevailed for centuries.

If it were true that history is a straight line of upward development, then surely the humanist and rationalist ideals of the early Greeks would have resonated in the minds and hearts of mankind during descending Kali Yuga, as they have done in our modern era.

Instead, we see the pattern of inexorable decline and then resurgence of human awareness that is the Kali Yuga footprint of the cycle of the yugas. Mankind was once able to grasp and appreciate ideals, concepts, knowledge, and qualities of human behavior in descending Kali Yuga that, as dharma declined, became steadily dimmer until mostly incomprehensible.

Then, gradually, after mankind had passed through the worst of the dark times of Kali Yuga, reason came back to the fore. Human dignity was reclaimed. The laws of science re-emerged. Mankind was once again ready to enter Dwapara Yuga.

PART TWO

Our Emerging Energy Age

Chapter 3

Ascending Dwapara Yuga —
The Energy Age

Timeline

1700 AD Beginning of present ascending Dwapara Yuga

1900 AD End of the 200-year transition period (*sandhi*) from Kali Yuga

3900 AD Beginning of the 200-year transition period (*sandhi*) to Treta Yuga

4100 AD End of present ascending Dwapara Yuga

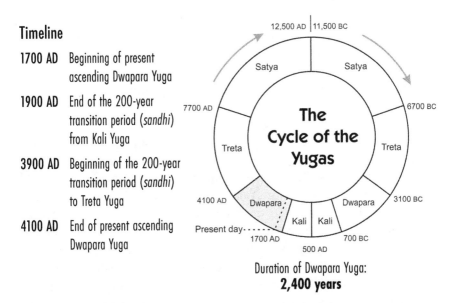

Duration of Dwapara Yuga:
2,400 years

In 1894, Sri Yukteswar wrote that during Dwapara Yuga, mankind would comprehend the "fine matters and electricities" underlying matter. During the eighteenth and nineteenth centuries AD, which comprise the *sandhi*, or transition period, of Dwapara Yuga, there were many fundamental scientific discoveries which revealed that matter is composed of subtle structures (fine matters) that are affected by energy (electricities). These discoveries set the stage for our present age of energy.

In 1778, Antoine Lavoisier isolated and named oxygen and hydrogen as unique types of gas, revealing that air, at that time considered to be one substance, is actually made up of different gases. John Dalton published his proofs that all matter is made up of atoms in 1803, and, based on Dalton's work, Dmitri Mendeleev composed the first version of the periodic table of elements in 1869. In the 1860s Joseph Lister's and Louis Pasteur's work proved the role and effects of micro-organisms in disease, leading to pasteurization and vaccines.

In the nineteenth century, the behavior of electricity and magnetism was explored by many scientists, Michael Faraday and Georg Ohm among them. These explorations led to the discovery and formulation of laws regarding voltage, current, and resistance. Faraday's work, in such areas as magnetic fields and conductors, led to the invention of the electromagnetic rotary device—which formed the foundation for modern electric motors. Another notable scientist of this time was James Clerk Maxwell, whose discoveries and formulations still form the basis for our understanding of *electromagnetism*—the unification of the basic laws of both electricity and magnetism.

Rapid Expansion of Knowledge

While the *sandhi*, or transition period of Dwapara Yuga, did yield many key discoveries, Sri Yukteswar's 1894 prediction was that the twentieth century would see "the rapid expansion of knowledge in all departments."[1] While the number of new discoveries and the amount of new knowledge in the eighteenth and nineteenth centuries is impressive, the new discoveries, new knowledge, and especially the applications they led to in the twentieth century are truly staggering: nuclear physics (photons, quanta, nuclear energy, quantum physics, quarks), biology (DNA, microbiology, genetics, pharmacology), astrophysics (relativity, galaxies, big bang, black holes, quasars, pulsars, galaxy clusters, dark matter, dark energy), materials science (plastics, synthetic fibers, metal alloys, silicon, nanotechnology, carbon fiber materials), medicine (x-rays, electroencephalograms, CAT, PET and MRI scans, laser surgery), communication (radio, telephone, broadcast television, computers, digital transmission through the internet, fiber optics), and transportation (automobiles and trucks, both electric and internal combustion, high speed trains, magnetic levitation trains, submarines, airplanes, helicopters, and even rockets and spacecraft).

And that is just the short list of discoveries and developments made in the twentieth century and into the beginning of the twenty-first! The list doesn't include similarly rapid expansion of knowledge in geology, archeology, psychology, jurisprudence, education, agriculture, engineering, political science, history, philosophy, and religion—in fact, simply to *list* all the areas of expanding knowledge would require several chapters, if not an entire book.

The amount of information available to us today has been expanding at a rapidly accelerating rate. Estimates have been made that from 1900 to 1950 the sum total of mankind's knowledge doubled, and then doubled again by 1970, and again by 1980, and again by 1985, and so on. Even if these estimates overestimate the pace, there is no question that we are seeing the rapid expansion of knowledge that Sri Yukteswar predicted in 1894.

Knowledge has expanded to such an extent that leading educators are wondering what school-age children *should* be taught—there are simply too many subjects, and too much information in all of them, to even address them all, let alone teach them as subjects. These educators are advocating that, while a basic knowledge set is still desirable, the most important thing that can be taught is *how to learn*, since we all need to learn continually *throughout our lives* just to keep pace with new discoveries.

"Space Annihilators"

Where might the expansion of knowledge lead? In *Autobiography of a Yogi*, Paramhansa Yogananda refers to the current developments of transportation and communication as "space annihilators."[2] What other ways might we see mankind overcome the inherent limitations of space? One limitation of space is distance. In Kali Yuga, communication by written word, when carried from country to country, or even continent to continent, often took months. The oft-used phrase, "waiting for his ship to come in," referred to the experience of not knowing for months, even years, the fate of ships traveling around the world. Distance was a significant limitation. Today we have instantaneous communication. It is commonplace to be able to talk on the telephone to someone halfway around the world. We've even talked with men on the moon.

So far, instantaneous transmission has been limited to non-tangibles: the voice, images, and data, sent via modulated frequencies and digitized bits and bytes. But in 1993, a group of scientists at England's Cambridge University published a convincing paper [3] indicating the possibility of creating an exact copy of a particle. A matter copy machine, so to speak. This phenomenon is known as quantum teleportation. Star Trek's "beam me up, Scotty" may not be as farfetched as it seems! Just now, however, it would be hard to find a volunteer to be the first person dissolved and recreated in another place, given how tenuous the evidence is that such a thing is possible. But given what is already known today, can we rule out the possibility of such capability in the future?

Overcoming the limitations of distance on earth pales beside overcoming the limitations of interstellar distances. Even traveling at near the speed of light, a spaceship would take lifetimes to reach nearby stars. But physicists have posited for decades that there may be "wormholes" in space. Wormholes could be likened to shortcuts through space. Instead of having to travel millions of light years to arrive at a distant star, wormholes might allow a spacecraft (assuming we needed one!) to arrive in a fraction of the time.

It takes a physicist to appreciate how a wormhole could exist. Wormholes, should they exist, are unlikely to be like the slightly eerie and fuzzy subway tunnels that are depicted in science fiction movies. However, a person in Kali Yuga could never have imagined that it would be possible to talk with someone on the other side of the earth, yet we do so all the time. So why not shortcuts through space?

Ask any physicist and he will tell you that we are *just beginning* to understand the nature of the universe. In the 1990s a team of scientists concluded that the visible objects in the universe account for only 4% of the total gravitational effect known to exist in the universe. Only 4%! The other 96% of the universe's gravitational effect—theoretically comprised of so-called "dark matter" and "dark energy"—have yet to be even observed.

Another limitation of space is the seeming immutability of matter. Already man has learned, albeit to his peril, to convert matter to energy. Yet this conversion may be only the barest beginning of what is possible. Perhaps mankind will learn not only to convert matter to energy, but also to convert energy to matter. The conversion of energy to matter is already taking place at infinitesimally small scales in "atom smashers," the particle accelerators and colliders that particle physicists use for their experiments. When atomic particles are accelerated to near the speed of light, and then aimed at carefully isolated atoms or sub-atomic particles, the resulting collisions can often result, if only for nanoseconds, in the formation of new matter. Considered theoretically possible as early as the 1930s, this phenomenon was first confirmed at the Stanford Linear Accelerator in 1997. If tiny bits of new matter are routinely created in the laboratory, why not some day on a grander scale?

In light of the current pace of discovery, it is not hard to believe that instantaneous travel, interstellar travel, and the ability to manipulate the very structure of matter may become possible, and that eventually man will develop many more space annihilators — perhaps in ways not yet even conceived.

Dwapara — The Energy Age

The common theme of scientific discovery in the twentieth century, and now in the twenty-first, is *energy*. It is as if the material cover of matter has been peeled back to reveal a pulsating, ceaselessly vibrating world of what Sri Yukteswar described as "fine matters and electricities." Electricity, radio, telephony, television, and a host of other modern-day miracles are the result of science learning to harness the interactions of the "electricities" with atoms and molecules, the "fine matters" — by taking advantage of energy's predictable, wavelike, vibratory motion.

Further, it is the stunning insight that all matter is influenced by, and indeed composed of, radiant, vibrating energy — the quantum flux, or more poetically, the quantum foam of John Wheeler — that underlies nearly all scientific advances since 1900. You could say that mankind as a whole now understands that matter is not what it seems. Complex, wave-like interactions of energy underlie the reality of matter.

The best science of Kali Yuga, which was primarily engineering, was mechanistic. It relied on an understanding of the world that was based on the gross physical properties of matter: weight, strength, hardness. It was limited by the contemporary level of understanding of how to alter things: chiseling stone, cutting wood, casting metal. And finally,

Kali Yuga science was limited by the known ways to move matter: muscle power (animal and human), fire power, and water power.

Even the explanations for how forces affected matter during Kali Yuga were always very mechanistic. The Aristotelian concept of fire was that it was a *thing*, an element, like water, or stone. The careful separation of the concepts of matter and energy didn't take hold until the eighteenth and nineteenth centuries AD, during the transition period from Kali to Dwapara Yuga. During those two centuries, leading up to Dwapara Yuga proper, the natures of light and magnetism were explored by many scientists. But it wasn't until the beginning of the 1900s, when Dwapara Yuga's revelations really began, that mankind discovered not only that energy was not a *thing*, but that things themselves were actually made up of energy.

Thoughts Are Universal

It is commonly thought that civilization has advanced to today's level by mankind simply adding new knowledge to what was already known. If we see human development as a straight line upward, Einstein's theory of relativity came when it did because of a long line of earlier discoveries. Sri Yukteswar tells us, however, that in 1900 mankind attained a new *consciousness* that was more subtle, and one that, being more subtle, allowed mankind as a whole to appreciate that the world surrounding us is formed and held together by subtle, unseen energies.

Einstein often gets the credit for giving the world this fundamental insight. His was the good fortune to be the one who formulated the key insight, often expressed as $E=mc2$. But, according to Sri Yukteswar, if it hadn't been Einstein it would have been someone else who made the connections and formulated the theory at that time — because mankind was ready to understand it.

The history of science includes many instances of two or more scientists making the same discovery at nearly the same time. Darwin's theory of evolution, first published in the late 1850s, was almost *Wallace's* theory of evolution. Alfred Russel Wallace wrote a letter to Darwin outlining his own, and very similar theory of evolution, at or very near the same time Darwin presented his theory to the world. Had he not been 8,000 miles away in Malaya, and had his letter therefore not required months to arrive by ship, Wallace may well have gotten the credit for the theory. In fact, there are a number of scientists today who insist on calling it the Darwin/Wallace Theory of Evolution.

We see too many examples of simultaneous discoveries to explain them away as coincidences. In the early decades of the twentieth century, Thomas Edison and Nikola Tesla, while jealously guarding their discoveries from each other as much as possible, nonetheless ended up leapfrogging each other with discoveries about, and uses for, electricity. During World War II, during the race to create a nuclear weapon, scientists, working in strict isolation in both the United States and Germany, an isolation enforced by top secret clearances and guarded facilities, nonetheless duplicated many of one another's discoveries. In 1962, two scientists, Arno Penzias and Robert Wilson, working for Bell Labs in New Jersey, discovered the cosmic background radiation that eventually confirmed the Big Bang theory. When they published their findings, however, they narrowly beat out another team working on the same discovery at Princeton University, a research team they knew nothing about. Stories of simultaneous discoveries abound in the literature of science.

In the spiritual classic *Autobiography of a Yogi*, Paramhansa Yogananda explains that "thoughts are universally and not individually rooted."[4] He used the analogy that we tune into thoughts much as we tune a radio dial to find a particular station. The same discoveries are made by men and women who are "tuning in" to the same problem or concept, thus tuning into the same ideas, insights, and solutions. Ideas, therefore, can be said to exist outside of any one person's mind. Thoughts are *perceived*, not created.

The truth that ideas are universally rooted, not individually rooted, was as true in Kali Yuga as it is today in Dwapara Yuga. But Dwapara Yuga's effect on mankind is, essentially, that we now possess a qualitatively new and subtler *level of perception*. Just as radios can have multiple bands—AM and FM for example—mankind as a whole now has access to a "higher" frequency band, which allows us to "tune in" to more subtle ideas. Kali Yuga man had AM only, so to speak. Dwapara man has both AM and FM. The new "FM band" of Dwapara Yuga is capable of receiving more subtle ideas, qualitatively different from the "AM band" of Kali Yuga. Thus the average Dwapara Yuga man is capable of perception and understanding beyond that of the average person during Kali Yuga.

The Discovery of Man's Inner Energy
and Inner Consciousness

Just as our more refined perception has revealed the subtle, inner energies of matter, so too has it revealed subtle, inner energies within man himself. And just as greater awareness of matter's subtle energies has given us greater ability to transform the world around us, so, too, our greater awareness of our own subtle, inner energies has given us, as individuals, greater ability to transform ourselves.

The heightened level of perception brought about by Dwapara Yuga has made us more self-aware. For example, people today are demonstrably more aware of their own energy than they were in Kali Yuga. Phrases in common parlance include "having energy" to do something, "getting energy" from other people or situations, feeling "energized" by exercise or a good night's sleep, or feeling "empowered" to do something.

The phrases "will power," and "life force," weren't even used before the 1800s. Additionally, we have a host of new words coined in the twentieth century, or new meanings have been given to old words, all conveying our everyday awareness of the state of our own personal energy: dash, fire, get-up-and-go, juice, pep, pizzazz, zest, zing, and zip!

Oriental martial arts, once hidden in monasteries, are now appreciated and practiced all over the world. At the heart of most of the disciplines, such as karate, kung fu, tai-kwon-do, jujitsu, and other martial arts styles, is the control of one's *chi*, or life force.

Masters of the martial arts can perform acts that defy physical laws. A tai chi master, while giving a talk on the benefits of practicing tai chi, once invited four people to come up onto the stage to help him demonstrate the nature of the *chi* or life force. First he asked the volunteers to pick him up. He is a slight man, weighing no more than 120 pounds, and the four volunteers had no difficulty lifting him off the ground. After they lowered him back to the ground, he asked the volunteers to wait while he prepared himself. A few moments later, at a nod from the master, the four volunteers once again went to pick him up. This time they could not lift even one of his feet off the floor! They changed grips, they struggled and strained, but they could not pick him up. The master then performed an even more remarkable feat. He asked one of the volunteers to pick him up and keep him up. The volunteer, a large healthy-looking man, lifted him up, and then the audience watched as the master, with no visible effort, slowly and inexorably sank to the ground as the volunteer strained to hold him up.

Obviously not everyone has this remarkable degree of control over his inner energies. But the conviction that we do have inner energies to control is widespread. In practices ranging from martial arts to exercise, from meditation to yoga, from therapy to positive thinking, people have embraced the reality of a hidden, subtle realm that profoundly influences their lives.

Mankind has also accepted the knowledge that we each have an inner world of hidden *motives* that can affect us in profound ways. During the late 1800s and early 1900s the new science of psychology was born. Now commonly accepted, the notion that all people are profoundly influenced by hidden, inner forces (e.g. the subconscious mind, id, ego, and superego of Freud) only emerged when we fully entered Dwapara Yuga proper in 1900. Freud's seminal works on dreams and the subconscious mind, as well as contributions from scientists such as William James and Alfred Binet, were published between 1895 and 1905.

We can draw an analogy between our personal motivations and the concept of potential energy as defined by physics. In the science of physics, potential energy is the extra energy an object possesses but is not immediately using. For example, when a roller coaster car is at the top of the first big hill of the roller coaster track—even though it is barely moving, it possesses tremendous potential energy—which is then expended once it starts going, rapidly, down the other side of the hill.

We could say that our motives and our desires, whether subconsciously hidden or consciously known, possess the same quality of potential energy. Stored within us we have enormous energy bound up in specific motivations and desires. Once we have an opportunity for our motives and desires to manifest in some way, we experience the release of stored energy.

The notion that we can compare potential energy to personal motivation may seem only an intellectual exercise. But the purpose of the comparison is to show that the Dwapara keynote, *energy*, that so clearly defines modern scientific knowledge, is also the keynote that defines our modern day view of human behavior as well. We are aware that our personal motivations and life force can be considered separately from our physical bodies, just as Dwapara science separates energy from matter.

The Rise of the Empowered Individual

The average person in Kali Yuga was more interested in adapting to his circumstances than rising above them. Confucianism, for example, born in descending Kali Yuga (c. 500 BC), epitomizes this aspect of Kali Yuga. Confucianism is the meticulous description, along with meticulous proscriptions, of how any individual fits into the surrounding society. The underlying premise of Confucianism is that any person's happiness lies in conformance with the expectations of the position in which he finds himself. In Kali Yuga India, we find the same strong trend toward accepting the norms of society. The caste system, grossly distorted from its original expression, became a hereditary system. The caste one was born into (and the particular *jati*—or sub-group—within that caste) defined one's possibilities for life. Europe and the Middle East also had expressions of this same rigidity of social order and pattern—the feudal system, class systems, and religious teachings all reinforced the thought and practice that a man's fate was sealed at birth.

Religious teachings of an afterlife, both the Western conception of life after death in heaven or hell, and the Eastern conception of reincarnation, were deeply believed in Kali Yuga. Deeply believed, because the thinking of the day was that one's earthly existence was something to be endured, not enjoyed, that it was perhaps even a penance or punishment. Life in Kali Yuga, for the average person was hard: life spans were short, day-to-day life was uncertain, and one's destiny was determined by birth, not merit. As a result, people were drawn to religious concepts that emphasized a better life coming in the hereafter.

Dwapara Yuga man, by contrast, wants a better life in the here and now, not in the hereafter. Dwapara man actively seeks to alter his circumstances. Dwapara man is empowered and *self-interested*. Enabled by the shared convictions of the times, Dwapara Yuga individuals demonstrate much greater ability to affect the world around them, better their circumstances, and expand their knowledge and skills than did the people of Kali Yuga.

In Kali Yuga, priests and rulers represented powerful institutions that shaped the life and thought of every man. To disagree with the priests was to risk one's place in one's society, to risk expulsion and ruin. To disagree with the rulers was to risk death or detention. Today, the individual is considered equal to, if not actually more important than, the institutions of religion and government. Disagreement with the powers that be is today not merely possible, it is often considered a virtue.

The Ascent of Reason

It would be hard for anyone alive today to imagine a world where *reason*, rational thinking, did not dominate as the shared and accepted way of arriving at opinions, conclusions, and fact. We take for granted the process of observation, inquiry and logic, the scientific method, and the need to support conclusions with demonstrable facts. This does not, of course, mean that everyone agrees on everything today. The need to support conclusions with demonstrable facts is often honored in the breech, and not everyone is as able in his reasoning abilities, or as willing to be reasonable. *Self-interest*, the hallmark of Dwapara Yuga, has an all too familiar way of using reason to try to get its own way. But, by and large, rationality is the accepted *mode* of arriving at conclusions about most things, even if people use reason with varying degrees of impartiality.

As we will explore in later chapters, reason is not the only, or even the best, way to arrive at what is true. Intuition, or direct perception, is superior. Even in the field of science, considered to be a bastion of rational thinking, great scientific insights have come to scientists not only as the result of a step-by-step process, but in an intuitive "leap." Einstein, considered by nearly everyone to be a genius, experienced many of his insights coming to him in a flash—but subsequently devoted years painstakingly to prove his insights through the process and language of reason.

Intuition, alas, can be distorted beyond recognition by *self-interest*. From self-proclaimed but deluded "prophets" to darkly motivated leaders such as Hitler, powerful individuals, strongly *self-interested* and even obsessed, yet claiming intuitive insights, have led many people into error. Experiences with this sort of "intuition" have left mankind skeptical and mistrustful of claims of intuitive truth. Reason, for all its limitations, currently suits our awareness. The current state of man's awakened intellect is in tune with reason.

During Kali Yuga, neither reason nor intuition held sway. Kali Yuga was the time of commandments and unquestioning acceptance. The great majority of people were simply told what was and what was not true—and for the most part accepted what they were told. In medieval Europe we can see this acceptance of authority in the dominance of the Catholic Church. The notion that a person could draw conclusions that differed from those of spiritual authority was considered heretical in medieval Europe and, quite frankly, perilous—even on issues of natural science. Galileo, now considered to be the father of reason, spent his last years under house arrest until his death in 1642, as a result of his assertion that the solar system was heliocentric.

In Kali Yuga, most people accepted without question that the physical world, because of its divine origins, was incomprehensible to man. All knowledge of the physical world was considered to have been revealed by God's messengers. Revelation was interpreted and disseminated by priests who formulated dogmas that became the accepted knowledge of the time.

We see the same authoritarian dispensation of truth not only in Europe but around the world. Huang Zongxi, a Chinese philosopher and minister in the Ming court, died in prison in 1695 for asserting that rulers were not inherently divine, and that reason should be the determinant of truth. In India, the hold the Brahmins had on the minds of the people was so strong that reason, as an independent means of arriving at what is true, had no foothold until the British arrived in the seventeenth century AD.

One might think that, had there been schools, books, and teachers in Kali Yuga, people would have been as easily awakened intellectually as we are today, that the natural tendency to reason would have quickened just as it does today. But according to Sri Yukteswar, the average Kali Yuga man was not as *capable* of intellectual awakening. Dharma, or mental virtue as Sri Yukteswar described it, was only one-quarter developed during Kali Yuga. Kali Yuga man was not guided by intellect. The senses, not the intellect, were the dominant determinant of Kali Yuga man's actions—the simple calculus of maximizing pleasure and minimizing pain ruled man's nature. The AM band of Kali Yuga man's perceptual "radio" simply did not include reason and intellect. At the twilight of Kali Yuga and the beginning of Dwapara Yuga, however, mankind's intellect began to quicken—the higher and more subtle FM band of Dwapara Yuga man's perceptual "radio" became accessible, and led to reason's ascent. Dharma, or mental virtue, was becoming one-half developed.

We see evidence for the awakening of reason in the timing of the Enlightenment. The essence of the Enlightenment, beginning in the waning transition years of Kali Yuga (1600 AD) and coming to its full flower by 1800 AD, was the switch from a reliance on commandments and authority, religious authority especially, to a reliance on reason, and its champion, science. Enlightenment thinkers themselves referred to this period as the *Age of Reason.*

Enlightenment philosophers included: Hobbes (1588–1679), whose work *Leviathan* puts forth a rational framework for politics, often called the social contract; Descartes (1596–1650) whose dictum *cogito ergo sum* ("I think, therefore, I am.") is emblematic of *rationalism* as a philosophic position; Locke (1632–1704) a seminal thinker in the realm of political philosophy, a philosopher who espoused and expanded the concepts of the social contract; Spinoza (1632–1672), considered to have laid the foundation for the Enlightenment with his rationalist approach to science and ethics; Voltaire (1694–1778), who wrote extensively about the rights of man as an independent rational being, and who dared to criticize church dogma; Hume (1711–1776), who championed empiricism and scientific skepticism, and advanced the doctrines of naturalism and material causes; and Kant (1724–1804), who systemized critical philosophy based on the principles of reason.

By 1800 AD reason reigned supreme. The Age of Reason and the Scientific Revolution had swept the world. Careful application of reason, logic, observation, and experimentation was revealing nature as never before—lawful and explicable. Reasonable arguments were carrying the day in politics, philosophy, medicine, and even religion.

~~~~~~~~~~

Dwapara Yuga's influence has not merely given us new insights, it has changed mankind itself. Mankind as a whole is capable of more subtle perceptions. New abilities, largely dormant during Kali Yuga, have awakened. There are obvious reasons for calling Dwapara Yuga the *Energy Age.* Myriad scientific discoveries have led to the widespread use of energy and the understanding that there is a *subtler reality underlying all matter*, one imperceptible to our unaided senses, and governed by the laws of energy.

On the human level, mankind has discovered a subtler self, also governed by laws of energy, but highly personal and unique to each individual. This new awareness has awakened personal *self-interest*, and with this new awareness has come the conviction that one can, using *one's own energy*, affect one's circumstances and achieve one's goals. And so we might also call Dwapara Yuga the *age of the individual*. And finally, mankind's intellect has awakened. Rational thought and logical arguments are but the obvious expressions of a world in which *rational thinking* is the norm.

Energy awareness, the awakened intellect, and the empowered individual have already reshaped our world—and the process is just beginning. Dwapara Yuga is but 300 years old. There remains another 2,100 years of development!

Chapter 4

Ascending Dwapara Yuga —
Currents

Timeline

1700 AD Beginning of present
ascending Dwapara Yuga

1900 AD End of the 200-year
transition period (*sandhi*)
from Kali Yuga

3900 AD Beginning of the 200-year
transition period (*sandhi*)
to Treta Yuga

4100 AD End of present ascending
Dwapara Yuga

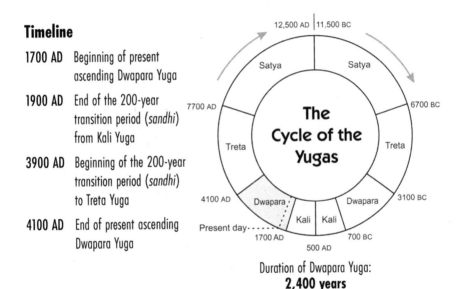

Duration of Dwapara Yuga:
2,400 years

Before describing some of the broad currents that are moving the affairs of Dwapara Yuga man forward, it is important to again point out that Sri Yukteswar employs the phrase *mankind as a whole* to describe who is affected by the changes of consciousness brought about by the yugas. The *majority of mankind* might also be the right phrase. But Sri Yukteswar strongly states that in any yuga there have been, and will be, both people who are more advanced in their consciousness than that prevailing in the yuga, and those who are less advanced.

In the world today there are people whose consciousness is more akin to Kali Yuga — passive, dull, and lacking in energy. There are also

51

people alive today whose consciousness is more in tune with the higher consciousness of Treta and Satya Yuga. If you don't see yourself flowing along with the Dwapara Yuga currents we are about to describe, then perhaps you will find yourself more in tune with those of the higher yugas. The currents described in this chapter are necessarily broadly generalized. You might think of these currents as flowing from the "center of gravity" of our world civilization. But any specific individual will always be unique.

In the last chapter we described the fundamental changes to man's consciousness that are the keynotes of Dwapara Yuga:

- Where Kali Yuga man was passive and accepting, Dwapara Yuga man is empowered and *self-interested.*

- Where Kali Yuga man was dull, with intellect asleep, Dwapara Yuga man's intellect is awake and reasoning.

- Where Kali Yuga man perceived only gross matter, the Dwapara Yuga man is able to perceive the subtle energies underlying gross matter and within himself.

- Where Kali Yuga could be seen to have unfolded to the formula of *passive acceptance* x *dull-mindedness* x *matter awareness*, Dwapara Yuga can be seen to be unfolding to the formula of *self-interest* x *awakened intellect* x *energy awareness.*

The formula for Dwapara Yuga is highly energetic; like an electrical turbine, it is sending out wave after wave of energetic currents. New ways of thinking and new motivations, new capabilities both positive and destructive, and new-found self-awareness are profoundly reshaping the world around us.

Cities and Commerce

If one could go back in a time machine to Kali Yuga and fly over the world, and then return from the past and fly over the world as it is today, one of the most striking differences one would see is the enormous increase in the size and number of cities.

Throughout Kali Yuga the overwhelming majority of people lived simple agrarian lives. Most people were tied to the land, and their very survival depended on farming and herding. Typically they lived together in small extended family groups, or small villages surrounded by farms. We see this pattern during Kali Yuga in China, India, the Middle East, Africa, Europe, and North and South America. We know that approximately 80% of the population in medieval Europe survived through subsistence agriculture.

Today the percentage is nearly reversed — for example, not only does over 80% of the population of the U.S. live in cities with populations of 10,000 people or more, but less than 1% of the entire U.S. population is involved in agriculture. Although large percentages of the populations of China, India, and Africa as well as other areas are still agrarian, the world trend is also clearly toward urbanization. Population scientists predict that during the period between 2050 and 2100 AD the great majority of the world population will live in urban environments and only a small percentage will live rural lives devoted to agriculture.

The high concentration of the world population in cities is only possible because of the worldwide explosion of business and commerce. Without a money-based economy it would not be possible to concentrate so many people so close together.

Most historians will tell you that this enormous shift from subsistence farming to urban living is the result of the Industrial Revolution of the eighteenth and nineteenth centuries. Or perhaps they will point to the Industrial Revolution as the beginning of the trend but to twentieth century technology as the real cause.

But, Are These Causes or Effects?

Sri Yukteswar writes that the 200-year transition period from Kali Yuga to Dwapara Yuga took place during the eighteenth and nineteenth centuries — exactly corresponding to the time period of the Industrial Revolution.

The bare facts of history often leave out the motives of the people who make the history. The simple fact is that people *want* to move to cities because *cities afford them the greatest opportunities to pursue their self-interest.* Self-interest is leading people to go where they can experience more than subsistence living, where they can find the best chance for education, advancement, discretionary wealth, and a wide variety of lifestyle choices. Right now, and for the past three centuries, those new experiences have been found primarily in cities.

Today we take it for granted that each person can, or soon will be able to, significantly improve his circumstances. But such was not the predominant way of thinking in Kali Yuga. Kali Yuga man tended to passively accept his lot. It was expected that one would live and die in the same class or caste or station one was born into. Social mobility did not exist. Education was for the very few.

Many historians lead us to believe that this was the result of conscious subjugation by the ruling classes. The implication is that always simmering below the surface was the common man's urge to break out of his subjugation. But history doesn't really bear out this notion. Rather, everyone, the subjected and the subjugator alike, saw his place as part of the natural order. People, even rulers, were fatalistic about their lives.

During the French revolution, which occurred in 1792 (during the transition period from Kali Yuga to Dwapara Yuga), Louis XVI and Marie Antoinette were genuinely shocked to learn of the *idea* that their subjects did not think they had a predetermined right to rule. Such an idea did not even arise during the preceding Kali Yuga centuries of royal rule in France. However, once Dwapara Yuga began to unfold, people everywhere began to reject the notion that the right to rule was hereditary.

The earliest stirrings of such thinking in the West occurred during the Enlightenment, which began in the 1600s (during the 100-year twilight transition of Kali Yuga) and lasted until 1800 AD (the middle of the Dwapara Yuga's 200-year transition period). John Locke, David Hume, Voltaire, and a host of other scientists and philosophers began to formulate and put forward the ideas we now take for granted—the rights of the individual and the importance of reason. But prior to the 1600s, not even the elite had such thoughts, let alone the common man.

People today, on the other hand, take for granted the idea that we can and should actively seek to improve our circumstances. As Sri Yukteswar writes, during the transition from Kali Yuga to Dwapara Yuga, "people began to have respect for themselves."[1] Or put yet another way, mankind woke up from the passive dream of Kali Yuga and set about to change the world to suit themselves.

Careful study of the Industrial Revolution and of the rapid expansion of technology in the twentieth century will reveal that commerce, accompanied by the desire to create wealth, was the driving force behind the industrial and technological development that so dramatically transformed our world—not the other way around.

Put bluntly, we enjoy the benefits of the wonders of the modern world largely because someone, or some group, was self-interestedly willing to invest in developing them. And, in turn, those people were willing to invest in the development of our modern wonders because they believed enough people would be sufficiently self-interested to *pay* for them.

In our times, we take the idea of money for granted. But in feudal Europe, and throughout the world during that era, the average person never accumulated more money than could buy him the few necessities he could not grow or make for himself. Barter was far more common than purchases made with money. There was a merchant population in Kali Yuga, but it was a very small proportion of the whole, and served largely the hereditary wealthy and the ruling class.

Today nearly everyone depends on money. The "merchant class" has in fact grown to include the majority of mankind. Not everyone is a merchant in the narrow sense of the word—directly buying and selling for profit. But the majority of mankind, and the proportion is steadily increasing, is involved in the design, production, manufacture, delivery, or provision of goods and services that comprise what we call the world economy. This world economy is in turn the result of the millions and millions of people making individual, self-interested decisions as to where to use their energy, creativity, time, and passion—and where to spend their money. The merchant class has expanded to include billions of people around the world. The merchant class no longer serves only hereditary wealth and ruling classes—it serves primarily itself!

The size and number of cities around the world is one of the most visible ways that Dwapara consciousness has reshaped the world. The dominance of commerce, driven by self-interested individuals, has freed most people from subsistence on the land. Now people earn their livelihoods in one manner or another through business. Business is generally most efficient—and most profitable—where people are concentrated.

The foundation of modern cities is commerce—and commerce is one of the primary manifestations of the formula *self-interest* x *awakened intellect* x *energy awareness* thus far in Dwapara Yuga.

The Pursuit of Happiness

Today, the average citizen in one of the world's prosperous nations has more wealth, more education, and thus more freedom to follow his or her interests, than nearly anyone who lived during Kali Yuga. If current trends continue, the vast majority of the world population, which currently still includes millions and millions who live hand to mouth, will eventually achieve prosperity and freedom of action as well.

Even now, a significant percentage of the world's people, who, because their basic needs are assured, are able to make many life choices purely for the sake of individual happiness. This may well be the single most powerful current motivating billions of people around the world today. And people are taking advantage of their newfound freedom to pursue their happiness with dedicated zeal!

Today's predominant pursuits are accumulating wealth, property, and other objects; experiencing endless varieties of sensory and mental experiences; and gaining and using personal power and striving for personal achievement. All of these pursuits were, perhaps, just as desirable during Kali Yuga, but now, during Dwapara Yuga, they are much more attainable—Dwapara Yuga is providing many more ways of pursuing them—and people are much more capable of trying and motivated to attain them.

The shear variety of things to do and experience today is astonishingly greater than it was even one hundred years ago. World travel, varied cuisine (myriad types of food, plentiful restaurants), endless entertainment (movies, television, radio, books, music, art), choices for personal possessions (the list goes on forever), personal achievement (from being promoted at work to gaining fame, from learning to cook to running a business) have exploded the number of choices people can make seeking personal pleasure and fulfillment.

Nor is this the whole picture. Dwapara man's *interests* are also legion. The World Wide Web, the world's exponentially growing repository of information, gives us glimpses of the enormous variety Dwapara man is exposed to. For example, Wikipedia, an online encyclopedia, attempts to address all known hobbies. Just the list of *categories* of hobbies numbers more than 300 — the categories include (in a more or less random sampling) falconry, soap making, dumpster-diving, collecting moths, collecting salt and pepper shakers, retro computing, hardware hacking, war gaming, Wild West reenactment, constructed languages, live steam models, ghost hunting, laser skirmish, plinking, erector sets, roadgeek, and train spotting.

Dive into any of these hobbies and you will find there are thousands or even millions of enthusiasts. For example, the phrase "train spotting" occurs on over 110,000 pages found on the web. "Ghost hunting" nets you over 650,000 pages, and "soap makers" will find over 1.4 million pages to explore. Put something better known, such as "tennis," into a search engine and you get 250,000,000 matches to your search.

Dwapara man's astonishingly varied pursuit of happiness also has its dark side. It is as if the restraints of the past have been removed. Dwapara Yuga's ascent of reason, science, and technology has led many people to reject all of the past — the wisdom along with the ignorance. Modern society is less accepting of the *commandments* of the past. "Thou shalt not," is no longer sufficient to convince people that many pursuits are unwise.

People are determined to find out for themselves, and often the result is self-destructive. Alcohol, drugs, and sex, taken to excess, still, as in Kali Yuga, lead to unhappiness. Ambrose Bierce's definition of a *debauchee*, in his wonderfully wry, yet insightful, *The Devil's Dictionary*, is: "One who has so earnestly pursued pleasure that he has had the misfortune to overtake it."[2] The definition says a lot about what many people have yet to learn. Over-satiety leads to dullness. Further stimulation requires ever-greater excess — truly a vicious cycle. Yet more people than ever pursue their happiness down this fruitless path.

Further, self-interest is, alas, often *self-centered*, and mankind is currently pursuing happiness without much regard for other people. When we watch a child grow up, we may lament some of the "phases" the child must go through on its way to maturity. So, too, with the rise of self-interest that we see in Dwapara Yuga, many of the results of this phase are lamentable: self-involvement, personal excess, amoral behavior, accumulation of extreme wealth at the expense of others, and greed untempered by ethical considerations. Much of Dwapara Yuga, so far, does not paint a pretty picture, and one can sympathize with those who think the world is going to the dogs.

The formula *self-interest* x *awakened intellect* x *energy awareness* explains the explosion of interests and pursuits we witness today. It doesn't, alas, guarantee happiness. Yet, according to Sri Yukteswar, man is developing toward greater dharma, or mental virtue. It is as if mankind as a whole is conducting an ongoing experiment in how to find happiness. Like Thomas Edison, who experimented with thousands of different types of filaments for the light bulb before finding the right one, mankind also is experimenting and, through trial and error (and perhaps by eventually regaining an appreciation for past sources of true wisdom), will eventually learn to seek happiness in ways that give more lasting results.

We also must keep in mind that at the same time that mankind's self-interested behavior appears to be leading us to an undesirable end, it has also led to improved standards of living, better health care, better education, and the thousands of ways that energy has been harnessed for mankind's benefit. These developments—no matter how self-centered the motives that conceived them—have vastly changed *everyone's* lives.

Dwapara Yuga brings with it both perils and pitfalls. But you would be hard pressed to find many people alive today who would prefer the conditions and consciousness of Kali Yuga over those of Dwapara Yuga—regardless of its shortcomings.

The Individual vs. the Institution

During Kali Yuga, institutions dominated the lives of individuals. The power of the rulers was nearly absolute. The influence of religions on the minds of the common people was paramount. From China to India, from Europe to South America, kings and emperors controlled their populations through might of arms, and priests and religious leaders wielded vast influence over the minds and hearts through dogma and the ability to inspire reverence or fear. Even at Kali Yuga's best, an individual had little possibility of influencing the course of government or the dogmas and tenets of the time.

Today the influence of individuals is on the rise. The balance has shifted from the individual being subject to the institution, to the institution being subject to the individual. In modern day democracies the individual can sue the government—and often win! Freedom of religion, a highly regarded right in America and other countries, continues to gain greater and greater acceptance throughout the world. The ability of individuals to create businesses, champion social causes, lobby the government, get elected to political office, or pursue an independent religious path, has given individuals much more influence over government and religious institutions than they ever had in Kali Yuga.

The institution however, is far from dead. Institutions are still very effective at organizing and channeling the efforts of large numbers of people to particular ends. And once these ends are attained, the institution, whether a corporation, a government, or a church, is still very effective at continuing its activities. But, although large institutions are still necessary today, their limitations are better understood.

E. F. Schumacher's book, *Small is Beautiful: Economics as if People Matter*, first published in the 1970s, was a thoughtful look at the advantages of small economic systems, from small businesses to small villages. Big governments and large businesses tend to reduce the individual to the status of a statistic, whereas small, innovative governmental programs and small businesses can respond to the ideas and needs of individuals much more effectively.

We also see a trend of individuals, from their own convictions and by marshalling their own resources and those of like-minded people, setting out to make a difference. From Mahatma Gandhi to Bill Gates, from Nelson Mandela to Bono, individuals are now shaping government and history, and taking on the causes and concerns that larger institutions will not, or cannot.

Democracy is perhaps the most obvious development in government in Dwapara Yuga. At the heart of democracy is the conviction that those who govern do so at the pleasure of those who are governed. If those who are governing displease enough people, they are voted out. As Abraham Lincoln, the sixteenth President of the United States put it in 1863, democracy is "government of the people, by the people, and for the people."

Many people will point out that democracy was born in ancient Athens. And it is fair to say that the idea existed then. The practice, however, was far less than what we mean today when we refer to democratic government. First, voting was limited to male landowners, a limitation that excluded soldiers, artisans, farmers, women, and slaves—the overwhelming majority of the population.

Second, Greece's admittedly noble, if limited, experiment in democracy failed miserably. In a few short years, Athens was in disarray as a result of a fickle crowd voting on everything. Any passionate speaker could sway the voters to take a vote, there and then, to do something—including exiling for life the very man who instituted democracy in the first place, Cleisthenes!

What Athens lacked, and what elevates modern democracy above voting alone, is the rule of law. The rule of law implies that there are rules defining the limits of conduct, rules that are *rationally* determined, and that pertain to all, regardless of rank, station, or wealth. Or as is commonly stated, and commonly understood, "no man is above the law." Without a body of laws, Athens' experiment with democracy was just a shade above mob rule.

The rule of law did not rise to its present level until after the end of Kali Yuga. Yes, there were laws in Kali Yuga, but the ruling class was not always subject to those laws, and could institute new laws, or overturn old laws, by edict. The idea that the law was higher than those who governed didn't really take hold until the transition from Kali Yuga to Dwapara Yuga, and was only fully established in the twentieth century. Though still not established everywhere in the world, there is now a majority of nations with democratic governments that have established bodies of law.

Put another way, and looked at from the point of view of the change of consciousness brought about by Dwapara Yuga, the individual's self-interest is now considered paramount over the government's interest. In the preamble to the American Declaration of Independence is the famous line, *"We hold these truths to be self-evident, that all men are created equal, that they are endowed by their Creator with certain unalienable Rights, that among these are Life, Liberty, and the pursuit of Happiness."* Not only the American government, but most governments, including the United Nations, also hold as self-evident that there are basic human rights.

The following is a list of documents, created by various world governments, starting in 1689, and continuing up to the present, which express the commonly held idea that all men and women everywhere are entitled, without question, to basic human rights.

- Bill of Rights 1689 (England) and Claim of Right (Scotland)

- Virginia Bill of Rights (June 1776)

- Preamble to the United States Declaration of Independence (July 1776)

- United States Bill of Right to the United States Constitution (Completed in 1789, ratified in 1791)

- Declaration of the Rights of Man and of the Citizen (France, 1789)

- Constitution of Greece (Epidaurus, 1822)

- Basic Rights and Liberties in Finland (1919)

- Universal Declaration of Human Rights (1948)

- European Convention on Human Rights (1950)

- Fundamental Rights of Indian Citizens (1950)

- Candian Bill of Rights (1960)

- Canadian Charter of Rights and Freedoms (1982)

- Artigo Quinto of the Constitution of Brazil (1988)

- New Zealand Bill of Rights Act (1990)

- Hong Kong Bill of Rights Ordiance (1991)

- Constitution of South Africa Chapter 2: Bill of Rights (1996)

- Human Rights Act 1998 (United Kingdom)

- Charter of Fundamental Rights of the European Union (2006)

Not only the rights of the individual are being championed today but also minority rights, women's rights, children's rights, and religious rights. We can see in these movements the natural unfolding of Dwapara man's self-interest; the shared conviction that individuals must be protected from restrictions of their freedom imposed by government, religion, and society.

An Uncertain World

Democracy is a noble idea that does not, however, always rise to nobility. It is no surprise to most of us that government and political processes throughout the world are rife with self-interest, true to the prevailing consciousness of Dwapara Yuga. It is difficult to read about American politics without encountering the phrase *special interests*. While far better suited to the Dwapara consciousness, democracy, the rule of law, and the protection of human rights, do not by themselves ensure that wise laws and decisions will be made.

The formula *self-interest x awakened intellect x energy awareness* is not inherently conducive to fostering wisdom, world peace, and harmony. The energy age is, alas, also the *unsafe and uncertain age*. As long as self-interest is the norm, and therefore the dominant determinant of behavior, we will continue to have a world made up of the haves and the have nots; the oppressors and the oppressed; those with more power and influence and those with less.

The selfish distribution of wealth and knowledge; fear and mistrust of others' motives; race hatred; class and religious prejudice: all these combine to create tension throughout the world — tension that, once it reaches the breaking point, turns into conflict, war, and uncontrolled violence at both an individual and national level. Couple this worldwide tension with weapons that can destroy millions of people, and we have a profoundly unsafe world.

Will we see the world destroyed? According to Sri Yukteswar's disciple, Paramhansa Yogananda, during a talk given in 1940, Dwapara Yuga man possesses enough enlightened self-interest to avoid complete destruction, but that "partial dissolution"[3] is quite possible — due not only to war and our own destructive weapons, but to natural catastrophe as well.

During the talk mentioned above, Yogananda described a law of cause and effect (which may be better understood in Treta Yuga) whereby the mental and emotional tensions engendered by our world subtly affect the weather, and even the structure of the earth. Our "bad vibes" result quite literally in destructive storms, hurricanes, floods — even earthquakes. Earthquakes, if severe enough, could fulfill the predictions of psychics and seers of earth changes of a magnitude to reshape the world at a continental level.

Will these changes happen? When might they happen? Understanding the yugas can give us only a millennial perspective. In Dwapara Yuga the possibility certainly exists for widespread destruction and catastrophe, but these are not foreordained by the age. At the same time, what an understanding of the yugas also offers is an optimistic view of the future. Mankind will improve. As Dwapara Yuga man's change of consciousness becomes fully established and matures, man will inevitably retreat from self-destruction and begin to realize the higher potentials of the age.

Ascending Dwapara Yuga —
Emerging Trends

Timeline

1700 AD Beginning of present ascending Dwapara Yuga

1900 AD End of the 200-year transition period (*sandhi*) from Kali Yuga

3900 AD Beginning of the 200-year transition period (*sandhi*) to Treta Yuga

4100 AD End of present ascending Dwapara Yuga

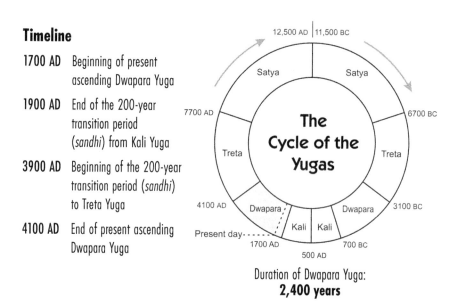

Duration of Dwapara Yuga:
2,400 years

The major Dwapara Yuga currents that are shaping our world, as we explored in the last chapter, may often appear to be of dubious value. *Self-interest* often leads to greed, *energy awareness* has brought us to the point where we could destroy ourselves, and *awakened intellect* is clearly not always synonymous with wisdom. Yet there are also more positive but less well-known trends influencing the unfolding of our age that may well lead us forward into a more enlightened expression of Dwapara Yuga.

Like Attracts Like

We often have nothing more in common with our neighbors than a street address. It is likely that we share nationality and language, but it is more surprising than not if we share interests, or have a similar outlook on life.

In Kali Yuga, assuming someone even had singular interests, the chances of meeting someone else with similarly singular interests were almost nil. The average person lived and died within a few miles of his birthplace. Books were few and extremely costly—and very few even knew how to read. The average person's choices were circumscribed.

Today, however, it is far easier to find people of like mind, to share thoughts, to get together—even to reside in the same location—than it was in Kali Yuga. Today's instantaneous communication, freedom to travel, and relatively greater prosperity, are enabling people to deliberately mix with people of like mind much more readily. We see this trend reflected in the explosion of groups, organizations, media, and websites that are devoted to specific interests. As cited as an example in the previous chapter, there are currently 1.4 million matches to the internet search "soap makers" alone.

This trend is by no means limited to hobbies. Professional, political, and educational associations abound. Thousands and thousands of groups can be found that facilitate communications and bring people together to focus on making money, raising children, maintaining a home, staying healthy, losing weight, and much, much more. Each group has its own approach, and that approach draws people with similar points of view.

Perhaps the most dramatic example of this trend is the rise of intentional communities. The Communities Directory, maintained by the Fellowship for Intentional Communities (FIC), currently lists over 3,000 communities worldwide, ranging in their focus from egalitarian, to ecological, to spiritual communities. Since the Directory is created by voluntary participation only, it is likely that there are thousands more communities not even listed in the Directory.

The communities listed in the Directory range from a dozen people sharing a house and a set of convictions, to communities comprising hundreds of individuals and including businesses, schools, cultural centers, and places of worship. Intentional communities allow individuals to focus on their core interests and pursuits to a depth that is difficult to achieve in a more heterogeneous environment.

Spiritually focused communities, especially, are spreading rapidly, and are not limited to faith, denomination, or other categorization. Thousands of people have organized into communities to buy land together, or near one another, in order to participate in a community that supports them living as their faith and convictions dictate.

Communities know no limitations of country or concept. There are Christian *mega-churches* in the southern United States that include residential areas. Auroville in India is home to scores of spiritual seekers. In Israel there are hundreds of kibbutzim—communal farming settlements. Italy is home to a vibrant new age spiritual community called Damanhur. The United States is home to communities from just about every spiritual tradition: Buddhist, Zen Buddhist, Christian, Jewish, Sufi, and to many, many communities inspired by Indian teachings—such as Ananda, a community focused on the teachings of Paramhansa Yogananda.

You might say that the United States started out as spiritual community for like-minded seekers. Early groups of settlers on the eastern coast of America often shared spiritual convictions. Among the first wave of settlers were the Quakers and the Puritans. In the centuries following settlement, new communities were formed—among these were the Shakers, Amish, and Mennonites.

Communities of like-minded people continue to multiply. It may be that the intentional community becomes the defining social structure of Dwapara Yuga. As more people experience the benefits of close cooperation, participation, and support, more and more communities will form around groups of people with shared convictions and shared goals.

If the trend continues, future Dwapara Yuga residents may see intentional cities, intentional regions and, who knows, even intentional countries. But the trend, no matter how it plays out, is very much an expression of Dwapara Yuga's formula of *self-interest* x *awakened intellect* x *energy awareness*—people shaping the world to further their interests, in energetic and creative ways.

Education

Almost all countries in the world today provide free education for their children. There are still numerous emerging nations that cannot support public education, but that nonetheless accept its value and importance. In Kali Yuga, by contrast, education was limited to the wealthy, or to those whose occupation required some education — such as scribes, who needed to be able to read and write.

It wasn't until the 1600s, during the 100-year transition period at the end of Kali Yuga, that the idea of education for everyone began to take hold. The Parliament of Scotland, in 1633, passed the first known law to levy taxes to support public education. The town of Dedham, in the Massachusetts Bay Colony, authorized the first public school in America in 1643. Throughout the 1700s and into the 1800s, the 200-year transition period at the beginning of Dwapara Yuga, the establishment of public schools in Europe and America became more widespread and organized. In 1837, Horace Mann became the first Secretary of the Board of Education for Massachusetts, and established an approach to public funding for public schools that by the 1870s was adopted by every state in the United States. By the early 1900s, mandatory education was established throughout the U.S. A similar pattern is found in all the prosperous nations of the world.

Higher education evolved along a similar timeline. Harvard College (now Harvard University) was founded in 1636. Although Oxford and Cambridge, founded in the 1200s, are considered to be the oldest universities in the world, they too went through a transition in the 1600s. Prior to the 1600s, Oxford and Cambridge were focused primarily on "scholastic philosophy," which was the study of classic philosophy and church doctrine. The "colleges" that made up Oxford and Cambridge had more in common with monasteries than with the higher educational institutions of today, and today one finds many of Oxford's and Cambridge's colleges still associated with the chapels and abbeys of their past, such as St. John's and Trinity College. In 1536 Henry VIII dissolved the monasteries in England, and with them the colleges, and set Oxford and Cambridge on a new course away from a purely religious and philosophical focus and into the classics, mathematics, and science. Today there are thousands of colleges, universities, and other institutions of higher learning throughout the world.

Public schools are a giant step forward in education, but are often seen as a mixed blessing. If public schools themselves were to be graded on their efficacy, many people might give them an F. When schooling is mandatory, all children may go to school, but not all thrive. Even gifted teachers cannot hope to bring out the best in every student when they have thirty or more in a classroom.

Leading educators, often found in private schools and in such progressive public school programs as charter schools and home schooling programs, are pioneering several trends in education, trends that address current needs and that are likely to gain momentum into the future of Dwapara Yuga.

Individualized learning: Children are just as unique as adults, yet the current public school model channels them all through the same basic subjects and teaches them in the same way in classrooms around the world. The groundbreaking work of Howard Gardner, *Frames of Mind: The Theory of Multiple Intelligences*, persuasively argues that all of us, children and adults alike, learn and process information in very different ways. Gardner refers to these as multiple intelligences: bodily-kinesthetic, interpersonal, verbal-linguistic, logical-mathematical, naturalistic, intrapersonal, spatial, and musical.

While these specific categorizations of people's natural intelligence may not stand the test of time, it has become clear that teaching thirty different children in the same classroom, all in the same way, will tend to resonate only with those children who *like* to learn that way—and will leave the rest at a disadvantage.

Home schooling programs, personalized learning programs, and schools where different educational methods are available, are soaring in popularity in California, and are spreading throughout the U.S. They provide not only a broader choice of subjects than the traditional public school, but allow for different learning styles as well.

Look for this trend to continue to expand and become more practical. Individualized learning is an obvious outcome of the formula *self-interest* x *awakened intellect* x *energy awareness*.

Effective learning: A frequent, and rueful, subject of conversation among adults is how little they remember of their public school and college educations. Studies have shown that retention of knowledge goes up enormously when that knowledge is *applied* in some manner as part of the process of learning. Conventional wisdom has known this for a long time. If you want to learn something well, go out and do it.

While not ground-breakingly new, making learning more effective dovetails well with the approach of individualized learning. Apprenticeships, internships, participation in activities, outings, travel, all may become part of an individualized learning experience for a particular learner, one tailored to his interests and his preferred way of learning.

Holistic learning: Current education for children addresses only the mind and the body. Through classes and mental pursuits, children are taught to use their intellect and reason, and are encouraged to use their bodies in sports and outdoor activities. But their emotional and spiritual natures are rarely addressed.

In America, this lack is in large measure due to the so-called separation of church and state. Teachers in public schools are forbidden to explore spiritual and religious issues, lest they be perceived as trying to win children to a particular religion. But even in so-called religious schools children rarely explore or experience their innate spiritual natures; instead they memorize religious tenets and dogmas.

Children's emotional natures are similarly left alone, but for different reasons. Only a few gifted teachers are able to help children gain emotional awareness and understanding. The majority of teachers are not given tools or training that could help them encourage emotional awareness among their students. Both the emotional and spiritual natures of children are considered to be the domain of the family, and teachers are told not to intrude.

Attitudes are changing, however: many parents and educators are looking for new ways to incorporate emotional and spiritual awareness into education. For example, in his book *Education for Life*, J. Donald Walters presents a seminal approach to helping children explore and learn about their emotional and spiritual natures, in ways that are neither religious nor subjective. His approach is to facilitate the process of children recognizing, considering, and learning about their own feelings and subtle natures—without conflict with their own, or their family's, personal or religious outlook.

Walters points out that there are *universal* emotional and spiritual experiences. Just as everyone has his heart in the same place, his liver in the same place, uses his legs in the same way to run, needs to eat when he is hungry and sleep when he is tired, so too there are commonalities of emotional and spiritual experience. Feelings are centered in the heart. Positive feelings are accompanied by an increase in, and upward flow of, energy in the body. Negative feelings are accompanied by a decrease in, and downward flow of, energy in the body. Happiness-producing actions are calming, relaxing, and move toward an inward sense of contentment and security. Unhappiness-producing actions make one nervous, tense, and restless.

Children can be taught to be aware of these universal experiences, and as a result, can learn to be more in command of themselves, and much more likely to make choices that lead to fulfillment. This approach, of fostering *innate* emotional and spiritual awareness among children, avoids the limitations of conventional religious education.

Health and Healing

Kali Yuga medicine was, not surprisingly, primarily material and physical. In Europe, during the Kali Yuga era, medicine focused on a balancing of the elements, or "humours" as they were called in the West: yellow bile (fire), black bile (earth), blood (air), and phlegm (water). Similar systems existed in China, Japan, and India. Health was restored to ailing patients when the proper balance of the elements was achieved.

Galen, a Roman who lived from approximately 129 AD to 200 AD, epitomized the Kali Yuga approach. He was among the first to perform dissections on animals in a desire to see how the body worked as a mechanism. He performed crude surgeries, and established many procedures that, due to his copious writings, influenced Western medicine for nearly a thousand years; his procedures included bloodletting, intended as a means to rebalance the patient's humours. While most of his specific practices have long been discredited, his accentuated view of the body as a physical object has persisted well into our present era.

Modern medicine remains focused on balancing the elements in the body, though with far greater sophistication than in Kali Yuga. Modern medicine still relies primarily on body chemistry and surgery. Illness is treated largely by introducing substances into the body that have a desired chemical effect on the patient. However, Dwapara

Yuga's insistence on verifiable and repeatable results, unlike Kali Yuga's mixture of superstition and ignorance, has led pharmaceutical science to create "miracle drugs" that have effectively eradicated many fatal or crippling diseases, including smallpox, tuberculosis, polio, and malaria. Research has led to the identification of thousands of drugs effective for thinning the blood or clotting the blood, for bringing a person to a high state of alertness or putting a person to sleep, for strengthening or weakening the immune system, for speeding or slowing the heart rate—in short, drugs that affect every organ and tissue in the body.

Medicine has also advanced in the care of trauma and catastrophic injury. Many people today are alive, and whole, because of emergency medicine and surgery. Additionally, medicine has reached the point where failing organs can be replaced by artificial and donated organs. Extreme mental and emotional conditions can also be alleviated. Our increasing life expectancy is due in no small measure to modern medicine's effectiveness.

However, modern medicine is focused on treating a pre-existing illness (such as cancer, heart disease, or diabetes), or on preventing death or disability caused by trauma (such as automobile accidents, broken limbs, spinal fractures, etc.) through surgery and drugs. In its emphasis on external treatment, modern medicine is, although far more advanced, not unlike Kali Yuga medicine.

Significantly, while modern medicine can keep you from dying, or can at least prolong life, it can't make you healthy. To be healthy is to have not only a physical condition that allows you to remain active, but abundant energy and positive mental and emotional attitudes as well. Health is not the absence of disease. Health is a vital and positive state of well-being.

Many people, while not actually sick, aren't very healthy either. They may have little energy to do things; they may be mentally dull and unhappy. These people may turn to modern medicine for solutions for their vague malaise, unhappiness, and lack of energy—hoping for a pill or a treatment that will bestow the vitality and mental and emotional well-being they lack.

In response, pharmaceutical companies are making massive investments in drugs that claim to treat conditions of malaise, lethargy, and unhappiness—conditions including anxiety, fear of social situations, poor sleeping patterns, restless legs syndrome, and eating disorders. All these "syndromes" now have drugs available for their treatment—but their success rate is limited.

More and more people are instead turning to alternative, energy-based methods of achieving health and well-being, methods that work directly with one's life force. As mentioned in an earlier chapter, life force, the inner, subtle energy flowing within the body, has only recently become commonly understood. This understanding is one expression of mankind's increasing awareness of energy in general in Dwapara Yuga.

The essence of an energy-based approach to health is that life force, when flowing freely and abundantly throughout the body, *keeps* us healthy, and is also accompanied by the *feeling* of health—strength, energy, relaxation, and well-being.

Chiropractic therapy is one of many alternative approaches that embrace the life force as the key to health and healing. First introduced by D. D. Palmer in 1895 (very near the significant date of 1900 when we fully entered Dwapara Yuga), chiropractic therapy works to allevi-ate blockages to the natural flow of life force in the body. In the early years of chiropractic medicine, practitioners focused attention on the spine in particular, but they have since developed many ways of reduc-ing energy blocks throughout the body.

Pertinently, acupuncture, another popular alternative therapy that embraces the power of life force to ensure health and healing, did not emerge in the current Dwapara Yuga, but in the *last* Dwapara Yuga (3100 BC to 700 BC). Acupuncture needles have been found in Mongolia dating as far back as 3000 BC; acupuncture has been in continuous practice (though it almost died out in Kali Yuga) for thousands of years.

Modern science, and particularly modern medicine, tends to reject the concept of life force because there is no known way to mea-sure it. Chiropractic care, acupuncture, and a host of other therapies (physiotherapies and massage therapies such as osteopathy, hands on healing, pressure point massage, acupressure, craniosacral massage, trigger point therapy, the Alexander method, and subtle essences such as homeopathy and flower remedies—the list goes on and on) are gaining in popularity—not because science has embraced them—but because they produce positive results.

Clinical studies, involving real patients in controlled environments, have shown that chiropractic therapy and acupuncture have measurable health benefits. Acupuncture, for example, has been found to be one of the most effective ways to reduce chronic pain—better even than painkillers. While modern medicine remains skeptical of the theory of life force, it cannot completely ignore the benefits. Thus we see chiropractic therapy and acupuncture not only an increasingly accepted and familiar approach to health and healing but even included in health insurance policies.

We are also seeing the re-emergence of yoga postures, another ancient science whose origins are in the last Dwapara Yuga (or perhaps even earlier). There are clay seals, dating back to at least 3000 BC, found in Mohenjo-daro and Harappa in India—ancient cities long abandoned—that depict people in the lotus and other postures.

Unlike chiropractic therapy, acupuncture, or other massage therapies, yoga postures do not require a therapist or practitioner to alleviate blocks to the life force or to stimulate life force with pressure or needles. Yoga postures are an ancient science of positions and stretches that allow one to maintain and encourage a healthy flow of life force in the body by relaxing and stretching skeletal and muscular points of tension.

Exercise, good diet, and consciously developing positive attitudes also contribute to the healthy flow of life force in the body, and they, too, are getting increasing attention. All—alternative therapies, yoga, exercise, good diet, positive attitudes—stimulate, or promote, the flow of energy in the body, and when the life force is flowing freely and strongly—a result that modern medicine cannot bestow through drugs or surgery—one feels *vital* and is less likely to develop disease.

Someday in Dwapara Yuga modern science may discover how to measure life force and will then develop its own ways to work with life force to promote health, thus combining the best of both worlds—the rigorous analytical method with the subtle power of life force. Whatever the place of science, look for this emerging trend to continue to gain acceptance and appreciation as Dwapara Yuga unfolds.

Paramhansa Yogananda, student and disciple of Sri Yukteswar, predicted that mankind would also begin to heal with "rays." Modern medicine already uses x-rays and other imaging technologies to see within the body. Also, radiation is used to kill cancer cells. But neither technology can be said to be *healing* with rays.

One example of actual healing through rays may be color therapy. Already many books on color healing explore the effects of particular colors on human health. A typical process involves bathing the patient in a particular color of light for a specific period of time over the course of weeks or months in order to bring out certain emotional, mental, or physical qualities.

Sound therapy is another example of healing involving rays. Music itself can have a soothing, healing effect on a person, but sound therapy goes well beyond music. Already experiments are being conducted on the effects on the body, emotions, and mind of extremely low and extremely high frequency sound waves.

There may be many as yet undiscovered "rays" that have, among other uses, a healing effect. Whatever specific discoveries await, Dwapara Yuga awareness should bring to the surface additional subtle, energetic ways to effect healing, which eliminate, or at least reduce, the need for gross methods of surgery and pharmacology. Uniting these methods of healing will be an unfolding understanding of life force — the subtle inner energies that manifest our bodies.

The Arts

The most dramatic change in the arts from Kali Yuga to today is how widespread the arts have become. In Kali Yuga the average person's exposure to "art" was limited to seeing great buildings, such as cathedrals, temples, palaces, and great homes, and watching traveling bands of performers giving simple plays, dancing, and singing popular fare. Only the wealthy and powerful saw the paintings and sculptures, read the literature and philosophy, and enjoyed the sophisticated dance and music that we think of as Kali Yuga's treasury of art.

Today the average person living in the more prosperous areas of the planet is continually exposed to art. Easily available to us are the visual and performing arts of the world. A college student may have a Van Gogh print on the wall, be listening to Mozart, and reading Plato all at the same time. The average home includes books, music, visual and decorative art. Most people can visit museums and galleries, and go to concerts, operas, ballets, and plays. Dwapara Yuga's awakened intellect and *self-interest* have brought what used to be the exclusive domain of the few within the reach of nearly everyone.

Art, during Kali Yuga, was almost exclusively influenced by its audience, the dominant powers of the age, political power or religious authority—and as a result art abounded with religious themes, military themes, or themes involving the ruling class. The world sometimes seems littered with busts of Hadrian, a Roman emperor who ruled near the peak of Roman power, and many museums display portraits galore of emperors, tsars, and kings. Kali Yuga era sculpture and painting of religious figures are even more numerous—from the ubiquitous statues of Buddha and the gods and goddesses of Hinduism, to painting after painting featuring the Holy Family of Christianity. Today, by contrast, the arts address the interests of the billions of awakened Dwapara citizens—which means all interests are represented—from high to low, in any realm, any style, any subject matter. Gone are the days when religion and power dominated art.

Not only was the *subject matter* of Kali Yuga art highly circumscribed, but the *form* also. Kali Yuga art was fixed and material—paintings, sculptures, buildings. Sculpture, which in Dwapara Yuga has receded in prominence, was highly prominent in Kali Yuga. In many ways Kali Yuga sculpture is emblematic of the age—solid, material, rigidly realistic in form, dominated in subject matter by political power and religious authority.

Even Kali Yuga music, though clearly not solid and material, was fairly rigid in form and was dominated by religious authority or political power. Music that was neither sacred nor courtly did exist—for example, the tradition of the troubadours in the West—but music was performed primarily in churches and temples and in the courtly halls of governing powers. Gregorian chant in Europe, chanting the Vedas in India, Chinese classical music—these comprised the main expressions of music during Kali Yuga.

Beginning with the Baroque period in approximately 1600 AD and moving through the Rococo, Classical, and Romantic periods, Western art passed through both the transition periods of Kali Yuga and Dwapara Yuga. During this transition, artists gradually left behind the restraints of both form and subject that existed in Kali Yuga. Rembrandt (1606–1669), in addition to his usual paintings of rich and important men and women and of religious subjects, also painted ordinary people and objects, in ordinary scenes, a practice considered unusual at the time. By the time of Van Gogh (1853–1890) and the

Impressionists, all previous restraints on both form and subject were nearly gone.

A similar progression took place in music. The soaring complexity of Bach (1685–1759) left behind the simple rules of plainsong, and burst out of the classic forms of the Renaissance. The Classicists (Mozart, 1756–1791) added humanist feeling, and the Romantics (Beethoven, 1770–1827) added power and vibrant emotion — not only leaving behind the simple, rigid musical forms of Kali Yuga, but embracing individual, human experience as well.

In China and India, as well as in other non-European cultures around the world, it is difficult to see a similar progression in the arts during this same period (1600 to 1900 AD), simply because their own development was obscured by the colonial expansion of the Europeans into these Eastern cultures. The more forward-looking elements of Chinese and Indian society embraced Western art, and relegated their traditional arts to a lesser importance. The desire to become westernized even led many colonial countries to actively suppress traditional forms of art and music. Traditional instruments such as the Thai ranat ek (similar to a xylophone), for example, were outlawed; they were considered to be inferior instruments because they weren't played from a chair, or while standing, as were Western instruments.

By the turn of the twentieth century, the restraints on form and subject that shaped art in Kali Yuga had vanished. Dwapara Yuga art forms and subjects ramified with bewildering speed — Modernism, Fauvism, Expressionism, Cubism, Synchromism, Surrealism, Futurism, Vorticism, Dadaism, Constructivism, Abstract Expressionism, Kinetic Art, Land Art, Minimalism, Post Minimalism, Lyrical Abstraction, Neo-Expressionism, New Realism, Pop Art, Op Art — each expanding the boundaries of form and subject — and all these ism's within the visual arts alone.

The performing arts have seen an even more dramatic transformation. While Dwapara Yuga's relative prosperity has made theater, opera, dance, and musical performances much more accessible to the average person, and as such no longer available only to the elite, it is movies, television, and modern popular music that are the dominant art forms of today.

It can be argued that movies, television, and modern music are not art. But time alone is the best judge of what should be considered art. Keep in mind that Shakespeare's plays were commercial ventures to entertain the average citizen, and that opera was developed to make sophisticated music more accessible to the common man. In their time, both opera and Shakespeare were not considered Art (with a capital A), yet time has judged otherwise. Not *all* movies, television programs, and popular music are likely to be judged, in time, as Art. But we must accept that movies, television, and modern music do comprise a new art form and that some of what has already been created will survive time's critical judgment.

These new art forms spring from Dwapara Yuga's discovery of energy and its myriad applications. Whether as the excitation of phosphors inside the screens of our televisions, or the reflection of a projection of light on a screen in the movie theater, motion pictures work directly with light, made possible by working the subtle laws of energy revealed in Dwapara Yuga.

Initially, movies and television programs were little more than filmed stage plays, but as time moved on, completely new visual experiences began to manifest, and with the advent of computer-generated special effects, movies were able to depict what had once been accessible only to the imagination. From dinosaurs to light sabers, from volcanic eruptions to ethereal beings, from fantasy worlds to outer space, movies express Dwapara Yuga awareness in ways that no other art form has been able to do.

By 1900, literature, too, had undergone significant changes in both subject and form. As mentioned earlier in this chapter, Dwapara man's awakening intellect has led to increased literacy, so that reading has become an everyday activity for billions of people. Mass printing techniques, developed as a result of the application of energy awareness to the manual printing process, now provides reading material to those literate billions. In the United States alone, there are currently more than *two billion books* sold every year.

In Kali Yuga, on the other hand, books were rare, expensive, and found only in churches and temples, monasteries and restricted libraries. Throughout Kali Yuga it was unusual for books to be privately owned. The subjects addressed in books were, almost exclusively, theological, philosophical, classical, academic, and historical. Kali Yuga authors were bound by formulaic strictures. For example, even as late as the 1600s in Europe, Latin was still the primary language for books, even though spoken Latin had died out a thousand years earlier. Complex rules dominated the written form. Shakespeare wrote in iambic pentameter in the late 1500s; even the "popular fiction" of Kali Yuga, *romances*, idealized tales of heroism and courtly love such as *The Song of Roland*, were written in verse rather than in prose style.

Sanskrit dominated Indian literature, just as Latin did European; also, Sanskrit, like Latin, had not been used as the common spoken language for over a thousand years. In China, *wenyan*, formalized classical Chinese, spoken, read, and written by only a small percentage of the population, even as late as the 1800s, was the language of literature, yet it too had emerged and died as a spoken language more than a thousand years before. Kali Yuga's material consciousness manifested as rigidity of form even in things less clearly material such as language and art.

By 1900, there was an explosion in the popularity of prose fiction and its main form, the novel. The primary intention of the novel, as of film and television, is to entertain; as with movies and television, time alone will tell which novels will be considered Art. Meanwhile, novels serve Dwapara Yuga man's *self-interest* and pursuit of happiness by catering to an enormous variety of personal interests and depictions of the human condition: from the sublime to the base, from the realistic to the fantastical, from the subtly insightful to the highly improbable—encompassing the collective imagination of Dwapara man.

Prose is not really a *form* of writing so much as it is a *lack* of form. The rules of verse, the formulas of style of Kali Yuga no longer apply today. In fact no rules apply today—except perhaps the rules of commerce. Grammar, syntax, length, spelling, structure are all rapidly evolving.

In Dwapara Yuga, new media and technology have also transformed the visual arts. New materials, or advanced variants of such traditional materials as plastics, metal alloys, ceramics, inks, dyes, textiles, paints, glass; new technologies, such as high-end printing (which allows for new forms of original production as well as quality reproduction), silk screening (which allows an image to be applied to irregular objects as well as to paper and textiles), the use of lasers (both to cut and shape, and as a medium), the use of computers (to produce digital art, both static and moving); and new venues, from a T-shirt to a computer screen—all these have created *thousands* of new ways to create and make visual art available, with the result that visual art has reached near ubiquity.

In Dwapara Yuga, not only do we see the rapid expansion of media, techniques, and venues for art, we also see mixing and combining in multi-media or multi-modal art forms, which for example may combine painting, music, and dance, or photography, music, and painting: the possibilities are all but limitless.

Art has also undergone the transformation from noun to verb—from an emphasis on the *object* created, to the *experience* of creation. Dwapara Yuga has heightened individual awareness of inner feeling and inner energy. We have today a more appreciative understanding of the creative process. Individuals are encouraged to take up artistic creativity—not because they are likely to produce great art—but because the process of creation has a positive, enjoyable, and healthy effect on the artist. Art therapy even exists as a formal methodology within psychology.

One result of art as *experience* is the trend to allow people to participate, with an artist or group of artists, in the creative process. Art installations, performance art, conceptual art, environmental art are all participatory; they allow a co-creation, a collaboration, a shared experience.

Where Will Art Go from Here?

Look for continuing experimentation to develop even more immersive experiences than movies provide today. Movies involve two of our senses—vision and hearing. Look for developments that involve the other three senses. We can already observe this trend. Theme parks, such as Disneyland, have combined the traditional movie experience with the sensation of motion. Star Tours, a "ride" at Disney's theme parks, employs seats that move, as does the entire room in which one is "riding." The end result is the sensation that not only are you watching a movie about a spacecraft zooming along and narrowly avoiding one catastrophe after another, but that you are actually in the spacecraft and feeling every hair-raising bump and turn.

We are also seeing the early stages of experiments that involve the sense of smell. To fit the scene on the screen in a movie theater, appropriate scents—perhaps the smell of pine during a walk through the forest—are released into the air. In addition, the air may be cooled, or warmed, or moistened to further the mood. Sound technology even brings in the sense of touch as well as hearing, and has advanced to the point that massive impacts depicted on the screen are felt as much as they are heard through powerful low frequency sound waves.

Video games too may evolve into an ever-more immersive experience. Today's leading edge video games are far more than animated games—they are worlds unto themselves. A single very popular game today is played by over 10,000,000 people! A player can develop an intricate character, which in turn can interact with other characters within the realm of the game. Players fight battles, go on quests, join groups, which in turn go on quests and fight battles together, such as complex "raids" involving 10, 20, 30 or more players, each with specific roles, to defeat powerful computer-generated characters. The game world has its own economy, with tradable value outside the game itself, and has spontaneously developed its own culture, including art, literature, movies, and music inspired by the world and characters of the game. For an idea of the appeal of today's immersive video game experience, imagine a fantasy movie that you can enter and leave at will, where you become one of the main characters, where you influence the outcome of the story, a movie that keeps evolving, adding more characters, more plot, and more interest all the time.

Yet another immersive experience is so-called "virtual reality." Unlike a movie, which provides a "canned" experience, virtual reality allows you to interact with a three-dimensional experience—including actually moving your own body within the experience. Still very crude, and for most people, uncomfortable, even disorienting, due to the constricting visual mask you need to wear, virtual reality is likely to improve and, given our times, prosper.

Look for more ways of depicting subtle, inner reality. Now that Dwapara man is becoming aware of the reality of inner energy we see it expressed in increasingly realistic ways. In Kali Yuga, we saw the stylized depiction of holiness as the halo: a rough, simple, and material way to represent the human aura. But today we can already see in movies and painting a truer expression of subtle light—from Obi Wan Kanobi shimmering in blue light in Star Wars, to paintings showing layers of subtle light around the human form and interpenetrating with centers of energy in the spine.

These trends — the forming of communities of like-minded people, education that fosters the natural interests and talents of individual students, healing through energy, and art as an increasingly immersive, personal experience — are just a few of the new and positive trends we can see emerging as Dwapara Yuga responds to the formula of self-interest x awakened intellect x energy awareness.

While not an exhaustive list of all positive trends, we hope that the trends we have described in this chapter have provided you a glimpse of the potentials that our age of energy and the empowered individual are beginning to manifest. As Dwapara Yuga unfolds we expect to see the positive trends of today grow stronger, and the shortcomings of Dwapara Yuga begin to fade or mature into positive directions.

Our world today shows both peril and promise, but the continued increase of dharma through Dwapara Yuga, according to Sri Yukteswar, will eventually, and inevitably, as these more positive trends illustrate, result in a better world.

PART THREE

Our Enlightened Future

Chapter 6

Ascending Dwapara Yuga —
The Future

Timeline

1700 AD Beginning of present ascending Dwapara Yuga

1900 AD End of the 200-year transition period (*sandhi*) from Kali Yuga

3900 AD Beginning of the 200-year transition period (*sandhi*) to Treta Yuga

4100 AD End of present ascending Dwapara Yuga

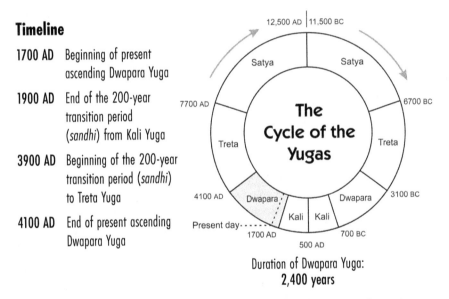

Duration of Dwapara Yuga:
2,400 years

The first three hundred years of Dwapara Yuga have already produced dramatic changes — in science, in society, and in human
awareness. While the previous chapters have been largely focused on
exploring present and emerging Dwapara Yuga trends, in this chapter
we will speculate on the more distant future.

New Types and New Uses of Energy

Paramhansa Yogananda described electricity as "the animal current
in the energy world,"[1] implying that there are other types of energy yet

to be discovered — or put to use. Today we have hydro power, geothermal power, solar power, fossil fuel power and nuclear power — but the
primary way that these different sources of power are channeled into
usefulness is by converting them to electricity.

In fact, there is some irony in the fact that so-called "nuclear power"
is really an extension of steam power, which was developed in the eighteenth and nineteenth centuries. Nuclear reactors serve only as the
source of heat for converting water to steam. The resulting steam is fed
at high pressure into turbine electrical generators, making them spin
at high speed and thus generate electricity.

Yogananda also said that mankind's current approach to generat-
ing energy is to force material objects into motion by the brute force
application of energy, and that someday, still within Dwapara Yuga,
mankind would learn to cooperate *with* forces, rather than working
against them. There may be some hints of this trend already.

Today there are trains that "float" on a magnetic field instead of having wheels on rails. Magnetic "push" not only keeps the train above the
ground, but, by a series of electromagnets having their polarity changed
in sequence, the train is also propelled forward by the "pull" of magnetism. The magnets that make these trains work are powered by electricity — but perhaps someday mankind will learn how to use the earth's
natural magnetic forces instead of producing our own with electricity.

The sun bathes the earth with prodigious amounts of energy.
Current attempts to use sunlight as an energy source involve converting it into electricity through solar cells or using the sun's heat to generate steam to spin turbines that then produce electricity. One day
perhaps, we will eliminate the middleman — electricity — and draw
power directly from the sun.

There may well be other manifestations of energy that we barely
understand today, manifestations that we may someday be able to cooperate with rather than fight. Gravity is a force that we currently have to
overcome. Cars require more energy to go uphill than to drive on a flat
road. Mechanisms that lift objects — such as elevators, forklifts, and airplanes — require extra energy to overcome the force of gravity. Eliminate
the force of gravity and (although we would all float off into space) we
would drastically reduce our energy consumption. Perhaps there is a way
that gravity can be manipulated to work in our favor instead of against
us, thus reducing the force needed to move things about.

Clearly, these examples are speculative. But, the length alone of Dwapara Yuga indicates that we would be unwise to dismiss the possibility of a future technological world unlike anything we know today.

Declining Population and Increasing Lifespan

Malthus got everybody worried. In his work, *An Essay on the Principle of Population*, first published in 1798, Malthus made the famous prediction that population would outrun food supply, a trend that would lead to a potentially fatal decrease in the amount of food available per person. Since then, many demographers have made even more alarming predictions of famine, starvation, and catastrophe.

These predictions, however, have not come to pass. Clearly there have been famines around the world. But the world's food supply has, in fact, kept pace with population growth. The famines have been the result of war, conflict, ignorance, and politics — conditions that have led to the unequal distribution of food — not the consequence of the lack of food itself. Equally clearly, however, the world's population has been growing at an alarming pace. In Malthus' day the world's population was approximately 800 *million*. Today the world population is over 6 *billion*.

The world's present population is putting tremendous strain on the earth's resources. We are contaminating our soil, air, and water, and as a result even altering natural balances. Nor do demographers predict that we have peaked. Estimates for the peak of world population range from 9 to 12 billion people — to be reached in fifty to one hundred years.

But most demographers also agree that if current world trends continue, the world's population will begin to decline — even if no epidemic, war, or other catastrophe were to strike us. The world's most prosperous nations are now declining in population. Europe has had a declining birth rate for over twenty years. America is showing the same trend, but immigrants from Mexico and other emerging nations still have cultural attitudes that foster high birth rates, and as a result the general trend in America toward population decline is offset by the immigrant population — at least for now.

The majority of continuing growth in our worldwide population is found in emerging nations such as those in Africa, South America, and India. China is an exception to the rule. Although still below the level of prosperity of other nations, China imposed government regulations, with strict penalties, limiting the number of children families are allowed to have. Even though these restrictions are now rescinded, Chinese families continue to choose small family sizes, perhaps because they have come to appreciate the advantages. Demographers predict that the populations of these emerging nations will naturally begin to decline when they reach levels of prosperity similar to those of wealthy areas such as Europe, America, and Japan.

As people become better educated, and have improved standards of living, they tend to have fewer children. Perhaps this is due to the availability of birth control, or is simply a result of *self-interest*. The demographers cannot tell us. But anyone who has raised children in a prosperous nation can tell you that it costs a lot to raise a child, a financial reality that makes it far more *self-interestedly* sensible to reduce the number of children for which you are responsible.

For those of us alive today, population decline can't happen too soon, but we are unlikely to see any significant decline in our lifetime. Barring catastrophe, we will see the world population increase for the next 50 to 100 years. But in the millennial view of the yugas, world population will probably drop off very quickly. Even an overall population decline of .5% per year would reduce the world population from 10 billion to a little more than 6 billion in only 100 years. In 450 years the population would decline to 1 billion. If the population were to decline at 1.0% per year, a population of 10 billion would be reduced to 3.6 billion in 100 years, 1.3 billion in 200 years, and down to 500 million in 300 years.

Other factors could easily influence the rate of increase or decrease in the world population, but if Dwapara Yuga man remains *self-interested*, energized, and mentally awake, as Sri Yukteswar predicts, it seems likely that the world's population will eventually decline dramatically. And, after two millennia, at the end of Dwapara Yuga, world population could be vastly less than it is today.

Another trend that counters continued population growth is that we are living longer. Although this reasoning may seem counterintuitive, it appears that the longer-lived a population, the lower the overall birth rate, with the result that population begins to decline. Whether there is a cause and effect relationship between increased longevity and decreased birth rate no one knows. But we do know that the trends tend to happen in the same populations.

The tradition in India has it that man's natural lifespan will increase in each ascending yuga — 100 years in Kali Yuga, 200 years in Dwapara Yuga, 300 years in Treta Yuga and 400 years in Satya Yuga. This could probably best be described as a rule of thumb. It was rare that anyone lived to be 100 in Kali Yuga, though it did happen; in fact, most people died far younger. But the rule of thumb suggests that as Dwapara Yuga progresses, there may well be people who reach the ripe old age of 200 years.

Corroborating studies and census information show the average life span steadily increasing around the world. In the beginning of the twentieth century the average life expectancy was only thirty to forty years; now it is approaching seventy. Thousands of people turn one hundred years old, *every day*, and the longest-lived person, *so far*, was 122 years old when she died.

Increasing Human Potential

The most obvious effects of Dwapara Yuga's increased awareness of energy are currently manifesting in man's increasing control over the *outer* physical world. We marvel daily at the wonders of technology. But the wonders to come may well manifest primarily through man's increasing control over his *inner* world—his mind, life force, and physical body.

We can easily see a trend toward greater and greater accomplishments in athletics. Records seem to fall every day. Athletes are getting faster, stronger, and more capable year after year. This change is no doubt due, at least in part, to a steadily changing gene pool, the result of natural selection favoring physical prowess and other physical characteristics. But if we take a closer look we can see underlying this trend another more subtle awareness.

Athletes are increasingly aware of their *life force*. In martial arts, as we have already discussed, the life force is called *chi*; in India it is known as *prana*. Whatever it is called, athletes more than ever appreciate that their physical bodies are only one part of the equation. They also need to tune into the flow of energy in their bodies.

In the 1970s Timothy Gallwey wrote *The Inner Game of Tennis*. Gallwey notes that many top athletes enter a "zone" when they are performing at their best. While in the zone, the usual rational processes we associate with being awake and alert recede, and choices are made in a flowing, intuitive manner. When asked later why they had chosen to try a particular shot, or initiate a particular tactic, their answer is simply that they just knew what to do. They achieve a kind of fusion of body, mind, and energy that is more capable than the sum of its parts.

Soon the concept of being in the zone, or in a flow, was recognized outside the world of sports. Exceptional business people, artists, authors—in any field—have similar experiences. A strong, centered, confident flow of high energy has its own guiding intelligence. Intuitive insight, hunches, creative excellence, body-transcending feats, often occur when in the zone, as Gallwey describes it, or, as others have come to describe it, in a strong, confident *flow*.

Many top athletes work with motivational coaches and use techniques that help them get into the flow. To help athletes, businessmen, or anyone wanting to achieve peak performance, motivational coaches focus on, in addition to the usual physical training methods and disciplined practice, the development of positive attitudes, physical relaxation, concentration, and emotional calmness while in competition.

Athletes are also increasingly aware that the *conviction* that they can succeed is as much, or more, important than physical ability and training. If athletes don't truly believe they can accomplish a feat—they won't. This negative conviction can come either from the individual athlete thinking himself not capable of succeeding or from fellow athletes thinking the feat impossible for *anyone* to accomplish. Either way the result is the same.

Conversely, once any athlete has accomplished a feat, say breaking the four-minute mile, or, astonishingly, doing a back flip on a motorcycle fifty feet above the ground, then other athletes often quickly accomplish the same feat. In 1954 Roger Bannister became the first man to run a mile in under four minutes. At the time, the four-minute mile was widely believed to be impossible. Sports reporters, trainers, doctors, scientists and, as a result, nearly everyone else held the strong thought that the human body simply wasn't capable of the physical effort required to run that fast, that far. However, once

Roger Bannister broke the four-minute mile barrier, many other run-
ners promptly broke the same barrier. Currently, the world record is
now almost seventeen seconds less than four minutes—and expected
to get broken again.

Although the breaking of the four-minute mile received worldwide
attention, similar breakthroughs happen frequently. A bizarre example
is doing a back flip on a motorcycle. At the end of the 1990s, the first
successful back flip was performed on an 80cc motorcycle. Now the
feat is routine. In fact, other riders have now done back flips on full-
sized motorcycles, four-wheeled ATV's, and snowmobiles! Not to be
left behind, in 2006 a motorcyclist performed a *double* back flip. As
recently as the 1960s people were impressed that Stein Eriksen, an
Olympic Gold Medalist in 1954, could do a back flip on skis! Such a
feat seems like nothing now.

What these anecdotes highlight is that, as Dwapara Yuga unfolds,
people will be able to do many things not thought possible today—
perhaps not even imagined. For example, there are currently being performed many feats, physical and mental, that are so far from the average
person's experience, that most people simply refuse to believe them.

High degree masters of the martial arts, by complete command of
their life force, have been able to prevent a sword point from penetrat-
ing their abdomen even when it was thrust against them by two and
three men at the same time. Although this feat has been frequently
described in print, and even captured on film, most people dismiss it
as a hoax or a freakish ability beyond the common man.

But the evidence of untapped human potential is simply too great
to ignore. Yogis in India have demonstrated an ability to levitate, go
without breathing for days, or calmly endure extremes of heat and
cold—all through the practice of *pranayama*, or life force control.
Savants, people who possess extraordinary mental abilities, have shown
that they can memorize pi to over 22,000 digits, mentally multiply say,
37 to the 6th power (37 x 37 x 37 x 37 x 37 x 37) in less than a minute,
or simply know the day of the week of any date you can name.

Mankind is currently enamored of the wonders of technology.
However, as Dwapara Yuga unfolds, the most wondrous "technology"
may well be our own ability to control our minds and life force. As
we are often reminded, we currently utilize only 10% of our brain's
potential. The performance of feats now considered impossible may lie

in Dwapara Yuga's future. If we could travel to the future, we might be more astonished by the everyday abilities of ordinary people than by any technological innovation we would see.

Psychic Abilities

The average person today tends to think of psychic abilities as a con job or as the misguided beliefs of the weak-minded. At least in popular culture, the debunkers appear to be in the ascendant. Most people would be surprised to know that the ability to perceive things at a distance, "remote viewing," as it is often described, and to perceive events in the future, have been proven to be real by hundreds of systematic studies conducted by highly reputable organizations, including the Princeton Engineering Anomalies Research Lab (PEAR Lab), the Stanford Research Institute (SRI), the U.S. and Russian military, and the American Central Intelligence Agency (CIA). No scientific establishment has been able to determine *how* psychic abilities work, but they have proven beyond question that genuine psychic abilities *do* exist.

During the 1970s and continuing to 1995, the CIA conducted the Stargate Project, a program to study psychic abilities. The program's purpose, not surprisingly, was to see if psychic ability to see and hear things at a distance could be used for collecting intelligence. The CIA had as many as twenty-two different labs set up to test and develop this capability.

Eventually, around 1995, the CIA's Stargate Project was abandoned because the intelligence gathered by the remote viewers was not consistently reliable enough to make it useful as an intelligence tool—although to this day the CIA continues to use psychics in certain situations. Many people have interpreted the program's demise as an indication that psychic abilities were found to be unfounded. Actually the program demonstrated just the opposite. They found that gifted psychics could see things at a distance with a high degree of accuracy—they just couldn't do so 100% of the time, but they could do so with a degree of accuracy that was far, far beyond chance.

For those still skeptical, it is both amusing, and emblematic of our commercial age, that some of the remote viewing methodology discovered by the CIA and SRI has been craftily co-opted by big business, the natural home of hard-headed skepticism. In his book, *The Synchronized Universe, New Science of the Paranormal*, Dr. Claude Swanson notes that DuPont has trained some scientists to look into the future and "see" what new inventions and applications they may find. If they "see" something promising, and with enough detail, DuPont applies for a patent on it![2]

Psychic abilities are not limited to remote viewing and looking into the future. An increasingly common use of psychic abilities is in health and healing. "Medical intuitives" use their abilities to "see" into the patient. In Dr. Claude Swanson's book mentioned above, he tells the story of an eleven-year-old boy in China who was able to successfully diagnose 93 out of 105 patients just by looking at them from a few feet away.[3]

Our modern culture is just beginning to embrace psychic abilities as genuine. From a scientific point of view, the big stumbling block to their acceptance is that they appear to violate the laws of space and time as these laws are currently understood. In controlled experiments, the abilities demonstrated by psychics are undiminished by distance. Remote viewing has proven equally accurate whether the object or person viewed is on the other side of the earth or in the room next door. All forces now known to physics rapidly diminish over distance. The anomaly of psychic ability indicates that science has yet to discover the more subtle level of energies that can be perceived and felt—even controlled—by people with psychic abilities.

In the centuries ahead, according to Sri Yukteswar's description of the yuga cycle, more and more people will become sensitive to subtle energy. More than any other development, this change in man's awareness and abilities may shape our future.

Spiritual Practices

Kali Yuga was dominated by religions that were highly orthodox (i.e. adhering to beliefs or practices approved by authority or tradition) and that required the intercession of priests, brahmins, mullahs, etc. with higher powers for its followers. True to the matter consciousness of Kali Yuga, the religions of the time were form bound. To be a true follower required obedient practice of certain rituals—prayer, offering, confession. The rituals were formulaic—a certain number of repetitions of prayers, the proper offering performed in the proper way, confessing the right number of times, etc. Those faithful to the rituals, whether they understood them or not, whether they sincerely felt them in their heart of hearts or not, were assured they would go to heaven or gain merit for their next life.

In Kali Yuga, obedience and unquestioning acceptance of the tenets or dogmas of religion were expected. Understanding those tenets and dogmas, however, was not required. In fact, it was almost impossible for the average man to understand them. In India, the chants and prayers performed by the Brahmins were in Sanskrit, a language seldom understood or spoken during Kali Yuga. Similarly in Europe, the Christian masses, prayers, and especially the Christian Bible itself were in Latin, also a dead language. It wasn't until nearly the end of ascending Kali Yuga, in the 1500s that Martin Luther's "protests" brought about the translation of the Bible into the languages understood by the common man.

Form was of far greater importance than understanding. Saying a prayer in Latin, even if ignorant of its meaning, was enough. Form was served. Rituals performed. Priests obeyed. The matter consciousness of Kali Yuga imparted rigidity of form and thought to religious practices.

Nonetheless there were those who persevered in the practices of their religion and gained solace, inner peace, and some measure of contentment—even transcendence. Saints and sages arise in any yuga. However obscured the spiritual realities may be by the commonly held ideas and attitudes of the time, there will always be some who experience these realities clearly. Those of high realization, however, were able to pass on their knowledge only in ashrams, monasteries, and protected enclaves where inward teachings could be practiced.

The dominant world religions of Kali Yuga excluded any religious thought other than their own—to the point of extreme intolerance and war. The religious Crusades fought by European Christians against the Moslems of the Middle East, the Moslem conversion "by the sword" of millions of Brahmins in India during the Middle Ages, and the Spanish Inquisition are but three examples of the extremes of intolerance and rivalry brought about by Kali Yuga's fixed consciousness.

The religious traditions born in Kali Yuga, such as the insistence on belief and unquestioning acceptance of dogma, the need for priestly intercession between man and God, and continuing intolerance toward other religions, do not sit well with the new consciousness of Dwapara Yuga. Kali Yuga religion's inability to satisfy the minds of people now steeped in reason and science has led to a widespread rejection of religion and religious belief of any kind in our time.

At the very least it is clear that the influence of the world's religions over the actions and thoughts of the average person has diminished significantly. Compared to its power in the Middle Ages, where men could be excommunicated for heresy, tortured for suspected witchcraft, and taught to live in fear for their soul, the Catholic Church has far, far less sway today.

Although millions of people still find inspiration and guidance in the lives of saints and saviors such as Jesus and Buddha, they do so less through the formulaic practice of religion and more from personal experience.

Atheism, or at least agnosticism, increased significantly in the eighteenth, nineteenth, and twentieth centuries. Literal and orthodox religious beliefs, such as that God created the cosmos in seven days, and that the world is only four thousand years old, have not stood up well against scientific discoveries that indicate the universe is perhaps thirteen billion years old and contains over 100 billion galaxies.

Since the beginning of Dwapara Yuga, mankind has been going through a transition phase in which old modes of religious belief and practices are less and less accepted — and yet in which a new religious expression has yet to fully establish itself. Thus, many people, with nothing they can believe in, choose to believe in nothing higher or more subtle than the empirical facts of science.

Traditional Kali Yuga religions simply do not resonate well with the three hallmark trends of Dwapara Yuga — *self-interest, awakened intellect, and energy awareness*. As a result, there has been a resurgence of interest in spiritual practices that were developed and practiced in the preceding Dwapara Yuga, and of interest in new Dwapara Yuga expressions of spiritual practices similar to them. These spiritual practices range from physical and energetic disciplines, such as hatha yoga and Tai Chi, to techniques for life force control, such as breathing techniques, to meditation practices, such as Zen meditation, Buddhist meditation, and various techniques of meditation from India.

These practices, and the teachings that accompany them, are more satisfying to the Dwapara Yuga person's natural self-interest — with these practices they can direct their own spiritual exploration without the need for religious authority. Unlike traditional religions born in Kali Yuga, in which man is considered to be separate and unequal to the Creator, Dwapara Yuga spiritual practices allow the practitioner, by applying his or her own will, to have direct experience of higher consciousness.

Many practitioners experience an expanded sense of self, a transcendent awareness of their own intrinsic inseparableness from higher consciousness. Paramhansa Yogananda called this the process of self-realization, the expansion of our own limited awareness into an awareness of our own higher nature. He predicted that the process of self-realization, and the techniques that support the process, would essentially become the unorganized and highly personal "religion" of Dwapara Yuga.

These practices, and the teachings that accompany them, are also more satisfying to the *awakened intellect*. There are many books out today that explore the amazing conformance between the ancient Dwapara Yuga spiritual teachings and modern scientific discoveries. Ancient texts in India accurately describe the nature of the atom and the vastness of the universe. But more importantly, Eastern teachings, and we must generalize here, are universal, not exclusive. Rather than creating division among religions, as the convictions of Kali Yuga religionists did, Eastern teachings stress the unity of all religions. The philosophies of Dwapara spiritual teachings embrace the notion that if there is indeed one infinite consciousness of which we are an inextricable part, then other religious and spiritual teachings must be appreciated as but different ways to arrive at the same experience of the same reality.

Finally, and especially, these practices are also more satisfying to the energy awareness of Dwapara Yuga, because at the heart of these practices are techniques for becoming aware of and then controlling our own inner, subtle energies. Instead of allowing their life force to flow through sensory channels only, practitioners learn to withdraw from the senses and focus their life force inwardly. The practitioner then discovers, directly, that his or her own life force is but a small part of a blissful sea of divine energy.

The Lessons of Dwapara Yuga

According to Sri Yukteswar's description of the yugas, the arc of human development we see in ascending Dwapara Yuga will be marked by the increasing use of personal power and individual will to control the world. The years to come will produce ever more powerful people and ever more powerful technology; coupled with mankind's exploration of *self-interest*, the result will be a continuing and perilous vying for control around the world for some time to come.

Mankind's vying for control in the world may play itself out through conflict and war, or through the continued expansion of multi-national, even trans-national (owing no allegiance to any one country) corporations on the battlefield of market economics. These conflicts we already know. In future, there may emerge battlefields that we cannot even imagine today.

The years to come will also be marked by increasing prosperity and by mankind's subsequent headlong pursuit of happiness through material goods, sensory experience, and the expression of personal power and accomplishment. The fortunes of Bill Gates and Warren Buffett, considered the richest men in the world today, may pale in comparison to what fortunes may be amassed by some business mogul in the future. The products created to help us, or entertain us, will likely exceed anything we can envision today, and the range of pleasures available will expand as well.

However, according to Sri Yukteswar, before Dwapara Yuga reaches its end over two thousand years from now, mankind will learn two overarching lessons.

One—the experience of happiness, the feeling *of being happy, is the result of movements of our life force in our bodies.*

Nearly everyone would agree that a mean-spirited, hard-hearted miser is not going to be a happy person. Grasping at material wealth with a focus on self-centered material desires does not result in happiness.

At the time the British were relinquishing India as a colony, around 1948, the richest man in the world was a maharajah living in northern India. He was, indeed, a mean-spirited, hard-hearted miser. When he discovered that it was expected that he serve champagne for the English Viceroy when he visited, he provided only one bottle—placed neatly in front of the Viceroy—and provided none for all the other guests. After his death, it was discovered that he was even wealthier than anyone guessed. He had been hiding money and jewels in desk drawers, cabinets, and wardrobes for years. He died unloved and unlamented—a sad human being indeed.

Many people, if not most, would agree that he was obviously unwise and unhappy—yet many people, if not most, pursue the same ends, even if with less obsession. There is a hypnosis, a mass conviction, that if we can just accumulate enough things, enough money, enough pleasures, that we will break though into feeling truly happy.

Material happiness is the shared myth of our time.

The conviction is constantly reinforced by movies, books, television, and especially advertising—like a perpetual echo chamber. The people in the ads look *so happy* with their new car. The hero and heroine are obviously *over the moon with joy* when they finally gaze deep into each other's eyes at the end of the movie. But mostly the conviction is reinforced by the thoughts and actions of those around us. Year by year, generation by generation, an unspoken but clear message is passed on that the best way to find happiness is more and better stuff, better relationships, more wealth.

Most people are aware that it doesn't always work to pursue happiness in this way—yet they persist. Why? Because it appears to work at least sometimes! If someone gives us a thousand dollars, most of us will *feel* good. If someone is kind to us, or loves us, or admires us, we *feel* good.

The obvious conclusion is that since those experiences made us happy, more such experiences will make us even more happy, and a continuous supply of such experiences will make us perpetually happy.

But the system doesn't always work. The thousand dollars that made us happy yesterday, takes ten thousand dollars tomorrow. People we find enchanting today, drive us crazy tomorrow.

Put simply, if things outside ourselves actually possessed the power to make us happy, we would stay happy as long as we had those things. But the truth is that it has always been our inner *reaction* to things that has made us feel good, because our reaction releases a flow of *our own life force* in the body. In a very real sense, we *allow* ourselves to feel good. It is we ourselves who possess the power to feel good.

Furthermore, people often weave complex webs of conditions that they think will catch happiness for them. But instead they have put so many conditions on their own happiness that they make it almost impossible to allow themselves to be happy—so many conditions can never all be met. In fact, more often than not, the conditions people put on their happiness result in a lifetime of tense, anxious striving to meet all the conditions; or in a lifetime spent regretting opportunities they think they've missed; or being jealous, angry, or despairing that other people have what they so strongly desire.

The good news is that mankind's newly emerging awareness of energy, of the inner *life force*, is the seed that will eventually grow into the understanding that happiness, well-being, and prosperity are *feelings* that come about as the result of *life force* flowing positively and abundantly through the body. Learn to properly direct your life force and you will be able to experience positive feelings at will. Increase the flow of energy, and you will experience them even more generously—a principle that brings us to the second overarching lesson of Dwapara Yuga.

Two—the experience of personal happiness is enhanced through the expansion of one's awareness and sympathies.

Once people become more aware and more able to direct their life force, they will begin to further refine their awareness and they will discover that a focus only on one's own happiness *contracts* the flow of life force. A generosity of spirit, an open-hearted way of dealing with others, an awareness and concern for the welfare of others, a willingness to sacrifice for the benefit of others: these expand the flow of life force.

Even now, even if only dimly, most people recognize this. People honor Mother Teresa not just because of her accomplishments, but because they recognize the wisdom of her life, so evident in her shining eyes and joyful face. Gandhi is admired not solely because he liberated India by peaceful means, but because he radiated peace and joy.

Mankind knows this, but does not yet trust it enough. In time, as the lessons of the years are learned, people will come to take for granted that contributing to the well-being of others is as important to their own happiness as are their own circumstances. We can call this understanding *enlightened self-interest* because the core motivation will still be personal happiness, and yet it will lead to the joy of altruism, fair-mindedness, and service.

Human motivations, as you will see in the upcoming chapters on Treta and Satya Yuga, are the most significant and transformative aspects within each of the yugas. In the low point of Kali Yuga, human motivations had sunk to the level of simple survival. The stronger imposed their will on the weaker. Might was the only arbiter. By the end of Kali Yuga, mankind had once again awoken to an appreciation of the inalienable rights of each human being.

In ascending Dwapara Yuga, the yuga began with the rise of the individual, and the headlong pursuit of personal happiness without regard to its impact on others. Today, unfortunately, mankind generally turns a blind eye to exploitation, inequity, and injustice. But, according to the insights of Sri Yukteswar, by the end of Dwapara Yuga mankind will learn that the well-being of others is essential to each individual's happiness; as a result, the exploitation, inequity, and injustice we see around us today will gradually come to an end.

～～～～～～

According to Sri Yukteswar's explanation of the yugas, by the close of Dwapara Yuga, when dharma is fully one-half developed, *self-interest* will have moderated into *enlightened self-interest*; the awakened intellect and energy awareness will have merged, in a sense, into *high-energy, flowing, intuitive awareness*. Reason and logic, so entrenched today, will be seen as too slow, cumbersome, and rigid to move with the *flow of ideas* that accompanies the *flow of energy*.

Physical, mental, and psychic abilities that are unusual today will be commonplace. In any large population, not everyone will be equally talented or able. But the majority of mankind will routinely accomplish things we only dream of today.

Personal power will not always be used for good. Through the arc of Dwapara Yuga, increasingly more powerful people will often be in conflict. But people will eventually learn to appreciate that happiness is essentially non-material and will realize that within themselves is an inexhaustible source of happiness—their own life force. As people become more aware of their inner energy, and learn to direct it properly, they will discover that their own life force is not only the source of their happiness, but is *subject to their will*. No longer will they need to vie with one another to try to control an external source of material happiness.

Sounds simple doesn't it? Many people alive today already know this simple truth. There are many teachers who have extolled this simple truth both now and in the past, and many people have learned the secret of happiness. But for mankind as a whole, alas, the lesson will take centuries to learn. Nevertheless, the ascending yuga's effect is inexorable. According to Sri Yukteswar, the minutely changing awareness of mankind, brought about by dharma's steady advancement, can have no other outcome.

Chapter 7

Ascending Treta Yuga —
The Age of Thought

Timeline

4100 AD Beginning of the next ascending Treta Yuga

4400 AD End of the 300-year transition period (*sandhi*) from Dwapara Yuga

7400 AD Beginning of 300-year transition period (*sandhi*) to Satya Yuga

7700 AD End of the next ascending Treta Yuga

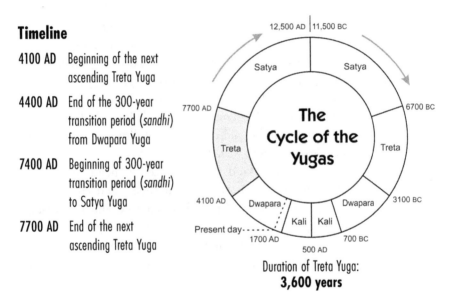

Duration of Treta Yuga:
3,600 years

According to Sri Yukteswar, it is far easier for us to understand the present and previous ages of Kali Yuga and Dwapara Yuga than it is for us to understand Treta Yuga — if we can understand it at all. Sri Yukteswar does not specifically describe what life might be like in Treta Yuga. In fact, referring to Treta Yuga in The Holy Science, he wrote, "the grasping power of the human intellect is at present so limited that it would be quite useless to attempt to make the matter understood by the general public."[1]

We probably can't *truly* understand Treta Yuga at all. Kali Yuga man's awareness and capabilities were less expanded than our own, and so, just as adults can understand a child, we can easily relate to Kali Yuga man. We can also understand much of Dwapara Yuga man's awareness and capabilities because we share that awareness. We may be able only dimly to perceive the future of Dwapara Yuga, but its future is at least an extension of what we now know.

Treta Yuga, on the other hand, is far more challenging for us to comprehend. In this instance, we are the children trying to comprehend the adult. We simply don't have enough direct experience to be able to truly understand Treta Yuga. Further, Paramhansa Yogananda said that both Kali Yuga and Dwapara Yuga have a common theme of *materialism*—in Kali Yuga it is most pronounced, but in Dwapara Yuga, too, mankind's values are fairly materialistic. But the motivations, awareness, and capabilities of those living in Treta Yuga will take a quantum leap beyond our current, more materialistic understanding.

The analogy, which we used in an earlier chapter on Dwapara Yuga, of man being like a radio, remains apt for the higher yugas as well. If Kali Yuga man can be said to have the capability to tune into only AM frequencies, and Dwapara Yuga man additionally into FM frequencies, then Treta Yuga man can be said to gain the ability to tune into even higher frequencies, say, short wave (SW).

In Dwapara Yuga, mankind is able to comprehend that energy underlies all matter and so is able to manipulate and control matter. In Treta Yuga, mankind will be able to comprehend that *thought* underlies all energy; he will comprehend that everything is made up of *ideas* or *thoughts*. As a result, mankind will be able to manipulate and control energy—and by extension, matter—even more dramatically than we can today.

Dwapara Yuga man currently relies on technology to work the wonders that energy awareness makes possible; Treta Yuga man will require no technology to accomplish far greater feats. The arc of human development that in Dwapara Yuga will result in increasingly powerful individuals, will continue in Treta Yuga. Highly advanced individuals in Treta Yuga will become capable of altering, or even *creating* material objects, as well as of controlling natural forces, and sharing thoughts directly with other people—capabilities the average man today would consider miraculous, magical, or fantastical.

In Dwapara Yuga, mankind is developing "space annihilators." In Treta Yuga, mankind will develop "time annihilators."[2] In Dwapara Yuga, mankind is motivated primarily by *self-interest*. In Treta Yuga, mankind will be motivated by the desire to achieve personal perfection or *self-mastery*. In Dwapara Yuga, mankind relies on reason and intellect to explore knowledge. In Treta Yuga, mankind will rely on *intuitive attunement*—a higher octave of intellect and perception, one that includes both thought *and* feeling.

Awareness of Thought

Can we truly grasp such a world? Perhaps not fully or deeply, but there are people in any yuga who manifest the qualities of the higher yugas, and from whose lives we can gain insight. We may not be able to fully understand these insights, but at least we can attempt to articulate them. Also, some aspects of Treta Yuga may strike a resonant chord within us, because the truths that are revealed in the higher yugas are just as true today as they will be then. It is just that mankind *as a whole* will only become aware of these truths in the higher yugas.

It is important to realize that, even today, people are unconsciously using the same powers that will be used *consciously* in Treta Yuga—but today most people simply don't understand that they are using these powers! Even today, healers and spiritual teachers tell us that our innermost convictions, our *core thoughts*—usually held at a subconscious level—are, moment by moment, determining every condition of our physical body. Healers and spiritual teachers tell us that the moment we change our innermost thoughts about our body, our body changes immediately. But most people either don't believe this mind-body relationship, or if they do, are unable to change their innermost thoughts at will, and therefore never really see the power of their thoughts at work. Without clear cause-and-effect confirmation of the power of thought, most people regard the concept as unfounded or beyond them.

Nonetheless, if we look for it, we *can* see the power of thought at work. One of the more fascinating demonstrations of this power can be seen in the lives of people with multiple personalities. Many books have been written on the subject. *The Three Faces of Eve*, by Dr. Corbett H. Thigpen and Dr. Hervey M. Cleckley, came out in the 1950s, and *Sybil*, by Flora Rheta Schreiber, in the 1960s. Both books were so popular and intriguing that they were made into movies of the same title.

These books and movies brought the condition of multiple personalities to the public's awareness. Since then, psychiatrists and psychologists have documented numerous accounts of people who radically change personalities. Some people with this condition manifest dozens of personalities. These personalities aren't simply different expressions of strong character traits. Rather, each personality is unique and consistent. Each personality has unique memories, and is not aware of the memories of the other personalities. Each personality has unique brainwave patterns. Each personality has unique "voice prints," impossible to fake even by gifted impersonators. These personalities are, by almost any measurement, separate people.

As these personalities "come" and "go," the person undergoes sudden, and at times radical change. Usually the person does not even realize that a personality change has occurred. People suffering from multiple personality disorder often seek the attention of psychologists. Ironically, however, they don't often do so because they realize that they need help dealing with multiple personalities, but because they believe they are suffering from *amnesia*, since any one personality does not remember anything about the large gaps of time when other personalities were present!

Not only does each personality undergo changes due to his or her unique *psychological* characteristics, each personality also undergoes changes of his or her unique *physical* characteristics also. As each personality comes into control of the body, his or her unique physical characteristics manifest *instantaneously*. From the many documented cases of multiple personality disorder, studied in clinical environments, psychologists have compiled an amazing list of physical changes that occur. One personality had a mole that appeared when she appeared, and disappeared when a subsequent personality appeared. When previous personalities have taken drugs, such as sleeping pills, the drugs have no influence on the subsequent personality. One personality was allergic to bee stings and had to be taken to the emergency room to save his life, while the other personalities were not allergic. Some personalities needed to wear glasses while others didn't. Some personalities even had different eye color than the others!

Think about that for a moment: different eye colors, moles, allergic responses. People are materializing and dematerializing actual physical atoms *instantaneously*—but they have no idea that they are doing so, or how. In fact we all use this power. But because the innermost convictions that form our bodies change very slowly over the course of our lives, we don't tend to see the cause-and-effect relationship between thought and physical change.

Yet even if we are unaware of our ability to do so, we frequently work miracles with our thoughts. Lyall Watson, in his book *Supernature*, describes several experiments that demonstrate our mental power. In one experiment, ten test subjects were told that they had been given sleeping pills. However, one of the ten had been secretly given a stimulant instead of a sleeping pill. Nonetheless, the tenth test subject, *believing he or she had been given a sleeping pill*, slept through the night with the rest of the test subjects. The same experiment was conducted at the same time in another room, but in reverse. In this experiment, the ten test subjects were told that they had been given a stimulant. However, the tenth test subject was secretly given a sleeping pill. Nonetheless, the tenth test subject, *believing he or she had been given a stimulant*, stayed up all night with the rest of the test subjects.

Another dramatic confirmation of the power of our thoughts is seen in the *placebo effect*. New drugs are commonly tested using double-blind studies. In these studies there are two groups. One group gets the drug being tested and the other group receives a placebo — an inert substance that appears identical to the real drug. Neither the test subjects, nor those administering the drug to the test subjects, know who is getting the real drug and who is getting the placebo — thus the meaning of the term *"double-blind."*

About fifteen years ago, as described in the book *The Holographic Universe*, by Michael Talbot, a double-blind study was conducted to test a new chemotherapy drug. As with the typical approach to chemotherapy, the new drug and the placebo were tested over a period of weeks involving multiple chemotherapy sessions. During the weeks of the test, 30% of the control group, the group that received no actual drug — but were convinced they were receiving one — *lost all their hair*.[3]

All of us are using the power of thought to determine the physical characteristics of our bodies. But most of us simply don't know it because we are doing it at a subconscious level. Among those who do know, only a few are able to control their thoughts sufficiently to consciously affect the kind of changes described above. In Treta Yuga, people will first gain greater awareness of their thoughts, and then gradually the ability to control and direct their thoughts at will.

Communication and Learning

As in any large group, some people in Treta Yuga will have greater awareness and control of thought than others. Additionally, different individuals, each one unique, will be drawn to use their ability in different ways. As today, where people become politicians, scholars, artists, athletes, soldiers, teachers, scientists, etc., so in Treta Yuga, the natural affinities of different people will lead them to explore and use their mental capabilities in different ways.

According to Sri Yukteswar, one *specific* mental ability most Treta Yuga men and women will share, however, is the ability to be aware of one another's thoughts. One would expect that some would be better able to tune into people's thoughts than others, but, even so, if the majority has even *some* of this ability, the implications are far-reaching — both for individuals and for society.

Communication, in the early centuries of ascending Treta Yuga, would, therefore, likely be a mix of spoken language and mental telepathy. The communication process may resemble the way two people who share the ability to speak the same two languages, often flow from one language to the other, even in mid-sentence, choosing the language that provides the best way to express their thoughts. Such a bilingual conversation seems confusing to someone who knows only one of the languages, but the two people in the conversation may not even realize that they are switching back and forth.

One can imagine a similar experience with speech and telepathy. People sharing information, having conversations, teaching others, may flow between communicating their ideas telepathically when the other person can understand them, and where doing so would communicate the idea more fully, and using spoken language where that better suits their recipient's abilities. Eventually, one would expect the majority of communication to be conducted mind-to-mind, as more and more people became comfortably able to communicate without spoken language.

It is unlikely, given the testimony of present-day telepaths, that one would receive the equivalent of a spoken sentence from someone else's mind. Rather, what psychics with telepathic abilities tell us is that they receive mental pictures, images, seed thoughts, even sounds, from the minds of others.

Each of us has probably "gotten an idea" from time to time. Usually it comes into the mind full-blown. We may require time to "think it through," to contemplate the implications of the idea in relationship to other realities; nonetheless, the core idea arrives in an instant. Each of us today has probably also then tried to share our idea with others and encountered the difficulty of conveying the totality of the idea using just words. It can take hours to share such an idea, even with friends with whom we share basic points of view. It might require writing a *book* to convey the idea to someone with whom we have *no* shared understanding. Imagine if we could simply convey, directly to another person's mind, the same core idea in the same instantaneous way it came to us.

As the old saying goes, "a picture is worth a thousand words." Ideas, concepts, or subtle understanding would be conveyed more fully and effectively mind-to-mind, rather than through the relatively cumbersome medium of the spoken or written word. In Paramhansa Yogananda's *Autobiography of a Yogi*, he describes a deep learning experience he had with his teacher, Sri Yukteswar: "My mind was now in such perfect attunement with my guru's that he was conveying his word-pictures to me partly by speech and partly by thought-transference. I was thus quickly receiving his idea-tabloids."[4] Imagine the speed, fluidity, and depth of communication possible if an entire society were to communicate in this manner.

During the centuries of ascending Treta Yuga one expects the efficacy, clarity, and accuracy of telepathy to gradually ensure that it become the primary method of communication. Although it is hard to imagine the spoken word dying out altogether (even harder to imagine an entire society using mental telepathy in the first place!), still we may reasonably expect speech to be relegated to a secondary role.

Not only can we expect telepathy to transform *how* people communicate, but also *how far apart* people can be and still communicate. Distance has proven to be no barrier to telepathic communication. As we mentioned in the last chapter, experiments in "remote viewing," conducted by the CIA in the 1990s, have shown that there is no diminishment in the accuracy of remote viewing because of distance. Today's complex, instantaneous, and worldwide communications technology may well be replaced, in the future, by people's innate ability to simply know one another's thoughts — regardless of distance.

The implications of mental telepathy for learning are fascinating. Imagine being able to learn by direct transference from the mind of a teacher. It is doubtful that one person would simply be able to receive *all* the thoughts of another person, like copying all the files from one computer to another. Just as children today need to learn in stages, gradually building up their understanding of a subject, people in ascending Treta Yuga would probably still need to develop their understanding in stages. But the process of learning may be vastly accelerated. What was learned would also be more likely to be remembered and integrated, rather than forgotten, as is so much of what we now learn in school.

As we know, we don't stop learning once we've reached maturity. In Treta Yuga, the learning process could achieve heights not possible today. Highly advanced teachers in any field could vastly accelerate the transference, understanding, and integration of knowledge for students who make the effort to attune themselves to the thoughts of their teacher. Not only would this process accelerate learning, it would increase the depth of learning as well. Combine that with the longer life spans expected for Treta Yuga—up to 300 years—and we have a picture of the future in which the potential development of each person goes well beyond anything we expect today. Imagine what Einstein or Bach might have accomplished had they lived another 200 years!

Self-Mastery and Intuitive Attunement

Most athletes today train and practice to achieve mastery over their *bodies*. Yogis and tai chi practitioners today train and practice to achieve mastery over the body and *life force*. Treta Yuga people will train and practice to achieve mastery over body, life force, and *mind*. While Treta Yuga's elevated consciousness will bestow the *awareness* of thought, Treta Yuga man will require increasing *self-mastery* if he is to develop the concentration resulting, finally, in the ability to *direct* thought.

The more deeply anyone concentrates, calmly and steadily, on any idea or concept, the more he or she becomes intuitively attuned to it. Intuitive attunement involves not only mental awareness, but calm, centered feeling as well. Our feelings can be compared to a pond. When the surface of a pond is perfectly still, we can see a perfect reflection of the surrounding area in its mirror-like surface. When the surface becomes disturbed by wind, or by tossing in a stone, the ensuing waves and ripples, crossing and re-crossing each other, obliterate any image we might try to see.

Similarly, when our feelings are calm, and united with our focused mind, we can "see" with great clarity into the nuances and subtleties of anything on which we choose to concentrate. The resulting intuitive attunement goes beyond surface facts. Intuitive attunement takes us *within* the very essence of what we focus upon. Insight comes from being one with the object of focus. The knowledge gained is as much *felt* as thought. With only the mind alone we tend to only deal in facts and logical deduction. Add calm feeling however, and we gain the ability to understand with greater depth and certainty.

Even in Dwapara Yuga there are those who have developed intuitive attunement to such an extent that they see truths no one else has even glimpsed. We call such people geniuses. Einstein's theory of relativity came to him in a "flash." But the flash came as a result of profound absorption in his subject. Even so, it took him years to work out the mathematical proofs of the insights that he knew, by intuitive attunement, to be true.

Nikola Tesla, considered to be the father of modern electrical engineering, had extraordinary powers of concentration. Born in Serbia, in 1856, Tesla was deeply fascinated with electricity. He was born during an electrical storm, and even from childhood believed that electricity was his destiny. In his youth, he thought constantly about electricity and its properties, and eagerly read everything he could find on the subject. So completely absorbed did he become that he began to understand ways to put electricity to use that his contemporaries were not even considering. Idea after idea poured into his mind.

In his youth, he told all who would listen that he had keen insights into electricity, and how it might be harnessed to benefit mankind. However, he couldn't demonstrate his insights, because he was not able to perform experiments. Laboratories weren't available to him and, at the time, he did not have the means to build a laboratory for himself.

Even without scientific equipment, however, his concentration and visualization abilities were so advanced that he was able to "build" his first invention completely in his mind. Tesla designed the world's first electrical motor without even using drawings. So clearly had he visualized the principles and physical structure of his motor, that when he finally had access to a laboratory, he was able to manufacture each piece of the motor, one by one, from the exact dimensions he had in his mind. When he put the pieces of the motor together, they fit perfectly—an amazing feat in itself. Even more amazing, the motor worked perfectly the very first time! Tesla's intuitive attunement to electricity was so profound that he simply knew how it would behave.

Tesla's invention of the electric motor revolutionized the world. Tesla went on to conceive and then develop the basic system of electrical generation (turbines), transmission (alternating current) and use (electric motors) that is still the norm today. So far-reaching was the impact of his inventions that he has been called, "the man who invented the twentieth century."

Total focus, concentration and absorption in their work are the hallmarks of those we consider to be geniuses. From the humble peanut, a crop widely considered good only for feeding livestock, George Washington Carver developed over one hundred products, including many food products (peanut butter being his most famous), cosmetics, dyes, paints, plastics, and ethanol. Carver was known to spend long periods alone praying and opening his feelings to the Divine, asking God to reveal to him the secrets of the peanut.

Intuitive attunement to a specific subject is not easily achieved. Genius is rare in our day and age. Most people today are pulled by their interests and feelings in a variety of directions—sometimes even in opposite directions. Rarely do people *choose* to be attuned to specific thoughts or feelings. Instead they tend to more or less haphazardly adopt the interests and convictions of their families, friends, and co-workers. As a result, most people never achieve the one-pointed focus of genius. In Treta Yuga, however, the principle of genius, the ability to achieve intense focus and intuitive attunement to a particular subject or discipline, will be recognized, encouraged, and taught.

Today a few people work in this way, and we describe them as *master craftsmen, master gardeners, musical virtuosos,* and, as we've already explored, *scientific geniuses.* All of these terms describe people whose lifelong focus and intuitive attunement to their particular field has made them extraordinarily good at what they do.

Imagine a society where *everyone* is encouraged to go deeply into a chosen pursuit, and is given the tools to develop *self-mastery* and intuitive attunement. Imagine singers who not only train their voices, but who attune themselves to music by continuous concentration on the nuances and feeling of the piece they sing; who focus with one-pointed concentration not only on producing the sound, but on the words of the song and the meaning from which the words arise. Perhaps such singers could even perform without producing an outward sound, by sending images, tones, and meaning directly to the minds of other people.

Artists, having become so attuned to their medium and to what they want to express, would be able to create transcendent works of art. Healers might be able to heal by going deeply into the minds of their patients. Feeling their way to the particular mental and emotional convictions at the core of their patients' illness, they could help their patients change the underlying causes of their illness. A master cook, with intimate knowledge of the range of tastes of every food, and intimate awareness of the thoughts of another person, might be able to prepare food *specifically* for the palette of one individual.

The Power of Thought

If we continue this line of thinking, and consider the effect of thought awareness and intuitive attunement on any human endeavor, we can envision a Treta Yuga society filled with extraordinarily capable people. But intuitive attunement to a particular realm of thought leads not only to great accomplishment, but can lead to great power as well. As a person becomes intuitively attuned to thought, he or she will be able to direct thought, and as a result *manipulate energy and matter*, by affecting the very thought forms that give rise to them.

Here we truly part company with the world with which we are now familiar.

Even so, there are those rare examples of people even in our age who have demonstrated the ability to manipulate energy and matter by their directed thoughts. Luther Burbank is known to most people as the scientist who pioneered the process of plant hybridization, and who developed hundreds of hybrid fruits and vegetables during his lifetime. But Luther Burbank was also a man of higher awareness, who in his hybridization experiments consciously used the power of intuitive attunement to directly influence the *outcome* of his work.

In the 1920s, Paramhansa Yogananda visited Luther Burbank at his home in Santa Rosa, California. As he was being shown a variety of "spineless" cactus, Luther Burbank told him an amazing story: "While I was conducting experiments to make 'spineless' cacti, I often talked to the plants to create a vibration of love. 'You have nothing to fear,' I would tell them. 'You don't need your defensive thorns. I will protect you.' Gradually the useful plant of the desert emerged in a thornless variety."[5] Luther Burbank, using both his focused mind and calm feeling, developed an intuitive attunement to the essential consciousness, or thought form, of the cactus plant, and was able to influence the plant to grow without thorns.

Imagine, if you will, a Treta Yuga master gardener, deeply attuned to his plants and to the processes of growth, using his mind and heart to coax an apple tree to bear fruit. His awareness and concentration could become so deep that he would feel no separation between himself and the tree. The thought form of the tree would then respond to the thought of the gardener. The Treta Yuga master gardener might be able to create new plant varieties, with more beautiful flowers, tastier vegetables, or more succulent fruit.

Treta Yuga citizens may be able to attune themselves to the natural forces around them and, as a result, be able to bring rain, stir up a gentle breeze, or create clouds on a day too hot for comfort. There is really no *definable* limit to Treta Yuga man's powers. (What they might *choose* to do is another matter.)

Heady stuff—and hard to imagine. As we've already explored in the examples of multiple personalities, we already have the power to manipulate matter and energy—we just aren't able to use it deliberately and consciously. But in Treta Yuga, people will be able to do deliberately and consciously what most people today would consider miraculous.

Divine Magnetism

In *The Holy Science*, Sri Yukteswar writes that in Treta Yuga "the intellect of mankind will become able to comprehend the *divine magnetism*, the source of all electrical forces on which the creation depends for its existence."[6]

Paramhansa Yogananda describes *divine magnetism* as "the power of all powers."[7] Not, however, a blind or impersonal power. *Divine magnetism* is conscious and aware, and therefore will respond consciously to the intuitive attunement of Treta Yuga man.

As those in Treta Yuga become more able to calm and center their feelings, and thus to use intuitive attunement to gain knowledge, insight, and power, they will also become aware that their own existence is only part of a much greater *conscious* reality. They will be able to perceive, in the intuitive center in the heart, that divine thought, *divine magnetism*, gives rise to everything they experience.

Dwapara Yuga man, even at the eventual height of his awareness, will still believe that his body and life force constitute his sole reality. He will still experience his sense of self, his ego, as being separate and distinct from everything else. Mankind will begin Treta Yuga with this awareness as well, but as Treta Yuga goes through its arc of development, Treta Yuga man will discover, through *direct experience*, that the *real* self is far greater than the limits of body and life force.

Treta Yuga man's perception of the *divine magnetism* will be as direct as our sensory experience of matter. When a Treta Yuga citizen turns his intuitive perception *within*, he will be able to consciously interact with a conscious Divinity, who in turn can interact with him.

Overcoming the Limitations of Time

Another facet of Treta Yuga difficult for us to comprehend is that in Treta Yuga, mankind will overcome the limitations of time by developing "time annihilators,"[8] as Paramhansa Yogananda explains in *Autobiography of a Yogi*.

One of the limitations of time that we accept today is that it "takes time" for certain things to happen. Plants grow at a certain pace, healing requires time to happen, children need a lengthy childhood to grow up, people need time to learn. In Treta Yuga, it may be that many processes we now believe absolutely will "take time," could be sped up or even eliminated by the agency of thought.

Perhaps, by the power of thought, a tree could be induced to grow a fruit more or less instantaneously. Healing in Treta Yuga may be accomplished immediately by helping others change their thoughts, rather than by relying on slow, "natural" processes that require more time. The long journey of youth may be sped up or eliminated as well. Childhood is in many ways a crash course in coming into attunement with the body, mind, and feelings. If a child's attunement could be sped up by direct transference of knowledge from adults, perhaps, as a result, the body's growth would be sped up as well.

Another limitation of time is that we seem able to experience only the *present*. Perhaps Treta Yuga man will be able to experience the future and the past as well—and perhaps even be able to affect them.

There are men and women alive today, and many who have lived in the past, who claim the ability to foretell events. Controversy always surrounds such claims, yet there do appear to be genuine predictions. From prophets of the ancient past, to Nostradamus, a sixteenth century AD healer who made predictions through poetic metaphor, to Gordon-Michael Scallion, a modern-day psychic, such people have "seen" future events. What they see is not always very clear. Sometimes they see actual people and places, but other times what they see is more symbolic. In either case, interpretation is required in order to translate the images into specific predictions.

However, Scallion did accurately predict the 1984 Mexico City earthquake, the 1987 stock market crash, and numerous earthquakes in California; Nostradamus is credited with predicting the death of several historical leaders and popes. One would be hard-pressed to credit them with a high degree of accuracy, but they, and others, have been able to foretell future events with *enough* accuracy to rule out mere chance. We have to conclude that seers and prophets do perceive, however dimly, something of the future, which should at least admit the possibility that the future *can* be perceived.

On the scientific front, particularly in the world of physics, there is significant speculation about the nature of time, speculation that gives further credibility to the notion of time's mutability. Physicists who study the larger universe understand time to be a dimension in some ways similar to height, depth, and width. They see time as an inextricable part of space—without space, time cannot exist, and without time, space cannot exist. In fact physicists often use the phrase *the space-time continuum*, or simply *spacetime*, to communicate the inextricable interconnection of the two.

Einstein is quoted as saying, "Time is not at all what it seems. It does not flow in only one direction, and the future exists simultaneously with the past." Physicists, speaking from the point of view they achieve by reducing the universe to equations on a white board, often ask the question, "Why does time flow forward?" It appears from their equations that, theoretically at least, it could just as well flow backward!

Many experiments in quantum physics have been conducted using a *double-slit* apparatus that breaks a beam of photons into two streams. The experiment has been conducted for numerous purposes to help prove out various aspects of the nature of light and quantum mechanical theory. One unexpected result of a particular double-slit experiment (too complex to describe here) is that observers appear to be able to determine the path of a photon *after the photon has already passed through the slit*. Observers, in other words, appear to be able to affect the past.

Could man time travel in Treta Yuga as he does in many science fiction stories? In strictly rational terms, time travel is problematic. The old conundrum: If one goes back in time and kills one's grandfather would one still exist? implies that a rigid cause and effect is at work—if this, then that. However, time travel, if indeed it is possible, may be accomplished *within the realm of thought*, rather than within the realm of matter, and so not be subject to the same causality.

Thinking along these lines tends to make one's head hurt! But it does illustrate that we by no means understand all there is to know about time. These examples of how mankind might overcome the limitations of time are obviously even more speculative than the previous examples of how in Dwapara Yuga mankind might overcome the limitations of space. But they do remind us that we, here in the early centuries of Dwapara Yuga, are at only the relative beginnings of human understanding and development.

~~~~~~~~~

While Dwapara Yuga is currently unfolding according to the formula of *self-interest* x *awakened intellect* x *energy awareness*, Treta Yuga will unfold according to the formula of *self-mastery* x *intuitive attunement* x *thought awareness*.

Treta Yuga's unfolding possibilities suggest a world, a society, an individual's personal daily experience, very different from what we are familiar with when we wake up in the morning. Treta Yuga man may experience, and *feel*, the world as currents of thought! In the next chapter we will explore some of the trends that *might* come about as a result of these profound differences.

Chapter 8

Ascending Treta Yuga —
Trends

Timeline

4100 AD Beginning of the next ascending Treta Yuga

4400 AD End of the 300-year transition period (sandhi) from Dwapara Yuga

7400 AD Beginning of 300-year transition period (sandhi) to Satya Yuga

7700 AD End of the next ascending Treta Yuga

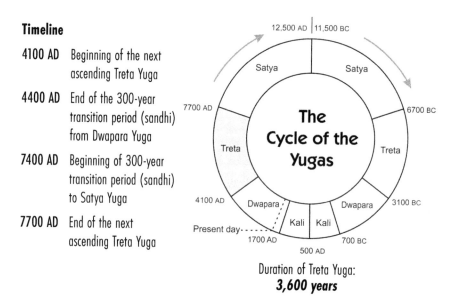

Duration of Treta Yuga:
3,600 years

In an attempt to give ascending Treta Yuga more shape and texture we will explore several *possible* trends reflecting the natural expression of the awareness and capabilities of Treta Yuga man. The trends we will explore are highly speculative. As we quoted in the previous chapter, Sri Yukteswar wrote this about Treta Yuga: "the grasping power of the human intellect is at present so limited that it would be quite useless to attempt to make the matter understood by the general public."[1] We only hope that you, our reader, are not part of the *general* public!

A Truly Civil Society

In a society where everyone has at least some ability to perceive the thoughts of others, we would expect to find a level of awareness of and sensitivity to others, unparalleled in our age. Awareness of and sensitivity to others would naturally lead to a more civil society.

We expect that people in ascending Treta Yuga will be much more aware of what everyone else is "really like." Today, it is easy to be fooled by people. We've all met someone who is charming and, seemingly, kind and thoughtful, only to have later encounters that reveal that the person has a mean streak, is prone to lie, or has other undesirable characteristics. Had his thoughts been more "visible" to us, we would probably have detected all the aspects of his personality immediately.

As an analogy, today we have mounting problems with pollution. Our air, our water, our food, are all increasingly contaminated with pollutants. But people's behavior, which is the root cause of the pollution, doesn't tend to change, because most people don't experience, moment by moment, the direct relationship between their behavior and the pollution they are helping to create. But, what if every bit of pollution each of us was responsible for creating were to accumulate in our homes, on our clothes, or on our bodies — visible as ugly, dangerous substances? It is easy to imagine that we would take more personal responsibility for the pollution we create, and it is even easier to imagine that, as a result, most pollution would be eliminated in short order!

Similarly, if negative character traits were an unattractively visible part of what a person "looked like" to others — if their thought "pollution" clung to them like a rash — people would probably make every effort to "clean up their act." Today, others' negative character traits, such as meanness of spirit, unkindness, self-centeredness, avarice, and greed are difficult to spot right away. Imagine a world where everyone could perceive them. Being untruthful would become more and more difficult. Saying one thing but meaning another, or making promises with no intention of keeping them, would be more clearly revealed to those whose perception is sensitive.

Beauty would no longer be only "skin deep." People would be thought beautiful because of the beauty of their thoughts, motives, and convictions. Men or women harboring selfish thoughts and negative emotions would be thought unattractive, even if physically beautiful, because the average person in Treta Yuga will be more able to see them as they truly are.

Equally significant will be the ability to see the impact one's own thoughts and words have on other people. Today, the results of speaking an unkind word, acting in an insensitive way, or harboring negative thoughts toward another person often go unnoticed by the person responsible for them. In Treta Yuga, people will be able to "see" the subtle impacts of their thoughts, words, and deeds on others, as clearly as today we see the impact of our physical actions.

Truthfulness, sincerity, and sensitivity to the needs of others will have high value in such a society. As a result, a civil society, which many of us long for today, is likely to finally, and naturally come into being. People who contribute positively and cooperatively to the betterment of society would be praised and admired. Those who have negative qualities, who exhibit characteristics that today are hidden behind various masks and justifications, would be encouraged to change their ways.

Leaders and Government

It would, therefore, be less and less likely, as Treta Yuga unfolded, to have leaders with hidden motives or significant character flaws. Today we are essentially *guessing* about the true character of our leaders; in Treta Yuga we could *know* their true character. As a result, it would be more and more likely that only men and women of true worth would end up in positions of leadership. Cooperation for the overall benefit of society would become the accepted goal of government. Men or women who are drawn to leadership because of the desire for power, wealth, or selfish interests only would, by their own thoughts, be revealed for what they were, and would not be entrusted with the public's business.

Society would probably find it impossible to ignore exploitation, injustice, and inhumane behavior. Today's self-interested, and twisted political logic, which allows people to starve, live in crushing poverty and dismal circumstances, would simply evaporate. The sensitive awareness of others, shared by all people in Treta Yuga, would not allow it. Treta Yuga man could no more ignore the suffering of other people than he could ignore pain in his own body.

Democracy, certainly democracy as we know it today, will likely have ended by ascending Treta Yuga. Democracy today is in many ways a reaction to the often-grievous failures of the hereditary and dictatorial rulers of Kali Yuga. While there were notable exceptions, such as the reign of Ashoka in the third century BC, or the rule of Charlemagne in the eighth century AD, most hereditary rulers, or those who achieved rule by conquest, did not do well by their subjects, to say the least. Some were out-and-out monsters. Emperor Nero of the Roman Empire is perhaps the epitome of despotic rule—self-absorbed, depraved, uncaring—fiddling while Rome burned. But there are many others that could be put in mankind's hall of shame.

It is no wonder then that, when Dwapara Yuga's influence began to be felt, one of the first waves of change was the end of hereditary rule and the establishment of democracy and the rule of law. In our ascending Dwapara Yuga we have yet to eliminate *all* despotic rule. Fear and force of arms still allow many to rule nations without the consent of their people. But we expect and hope soon to see, as Dwapara Yuga unfolds, these still oppressed nations gain the benefits of democracy.

Democracy for the most part prevents the excesses and wrongs committed by dictators interested only in personal power. As Friedrich Nietzsche is quoted as saying, "Democratic institutions form a system of quarantine for tyrannical desires."

But democracy does have its faults. As Winston Churchill is quoted, "No one pretends that democracy is perfect or all-wise. Indeed, it has been said that democracy is the worst form of Government except all the others that have been tried." Democracy, as it is practiced today, depends on compromise to make laws. In compromise, almost no one really gets what he wants, and, as a result, what progress is made is very slow. Democracy does prevent really egregious misrule, but does so by achieving sometimes internally conflicted laws and regulations, and thus makes very little forward progress.

Democracy's weaknesses are compounded by the reality that in order to move forward at all, lawmakers must cater to the largest common denominator of the public's interests and motives. Currently these are variations of *self-interest*—greed and fear. Justice, equality, and vision are nearly always left out of the equation.

By ascending Treta Yuga, most people will probably have left behind their previously justifiable fear of despots and dictators, and will realize that the best government, one that effectively improves the lives of its citizens, will be one run by wise and enlightened men and women with both the material and spiritual welfare of others uppermost in their hearts and minds. And as Treta Yuga citizens will be able to *directly perceive* the qualities of others, they will not fear that the wrong people will be given such power by mistake.

The Pursuit of Happiness

The increase of joy, the attainment of inner security, the experience of love—these remain the unchanging goals of man. Each yuga gives people different abilities with which to seek happiness—but no yuga guarantees that they will find it. Treta Yuga man will also pursue joy, security, and love. The awareness of thought, with its greater subtlety and refinement, will bestow on Treta Yuga man greater *potential* for experiencing happiness than we now enjoy in Dwapara Yuga, but it will still be up to each individual to achieve that happiness.

According to Sri Yukteswar, Treta Yuga man's natural attunement to thought will bring with it extraordinary awareness and abilities. Those living in Treta Yuga will eventually learn that their greatest happiness lies not simply in *self-mastery*—as an end in itself—but in using their *self-mastery* to attune themselves to *expansive* flows of thought.

Attunement to any thought brings with it an accompanying and specific experience and feeling. Attuning yourself to a particular flow of thoughts is like swimming in a river. Like the river's current, your thoughts take you on a journey. As people attune themselves to thoughts they become deeply immersed in these thoughts, and therefore influenced by them.

For example, thoughts of power, domination, and self-importance can bring an accompanying *feeling* of being powerful and energized. Initially this feeling can seem agreeable. But pursuing personal power for self-interested ends alone puts one into a flow that will end in attunement to thoughts with less agreeable accompanying feelings—vengeful and angry toward those who thwart your will, fearful that others are conspiring against you, indifferent toward those whom you feel are of lesser importance. One may have begun the journey with the agreeable feeling of self-centered power, but one will end in the feelings of anger, fear, and indifference.

Once you immerse yourself in a particular flow, your thoughts, like a river will take you along to their inevitable destination—regardless of what you might have hoped or expected. We don't produce thought inside our minds—thought exists independently of our minds. We attune ourselves to currents of thought that exist apart from us, and only *receive* them in our minds, as when we tune a radio to particular station. Our mind is the radio and thoughts are the myriad "stations" we can "tune into."

Attunement to positive and selfless thoughts expands our awareness beyond the ego—and is accompanied by agreeable feelings of joy and well-being. Attunement to negative and self-centered thoughts contracts our awareness within the ego—and is accompanied by diminished feeling and unhappiness.

The arc of Treta Yuga development, therefore, will be one of people learning to attune to thoughts that will lead to greater happiness. Mankind will learn that—fundamentally—joy, security, and love are experienced by *intuitive attunement* to expansive and uplifting flows of thought.

Further, perceiving that the flows of thought lie outside themselves, the people of Treta Yuga will come to appreciate that their ultimate happiness lies beyond the confines of their egos and limited minds. This awareness will form the essence of their spiritual experience.

Divine Magnetism and Spiritual Development

We wrote in the last chapter that Paramhansa Yogananda describes *divine magnetism* as "the power of all powers."[2] Not a blind or impersonal power, *divine magnetism is conscious*, and therefore will respond *consciously* to the *intuitive attunement* of Treta Yuga man.

Direct, personal experience of the divine is beyond the expectations of most people today. Such an immediate experience of the divine is often considered a sign even of mental instability. For those of you with an impish sense of humor, just mention casually to people that God has been talking to you, and watch the reaction of shock and wariness spread across their features!

Currently mankind is moving away from narrow or anthropomorphic conceptions of God. Just as the coming of democracy was an antidote to the grievous failures of the rulers of Kali Yuga, a conception of God as impersonal, universal, and infinite is an antidote to the rigid, sectarian, and anthropomorphic conceptions of God in Kali Yuga.

Philosophies that posit each person's essential divinity, and that, at the same time, allow room for each person's individuality, are very welcome at this time in mankind's development. For example, some kinds of Buddhism are widely embraced in the West, because they combine a divinity so impersonal as to approach non-existence, with an emphasis on the individual's thoughts and actions as more important than formulaic spiritual practices.

Certainly by Treta Yuga, if not before, we expect mankind once again to embrace the possibility of a *conscious and personal* relationship with the divine, a divine that is at the same time universal and infinite. Treta Yuga man will come to understand that spiritual advancement can be achieved through *intuitive attunement* to *specific, conscious expressions* of the infinite divine consciousness.

Just as we understand that the different colors of light in the rainbow are distinct from each other, we also understand that each color is itself an inextricable part of the phenomenon of light. So too, Treta Yuga man will comprehend that the divine can be experienced through a *particular and conscious personal relationship*, and that such a relationship is itself an inextricable part of a vast and all-inclusive divine consciousness.

In the last chapter we explored the idea that individuals may become so intuitively attuned to the thought form of a tree that they might be able to influence the tree to change into an entirely new species. Those who did not naturally attune themselves to growing things might be drawn to other pursuits—healing, teaching, music, governance, building, martial arts. Each pursuit would have its own core thought forms to which its practitioners would attune themselves.

Each of these pursuits is governed by a higher octave of thought forms. Music's highest octave could be described as the source of all harmonious vibration—the essence of music if you will—and in Treta Yuga this essence will be experienced as both divine and *conscious*. Attuning oneself to the essence of music, therefore, would be attuning oneself to a divine consciousness—a consciousness, moreover, that could respond, communicate, and interact. We might think of such a conscious essence as a god or goddess.

Treta Yuga man's extraordinary abilities will allow him to tune in so deeply that he can manipulate energy and matter—to achieve a state wherein his intuitive attunement to the thought form is so deep that he will become almost a part of it. In the same way, when someone's *intuitive attunement* is focused on a conscious expression of divinity, as described above, that person will be able to experience himself as part of the divine consciousness itself.

This then will be the "religion" of Treta Yuga.

The "priests" will be those who have mastered *intuitive attunement* to the divine. People living in Treta Yuga, because of their heightened awareness of the thoughts and feelings of others, will naturally gravitate to teachers who demonstrate the spiritual understanding they wish to develop in themselves. Treta Yuga citizens will seek to learn from enlightened sages, living exemplars of the truths they seek to master.

Dwapara Yuga man's awakened intellect and increased individualism tends to convince him that he doesn't *need* a spiritual teacher. In time, this inclination will moderate, and mankind as a whole will appreciate the benefits of learning higher truths directly from those who know them. By Treta Yuga such an attitude will be commonplace. If Treta Yuga citizens can already learn directly from the mind of another person, why would they want to learn their spiritual lessons from a book, however enlightened its author?

Conflict and War

Despite Treta Yuga man's advanced state, it is likely that there will still be conflict and war. Treta Yuga man will still be motivated by some degree of *self-interest*. Enlightened self-interest surely, but nonetheless each individual will still be seeking personal fulfillment. And although considerably more refined than Dwapara Yuga man's search for happiness, Treta Yuga man's search, in the beginning of Treta Yuga at least, will still be *self-centered*. Treta Yuga man's understanding that fulfillment lies beyond the narrow confines of ego will not fully mature until nearly the end of ascending Treta Yuga.

Additionally, as in every yuga, there will be those whose consciousness is more in tune with lower yugas, even though the majority of mankind will be in tune with Treta Yuga. There will still be some part of the population that remains centered in the more *self-interested* consciousness of Dwapara Yuga, especially during the initial 300-year transition period, or *sandhi*, of Treta Yuga. Also, Dwapara Yuga consciousness, though steadily diminishing during Treta Yuga, may well play a role in the affairs of Treta Yuga for many centuries beyond the *sandhi*.

The combination of Treta Yuga man's remaining *self-interest*, however enlightened, combined with the residual Dwapara Yuga awareness of some portion of the population does suggest that conflict will be likely. Not all Treta Yuga citizens will embrace their higher potentials and strive to rise above selfish interests. Treta Yuga man's awareness of the *divine magnetism* will not *compel* people to seek deeper attunement to it. People, whatever the age, have free will. Some may seek, instead, to see how powerful they can become. They may still seek expansion, growth, and power, but with their egos as the focus, and with their personal ambitions as their goals.

Still ruled by narrow self-interest and possessing vast personal power, highly advanced Treta Yuga men and women would inevitably clash. But Treta Yuga man's greater awareness of his fellow citizens may significantly change the way conflict and war play out.

War today is often waged indiscriminately. Civilian populations are frequently the victims of war. Mankind's enlightened self-interest, which should develop even before the end of Dwapara Yuga, may well eliminate much of this behavior—after all, what is gained by either side if much of the world is destroyed in the process of waging a war. But for now "mass destruction" is a common approach to war.

By Treta Yuga we expect that war would be waged among *warriors* only. No longer relying on technological weapons, but on mentally directed power, combat would likely be fought warrior to warrior. Warriors of the future may use concentration and attunement to directly control forces, forces they might unleash with great accuracy. Strength of mind, rather than might of arms, would become the mark of the accomplished warrior. Battles involving such warriors might unfold entirely differently than what we know of war today.

War might finally be waged in the idealized manner envisioned in the tales of the Knights of the Round Table and the Age of Chivalry. In Kali Yuga, the rules of chivalry were mostly honored in the breech—idealized but rarely followed. Knights were supposed to fight only knights. In practice, foot soldiers were encouraged to pull them from their horses, if they had the chance, and dispatch them on the ground. Knights were to be allowed to withdraw if wounded, or if they lost their weapons. Since this is when knights were the most vulnerable, they were often killed or captured and held for ransom. Non-combatants were never to be harmed. In practice, villages were burned to the ground, and looting and rape were the *perks* of the soldier.

In Treta Yuga combat, such rules would perhaps actually be followed. Even when affairs have reached the stage where combat seems the only solution, nonetheless, it may be that Treta Yuga man's advanced awareness will ensure that such noble rules will be adhered to—even in the heat of battle. Certain actions may simply be beneath the warriors of Treta Yuga. Even in the way war is fought today, some things are morally repugnant to both sides, and simply are not done. In Kali Yuga warfare, bodies were dismembered, heads displayed on pikes, and even hurled back at the enemy by catapults. Such actions are now considered beneath contemporary soldiers. We expect that by Treta Yuga the moral bar will have been raised even higher.

Daily Life

Even though man will be more highly advanced in many respects in Treta Yuga than in Dwapara Yuga, we will probably still find much that would feel familiar to us—relationships, raising families, pursuing vocations, maintaining friendships, going through hard times and good.

By Treta Yuga, one would expect the world population to have leveled off or continued to decline. The value attached to quality of life that is currently leading to declining population in prosperous nations will, if anything, accelerate in Treta Yuga. Treta Yuga people will have the higher awareness and the knowledge to allow them to live nearly perfect lives. We could liken them to the Swiss of today—prosperous, settled, desirous of peace, orderly and civil, surrounded by beauty.

Their homes, public buildings, and temples probably won't be overly large or ostentatiously ornate. Beauty of form, and harmony in relation to nature, will most likely shape their architecture, since their expanded awareness will make them keenly aware of such subtleties. With Treta Yuga's much smaller population, one could also expect that they will settle into the best "real estate" available — beautiful, healthful, and bountiful. Treta Yuga man may well spend a considerable amount of time out of doors in close touch with nature.

Individuals will be guided to develop along the natural lines of their innate qualities. As a result, society may stratify. Those with Treta Yuga consciousness will need to develop their abilities in accordance with their awareness. Those who are still primarily in Dwapara Yuga consciousness will need to develop their abilities in accordance with their awareness, as will those individuals who are more in tune with a Satya Yuga or Kali Yuga level of consciousness.

In the far more aware and enlightened society of Treta Yuga, such stratification would likely not be exploitative or unjust as what we see today. The hereditary caste system of India today is a millstone round the neck of its citizens. The hereditary class systems we still find all over the world typically have nothing to do with merit, ability, or awareness. In Treta Yuga, mankind's *actual awareness* of the thoughts and consciousness of other people will make it more likely that people will be allowed to develop because of who they are, not merely because of the family into which they were born.

Treta Yuga man will appreciate the value and benefits of serving others. Today there are many millions who are drawn to work and to professions that allow them to be of service to other people — teachers, nurses, policemen, firemen, soldiers, social workers — because they derive personal satisfaction from being of service to other people. Our Dwapara Yuga society, however, does not in general value such service nearly as much as it values accumulating wealth. People in the service professions are notoriously underpaid; they are often referred to as the "unsung" heroes of our society.

In Treta Yuga this balance may well be reversed. Those choosing a life of service may be more valued than those choosing to accumulate wealth or power merely for self-centered ends. Treta Yuga people will probably be acutely aware of the satisfaction that comes with placing the welfare of others ahead of their own. Today, the benefits of a life lived in service to others tends to be honored by lip service; in Treta Yuga it will be truly understood.

Although our description of Treta Yuga may sound like the Garden of Eden, still Treta Yuga man will not be perfect. Treta Yuga man will be *striving* for perfection, rather than simply seeking outward pleasure as most people are today, but much imperfection will remain. Self-interest, pride, insensitivity, unrequited love, anger, attachment, temptation—all these will still be present—grist for their mill of self-improvement.

We would, however, expect Treta Yuga man to be happier and more at peace than we are today, because Treta Yuga man's *starting point* of awareness—*intuitive attunement* to thought—provides a greater *possibility* for inner fulfillment and divine attunement than we have in Dwapara Yuga.

The Lessons of Treta Yuga

Treta Yuga man will become powerful beyond anything we comprehend today. Highly advanced individuals in Treta Yuga may have the power to create and destroy with their minds, to bring down lightning from the skies, or to magnetically draw to themselves what they desire. Their powers will be potentially unlimited, because thought underlies the very structure of the universe.

Learning the *right use of power* will therefore be the lesson of Treta Yuga. *Self-interested* use of such powers will ultimately be understood to boomerang on the wielder. Only when the wielder accepts that his purpose should be to use his powers to serve others will he find greater happiness. Until then, no matter how powerful the individual becomes, happiness, contentment, and fulfillment will always elude him.

By the end of the 3600-year arc of ascending Treta Yuga, people should be well on their way to the realization that there is no reality separate from the Divine. Not only will they realize that their highest fulfillment lies in service and attunement to the Divine, but they will begin to comprehend that they *are* divine in their very essence.

Chapter 9

Ascending Satya Yuga

Timeline

7700 AD Beginning of the next ascending Satya Yuga

8100 AD End of the 400-year transition period (*sandhi*) from Treta Yuga

12,100 AD Beginning of 400-year transition period (*sandhi*) to descending Satya Yuga

12,500 AD End of the next ascending Satya Yuga

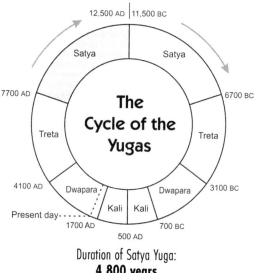

Duration of Satya Yuga:
4,800 years

The awareness, motivations, and abilities of mankind in Satya Yuga are nearly beyond our comprehension. If in our attempts to comprehend Treta Yuga we are like a child trying to understand an adult, in our attempts to comprehend Satya Yuga we are like a child trying to understand a saint.

Sri Yukteswar writes in *The Holy Science* that, in Satya Yuga, "the human intellect can comprehend all, even God the Spirit beyond this visible world."[1] Returning to the analogy of the radio, in Satya Yuga mankind will gain yet another radio band, a higher and more subtle frequency will become accessible—an ultra-high frequency band, if

128

you will—that makes it possible for Satya Yuga man to comprehend "all, even God the Spirit."

Pure Consciousness

"God" is a loaded word today. It conjures up different meanings for different people, depending on their backgrounds and cultures; often it conjures up a wide variety of positive and negative feelings. As previously discussed, many people today have turned to atheism and science in reaction against limiting conceptions of God that originated in Kali Yuga. Not surprisingly, Dwapara Yuga man often finds difficult to accept or understand the idea that mankind as a whole could live in day-to-day awareness of God the Spirit.

Sri Yukteswar wryly observes that God is not "a venerable personage, adorning a throne in some antiseptic corner of the cosmos!"[2] God is *pure consciousness*, beyond form and limitation, and our own consciousness, our very being, is an inextricable expression of this consciousness. Thus, the more deeply we understand ourselves, the more deeply we understand our consciousness as part of the pure consciousness of God.

One can describe the development of mankind through the yugas as the process of discovering deeper, more *subtle* aspects of the reality of who they have been all along. Advancing through the yugas is like removing layers of wrappings from a package, layers that are hiding the gift within. By Satya Yuga, most of the wrappings will have been removed, and the gift within will be visible, as though seen through one final, faintly obscuring, layer of tissue. In Satya Yuga, each individual will still need to remove that final layer, but he will also know that once he has done so, he will experience "God the Spirit beyond this visible world."

There are men and women alive today, as indeed there have been in all yugas, who have removed the final layer separating them from God. We think of these men and women as extraordinary, but in fact they demonstrate *everyone's* potential to realize unity with the pure consciousness of God.

The true nature of the consciousness possessed by saints, sages, holy men—by all people of advanced realization—is often obscured by the accretions of time, changing language, evolving cultures, differing symbolism, simple misinterpretation, and the lamentable tendency of groups of people to put *their* enlightened ones forward as the only true exemplars of Divinity. But the discerning seeker perceives that the underlying consciousness of all men and women of true realization has the same origin — pure consciousness.

An often told story in India has five blind men describing an elephant. One, touching the trunk, describes the elephant as a hose. The second, touching an ear, describes the elephant as a fan. The third, touching a leg, describes the elephant as a tree. The fourth, touching the side, describes the elephant as a wall. And the fifth, touching the tail, describes the elephant as a rope. All five blind men are correct. Each one is accurately describing what he has experienced of the elephant.

Yet the elephant is obviously more than any one of the blind men has been able to experience or describe. Conceptions of God likewise vary with the conceiver. Not all who perceive the consciousness of God do so fully. Even those rare people who do fully comprehend the consciousness of God must describe their experience using the language, symbols, and level of understanding of their time, making their descriptions of the consciousness of God seem to differ.

Jesus told his followers, "The kingdom of God is within." Buddha told his followers that by eliminating all false conceptions they would achieve nirvana. Krishna taught his followers to strive for yoga, or union with God. Three teachings that sound different from one another, and that yet all describe the same truth.

Direct Intuitive Perception and Self-realization

Sense perception, intellect, intuitive reason, intuitive attunement — the means of perception of the lower yugas — are all indirect means of perceiving reality. Each capability is more subtle than the previous one, and each capability allows us to perceive ever more subtle layers of reality. But to actually perceive God one must develop *direct intuitive perception*.

Direct intuitive perception requires no indirect mental or emotional processes. It is as if, until we achieve the ability of direct intuitive perception, we are always somewhat blind. Those who *are* blind need to use other senses, engage in other processes, such as stroking, smelling, lifting, rattling, even tasting an object, to put together a mental picture. They arrive at their mental picture indirectly. Whereas those who can see, simply see.

In the *Autobiography of a Yogi*, Paramhansa Yogananda describes his first experience of pure consciousness. Too long to fully quote, in this brief excerpt, Yogananda describes his experience as both inner ineffable bliss, and an outer vision of God's consciousness creating and sustaining the world:

> All objects within my panoramic gaze trembled and vibrated like quick motion pictures. My body, Master's, the pillared courtyard, the furniture and floor, the trees and sunshine, occasionally became violently agitated, until all melted into a luminescent sea; even as sugar crystals, thrown into a glass of water, dissolve after being shaken. The unifying light alternated with materializations of form, the metamorphoses revealing the law of cause and effect in creation.

> I cognized the center of the empyrean as a point of intuitive perception in my heart. Irradiating splendor issued from my nucleus to every part of the universal structure.[3]

When we fully calm the tumult of our senses and emotions, we intuitively perceive the subtlest realm of reality—pure consciousness. Our heart, the center of our direct intuitive perception, must be still in order to perceive with subtlety and clarity, as when we see the clear reflection of the moon in a perfectly still pond.

The achievement of inner stillness, and the refinement of *direct intuitive perception*, will be the focus of development for Satya Yuga man. The people of Satya Yuga will strive to calm the waves of emotion that disturb the heart's natural stillness. Once stilled, the heart reveals the consciousness of God, clearly and effortlessly.

All men and women who have perfected their direct intuitive perception realize that their own consciousness is inseparable from the consciousness of God. When they remain unshakably fixed in that awareness they can be said to be *Self-realized*.

Those who attain *Self-realization* retain their awareness of individuality, and at the same time are conscious of their oneness with God. *Self-realization* means that they no longer act from any sense of separateness. Their every thought, feeling, and action arises from their attunement with divinity, not from the limited consciousness of ego.

However, even a short study of the lives of *Self-realized* individuals reveals them to be unique in how they express their unity with the consciousness of God. Far from popular misconceptions of being mindless, robotic mouthpieces for a serious and humorless God, *self-realized* men and women are delightfully alive, full of joy, compassion, humor, and are each uniquely individual in expressing the consciousness of God.

Life as a School

The comprehension of "God the Spirit beyond this visible world," bestowed by the influence of Satya Yuga, will naturally incline Satya Yuga man to try to perfect his awareness of God. But he will still need great effort and focus to attain perfect and continuous *Self-realization*. Not everyone, even in Satya Yuga, will fully attain *Self-realization*. But most will strive for it.

Like Treta Yuga's society, Satya Yuga society will naturally organize itself around those of the highest advancement. In a sense, all of Satya Yuga society will become a school. Teachers will not so much teach people *about* divine consciousness, as help them to *deepen* their own perception of divine consciousness.

In a lifetime that might reach 400 years, it is possible to imagine people in Satya Yuga devoting decades, perhaps *centuries*, to intensive study and practice under the guidance of a *Self-realized* teacher. No longer practicing a religion that is only theoretical or intellectual, Satya Yuga man will know without any doubt that deeper attunement to God brings the greatest measure of joy, contentment, and love. The motivation to achieve deeper attunement to God will be both clear and strong.

We would expect to find the structure of society formed around centers of spiritual advancement. These centers might resemble the monasteries, convents, and ashrams of today, but would be located not on the remote fringes, as they are in our era, but in the heart of society. The process of government, teaching children, health and healing, daily work, artistic expression, raising families would all be deeply influenced by the wisdom and direction of *Self-realized* teachers.

In our society, the motivation that drives and informs government, schools, careers, medicine, raising families, artistic expression — the whole gamut of human endeavor — is the belief that the result of these pursuits will be fulfillment and personal happiness. In Satya Yuga, the gamut of human endeavor will be understood as learning opportunities to deepen one's attunement to God. Thus one person might allow himself to be guided by an advanced teacher into working as a humble gardener in order to calm an overactive mind, while another person might be encouraged to do mental work because his need was for deeper concentration. The goal in both examples is to grow spiritually, rather than to grow in wealth or position.

Relationships of all kinds, marriage, family, friendship, may be seen as opportunities to perfect the ability to love others, not, as we tend to live them today, as opportunities to *be* loved. Artistic expression may be seen as an opportunity to channel divine qualities, such as harmony and beauty, rather than as the opportunity for individual expression. Accomplishment may be seen as an opportunity to perfect will power, concentration, and creative attunement, not as an opportunity to get ahead in life.

Mankind's shared direction of *Self-realization* will shape all activity in Satya Yuga. The primary activities will be learning and practicing ways to achieve *Self-realization* — learning from men and women who have already achieved *Self-realization*, spending time in communion with God, and practicing techniques that will deepen awareness, concentration, and focus. Thus all activity, the sublime and the prosaic, will be infused with the same purpose.

Heaven on Earth?

It is understandable if one imagined Satya Yuga as a heaven on earth. More accurately, however, we could think of Satya Yuga as a time when many people could *experience* heaven, *while* on earth. The consciousness of a person immersed in God is vastly expanded, and that person's awareness would go well beyond "this visible world," as

Sri Yukteswar expressed it. The experience of heaven is transcendent, not earth-bound. Satya Yuga citizens will share with each other the heaven they experience within themselves, but the earth, the world of physical necessity, and all the imperfections that go with it, will still need to be dealt with.

We would also expect Satya Yuga man to lead a full, active life, with lively interests and keen appreciation — not as ends in themselves — but rather as the natural overflowing expression of the highly energized, highly refined awareness of one who lives in the consciousness of God.

Active lives in an imperfect world are bound to lead to issues with other people. Misunderstandings and disagreements will undoubtedly still occur. Nonetheless, we can certainly expect that life in Satya Yuga will be more peaceful and harmonious than life today, free of the deeper tensions that exist between people who are primarily self-centered. We would also expect life in Satya Yuga to be full of joy, laughter, and love — because all the highest aspects of dharma, man's perfected nature, would be given expression. Music, art, learning, teaching, health, healing, relationships, all will be imbued with higher consciousness and will reach their peak of expression.

Simplicity

We can imagine that the ordinary necessities of life will be kept simple so as not to distract from the main focus of uniting with Spirit. Growing and preparing food, maintaining homes, teaching the young, healing the unwell, making clothes, creating art, all would still be necessary and desirable, but it is equally probable they would be nothing like we experience today.

Our emphasis today is on seeking personal happiness outside ourselves — what we eat, what we wear, the home we live in, the car we drive, the job we have. These externals are not only considered necessary for our lives — but also essential to our happiness. As such they take on an importance far beyond their basic purpose. A significant portion of our technological advancement has occurred because mankind is infatuated with new and better consumer items — from toasters to townhouses. It is not easy for us to imagine a society in which the material life is unimportant.

Simplicity need not imply plainness or utilitarianism. Satya Yuga man's expanded awareness will make him keenly sensitive to beauty, balance, and harmony in all things. He will naturally wish to surround himself with these qualities, but doing so would not imply opulence, luxury, or ostentation. Beauty need not be created self-consciously. What could be more beautiful than a rose or a flowering tree?

Nor need simplicity imply boring conformity. Sri Yukteswar taught that "divine perception gives rise to the keenest intelligence."[4] It is hard to imagine sparkling, creative intellects falling into sameness. Rather, those living in Satya Yuga, in their uniqueness, would share and enjoy the bounty of their perceptions and thoughts. One imagines lively wits and vital minds.

Simplicity need not imply solemnity. The last phrase of Paramhansa Yogananda's poem *Samadhi* is, "A tiny bubble of laughter, I am become the Sea of Mirth Itself."[5] People in attunement with God overflow with joy. St. Francis de Sales, a medieval Catholic saint, said, "A saint that is sad is a sad saint!"[6] One imagines Satya Yuga ringing with good-natured laughter and humor.

Simplicity need not imply lack of refinement. The arts would reach their peak in Satya Yuga. Imagine a concert in which the singer could convey not only sound but *consciousness* to the audience. Imagine a weaving that revealed not only beautiful color and texture but beautiful feeling as well. Imagine art created by artists who might have dedicated *two hundred years* or more to perfecting their craft.

Simplicity need not imply isolation. The highly developed mental powers of Treta Yuga man will carry over to Satya Yuga, allowing instant communication with others, even at a great distance. Even though scattered across the world in small populations, Satya Yuga man will be aware of and able to communicate with his fellow world citizens at any time.

Simplicity need not imply primitiveness. While Satya Yuga citizens may reduce the complexity of their world, they will not lose their knowledge of the past. The best of centuries of development will remain. Sanitation, personal hygiene, disease prevention, agriculture, and much more, will all incorporate the benefits of past knowledge. Also, Satya Yuga residents may well be able to manifest many things by the power of thought and attunement to the consciousness of God, as we've already explored in the chapters on ascending Treta Yuga.

During Treta Yuga, as mankind develops the mental abilities to affect the world, technology may gradually die away. Knowledge of the principles behind today's technology will not die away, but the *need* for technology will. By Satya Yuga, the thousands of factories, myriad manufacturing processes, rapacious mining of raw materials, relentless transporting of goods, and the massive infrastructure that makes our consumer economy work, may be a dim memory, no longer needed by people who seek happiness within rather than without.

The trend toward a declining population, which we are already seeing signs of in Dwapara Yuga, will, in all likelihood, continue on into Treta and Satya Yuga. The world population could easily decline to tens of millions only—perhaps even less—during the nearly 6,000 years between now and Satya Yuga. Fewer people, living longer lives and bent on inner development, suggest a world without most of the complexity of today. Rather than bustling cities, there may be quiet villages. Rather than a large and complex economy to supply a bewildering variety of things such as we have today, there may be self-sufficiency and barter.

For the science fiction buff, this vision of the future may be a bit of a letdown. Science fiction's often imagined future includes entire planets that have become covered with one continuous city. Machines and technology so powerful they can move mountains and destroy armies. Computers so vast and sophisticated that everything is run by them, and everything is known to them.

Science fiction's vision of the future is a straight line extrapolation of many of the values and motivations of today—and some of science fiction's grandiose and technological visions may yet come to pass before Dwapara Yuga is over. However, according to Sri Yukteswar, many of mankind's basic values and motivations will change in Treta and Satya Yuga. As mankind's values and motivations change in the future, then much of what we take for granted today as having self-evident value and desirability will simply fade away, *for lack of interest.*

Conflict and Strife

Could there be conflict or strife in such an environment? Although mankind in Satya Yuga will have the clear *opportunity* to seek perfection, people will not yet *be* perfect. What each individual does with the opportunity will be up to him. Perfection, then as now, will only be attainable by sincere effort and determination.

It is certainly hard to imagine war or physical combat during Satya Yuga, but, as in the other yugas, there will be those whose awareness is more in tune with previous yugas. In Satya Yuga, one would not expect to find many whose awareness is like that of Kali Yuga man, but Dwapara Yuga and Treta Yuga consciousness could well be present. As a result, serious disagreements, differences, and disputes could arise.

As discussed in an earlier chapter, mankind's consciousness affects the very earth. The negative thoughts and emotions reverberating in the world mind today may yet result in catastrophic natural upheavals in our not too distant future. Satya Yuga's far more harmonious thoughts and feelings, on the other hand, will result in greater harmony in the natural world as well. The weather may be moderate and beneficial, and the lion may lie down with the lamb.

But the natural world, even in Satya Yuga, will still be an imperfect place. We would not expect Satya Yuga's harmony to overcome long-term natural processes such as ice ages, continental movement, earthquakes, and volcanic eruptions. Furthermore, Satya Yuga's population will not be immune to the inevitable ills, old age, and death of the body. Heavenly perfection transcends the physical realm; it won't be found here on earth.

The Lessons of Satya Yuga

The challenge of Satya Yuga will be to strive for perfection, and not simply passively to enjoy the peace, harmony, and joy of the age. Surely we would be excused for thinking that enjoying such a wonderfully high-minded world would be an end in itself! Yet the challenge for those in Satya Yuga will be to avoid becoming too complacent, and not to waste the opportunity that living in such exalted times gives them to make significant spiritual progress. Ultimately man's destiny lies not on the earth, but in the Infinite consciousness from which the earth was created.

By 12,500 AD, after 12,000 years of upward development, mankind will have reached the pinnacle of human development on earth.

The End of the Ascending Arc

Yuga	Motivation	Perception	Comprehension	Dharma
Kali	passive acceptance	dull mindedness	matter	one-quarter developed
Dwapara	self-will	awakened intellect	energy	one-half developed
Treta	self-mastery	intuitive attunement	thought	three quarters developed
Satya	Self-realization	direct intuitive perception	consciousness	fully developed

Figure 8 — Table of the evolving motivations, perceptions, comprehensions, and dharmas of the yugas

In 500 AD, at the start of ascending Kali Yuga, mankind as a whole was in a low estate; dharma was only one-quarter developed. The average man was able to comprehend only gross matter, a level of understanding that led to a life lived primarily through and for the senses. The intellect of mankind was dull. The motivation of mankind was passive acceptance. Most people made only simple, basic choices to minimize pain or to maximize pleasure.

By the end of ascending Kali Yuga, mankind was beginning to awaken to a higher potential. As Sri Yukteswar puts it, people began to have respect for themselves once more. The brutal ways in which man had treated his fellows gave way to an appreciation of the dignity of man, to humanism and enlightenment.

By 1700 AD and the start of Dwapara Yuga, mankind had progressed; dharma was one-half developed. The average man would soon be able to comprehend the energy that underlies matter and the subtle energy within himself — his life force. The intellect of man had awakened, and reason had come to the fore. The motivation of man was to develop self-will, to break free of the passive acceptance of the past, and actively to try to shape the world to his liking.

By the end of ascending Dwapara Yuga, mankind will have explored the pursuit of material happiness to its unfulfilling end. But people will discover, in the process, that their real source of happiness is their own life force. In the process, mankind will also have developed physical, mental, and energetic abilities well beyond those we know today. Man will also harness the natural world's energy, which underlies all matter, in order to overcome the limitations of space. Mankind's awakened intellect and awareness of life force will have evolved from the cumbersome step-by-step use of reason into the beginnings of intuition.

Beginning in 4100 AD, with the start of Treta Yuga, dharma will be three-quarters developed, and the average man will be able to comprehend thought, the divine magnetism underlying all energy. Mankind will still be using reason, but it will be tempered with feeling: to understand subtler realities, he will rely on calm inner intuition, rather than on the reasoning process alone. The motivation of mankind will be to achieve self-mastery—the honing of body, mind, and feeling in order to master the powers of thought.

By the end of ascending Treta Yuga, mankind will have explored the potential of personal power through mastery of thought, and some will have achieved extraordinary abilities as a result. Man will develop many ways to overcome time's limitations. People's attunement to one another, through the shared awareness of thought, will result in a truly civil society, enriched by genuine concern for, and service to, their fellow man. As Treta Yuga's citizens deepen their awareness of thought through intuitive attunement, they will discover that the origin of all thought is not themselves, but rather the Divine Source of all thought.

Beginning in 7700 AD, with the start of ascending Satya Yuga, and with dharma fully developed, the average man will soon be able to comprehend all, even God the Spirit beyond this visible world. Man will be capable of direct intuitive perception of reality, and will no longer require the mental process of reason, or any other indirect means of perception. The motivation of man will be to achieve Self-realization.

By the end of ascending Satya Yuga mankind will have reached the full potential of life on earth. Simplicity, harmony, beauty, and love will be the natural expressions of inner communion with Spirit. People's relations with others will be, in essence, sharing the bounty they find within. But it will not be heaven on earth, simply because the earth is too imperfect to allow the full expression of Divinity. Heaven can only be fully experienced within ourselves.

And thus we can understand the complete arc of mankind's upward development. However, it is important to know that while mankind as a whole must wait upon the slow moving cycle of the yugas for spiritual development, there are men and women alive today who have achieved Self-realization. One need not wait upon the yugas. There are to be found now teachers and teachings that will help anyone quicken his natural spiritual evolution.

In the last seven chapters, we have been exploring the upward arc of the yugas. In the following chapters we will explore our hidden past and the descending arc of mankind's development. What appears to the historians and archeologists of today as evidence of a straight line of development of man — from primitive, skin-wearing spear-throwers, to anxious, clothes-wearing car-drivers — will take on new shape and meaning in the light of your understanding of the more enlightened awareness, motivations, and capabilities of mankind revealed in our previous exploration of future yugas.

PART FOUR

Our Hidden Past

Chapter 10

Descending Satya Yuga —
Three Misconceptions

Timeline

11,500 BC Beginning of the most recent descending Satya Yuga

11,100 BC End of the 400-year transition period (sandhi) from ascending Satya Yuga

7,100 BC Beginning of 400-year transition period (sandhi) to descending Treta Yuga

6,700 BC End of the most recent descending Satya Yuga

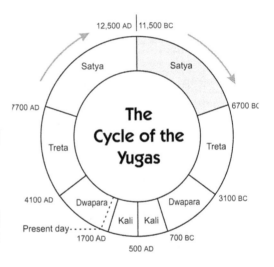

Duration of descending Satya Yuga:
4,800 years

In the following chapters we will explore how the yugas unfolded in the past—from descending Satya Yuga, through Treta Yuga, into Dwapara Yuga, and finally into Kali Yuga—taking us through the span of 12,000 years. We will present the past in a new light—sometimes presenting new evidence, sometimes demonstrating that old evidence admits of new interpretation. We believe there is clear evidence that, from its height in 11,500 BC, mankind gradually lost its exalted,

145

enlightened consciousness, and, by 500 AD, was most fully in the matter-engrossed consciousness of Kali Yuga.

According to Sri Yukteswar's explanation of the cycle of the yugas, mankind's consciousness would have been at the peak of enlightenment in 11,500 BC, even though most people consider this era to be primitive—its people ignorant, superstitious, and nearly savage. However, there is already significant accepted evidence indicating man's development in 11,500 BC was very different than is popularly believed. Three well-established misconceptions perpetuate the popular vision of the ancient past—the stone-age cave man, the frigid ice age, and the superstitious primitive.

The Stone Age Cave Man

The commonly held view of the world in 10,000 BC is of nomadic bands, grunting to communicate, using crude stone tools, wearing furs, eking out a miserable existence. This image is almost indelible. We see it in natural history museum dioramas, in textbooks, in movies, in literature, in advertising, in comics and cartoons, even in the idioms we use. To say the notion of the cave man is thoroughly accepted is an understatement—it just doesn't happen to be true—or at least not when most people think it was true.

What gave birth to the notion of the cave man living as recently as ten thousand years ago were two powerful ideas. The first and most influential idea was the theory of evolution. Darwin's *On the Origin of Species*, published in 1859, established the concept that all species—including man—evolve, a premise suggesting that an earlier and more primitive version of man had to have existed in the past. The second idea, the importance of which is less appreciated today, had to do with the common opinion at the time of Darwin of the age of the earth.

At the time when Darwin's theory of evolution was taking hold of Western science, in the 1860s and '70s, only a handful of natural scientists thought the earth was even as old as 50 million years, let alone the 4.5 billion years believed today. In the late 1800s the average person, even the average scientist, thought the earth was even far younger than 50 million years. Most people assumed that the earth's age was measured in hundreds of thousands, or at most a few million years.

Combined with Darwin's theory of evolution, the assumption of a very young Earth is significant, because this assumption led the scientists of the day to the conclusion that if man had in fact evolved from the apes, then man must have evolved *very* recently. Speculation among many scientists in the late 1800s was that a "missing link" must have existed, a new species that branched off from the apes as recently as 20 to 50 thousand years ago, and which evolved from ape-like man to modern man in the short span of a few thousand years.

If the natural scientists of the 1860s and 1870s, when the idea of the cave man took root, had had the perspective of a 4.5 billion-year-old earth, they might have theorized a much longer timeline of human evolution, and assumed a cave man period perhaps millions of years ago, rather than thousands of years ago. But because of the state of scientific understanding at the time, the cave man idea formed as it did — including cave men running around as recently as 10,000 BC — and, unfortunately, the idea still persists in the popular mind today.

In response to Darwin's theory, in the late 1800s a new branch of science now known as paleontology began to form. Hundreds of mostly amateur scientists went out into the field to find evidence of cave men and missing links, which they assumed existed within the last 100,000 years. Not surprisingly — given human nature — they found what they were looking for. The world was spellbound by such discoveries as Neanderthal Man, Cro-Magnon Man, Piltdown Man, and Java Man, all of which seemed to corroborate the theory that modern man had evolved from the apes within the last 100,000 years.

Most of these discoveries have since been discredited or significantly reassessed. The Piltdown Man was proved, famously, to be a deliberate hoax, made up from a modern human skull and the jaw of an orang-utan. Java Man was shown to be "put together" from bones found up to 10 meters apart, one of which, many authorities believe, was from an ape, and some of which are now known to be thousands of years apart in age. Neanderthal Man, as a species, is now believed, based on genetic analysis, to be at least a million years old, and there is growing opinion that the Neanderthal were, in fact, the same species as modern man, rather than an earlier and more primitive one.

Perhaps even more intriguing, from the point of view the yugas provide us, is the reassessment of Cro-Magnon Man. Initially Cro-Magnon Man was considered to be a separate species from modern man and was dated as having existed for only 30,000 years—from 40,000 to 10,000 BC. Current opinion among most paleontologists is that Cro-Magnon man was in fact "early modern human" and the same species as modern man. What led early paleontologists to their initial assessment, that Cro-Magnon Man must have been a different species, is the fact that the skulls of Cro-Magnons were significantly larger than ours— indicating that they had much larger brains. Yet another "Man," found in Africa, called Boskop Man, and dated at approximately the same time as Cro-Magnon Man, had an even larger brain. From this evidence we might conclude that instead of rapidly evolving from cave men living 10,000 years ago, mankind has instead devolved.

Nor is it just the examination of ancient bones that makes the idea of primitive stone-age cave men living in 10,000 BC highly unlikely. Over the last ten to twenty years especially, and in part because of increasingly more accurate dating methods and other means of scientific analysis (often called the New Archeology), a great many recent finds demonstrate that intelligent man's history on earth is much longer than previously assumed. For example, archeologists have found ancient stores of cultivated grains in Israel, at a site called Ohalo II, which indicate mankind has been growing and milling grains for at least 23,000 years.[1] Similarly, archeological digs in Afghanistan show that goats and sheep have been domesticated for at least 15,000 years.[2] Sophisticated settlements such as Gobekli Tepe and Catal Huyuk in Turkey, and Jericho in the West Bank existed as far back in time as 9500 BC; fired pottery has been found in Japan, attributed to the Jomon culture, that dates back to 12,000 BC.

In her meticulously researched work, Plato Prehistorian, author Mary Settegast surveys the latest archeological research and findings regarding the time from 10,000 to 5000 BC, and comes to this conclusion:

> The more we learn about early man, the more difficult it is
> to describe him as primitive. Even with the new and rightly
> placed appreciation of the so-called primitive peoples of
> today, it is becoming increasingly clear that at least some of
> the cultures of the Old Stone Age were both other and more

than the gatherer-hunter societies of recent times, and their members very far indeed from the savage creatures that all Paleolithic men were once assumed to be.

As a result, the existing model of prehistory — the view that sees the development of human culture as a unilinear series of stages, rising from primitive Upper Paleolithic hunting and foraging, to Neolithic farming villages, to the high civilizations of the Bronze Age and ultimately the urban societies of today — is losing its fundamental premise.

Archaeologists are aware of the inadequacy of the existing framework of thought. For almost two decades prehistorians have been seeking a new paradigm, a wholly new way of looking at the early world that would accommodate the growing number of contradictions to the present point of view.... If an authentically new vision of man's past is to be achieved, our most basic assumptions about the way things were may have to be uprooted, at least temporarily, and the old model let go in its entirety.[3]

What we can conclude from the finds of the New Archeology is that the "footprint" left by the so-called Stone Age hunter-gatherers, now considered to be much more advanced than previously thought, could be the same as the "footprint" left by people living in descending Satya Yuga, as we can envision their lifestyle from the description given us by Sri Yukteswar. A small population of spiritually enlightened people, living simply and lightly on the earth, would leave behind the same evidence of their presence in the past — small settlements and simple artifacts — as we associate with early man.

Even if Satya Yuga man had had more advanced capabilities than the archeologists ascribe to this era, such as metallurgy and the manufacture of textiles, no evidence of these capabilities would likely have survived. Even the artifacts of our "mighty" modern civilization cannot withstand the natural forces of disintegration arrayed against them, let alone the simple structures and artifacts of 10,000 BC. About the only material that lasts through thousands of years is stone — thus the term, the *Stone Age*.

As we will explore thoroughly in a later chapter, items made of fabric, wood, metal, plastic, even concrete, will last only a few thousand years, and will leave behind almost no trace of their existence. To the naked eye, 12,000 years from now, all that will be left of *our* technology, buildings, and artifacts will be, if anything, the parts made of stone.

The absence of evidence of fabric or looms, therefore, does not conclusively prove that early man wore ragged furs. It is possible that woven cloth and wooden looms did exist and have simply disintegrated with time. The fact that the earliest art works we know of are cave paintings does not preclude that other paintings were done on other materials that have long since turned to dust. The absence of jewelry or metal tools does not necessarily mean early man did not know how to work metal; it simply means that none has survived corrosion, oxidation, and disintegration — or they could simply have been handed down, reused, or reformed for millennia, as things of value tend to be.

Even if it *were* the case that the only tools, artifacts, and structures made by Satya Yuga man were made of stone, we need not therefore assume that the people of that time were ignorant and primitive cave men. It is difficult for us to imagine intelligent people choosing to live in Stone Age conditions — but that is just because it is difficult for us to imagine.

During Satya Yuga, the ability to control the environment and even to manipulate matter to satisfy simple needs, might have naturally led people to a disinterest in physical possessions and personal comfort, and they might have been content to use the simplest of tools when and if they needed them.

Ours, on the other hand, is a time when technology = good, physical comfort = obviously good, and more technology and more comfort = even better. Given our current fixation with material prosperity, it is ironic that when people want to take a vacation, they often want to go somewhere well away from the hustle and bustle of our "modern" life, away from telephones and computers, somewhere they can swim, hike, lie in the sun, be in nature, try to relax and revive their flagging energies, and, they hope, find some peace of mind. To a greater or lesser degree, most people know, without always fully understanding why, that true happiness is a state of being, not a state of having.

In Satya Yuga, peace of mind = good, relaxation = good, simple living = good. Why one would trade a transcendent joy-filled consciousness for stress and toil, so that one could have a big house with the latest conveniences, would be as difficult for the Satya Yuga man to imagine, as it is for Dwapara Yuga man to imagine he could find happiness without them.

At the very least, recent finds, as well as accumulating evidence from the past, seriously call into question the commonly held view of primitive, stone-age cave men roaming the world 10,000 years ago. Indeed, more and more evidence, as we will explore in a future chapter, points to a far longer history of civilized man than is currently assumed. In any case, the picture of man in 10,000 BC should now be drawn far differently than the cave man of popular conception.

The Ice Age

We often hear that the last ice age ended about 13,000 years ago. This is not an entirely accurate statement. We are, in fact, still in an ice age that began 2.6 million years ago when ice began to remain permanently at the poles. There have been other ice ages prior to the current one. In fact, geologists believe that in previous ice ages, the earth has twice been completely covered in ice, although that has not occurred during the current ice age. Geologists also believe that there have been many periods, some lasting hundreds of millions of years, when there was no permanent ice on the earth at all.

In the course of the over two million years of the present ice age, permanent ice has extended closer to and farther from the equator many times. These recurring extensions and retreats of glaciers and other permanent ice are known as glacial maximums and glacial minimums. What *ended* approximately 13,000 years ago, when permanent ice had again begun to retreat toward the poles, was the last glacial maximum, not the ice age itself.

It is significant to our subject to underscore that we are still in an ice age because many people think that our climate began to change *radically* for the better 13,000 years ago when the "ice age" ended. Many people envision all or most of the earth as having been frigid and highly inhospitable during the last glacial maximum, when in fact it was, in many regions, more verdant and hospitable than it is today.

Concerns about global warming have made us all more knowledge-able about global climate change, and more and more people appre-ciate that even a one-degree increase in average annual temperature around the world can have a massive effect on climate. So too, a one degree decrease. We now understand that just a few degrees decrease of average annual temperatures could result in the beginning of another glacial maximum.

But, even though there was more permanent ice on the earth dur-ing the last glacial maximum (roughly 23,000 BC to 13,000 BC) than there is now, *the day-to-day temperatures around the earth were only a few degrees cooler than what we experience today.* Most of the earth was comfortably habitable. The equatorial regions, especially, between the Tropics of Cancer and Capricorn, including India, Southern China, the Near East, North Africa, Central America, and a large part of North and South America, would have been ideal for human habita-tion, and far from any glaciers.

The areas in this central band around the earth, many of which are dry and arid today, such as the Near East, and the Sahara Desert, were green and fertile in 10,000 BC, and free from the extreme high tem-peratures that occur there today. In the last Satya Yuga, many river val-leys, such as the Yangtze, Yellow, Ganges, Indus, Tigris/Euphrates, and Nile, would have been regions of natural abundance, with healthful temperatures and long growing seasons. In many ways, even though less land was accessible because of the encroachment of permanent ice, worldwide conditions at the end of the last glacial maximum were more beneficial to man than those we experience today.

In 10,000 BC, mixed forest and grasslands stretched from India to Egypt. Northern Africa was semi-tropical savanna, and received significantly more rainfall than today—desertification and the resulting Sahara desert did not begin until thousands of years later. Much of Northern Mexico, now hot and arid, was cooler and wetter. Central America and the northern regions of South America, today primarily covered by tropical rainforests, were also cooler and con-tained more grasslands.

Food was abundant. Spanning the time from 17,000 to 7000 BC, roughly the time of ascending and descending Satya Yuga combined, archeologists have found evidence that man had plenty of both wild and cultivated foods. Fruits such as figs, dates, grapes, pears, bananas, plantains, and berries were abundant. Evidence of wild grains, nuts, seeds and cereals such as emmer and eikorn wheat, sorghum, spelt, rye, barley, rice, lentils, peas, chickpeas, flax, oats, sunflowers, hazelnuts, almonds, pistachios, and many kinds of millet, as well as of vegetable and root foods such as yams, taro, maize, beans, squash, potatoes and manioc, has been found in settlements around the world dating to this period.

In addition, game was plentiful, although today there is significant debate whether early man was as much a hunter as has been generally assumed. The assumption that early man survived primarily as a hunter arose from the thought that he had little alternative, a conclusion contradicted by increasing evidence of a veritable cornucopia of other foods, and by today's better analysis of fossil remains. It appears now that ancient man leaned more toward a vegetarian diet than a meat-eating one — some archeologists even think ancient man may have been almost exclusively vegetarian.

It is often assumed that ancient man was malnourished. Recent studies comparing the fossil remains of ancient man to the remains of early (circa 5000 BC) farming cultures in Mesopotamia and Egypt show an actual *decline* in nutrition and health once man began wide-scale agriculture.[4] Once animal domestication took place on a wide scale, general health also declined because of the transfer to humans of such animal diseases as beri-beri, rickets, leprosy, and diphtheria.

We can, at the very least, conclude that throughout the last glacial maximum, that is, during much of ascending and descending Satya Yuga, the earth enjoyed ideal conditions for human life. The last glacial maximum was not a story of frigid temperatures and grim survival throughout the world. Quite the contrary. Most of the earth was a natural paradise.

The Superstitious Primitive

Western science is currently wedded to a strictly material approach to the study of any subject, and therefore assumes that all claims to the existence of non-material realities must be considered fundamentally false. Therefore anything, past or present, that involves religion, spiritual belief, or higher states of awareness is explained in one of three ways — as function, delusion, or deception — or as a blend of all three, but is never taken at face value.

The explanation of religion as function is that many spiritual beliefs, though unfounded, nevertheless survive and evolve because they provide a benefit to society. These beneficial functions include keeping people from killing one another, creating a justification for altruism that encourages social cooperation, allowing the peaceful exercise of control over large populations by religious leaders, explaining natural forces, giving leaders an out when things go wrong, etc., etc., etc.

The explanation of religion as delusion is that even though some instances of spiritual experience appear to be genuine, these instances are essentially delusions experienced solely within the mind of the person having the experience, and are caused by drugs, emotional hysteria, or madness. Emerging from the *science* of psychology, such concepts as the collective unconscious are often embraced as the ground from which these experiences spring, and yet still negate any claim to the actual existence of subtle or non-material reality.

Finally, the explanation of religion as deception is that many priests, shamans, and other spiritual leaders are con men knowingly deceiving their gullible followers for their own personal gain. There is no doubt that this does happen, but the explanation is applied across the board to *anyone* who personally claims access to subtle knowledge or divine revelation.

These three explanations for the belief in subtle reality or spiritual experience, when applied to the past by modern archeologists and anthropologists, leave us with the overwhelming impression that early man was superstitious, gullible, and, well, pretty stupid. Theirs is a perfect argument in a circle. Since claims of subtle, non-material reality cannot be true, anyone believing these claims must be gullible, deranged, or stupid, and anyone making these claims must be deluded or deliberately deceptive, and therefore all of them must be ignorant and primitive.

Many of the best-preserved structures, the most sophisticated artifacts and, especially, the most cherished written and oral traditions have religious or spiritual significance. Yet, ironically, these are viewed by modern archeology as *proof* of primitive superstition, and further *confirmation* of early man's ignorance, rather than as indications of the presence of subtle knowledge and enlightenment in the ancient past.

In the introduction to his book *The Lost Civilizations of the Stone Age*, a compendium of information drawn from current archeological and paleontological studies, author Richard Rudgley writes,

> A near-universal theme in the mythologies of the world is that the present state of the world, and more specifically the social world, is in decline—a fall from the Garden of Eden or from a Golden Age. Modern civilisation has turned these traditional mythological assumptions on their head and written a new script, one based on the idea of social progress and evolution. In this new mythology the notion of civilisation (as it is generally understood) replaces Eden and this novel paradise exists not at the beginning of time but, if not right now, then just around the corner. Civilization is, in the plot of this new mythology, envisaged as a great success story—from prehistoric rags to civilised riches—and it is presented as the final flowering of human achievement born out of a long and interminable struggle against the powers of darkness and ignorance that are represented by the Stone Age.[7]

A recent example of how the "new script" is put to use is its application to a find made in 2006, in the Tsodilo Hills of Botswana, Africa, where a cave was excavated containing a very large sculpture of a snake.[6] It is an extraordinary find. The sculpture is well made, and shows an unexpected level of sophistication—and it could be 90,000 years old! But already the usual interpretations are being offered. Pieces of burnt terracotta pottery found near the sculpture, according to the principal archeologist, Dr. Sheila Coulson, indicate ritual offerings were probably made to the snake sculpture as a form of primitive behavior (a.k.a. superstitious nonsense). Further, Dr. Coulson says, the snake probably symbolized a primitive myth that the hills were protected by a Snake God (a.k.a. superstitious belief). Another expert, observing a small, somewhat hidden niche farther back in the cave beyond the sculpture of the snake, suggests the local shaman hid in the niche in order to make noises, or to speak in strange voices, to con the members of his tribe into trembling before the Snake God.

There is nowhere near enough evidence to support the conjecture that the sculpture of the snake was *worshipped*, and no evidence at all of shamans hiding out in the back of the cave and making eerie noises. Nowhere in the officially sanctioned material is the thought expressed that the sculpture could have been carved for purely aesthetic reasons, or as a symbol of a subtle reality. In many Eastern religions, for example, the snake is used to represent the inner energy "coiled" in the spine.

Scientists are encouraged to apply Occam's Razor to their theories: the principle is that the simplest explanations, requiring the least number of assumptions, are usually the true ones. The convoluted arguments used by sociologists, anthropologists, and archeologists to account for spiritual beliefs do not pass the test of Occam's Razor. The simplest explanation for the fact that all cultures, current, past, and anciently past, hold beliefs in subtle realities—is that subtle realities exist.

Paramhansa Yogananda compared spiritual knowledge to mathematical knowledge. He said that if all the textbooks on mathematics were destroyed, all the laws of mathematics would soon be rediscovered. So, too, with spiritual truths. Destroy all the scriptures and writings about religion and spiritual experience, and man will soon rediscover the same truths.

Whereas mathematical truths are derived from *logic*, highly valued in our day, spiritual truths are derived from personal *experience*, highly suspect in our day. Doubly suspect in our day because the historic record of spiritual experience appears to be an impossible confusion of often contradictory claims.

Logic would seem to dictate that if there is genuine spiritual experience then everyone should have the same experience. And in a very real sense everyone *does* have the same experience—a deep experience of upliftment, expansion, peace, and joy. Although these experiences are universally associated with spiritual practices, the reasons given for why these experiences occur, and what people need to do to achieve them, vary enormously. Science has yet to appreciate the simple essence of spiritual truth. Seeing the welter of confusion surrounding religion and spiritual experience, and finding no material proof of any subtle reality, science has chosen to dismiss spiritual reality altogether.

Just as mediaeval science placed the earth at the center of the solar system, our current science places matter at the center of the cosmos. Over time, it became increasingly difficult for astronomers to justify earth's position in the center of the solar system, because doing so required the acceptance of increasingly bizarre, looping epicycles, zig-zag movements, even backward movements of the planets. Once the sun was accepted as the center of the solar system, all the bizarre and improbable motions of the planets resolved themselves into simple circles and graceful ellipses.

In time, science will place spiritual reality at the center of the cosmos and will understand matter in right relationship to the vast and subtle forces that give rise to it—and which originate in Spirit. The seemingly bizarre and "backward" expressions of religion will resolve themselves into simple truths—Spirit reveals itself to man in countless ways and man responds as he is able. Nature worship, paganism, animism, poly-theism, deism, goddess worship, pantheism, monotheism, idol worship, shamanism, spiritualism, divination, yoga, miracles, meditation, and transcendence will all resolve themselves into explicable spiritual beliefs and practices (some more direct and effective than others) for the pursuit of a personal experience of "God the Spirit beyond this physical world."

In the well-researched and highly insightful work *Memories and Visions of Paradise: Exploring the Universal Myth of a Lost Golden Age*, author Richard Heinberg writes:

> As I came to see through the eyes of the primordial myth-makers, my own view of life and human culture was trans-formed. I began regarding modern religions as remnants of a formerly universal spiritual tradition, and the history of civilization as the record of humanity's progressive loss of its original egalitarianism and spontaneity.[7]

The sheer number, variety, careful preservation, and pervasiveness of spiritual traditions throughout the world, from as far back in time as we have knowledge, should earn these traditions at least the benefit of the doubt, rather than the summary dismissal accorded by modern science and archeology. If we view the past with openness to spiri-tual reality, a view that is fundamental to understanding the cycle of the yugas, much of the evidence, currently dismissed by archeology as ignorant superstition, will instead be seen to indicate that man pos-sessed a high degree of spiritual knowledge in Satya Yuga, and that the era was a time of wisdom, harmony, and grace.

~~~~~~~~~~~~~~~~~~~~~~

If we remove these three obscuring misconceptions from the lens with which we view the past—the ignorant cave man, the inhospitable ice age, and the superstitious and gullible primitive—we see the possibility of a very different past than is popularly assumed.

We do not have to assume, for example, that man was less intelligent than he is today. Nor do we need to assume that environmental conditions were so brutal that all of man's focus had to have been on survival alone. And finally we do not have to make the circular argument that because man held various spiritual beliefs in the past—none of which could be true—he was therefore primitive, ignorant, gullible, and superstitious.

We would do well to consider what ancient man said about himself, and not to rely only on what our current worldview insists must be so. The new script written by our modern society—from prehistoric rags to modern riches—is the prevailing interpretation of the past. *But it is important to keep in mind that it is just an interpretation.* Many of the known facts from the past do fit this interpretation, but those same facts fit other interpretations equally well. And, most tellingly, many facts from the past simply do not fit mainstream archeology's new script at all.

Chapter 11

Descending Satya Yuga —
Paradise

Timeline

11,500 BC Beginning of the most recent descending Satya Yuga

11,100 BC End of the 400-year transition period (sandhi) from ascending Satya Yuga

7,100 BC Beginning of 400-year transition period (sandhi) to descending Treta Yuga

6,700 BC End of the most recent descending Satya Yuga

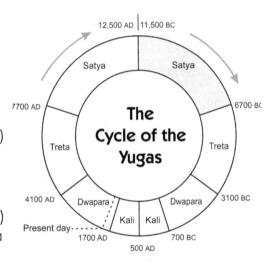

Duration of descending Satya Yuga:
4,800 years

Even a brief study of mainstream texts devoted to the ancient past will reveal that current archeology and paleontology, firmly wedded as they are to the prehistoric rags to modern riches story, give no credibility to almost anything ancient man has to say about his past. *It is assumed from the outset* that all past history and past traditions are murky distortions of what really happened. Ironically, it is because the histories and traditions of ancient cultures include descriptions of higher knowledge and spiritual capabilities that they are considered especially suspect!

We are told that there is no reliable recorded history before Greco-Roman times, and even then, most of the texts that have survived from, say, Plato's time (third century BC) are not considered to be entirely reliable sources of information, especially in describing their own past.

Any records from before the Greco-Roman era, the time of the ancient Egyptians, and the mist-enshrouded dynasties of China and India are considered so suspect and unreliable that scholars have made careers out of *interpreting* what the recorded fragments of these old cultures *might actually mean*. And it should come as no surprise that the interpretations bear little resemblance to the original source material.

What Satya Yuga Man Tells Us About Himself

So, what *did* Satya Yuga man say about himself? First, you might ask, how could Satya Yuga man have told us anything about himself at all? The oldest generally accepted date for writing of any kind dates to about 3500 BC, just before the beginning of descending Dwapara Yuga, and thousands of years after Satya Yuga ended. The Sumerians are generally credited with the first writing, but early pictographic symbols have been found that predate Sumerian. Even before there was evidence of written language, we find several traditions of oral transmission, the most significant of which is the Vedas of India. The four Vedas have been memorized and passed down by recitation, from one generation to the next, for thousands of years. Based on astronomical references made in the Vedas themselves, their origin may go back in time as far as 6000 or even 7000 BC, yet even this early date does not reach back as far as descending Satya Yuga.

Before the Vedas, however, there existed another form of communication passed down from one generation to the next. It is far older, found worldwide, and employs a universally understood vocabulary—a universal language we might say. Though not recognized as a language, as such, the *mythic lore* found in cultures around the world may well be the surviving remnants of the oldest language on earth.

The Language of Satya Yuga

According to Sri Yukteswar, during Treta Yuga and Satya Yuga mankind would have been able to communicate telepathically, and would therefore not have needed to rely on a spoken, let alone a written language. Based on the testimony of people living today, who have demonstrable telepathic abilities, communication mind-to-mind is rarely experienced as words sounding in the mind, but more often by images and symbols that appear in the "mind's eye" and whose meaning is intrinsic to the images and symbols themselves.

Studies indicate that images appear in everyone's minds as a natural accompaniment to the process of thought. Images are part of how we think. It may be that the best way to understand telepathy is to see it as the *sharing* of one's natural thought processes with another person. As we think about a concept, images, stories and personal experiences weave together with the *meaning* of our subject. Images would, therefore, naturally be bound together with the meaning of what we might communicate telepathically to another person.

Most people assume that telepathic communication would, as a result, be vague and fuzzy, unsuitable as a means of conveying the precision of meaning we enjoy in our present mode of communication. This assumption may simply be because we are not familiar with telepathy. Daniel Tammet is a modern day *savant*, and author of *Born on a Blue Day*. Tammet gained recognition because he recited the value of pi to 22,514 decimal places and is unusual among *savants* in that he can describe how he does his amazing feats. Most striking is that he describes *seeing* everything, even numbers, as images in his mind. He has even attempted to draw what *pi* looks like as it appears in his mind. According to Tammet, his extraordinary ability to know pi to 22,514 places arises not from an exceptional *memory*, but from his ability to *visualize* pi, and as he does so, recite it as a string of numbers.

A picture is worth a thousand words because it *concentrates* information. Images can often more effectively convey meaning, simply because the images chosen already contain metaphoric and subtle connotations. Some images take on shared meanings over time; many carry intrinsic meaning as well because drawn from nature and thus draw from shared experience. For example, water can convey subtleties of meaning simply by being pictured in different forms. Flowing rivers, gentle rain, stagnant ponds, restless brooks, crashing waves, powerful waterfalls, and oceanic immensity all provide different metaphors to carry different meanings, while at the same time they all suggest water's potential to flow and change form. Poetry is perhaps as close as we come today to this form of communication.

We can surmise that, as mankind gradually lost telepathic ability, and more and more people needed to communicate verbally, the wisdom and knowledge passed down from Satya and Treta Yuga would have taken the form of *verbal* descriptions of imagery formerly conveyed telepathically. Satya Yuga's wisdom and lore would, therefore, come down to us in stories rich in images—what we know as myth.

The argument for this being the case rests not on the simple fact that myth exists, but primarily on the striking similarity of myths around the world. The number of mythic themes is amazingly small, given that they occur in thousands of forms, among disparate cultures on far-flung continents, in populations that, according to currently accepted archeological theory, *could not possibly have known about one another, let alone communicated with one another, at the time the myths originated.*

Quoting again from *Memories and Visions of Paradise, Exploring the Universal Myth of a Lost Golden Age,* by Richard Heinberg, "we are confronted with what is emerging as the great problem of myth—the worldwide similarity of mythic themes."[1] This similarity is the heart of the anomaly that myth presents to modern archeology. Stories very similar to one another (often using the same images and metaphors) are found not only worldwide, but originated at a time when man was supposed to be isolated, ignorant, and unable to communicate.

The existence of such extraordinarily similar mythic themes strongly suggests that there existed a *shared world culture,* and a *universal language,* which was used to describe and convey the important thoughts and teachings of the age. The divine origin of the universe, the golden age of paradise on earth, and man's inevitable rise to enlightenment, all are told and retold around the world in myths, even though the particular images and stories used have become diffused and distorted over time.

We could say that myths are the *writing* left from a language that is no longer spoken. Like linguists who study Latin or ancient Greek, mythologists are those who take the time to learn and understand the language of myth. Mythology as a discipline is not merely the process of reading and remembering many different stories, but of uncovering the common meanings found within the myriad images that make up the stories. Once mythologists learn the vocabulary of myth, they often speak, and with a certain reverence, of the amazing conformance of higher meaning among the myths of the world, regardless of their cultural or geographic origin.

Joseph Campbell, one of the best known and respected mythologists, known in large part through his six-part PBS television series, *The Power of Myth*, was a pioneer in parsing the seemingly bewildering variety of myths into their essential forms. Finding that the same *meaning* emerged again and again from thousands of seemingly disparate myths, Joseph Campbell said that the myths of the world "resemble each other as dialects of a single language."[2]

If myth is the surviving expression of the telepathic language of Satya Yuga, it is quite possible that it includes *actual* descriptions of life in Satya Yuga. Most of the mainstream's skepticism toward there being any reality to myth comes from a circular argument: mankind wasn't advanced enough in the past for its myths to be literally true. Consequently, the similarities in myth must be attributed to allegory or archetypal subconscious patterns.

But the skeptics have been proven wrong before. Although the city of Troy, the setting of the Greek epic the *Iliad*, was long thought to be a fiction, in 1871 Heinrich Schliemann uncovered the actual ancient city in what is now Turkey. Similarly, the site of *Kurukshetra*, the famous battlefield in India's great epic the *Mahabharata*, has been determined to be an actual location in northern India.

It would be too much to suggest that *all* myths describe actual events. Clearly, myth conveys universal knowledge not tied to a particular time and place. But myth can have layered meanings. As we find in the *Iliad* and the *Mahabharata*, historical events and actual places can provide a *framework* for universal truths of human experience.

It would therefore be equally unwise to maintain, as archeology and paleontology do today, that there could be *no* historical veracity to the ancient myths that predate the Indian and Greek oral traditions of epic poetry. Many myths may contain more factual content than is popularly believed, may tell us about *actual life experience* in Satya Yuga, and should be considered at face value and not only as metaphor.

For example, in our first chapter, we presented numerous myths that described a past Golden Age. The myths came from all corners of the earth, including Greece, Egypt, Norway, India, Persia, Ireland, Australia, Mexico, and North America; they were found in over forty different cultures, with over two hundred variations.

Not only were the Golden Age myths found throughout the world, but they were remarkably similar in structure. The myths had a surprising number of commonalities: all of the myths express the belief that the myth tellers lived in the lowest of the ages they describe; most of the myths describe a sequence of descent from higher ages; and, lastly, all of the myths describe the highest age as a time of spiritual harmony, physical plenty, and heightened spiritual awareness.

The remarkable similarity of the Golden Age myths is perhaps nowhere so striking as between India's myth of the Bull of Dharma, and the Lakota (Sioux) myth of Buffalo Woman and the White Buffalo, which we presented in Chapter 1.

In the myth of the Bull of Dharma, Indian tradition records that in Satya Yuga the Bull of Dharma stood on four legs, while in Treta Yuga, the Bull stood on only three legs, in Dwapara Yuga, two legs, and in Kali Yuga, one leg.

The Native American Lakota (Sioux) have a traditional story of a visit by a celestial "white buffalo woman." She taught that there were four ages, and that in the highest age, the sacred White Buffalo, which figures prominently in Lakota myths, stands on all four legs. During the second age, White Buffalo stands on three legs, and in the third and fourth ages, it stands on two and then one leg.

The degree of similarity, the number of instances of the Golden Age myths, the matter-of-fact way in which they are described, all suggest that the myths of a Golden Age are more than allegorical, that they describe actual events. The same remarkable degree of similarity that we find among the myths of higher ages, also exists among the various descriptions of the Golden Age itself—or as most myths present it—paradise.

The paradise myth most familiar to Westerners is the story of the Garden of Eden, where the first man and woman lived in harmony with nature; they needed no clothes, no shelter, no farms, no protection, and lived in peace and in close harmony with their Creator. There are hundreds of other traditions of earthly paradise. The Sumerians, and later the Babylonians, living in the Tigris and Euphrates River Valleys as early as 4000 BC, have the similar myth of an earthly paradise called Dilmun, where first man and woman dwelt in complete happiness. The Avestan (Old Iranian) myth speaks of Yima's Age, when there was no disease, no old age, no death, where sons and fathers looked equally youthful.

The Egyptian tradition of paradise was called Zep Tepi, the first times, where everyone lived like gods. The Greek tradition of the Golden Age says that men lived without discord and war. The Taoist tradition in China speaks of a time when all mankind lived in a state of happiness. And the Vedic tradition of Satya Yuga, or Krita Yuga, as it is also called, describes a time when all mankind lived in awareness of Spirit.

The Lakota (Sioux), Cheyenne, and Hopi speak of a higher age of surpassing harmony with nature. The native peoples of Central and South America, Asia, Australia, and Africa similarly describe a higher, paradisiacal age. According to Richard Heinberg, *paradise is the single most common mythic theme.*

Although the myths of the Golden Age do not all share all of the same features, they do share a significant number of similarities:

1. People lived like gods, had miraculous powers, and were often considered to be "demi-gods," or the "first gods." They were described as luminous, able to fly and to perform miraculous acts of creation

2. People were not subject to disease and old age, and kept a youthful appearance.

3. People lived in harmony with nature, had an abundance of food (most paradise myths say man did not hunt or eat animals), perfect weather, lived peacefully in close proximity with even fierce beasts, and could communicate with all animals.

4. People could communicate in one language with all other men.

5. People lived in harmony with one another, without wars or discord.

While these descriptions of life in paradise may seem otherworldly, they apply equally well to Sri Yukteswar's description of the world in Satya Yuga. Since these descriptions have come down to us from the distant past, and since most of them have taken their final forms in Kali Yuga, they understandably reflect a limited understanding of man's spiritual potential. If someone today attempted to describe the state of *Self-realization* to tribal people in Amazonia, the tribesmen too would probably think they were hearing of a state so far beyond their daily experience that it must belong to another world.

But while the mythic descriptions of paradise are, indeed, extra-ordinary, we need not conclude that they are extra-human or extra-worldly. There are people living today and in the recent past, who possess the same abilities and level of awareness ascribed by various myths to the people of paradise. Numerous verified accounts describe attainments of men and women of high spiritual attainment:

1.   Levitation, or the ability to fly; a luminous aura, visible to others; the ability to perform miracles

2.   Radiant health well into old age

3.   Profound attunement to nature

4.   The ability to communicate telepathically

5.   The ability to influence those around them with their expanding aura of peace

1. Levitation, auras, and miracles

In the 1600s St. Joseph of Cupertino was seen levitating by hundreds of people and on numerous occasions; he was even given the nickname "The Flying Saint." In moments of great inspiration, Joseph would rise into the air and hover for long periods of time. During an audience with Pope Urban VIII, he soared above the entire papal court and only came down when ordered to by the head of his order.

Accounts of levitation are not limited to Christian saints. Yogis, shamans, and holy men around the world have demonstrated this ability, often before large crowds. Usually dismissed by skeptics as a cheap trick, the phenomenon has been witnessed by too many reputable men and women to be denied.

The depiction in paintings and engravings of Christian saints often includes a golden circle hovering above their heads—the halo. The halo became the stylized way of representing the aura of light around spiritually advanced people. Descriptions of the aura became so numerous that medieval monks broke the descriptions down into types: the Halo; the Nimbus, which surrounds the head; the Aureola, which surrounds the body; and the Glory, which is a combination of all three.

Today many healers and psychics can see the human aura. Healers can often gauge where in the body a person is carrying an illness by seeing darker (therefore less energetic) areas in the aura. Among those who do see auras there is consensus that the aura is much brighter and larger around spiritually advanced people. Even to those who do not ordinarily see auras, spiritually advanced people will often appear to be glowing with a soft luminosity.

Many highly developed souls are reputed to have miraculously manifested healings, medicines, food, even money, for those in need. Because these high souls rarely want attention brought to their feats, lest they attract the wrong kind of attention, we are told about them only second hand. There are exceptions, however. Sathya Sai Baba of India is renowned for both the almost casual and the highly public manner in which he performs miracles.

Sai Baba performs a daily walk (*darshan*) among those who seek his blessings. He will often throw handfuls of paper-wrapped candies into the crowd, place small quantities of "sacred ash," or *vibhuti*, into the hands of his devotees, and will sometimes put messages, written on paper, onto the palms of those who have asked, or prayed, for answers to questions. Yet none of these things—the candy, the *vibhuti*, the messages—come from any pocket or bag. Sai Baba, without any discernible effort, makes a circular motion with his hand and the items appear. Sai Baba's miraculous abilities have confounded many a skeptic. Indeed, after making an attempt to catch him out, many would-be debunkers have instead become admirers.

2. Radiant health and longevity

Health and longevity are also known to accompany those with spiritual advancement. Doctors attribute as much as 80% of all illness to the effect of stress. Freedom from emotional stress alone greatly increases one's health and sense of well-being. Even beyond simple relaxation, spiritual advancement in itself increases the flow of energy through-out the entire body. Paramhansa Yogananda often said that high energy electrocutes disease germs before they have a chance to cause harm.

Advanced yogis have demonstrated amazing control of their life force. Paramhansa Yogananda was able to maintain two *different* pulse rates, as two doctors simultaneously held his arms and felt his pulses. Sri Chinmoy, an Indian teacher who lived in the U.S., reveled in dem-onstrating the unlimited nature of life force. When he was 75, Sri Chinmoy was able to lift a baby elephant weighing over 2,000 pounds. Consciously applying life force to one's health often results in a youth-ful appearance well into old age.

3. Attunement to nature

Harmony with the natural world is a quality attributed to nearly all spiritually advanced people. In his *Canticle of the Creatures*, Saint Francis of Assisi rejoiced in the brotherhood of all beings. Birds were said to fly down from trees to perch on his shoulders and arms, and even wolves would follow him like pets. Paramhansa Yogananda's har-monious influence was so strong that a wild Bengal tiger rolled over like a kitten and let him scratch its belly.

We, the authors of this book, live in a spiritual community that is completely vegetarian. We often smile at visitors' expressions of aston-ishment and delight on seeing deer fearlessly wandering close to peo-ple and public places. Even a few hundred people living harmoniously can create a tranquil environment in which wild animals can feel safe.

Even plants respond to harmony. Many experiments have shown that plants grow more vigorously when they are sent positive thoughts. Perhaps most famous is an experiment in which plants flourished when Mozart was played nearby.

Nature responds to man's state of consciousness. If everyone liv-ing were as harmonious as Saint Francis, one could easily imagine a paradise in which food grew abundantly, the weather was calm and healthful, and the lion lay down with the lamb.

4. One language

We need explore no further how people in paradise might not only share one language but be able to communicate telepathically with anyone. Although we have covered this subject in depth in this and previous chapters, it is worth stating again that there are people alive *today* who have demonstrated, in clinical conditions, such as the CIA experiments, that information can be transmitted from mind to mind.

Science today has no explanation for telepathy, and as a result remains skeptical, and yet the results of the experiments are irrefutable. The Princeton Engineering Anomalies Research (PEAR) program was conducted for nearly thirty years at Princeton University and proved, conclusively, that individuals could not only send and receive information from mind to mind but could affect material objects as well.

Further, PEAR experiments proved that everyone's thoughts, not only those of "advanced" individuals, can affect physical objects. In experimental situations involving random effects and motions, such as water fountains, cascading steel balls, pendulums, and sounds, all test subjects were able, even if only slightly, to change the outcome of the experiment from a truly random distribution, simply by concentrating in a certain way.

One of the first skills many psychics have to learn isn't so much how to tune into other people's thoughts and feelings but how to tune out the cacophony of thoughts and feelings they receive when in a crowd of people. We are all *broadcasting*, but there are only a few who can *receive*.

5. The power of peace

There is a sweet story told of the poet Emerson. One day at a public park, a mother lost sight of her toddler and, in a worried frame of mind, began looking for him. After searching for a few minutes, she found her son fast asleep in Emerson's lap, as Emerson sat cross-legged by the side of a small stream running through the park. Such was the poet's aura of peace that a small child would as trustingly fall asleep with him as with his own parents.

Peace is not the absence of conflict. Peace is a positive power that emanates from such people as Emerson, the Dalai Lama, Mother Teresa, and Gandhi—anyone who consciously attunes himself to peace. Experiments conducted by the Transcendental Meditation organization showed that if a sufficient number of people actively prayed and meditated in a densely populated urban area, the crime rate would actually go down. If the conscious application of peace by a relative handful of people can affect thousands of others, imagine what effect there could be if *everyone* was deeply attuned to peace.

The common understanding of paradise is that the Divine provides the miraculous power, the blessing, that makes paradise, well, paradisiacal, and that without this divine intervention, paradise will quickly vanish. This common understanding implies that paradise is an unnatural condition, and that, if people are left on their own, the world will quickly revert to a state of self-interest and discord.

If, however, we look to the lives of spiritually advanced people living today and recognize the spiritual potential each of us possesses, we can appreciate that if all mankind were living in attunement with Spirit, in an advanced state of *Self-realization*, what we think of as paradise would result naturally. If we could gather together every saint, sage, and shaman ever known—such a gathering might in itself describe Satya Yuga—paradise would form around them regardless of the age. Paradisiacal conditions manifest *inevitably* when the majority of people live in high states of spiritual awareness.

~~~~~~~~~~~

The mythic lore of the world, at the very least, presents a mystery whose solution cannot be found in modern archeology's prehistoric rags to modern riches story. The reason for the amazing conformance of basic mythic themes, and within those themes, the amazing similarity of the way they are told, remains unexplained.

Archeology attempts to explain the worldwide recurrence of the same mythic lore in two ways: either the same myths were transmitted from one culture to another by direct contact some time before recorded history, or myths are archetypal knowledge that arises out of the subconscious mind of all mankind.

Archeologists trying to prove direct contact among ancient cultures have been unable to make a convincing case—based on known physical evidence and the knowledge and capabilities these ancient cultures are assumed to have had. The most difficult evidence to explain is the presence among Australia's Aborigines of myths similar to those of the rest of the world. According to current theory, the Aborigines became isolated from the outside world over 40,000 years ago, when various land bridges disappeared.

Archeologists and mythologists trying to prove shared archetypal knowledge end up having to assume an inner awareness so profound as to border on, or to cross the border into, a spiritual explanation — that all men share a consciousness that connects them in a non-material way.

Neither explanation — ancient contact between people believed to have been isolated, or shared non-material intuitive knowledge, which science believes to be impossible — has completely satisfied most archeologists, and the anomaly of myth remains, for now, on the shelf.

But if we change the story from prehistoric rags to modern riches to *prehistoric enlightenment to modern materialism*, then the universality of mythic lore assumes a simple clarity. Myth may well be the verbalized remnant of spiritual teachings, originally told using telepathic imagery, and including realistic descriptions of life, which have come down from Satya Yuga. Ancient man *has* told us about himself, but current theory simply cannot accept his telling at face value.

One thing we *can* say, myths *do* provide answers to what continue to be mankind's most frequently asked questions: where did we come from, how should we live our lives, and what is our destiny? These questions, and the answers, would naturally be the central concern of an age focused on spiritual truth, and it would be, therefore, quite natural for the main legacy of Satya Yuga to be spiritual knowledge — bequeathed to us in the enduring and universal form of image and story.

Descending Satya Yuga —
Unexplained Anomalies

Timeline

11,500 BC Beginning of the most recent descending Satya Yuga

11,100 BC End of the 400-year transition period (*sandhi*) from ascending Satya Yuga

7,100 BC Beginning of 400-year transition period (*sandhi*) to descending Treta Yuga

6,700 BC End of the most recent descending Satya Yuga

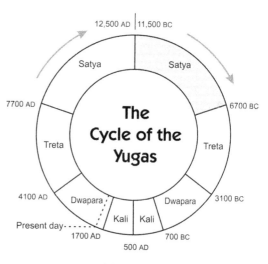

Duration of descending Satya Yuga:
4,800 years

As we have shown in Chapter 10, existing archeological evidence from 11,500 to 6700 BC, the span of descending Satya Yuga, can be used to support two very different views of the past—primitive hunter-gatherers, or enlightened people living lightly on the earth—that is, if all we take into account are the simple artifacts and structures that make up the bulk of the archeological record. However, there exists other *anomalous* physical evidence that simply does not mesh with the concept of the ignorant and primitive hunter-gatherer, but that *does* strongly suggest that a level of spiritual awareness and knowledge existed in the distant past for which current theory has no explanation.

Evidence from this period is scant to begin with, and the anomalous evidence we find is even more scant — but a little anomalous evidence goes a long way. At the close of the nineteenth century, physical scientists were supremely confident that they were combing out the last few tangles in the laws of electromagnetism. Once these last few knots were untangled, it was assumed, the laws of energy and its interaction with matter would be completely understood. There was however, one anomaly — the constancy of the speed of light — that was proving rather difficult to incorporate into their tidy picture of the universe.

Most scientists simply ignored the anomaly of the constancy of the speed of light; they considered it an odd but inconsequential fact, and remained confident that it would eventually be incorporated into existing Newtonian theory. The discovery in 1879 of the constancy of the speed of light lay on the shelf, so to speak, for twenty-six years, until Einstein described the special theory of relativity in 1905. In the end, the implications of the anomalous behavior of light brought about the complete unraveling of the prevailing theory. No longer could matter be seen as an immutable substance interacting with electromagnetic energy; instead the physical sciences had to accept that matter was essentially energy in another form, that matter itself was far less substantial than previously thought. The result was the ushering in a period of profound scientific discovery.

The anomalous facts we know from the ancient past could also one day turn current archeological and paleontological theories upside down. Mainstream archeology currently ignores many ancient anomalies, as physicists did the constancy of the speed of light, with equal confidence that the present-day theory will eventually explain them. But someone, perhaps archeology's Einstein — or some new or existing discovery that becomes impossible to ignore — may well bring about the unraveling of current archeological theory.

In this chapter and upcoming ones we will explore many anomalies. One thing they all have in common — whatever their age — is that they are not easy to explain away. And, if even *one* of these anomalies survives scrutiny, debate, new tests or new discoveries, then logic dictates that current theory must be reassessed.

Gobekli Tepe

The oldest known extensive manmade structure, dating to 9500 BC, is not, as you might expect, a village of simple huts. Rather, *the oldest known extensive structure appears to be a temple complex.* And not a small, crudely built hovel, but a multi-structure, well-crafted, complex construction, one that would have required years to build, and that remained in use for 1500 years!

Gobekli Tepe appears to have been devoted primarily to non-residential purposes. There is very little of the usual evidence of residential use. So far archeologists have not found the hearth fires or refuse middens that usually accompany residential settlements. Even mainstream archeologists conjecture that Gobekli Tepe must have been used for spiritual, healing, ritual, or religious purposes. The existence of a dedicated spiritual center is congruent with our view of Satya Yuga. Yet such a center is certainly anomalous in light of the current theory that during this time period the earth was populated only by small bands of subsistence-level hunter-gatherers.

Gobekli Tepe is located in southeastern Turkey near the Euphrates River. Aerial surveys show the entire complex to cover over 90 acres (36 hectares). Four structures have been thoroughly excavated; but there are indications of at least an additional sixteen structures of similar size and shape yet to be unearthed.

The complex consists of round structures, some as large as thirty meters in diameter, made solidly from stone and graced with *polished* terrazzo floors (see *Figure 9*). Some of the structures have a stone bench running around the inside of their circular wall. All of the structures contain many two-piece simple stone pillars, most along the walls, and some in the center of the room, perhaps serving as an altar or some kind of focal point. There is speculation that the pillars located along the walls served as roof supports, although the structures may also have always been open to the air.

Some of the pillars weigh ten to twenty tons. Many of the pillars have beautiful, one might even say elegantly stylized, depictions of animals in carved relief, such as the fox pictured below (see *Figure 10*). Other pillars have images of snakes, boars, foxes, vultures, spiders, scorpions, a centipede, and a three-dimensional figure that has been interpreted as a lion.

Figure 9 — One of four excavated "temples" at Gobekli Tepe, 9500 BC.
(Courtesy of DAI.)

Figure 10 — Stylized fox on pillar at Gobekli Tepe, 9500 BC.
(Public Domain, Zunkir.)

There are also some images that appear to have been chipped away. We can only speculate as to why. Perhaps the image was being removed so that a new image could be put in its place. Or, as some commentators have speculated, the images may have been removed to safeguard their significance, or to protect people from their power.

Such speculation is fueled by the fact that, after 1500 years of use, the entire Gobekli Tepe complex was *deliberately buried*. One of the twenty temples alone was deliberately buried under 500 cubic meters of soil. Speculation as to why, runs along the same lines. Was this a power center from which people needed to be protected? Was it buried to keep it out of the hands of those who didn't know its purpose? Were its creators concerned that it would be defiled?

Regardless why or how Gobekli Tepe was built, whether by the simple means of dragging stones from the quarry—a process that would have required hundreds of people and many years— or by other means unknown, the organization and effort that went into its construction is significant even by today's standards. The complex was obviously highly important to its builders. The organization required and the duration of focused effort suggest planning, intelligence, and a high degree of sustained commitment to a single purpose. The complex was in use for at least 1500 years. Fifteen hundred years is a very long time. Such longevity again suggests a level of importance to the complex that is not consistent with the notion of hunter-gatherers living on the edge of survival.

That the "altars" at Gobekli Tepe are adorned with animals leads many to immediately think "primitive religion." We need first to remember that what we see today is all that is left after 11,600 years. How the rest of the space may have been decorated—other images or symbols, fabrics and furniture— is lost to us. Second, a symbol drawn from nature does not preclude sophistication of thought.

In India today are temples that contain a *Shiva lingam*, or phallic image. One might assume this to be a primitive fertility symbol, but the *Shiva lingam* is actually an expression of the belief that *Divine creative power* manifested the universe, and is the simple, visible expression of a very sophisticated philosophical understanding of the nature of reality.

If our culture were to end today and a thousand years from now archeologists were to excavate Christian churches, it is difficult to guess what they would make of the altars: an emaciated man, cruelly nailed to a cross. Would they think Christians practiced ritual torture and sacrifice? Without an accompanying understanding of the subtle significance of Christ's sacrifice on the cross it would be nearly impossible to appreciate the symbol of the cross.

A symbol's purpose is to call to mind the meaning behind the symbol. What the figures of Gobekli Tepe called to the minds of those who worshipped or meditated there may never be known, but we can surmise that there may have been some focus on Spirit manifesting as Mother Nature or the Divine Mother.

Unfortunately, ancient spiritual practices involving Mother Nature are almost always considered to be fertility-oriented. In a nutshell, the thought is that the worshipper, or the supplicant, practices some form of ritual, an offering usually, asking Mother Nature, or the Mother Goddess, to grant a good yield to his crops, a child to his wife, a husband for his daughter. While this description may fit some of the practices of Kali Yuga, a closer examination of many currently practiced spiritual approaches to the feminine principle reveal much greater subtlety of thought.

Subtlety of thought, however, is almost never ascribed to the spiritual practices of the ancient past. When looking for authoritative works on ancient spiritual practices, we are once again subjected to the distortions created by the prehistoric rags to modern riches story of modern archeology. For a start, ancient practices are assumed to be rooted in superstition and ignorance, and consequently are simplistically compared to contemporary or recent examples of similar practices.

Furthermore, the assumption is made — given the concept of linear development inherent in the theory of evolution — that, even if fundamentally unfounded, religion nonetheless has gone through a process of evolution. Seen from the perspective of evolution, spiritual practices would have been at their most primitive in the past and became more sophisticated over time. Therefore, current theory holds, if really primitive expressions of religion can be found today, in say, Amazonia, then those of the ancient past *must have been at least as (or perhaps even more) primitive.*

But what if this assumption is not true? What if man's spiritual understanding was at its peak in 11,500 BC, and gradually devolved to what it became in Kali Yuga in 500 AD? What would we expect to find in Satya Yuga?

In Satya Yuga, everyone would have experienced for themselves the presence of Spirit everywhere and in all things. This direct, individual, intuitive perception of Spirit suggests not only that Satya Yuga man would have been aware of God the Spirit beyond material creation, but also that he would have had the awareness that *material creation is itself a manifestation of Spirit.*

In some ways the feminine principle suggests the *totality* of the divine presence more naturally than does the masculine. Steeped as we are in the West in the masculine-principled, monotheistic religions of our time, the feminine-principled view of Spirit seems foreign because it embraces nature as an inextricable part of Spirit, unlike most masculine-principled religions that focus on the presence of Spirit beyond this world.

In India, as well as in other cultures, there is an ancient and subtle tradition of the Divine Mother. Most people have seen the many-armed statues of Lakshmi, Kali, Durga, and other Indian goddesses, but few know that different principles, or aspects, of divine manifestation are represented by each arm, what each arm is holding, the position of the legs, and what each goddess is standing on.

One hand of the goddess bestows liberation, while another offers *maya* or delusion. One hand offers compassion; another destruction. The goddess dances the dance of creation while she receives power from the unmanifest Spirit on which she stands. Each goddess, though different from the others, represents all of creation, the process of creation, and the process of liberation. In the same way, when we look deeply into it, any facet of a gem reveals the whole gem, while the facet itself appears unique.

Although both the masculine and the feminine conceptions of Spirit are true, the emphasis on one principle over another can shape culture. In the West we consider the natural world to be merely a resource, governed by chemical processes, free for the taking; many of our world's problems reflect that thinking. Such thinking is the result not only of the current scientific, atheistic world-view, but also of the masculine-principled religions that dominate the West.

In Satya Yuga, we would expect the masculine and feminine principles to have been in balance. The Divine Mother in her many guises would have been naturally evident to Satya Yuga man's spiritual perception. Nature as Spirit manifested would have naturally awakened his reverence. We would expect, therefore, to find adorning places of worship, such as Gobekli Tepe, symbols drawn from nature and used to recall to mind the universal Mother. But, we would also expect to find, underlying simple images of nature, a high degree of philosophic subtlety rather than the primitiveness ascribed by mainstream archeology.

Gobekli Tepe could have been a place for worship and meditation, for spiritual healing or teaching, or for joyful celebration in song and dance of the presence of Spirit — we can't know for sure how the ancients used the site. But we do know that it was not residential, that it was built with great care and destroyed with great care, and that it was used for 1500 years. None of that fits in with current archeological theory and clearly presents us with an unexplained anomaly.

La Marche Cave

Most people have heard of the prehistoric cave paintings found in the Lascaux caves in France, as well as in a number of other caves in France and Spain. The Lascaux paintings are dated to approximately 14,000 BC, which would have been during the last ascending Satya Yuga; many of the paintings from other caves are dated consistently within the 9600 years of the last ascending and descending Satya Yuga.

The quality and techniques of painting found in Lascaux and in other caves is not seen again until the Middle Ages in Europe. Many of the paintings are polychrome, and, most significantly, employ the technique of perspective in their depiction, a technique that didn't come into known use again *for over 15,000 years*, not until the Italian Renaissance in the fourteenth century AD. The painting below (see *Figure 11*) is typical of many found in Lascaux and other caves from this time period.

The paintings and engravings found in Lascaux are largely of animals; only occasionally are there representations of people. When people are drawn, they are almost always shown as stick figures, apparently hunting. The viewer is left, notwithstanding the high level of artistic sophistication of the rest of the paintings, with a feeling that the cave artists were primitive. But there is another cave, little known to most people and disregarded by archeologists, that contains over 150 images of people, images reliably dated to 13,000 BC! Most amazingly, these images manage to convey a sense of people alive and very human — and a lot like we are today.

Figure 11 — Polychrome horse showing use of perspective 16,000 years ago in the Lascaux Caves in France. (Public Domain, Sevela.)

La Marche cave is located in eastern France; it was discovered and initially studied by Léon Péricard in 1937. So astonishingly modern seeming were the images he found that, when he presented his findings to the French Prehistoric Society in 1938, he was accused of fraud and deceit by his colleagues. This extraordinary evidence of the past, as a result, has been largely forgotten or ignored by archeology. But subsequent studies of the cave, and the images contained therein, were conducted in the 1960s by Léon Pales, and in 2002, by Dr. Michael Rappenglueck of Munich University. Both studies confirmed the dating and the authenticity of Péricard's original findings.

The images of La Marche cave are incised or engraved rather than painted. That most of the images are on free-standing stone slabs has led to conjectures that the engraving could have been done elsewhere and the finished work merely stored in the cave. Perhaps La Marche was the storeroom of a collective of Satya Yuga artists.

At first glance the images are confusing. What one sees is a number of incisions crossing and re-crossing each other; no clear image immediately presents itself. However, after careful study one can see many images emerge from the stone. As you study the examples below, we think you will agree that the images which are highlighted are not imagined, like seeing images in clouds, but that the images are very definitely there. Why the artist seemed to *scribble* on top of the images remains a matter of speculation. Perhaps it was simply easier to use the same stone over and over, or perhaps there is, lost in time, some deeper significance to the technique.

The images below are taken from *Les Gravures de la Marche* by Léon Pales and Marie Tassin de Saint Péreuse. The first two photos below (see *Figure 12*) show Pales' team at work studying the images.

Figure 12—Pales and his team at work on the La Marche Cave stones in the 1960s. (Figures 12–14 from Les Gravures de la Marche by Léon Pales and Marie Tassin de Saint Péreuse, Editions Ophrys; reprinted by permission of the publisher.)

As is evident in the sequence of images below, once the etched lines are highlighted one can see something similar to the drawings in an artist's sketchbook (see *Figure 13*).

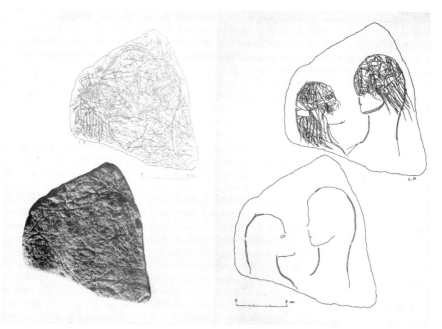

Figure 13—Sequence showing an etched stone, a drawing including all the lines from the stone, two heads emerging as lines are removed, and finally two heads in clear outline.

The following are images that resolve themselves out of the welter of inscribed lines found on scores of stone "tablets" found in the La Marche Cave (see *Figure 14*).

The images certainly do not look like the ragged cave man of current conception. Not only is there a high degree of skill in their execution, these images show people with cut hair, caps on their heads, and with distinct personality, intelligence, and character. Although most of the 155 human images are of heads and faces, there are also many in full torso, distinctly showing clothing, including what appear to be belts and perhaps even shoes.

This more "human" glimpse of Satya Yuga man does not by itself indicate spiritual advancement. But it is certainly easier for us to accept the possibility of *intelligent people* in Satya Yuga when looking at lifelike sketches thoughtfully and skillfully rendered and the images present modern archeology with an anomaly as yet unexplained. Even though the images themselves have been authenticated by two subsequent and thorough studies, the scientific establishment's initial angry rejection of Péricard's findings and of the images themselves as fakes has yet to be replaced with an alternative explanation.

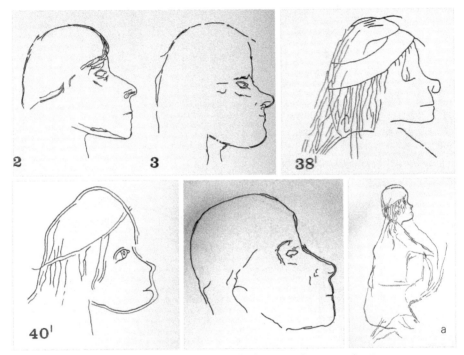

Figure 14 — Faces from the etched stones of La Marche Cave

In this chapter, we have chosen to present anomalous evidence that has long been known, even if not accepted, by mainstream archeology — and that can't easily be explained by the current prehistoric rags to modern riches story. We could have presented further evidence in support of our prehistoric enlightenment to modern materialism story of the cycle of the yugas. This evidence, however, is considered by modern archeology to be far less solid. We chose to omit any shaky evidence because, as we argued at the beginning of the chapter, all it takes is one anomaly—just one—that can survive the onslaught of criticism, doubt, or indifference from the mainstream thinkers of archeology. If even one anomaly survives, then the current prehistoric rags to modern riches story must be revised.

Chapter 13

Descending Treta Yuga —
The Vedas

Timeline

6,700 BC Beginning of the most
recent descending Treta
Yuga

6,400 BC End of the 300-year
transition period (*sandhi*)
from descending Satya
Yuga

3,400 BC Beginning of 300-year
transition period (*sandhi*)
to descending Dwapara
Yuga

3,100 BC End of the most recent
descending Treta Yuga

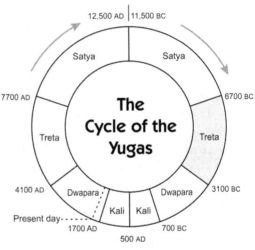

Duration of descending Treta Yuga:
3,600 years

The transition from Satya Yuga to Treta Yuga gives us our first look at the pattern of *devolution* that occurs during the descending arc of the yugas. This transition has characteristics that we will see again when we examine changes from Treta to Dwapara, and from Dwapara to Kali yugas. The *devolution* from Satya Yuga to Treta Yuga is marked by a move from greater to lesser awareness and capability—unlike our recent *evolution* from Kali Yuga to Dwapara Yuga, when we moved from lesser into greater awareness and capability.

In the recent transition from Kali Yuga to Dwapara Yuga we saw a pattern of change characteristic of the *ascending* arc of the yuga cycle. Old ways of doing things were improved to allow the expression of *new* awareness and capability. For example, the first automobiles were actually improved horse-drawn wagons or carriages—with the horse replaced by a motor. Only gradually did the old form of the carriage change to what we now know as the modern automobile. When the technology for television was first developed, it was often used to broadcast stage productions, a form that had been around for centuries. Only gradually did the old form change into the television programs we know today.

The goals of the Kali Yuga way of doing things and the new Dwapara Yuga way of doing things were often the same—the horse-drawn carriage and the automobile both serve the purpose of transportation, the stage play and the television program both serve the purpose of entertainment—but these goals are accomplished in very different ways according to the knowledge and abilities of their respective eras.

In the transition from Satya Yuga to Treta Yuga we see the same dynamic, but with a twist. Goals that were met one way in Satya Yuga were met another way in Treta Yuga—but not by improving on the old way of doing things, as we saw in the recent transition from Kali Yuga to Dwapara, but by trying to *maintain* the old way of doing things while employing the *lessened* capabilities of Treta Yuga. Put yet another way, one can see that in the beginning of descending Treta Yuga the capabilities of Satya Yuga were *approximated*, using the lesser awareness of Treta Yuga.

The paramount difference between Satya Yuga and Treta Yuga is that Satya Yuga mankind as a whole comprehended "all, even God the Spirit beyond this visible world," whereas Treta Yuga man lost this direct comprehension. It was the direct perception of God the Spirit which gave people living in Satya Yuga what we would today consider miraculous powers. People living in Satya Yuga were able to enjoy the fruits of an Eden-like world, or even to live without food altogether, by drawing life force directly from Spirit. Highly advanced souls could create, through the power of visualization and by attunement to Spirit, anything they needed or wanted. The paradise of Satya Yuga allowed people to live as described in the Biblical reference to the lilies of the field, "they toil not, neither do they spin."

When man descended into Treta Yuga, although he still comprehended *divine magnetism* and possessed advanced mental powers, a veil obscured his direct perception of "God the Spirit." The initial Treta Yuga response to this loss of awareness of Spirit and resulting loss of capabilities, was to continue trying to manifest their needs *miraculously* because that was the way in Satya Yuga. Therefore the people of Treta Yuga, at least initially, met their needs by *mimicking* the miraculous powers of Satya Yuga, *approximating* Satya Yuga capabilities as well as their mental powers and comprehension of the *divine magnetism* allowed.

We can see this expressed in one of the most important artifacts from Treta Yuga — the Vedas. Advanced souls, who still possessed the consciousness of Satya Yuga, showed the people of Treta Yuga practical ways to attain those Satya Yuga capabilities still accessible to their lessened awareness — specifically, through the use of the *mantras* of the Vedas. Or, in plain terms, they provided Treta Yuga man ways to *hang on* to the capabilities of Satya Yuga as long as possible.

The Vedas

David Frawley, a leading Western expert in Indic studies, and author of numerous works, including *Gods, Sages and Kings: Vedic Secrets of Ancient Civilization*, refers to the Vedas as India's Pyramids — a towering edifice of thought that defies easy explanation: they captivate everyone who studies them, and remain a glaring anomaly within mainstream archeological and anthropological thought.

The Vedas, a collection of over 10,000 Sanskrit verses, are the oldest known spiritual work in the world — and can be dated to as early as 7300 BC. Unlike the ancient records of China, Mesopotamia, and Egypt, which were destroyed in various deliberate destructions during Kali Yuga, the Vedas, the surviving core of Treta Yuga's spiritual legacy, survived Kali Yuga in India by virtue of an extremely methodical oral transmission from generation to generation of Brahmin priests — and of the deep cultural reverence they have inspired in India.

There were, in all likelihood, similar traditions in China, the Middle East, and indeed the rest of the world. Unfortunately very little direct evidence of these other ancient spiritual traditions has survived. The ancient Chinese concept of the *tao* and the Zoroastrian concept of *asha* are similar to the concept of *dharma* found in India's Vedas. These and other similarities suggest that the knowledge of Satya Yuga may have been the common well from which all of the world's spiritual traditions drew inspiration.

While the evidence of spiritual influence the Vedas may have shared with other cultures is fragmentary, we do know that Sanskrit, the language in which the Vedas were composed, significantly influenced the formation of languages as diverse as English, Germanic, Romance, Slavic, Celtic, Scandinavian, Iranian, Central Asian, and, of course, Indic language groups, forming together what are known as the Indo-European languages. More people today speak variants of Sanskrit than of any other language family.

There is a long-running debate whether Sanskrit is the mother of all these language groups or whether it, too, is a daughter language of a more amorphous *proto-language*, called Proto-Indo-European. The debate hinges on the dating of Sanskrit as a language, which in turn hinges on the dating of the Vedas.

In the last part of the nineteenth century, Max Müller, an extremely influential *Indologist*, proposed the date of 1500 to 1200 BC for the emergence of the Vedas. However, his dating was primarily based on the conviction that the world formed in 4004 BC, according to a chronology of the Christian Bible common in his day. Despite what seems today a significant flaw in Müller's reasoning, his dating of the Vedas to 1500 to 1200 BC persists in many quarters. There is, however, more recent archeological, historical, and archeo-astronomical evidence that argues for a much earlier date for the composition of the Vedas.

Archeological evidence found in Pakistan confirms that there were sophisticated settlements in the Indus River Valley dating back to the seventh millennium BC. In particular, the city of Mehrgarh, in modern day Baluchistan, a province of Pakistan, has been reliably dated to at least 6500 BC. Mehrgarh covers hundreds of acres and may have supported a population of 25,000 people or more.

Mehrgarh shows a surprising degree of sophistication. There is clear evidence of cultivated grains and domesticated animals. The exploration of the ruins of Mehrgarh yielded the first known example of *in vivo* dentistry[1], that is to say, dentistry performed on a living person.

The circular marks left in the teeth indicate that a drill of some kind was used to bore into the teeth.

Historical evidence also corroborates an earlier date for the Vedas as well. Megasthenes, a Greek geographer and traveler of the third century BC, spent considerable time in India and, in a work known as the *Indika*, faithfully recorded what he learned during his travels. Only pieces of the work survive today, but one fragment of great significance lists the royal succession in Vedic India. The list is similar to the dynastic lists found in Egypt and Sumeria, documents that enabled historical dating back to approximately 3200 BC. However, Megasthenes' list of 153 rulers is significantly longer than its Egyptian and Sumerian counterparts. Even a conservative estimate of the length of time each king ruled indicates a history going back to at least 7000 BC.

The Vedas themselves, however, may provide the best evidence for their proper dating. Many archeo-astronomical references are embedded in the Vedas. For example, the Vedas identify twenty-seven *nakshatras*, which, although similar to the twelve signs of the zodiac, are a finer division into twenty-seven sections, one for each day of the lunar cycle. Each *nakshatra* is marked by a constellation or a prominent star, all given names in the Vedas. Like the twelve signs of the zodiac, the *nakshatras* were considered to have esoteric properties, and are frequently referred to in the Vedas.

The stars and constellations that mark the twenty-nine *nakshatras* are still well known in India. Based on descriptions found in the Vedas of particular events—such as lunar or solar eclipses, occurring during solstices or equinoxes and falling "within" certain *nakshatras*—astronomical calculations can be made that give us accurate dating of those events.

Perhaps the most famous of the calculations was brought to prominence by B. G. Tilak, in his booklet, *The Orion: Or, Researches Into the Antiquity of the Vedas*, written in 1893. Tilak is best known as a social reformer and freedom fighter against the British rule of India, but he may also be rightly called the father of archeo-astronomy. Since he published *The Orion*, Tilak's scholarship and understanding of astronomy have frequently been questioned and his assertion that the Vedas date to at least 4000 BC has never been widely accepted. But since his time more systematic and better informed archeo-astronomical studies have been conducted; they have confirmed significantly earlier dates for the Vedas than are commonly accepted.

A recent study was conducted in 2005 by Dr. S. Balakrishna, a scientist whose main work has been wind tunnel experimentation for NASA. Dr. Balakrishna has a PhD in Aeronautics and Controls Engineering; he set out to see if modern computer simulations could provide an accurate date for the total solar eclipse described in detail in the Vedas by Atri, one of the composers of the Vedas. His article "Atri's Solar Eclipse" summarizes an extensive study using modern computer simulations and involving the input of several other astronomers. From his research Dr. Balakrishna concludes that the most likely date for the solar eclipse described in the Vedas by Atri is 4677 BC.[2]

Another configuration, studied carefully by Dr. B. G. Sidharth, an astronomer and director of India's B. M. Birla Science Centre, and described in his book *The Celestial Key to the Vedas*, involved positions of the sun and moon and a fixed point on the ecliptic, all occurring in the lunar *nakshatra* of *Tishya*. Dr. Sidharth calculated the date to be approximately 7300 BC.

There is significant debate whether scientists such as Dr. Balakrishna and Dr. Sidharth can ascertain clear indicators of astronomical configurations amidst the poetic and veiled language of the Vedas. However, more and more astronomical conformances are being discovered in the Vedas that confirm the findings of modern astronomy, and so support the arguments of Dr. Balakrishna and Dr. Sidharth.

The additional support lent by Megastenes' list of 153 Indic kings, and by the recent dating of Indus Valley settlements to the seventh millennium BC, gives us confidence to push the date of the Vedas back considerably earlier in time than mainstream opinion would have it. This earlier dating points to Sanskrit as the likely source of all the Indo-European languages and places the Vedas as the earliest known work of thought.

There is, however, still little acceptance of this much earlier dating for the Vedas, stemming in no small part from the Western bias toward Mesopotamia being the cradle of civilization. At the time that many of the theories of man's cultural development took form, Western thinking was that the races of India and China were *inferior* to those of Europe. The idea that European culture owed its beginnings to an Indian proto-culture was simply not acceptable. We see the same bias in the notion that Europe and Asia exist as separate continents—Europeans weren't willing to accept that they shared even the same land mass with India and China! As Dwapara Yuga unfolds, however, we expect this bias to shift.

Understanding the Vedas

The Vedas contain the names of their composers—the *rishis*. Atri, mentioned above in connection with the description of a solar eclipse, was one of the seven *rishis* or "seven sages" who composed most of the Vedas. There is no direct counterpart to the concept of *rishi* in Western culture. In simple terms, a *rishi* is a sage. But often *rishis* were also kings—or *rajarishis*. In the beginning of Treta Yuga, especially, we might naturally expect the rulers of a highly advanced society to be, themselves, highly advanced. Yet the *rishis* were not kingly in the sense we understand in the West. They didn't live grandly. Quite the opposite. Tradition has it that the *rishis* lived in Eden-like forest hermitages and ruled through wisdom, rather than through temporal power.

There are four Vedas—the Rig, which is the oldest, the Sama, Yajur, and finally the Atharva, which was probably written long after the first three. The Rig, Sama, and Yajur Vedas are very similar and share almost all the same content. However, the Atharva Veda, which may have been composed as many as three thousand years after the Rig Veda, is significantly different both in content and intent.

The Vedas were composed in Sanskrit, and for many thousands of years were memorized and passed on from generation to generation without a written form. The exactitude with which the Vedas were passed down was ensured in part by a long tradition of chanting the same verse in ten different ways—called *pathas*—which acted as an effective system for cross-checking proper pronunciation and word order.

The Rig Veda is comprised of over a thousand mantras. The concept of the Vedic mantra is often expressed in English as "hymn." While the word "hymn" does capture the sacred nature of the content of the Vedas, and does hint at the fact that the verses of the Vedas were often sung or chanted, it misses the essential meaning. The root words of *mantra* are *manas* ("mind") and *tra* ("tool"); therefore, *mantra* literally means "mind tool"—very fitting for Treta Yuga, when mental powers were the norm—and, as we will explain, the key to understanding the purpose and use of the Vedic mantras.

The first three Vedas form the original core of Vedic knowledge. Since their original composition, a large body of complementary scriptures have been composed to comment on and explain the Vedas. The complementary scriptures include three groups: the Brahmanas, which give specific instructions for ritual practices using the Vedas; the Aranyakas, which contain more difficult practices intended for those of advanced development; and the Upanishads, often collectively referred to as Vedanta, or the 'end' of the Vedas, which offer philosophic insight into and esoteric descriptions of the nature of man and Spirit.

To understand the descending arc of the yugas, we need to underscore that the Rig Veda mantras were composed *long before* explanatory works were added to the canon. The Rig, Sama, and Yajur Vedas are all but impenetrable to the contemporary rational mindset. It is the Upanishads, in particular, which provide the keys for us to understand the hidden layers of meaning in the Vedas. Today, without the philosophical insights offered by the Upanishads, we would likely find it very difficult to unlock the spiritual significance of the Vedas. Yet the Upanishads began to be composed hundreds, perhaps even thousands, of years after the Vedas.

Why would these mantras, these mind tools, be given to mankind without any explanation? Simply because, at the beginning of Treta Yuga, mankind didn't require any explanation.

When the Vedas were originally composed, the average person understood the purpose, use of, and the knowledge contained in the Rig Veda mantras because he was already attuned to *divine magnetism* and possessed advanced mental powers. The mantras are precise and specialized tools created for those with the awareness and ability to use them. Only after thousands of years, when the level of mankind's awareness declined, did it become necessary to explain their use and significance.

A prosaic comparison from our time is the phone book. If name after name and number after number from a phone book were recited by someone without any understanding of what a telephone is, the names and numbers would appear incomprehensible and useless. Yet the telephone book is provided to us today without explanation, on the assumption that everyone knows the purpose and use of the telephone. The phone book is a practical tool that meshes with a greater body of assumed knowledge.

In our era of *ascending* development we expect to see a pattern of theory, experimentation, and development, a pattern that leads to a practical application. For example, germ theory came before antibiotics, the practical application of the theory, were developed. E=mc2 came before nuclear power generation, the practical application of the theory, was possible. This is the pattern of the *ascending* arc of the yuga cycle.

The pattern of the *descending* arc of the yugas is just the opposite. The Vedic mantras, the practical application, came before the theory. Or put another way, the theory was already so well understood that no period of development from theory to practical application was required. The higher knowledge possessed by Satya Yuga man and by the enlightened rishis of Treta Yuga allowed them to immediately put forward a practical application—the one thousand mind tools of the Rig Veda—without the need for experimentation, *because they already knew the mind tools would be effective and why they would be effective.*

Also remarkable is that the Rig Veda and all subsequent Vedas and scriptures were composed in Sanskrit. Sanskrit is, even today, considered to be one of the most complete and internally consistent languages on earth. Its grammar, structure, syntax, and approach are so advanced that many linguists find it difficult to believe it could possibly have evolved, as have most other languages known today. Some modern computer programming languages—which require no ambiguity, perfect structure and clarity—were patterned after the Classical Sanskrit of Panini (who wrote its definitive grammar in the fifth century BC) simply because it was so exact and precise.

Additionally, there are no known precursors to Sanskrit. Sanskrit appeared, fully developed, in the Rig Veda. Languages that have evolved, such as modern English, reveal their evolution in their structure, spelling, grammar, and syntax. Sanskrit has very little evolutionary variation from the Rig Veda to the present, a span of perhaps as long as 8500 years. The biggest differences found over the millennia are in the accepted meaning of words, and in Panini's *simplification* of the grammar by eliminating some verb tenses and other syntactical forms. The Sanskrit of the Rig Veda is actually *more complex* than the Sanskrit defined by Panini.

Further, the Sanskrit language excels in the ability to describe subtle states of awareness and delicate shades of metaphysical meaning; it
includes hundreds of nuanced words used to describe Spirit. Sanskrit
appears to have been a language *deliberately created*, in a single, short
period, *for the purpose of expressing spiritual truths with subtlety and clarity.*

Use of the Mantras

It appears that the mantras, the "mind-tools" of the Rig Veda, were
used to enable Treta Yuga man to achieve, temporarily and approximately, the deep states of attunement to Spirit natural to man in Satya
Yuga. The Vedas could be seen as a tool kit for gaining the attunement with Spirit naturally enjoyed by Satya Yuga man, because once
attunement to Spirit was achieved by concentrated mental focus,
then miraculous abilities — the primary way Satya Yuga man met his
needs — followed naturally. The mantras allowed Treta Yuga man to
temporarily *mimic and approximate* the awareness and capabilities of
Satya Yuga man.

In order to appreciate how chanting mantras could bestow miraculous powers and deep attunement to Spirit, we need to remember that
early descending Treta Yuga man, from the perspective of our era, was
very highly advanced. Mental powers that are exhibited by only a few
people today were common at the time.

In order to understand the use of mantras we also need to try to
appreciate the worldview of Treta Yuga man. Satya Yuga man perceived *everything* — including himself — as an expression of Spirit.
Treta Yuga man lost this direct perception of Spirit, but he still saw
everything — including himself — as a manifestation of thought. In our
age, we are taught to see everything — especially ourselves — as separate
from everything else.

From Kali Yuga, modern man inherited many murky and often
superstitious beliefs in the existence of connections between the seen
and the unseen. Beginning in the eighteenth century AD, these were
rooted out and banished by the rigorous application of the scientific
method. Prior to the Scientific Revolution, there were thousands of
contradictory opinions about the physical world and how it functioned.
Aristotle is famous for believing that frogs sprang spontaneously from

mud. In medieval Europe, bathing was considered unhealthy. The world was popularly considered to be flat; what the sun and stars were and how they existed evoked a wide variety of opinions.

The Scientific Revolution insisted on separating opinion from fact—ruling out explanations that could not be empirically verified. The results were, indeed, revolutionary. The technology of today owes much to the rigorous and methodical discipline of science.

One of the effects of the scientific approach, however, is the perception of our world as composed of *disconnected*, discrete physical entities. Matter itself is considered to be composed of discrete disconnected atoms, which are in turn made up of even smaller discrete sub-atomic particles. Science's physical empiricism rules out, at least for now, anything that cannot be measured by physical instruments. Science therefore believes thought to be confined to the brain, and feelings to the body, and, further, that thoughts and feelings are electro-chemical in nature and can form no connection to anything or anyone else.

Steeped as we are in this worldview, we have difficulty imagining the world as inextricably *connected*. Yet such was the worldview of Treta Yuga man. Every thought was perceived as connected to every other thought in an all-pervasive matrix, an interconnected fabric of creation, which gave rise to all energy and matter. Treta Yuga man's own body and thoughts, his sense of self, were perceived as inseparable facets of a pervasive matrix of thoughts—impossible to be considered as separate, discrete realities. Further, Treta Yuga man perceived the pervasive matrix of thought, of which he was a part, to be an ineffable expression of *divine magnetism*.

Perhaps most difficult of all for us to grasp is that Treta Yuga man did not merely believe in but actually *perceived* this interconnectedness. Just as we can be certain that we are hot or cold, hungry or tired, happy or sad, Treta Yuga man *experienced* thought directly and without doubt; this direct experience was fundamental to his ability to use concentrated thought to affect both himself and the world around him. Thus the Vedic mantras, the mind tools, were supremely effective for Treta Yuga man.

Mantras, when chanted by a person of weak and unfocused mind, a person possessing no direct perception of thought, will not bestow anything remotely miraculous on the chanter. Even the finest bow in the hands of an amateur archer would not guarantee even hitting the target, let alone the bull's eye. In the hands of a skillful bowman, however, the finest bow could enable striking the *exact center* of the same target. The Rig Veda mantras are the finest mental tools, effective only in the hands of the finest mentalists.

If Treta Yuga man possessed such advanced awareness, why then were the mantras of the Vedas even necessary? Because mental powers are neutral. They are not inherently spiritual. Great mental concentration and attunement can be applied to anything, including actions that are harmful. People with great mental abilities are not necessarily wise. They can use their abilities to their own or other's detriment. The mantras of the Rig Veda were given to Treta Yuga man by enlightened sages to focus their minds positively and effectively — the mantras combined the higher wisdom of Satya Yuga with the powers of Treta Yuga.

Modern translations of the Rig Veda into English yield what appear to be descriptions of invocations and supplications to various gods, including Agni, Indra, Varuna, and Mitra. Western scholars, anthropologists, and mythologists often assume the Rig Veda is the expression of primitive animistic beliefs. Because the gods of the Rig Veda can be associated with fire, earth, water, air, the sun, the moon, and other elemental and astronomical phenomena, the Rig Veda itself is often seen as a collection of primitive invocations for rain, good crops, fertility, and wealth from the god of rain, the god of growing things, the god of fertility, the god of wealth.

Modern translations, however, are as many as nine thousand years — and several diminished levels of understanding — removed from the original intent of the Vedas. Western scholars often assume that the Upanishads express a positive, forward evolution of thought from the more primitive Vedas, while ignoring the frequent and clear statements in the Upanishads that they are only explaining and elucidating the subtle thought of the Vedas themselves — and that the Vedas are multi-layered and deeply symbolic. In the same way that the imagery of myth contains a rich matrix of meaning, more information than simple words can convey, so too the verses of the Vedas contain much more than a literal translation can convey.

Sri Aurobindo, a saintly and well-respected authority on Indian thought, authored numerous books and articles on the Vedas and other great Indian scriptures. A man of eloquence and spiritual insight, he described, in a 1920 article entitled "An Essay on the Vedas," the rishis' purpose in composing the Vedas:

> The poet [rishi] has to express a spiritual and psychical knowledge and experience, and he cannot do it altogether, or mainly, in the more abstract language of the philosophical thinker, for he has to bring out, not the naked idea of it, but as vividly as possible, its very life and most intimate touches. He has to reveal in one way or another, a whole world within him, and the quite inner and spiritual significances of the world around him, and also, it may well be, godheads, powers, visions and experiences of planes of consciousness other than the one with which our normal minds are familiar.
>
> The physical and the psychical worlds were to their eyes a manifestation, twofold and diverse, and yet connected and similar ... the inner and outer life of man, a divine commerce with the gods, and behind was the one spirit or being of which the gods were names and personalities and powers. These godheads were at once masters of physical Nature and its principles and forms, their godheads and their bodies, and inward divine powers with their corresponding states and energies born in our psychic being because they are the soul powers of the cosmos, the guardians of truth and immortality, the children of the Infinite, and each of them, too, is in his origin and his last reality, the supreme Spirit putting in front one of his aspects.[3]

Thus, when Treta Yuga man chanted or mentally focused on a mantra with the *intuitive attunement* natural to him, the mantra would have bestowed on him the inner awareness particular to that mantra.

The mantras of the Rig Veda were not, therefore, ritualistic or magic formulae intended, superstitiously, to manipulate the *outer* world, but instead provided a means for Treta Yuga man to manipulate his *inner* world. Through the mantras he achieved exalted states of awareness—he came as close to, he *approximated*, the direct perception of God the Spirit naturally enjoyed in Satya Yuga.

Once the adept practitioners of the mantras achieved an exalted state of awareness, they could in turn, if such was their intent, use the miraculous powers that attended their expanded awareness to accomplish whatever they needed or desired outwardly. Thus, a particular mantra was chosen to achieve a particular aim. The aim itself could have been, for example, simply achieving the exalted state itself, gaining deeper knowledge, increasing energy and power, or miraculously manifesting physical results.

The Vedic mantras were pragmatic tools used to achieve a more direct experience of Spirit. However, the experience was *temporary*. In time the practitioner would fall from his exalted state of consciousness and would therefore also lose any powers that attended his use of a particular mantra. The practitioner needed to employ a specific mantra to meet each specific need as it arose.

The Use of the Vedas Devolved

We can see the pattern of devolution typical of the descending arc of the yugas in the changing use of the Vedas through time. We can surmise that as Treta Yuga man's mental powers began to wane, so would the effectiveness of the mantras. We can clearly see this pattern in the composition of the three Vedas that followed the Rig Veda in time: the Sama, Yajur, and Atharva.

While there is no debate that the Sama Veda was composed after the Rig Veda, there is no reliable means of dating the Sama Veda relative to the Rig Veda. The Sama Veda contains almost exactly the same content. In fact the Sama Veda contains only seventy-eight unique mantras beyond the approximately one thousand mantras they share.

The *difference* between the two Vedas is that the verses of the Sama Veda have been slightly altered to make them easier to chant. It is possible that the initial use of the Rig Veda mantras was entirely mental, to be visualized rather than spoken. Perhaps, as the descending arc of the yugas made a purely mental use of the Rig Veda mantras less effective, the remaining enlightened *rishis*, to compensate, added sound vibration.

By tradition, Sanskrit is said to be based on *nama-rupa*, or name-form. The concept arises from the belief that all creation is vibrating at subtly different frequencies, the consequence of having sprung from the primordial sound, *AUM*, *pranava*, or the Word, as it is expressed in the Christian Bible. ("In the beginning was the Word, and the Word was with God, and the Word was God.")

The ancient *rishis* are believed to have *heard* the vocabulary of Sanskrit, each word corresponding to the way an object or concept actually "sounds" as it vibrates in the ether. Thus arose the concomitant belief that chanting the words of the mantras would energize them, making them more potent and effective.

The Yajur Veda, which was composed after the Sama Veda, also contains mostly Rig Veda mantras, but has a greater number of unique mantras than the Sama Veda. However, what primarily sets the Yajur Veda apart from the Rig and Sama Veda is that the order and presentation of the mantras has been reorganized as a guide for ritual. Yajur Veda groups the mantras according to the specific deities addressed — one group focused on Indra, another on Agni, and so on.

The Yajur Veda appears to represent a change in emphasis from the *personal* use of mantra for intuitive attunement to *priestly* use on the behalf of others. The words of the mantras also appear to be treated more literally. The word *yajna*, for example, is translatable as *sacrifice* and appears throughout the Rig Veda. In the opening centuries of Treta Yuga a sacrifice to Agni — now understood to be the god of fire — may have been understood as a way to personally *attune* oneself to Spirit by accessing the "fire" of one's own energy. However, by the time of the Yajur Veda, *yajna* was practiced as a physical sacrifice also, by offering symbolic objects into an actual fire.

By the time of the composition of the Yajur Veda, many of the Brahmanas and Aranyakas, detailed descriptions of how to conduct Vedic rituals, had also been composed, and a priestly class had come into being in order to perform the elaborate, often days-long rituals. The coming of ritual and a priestly class does not necessarily mean that the Vedic mantras were no longer effective. Even in the waning years of Treta Yuga mankind still possessed significant mental power and, relative to the consciousness of our time, heightened awareness. But the lessened mental power of later Treta Yuga man could have required more ceremony, more methodical and deliberate focus for him to use the mantras effectively.

The Atharva Veda may well have been composed in Dwapara Yuga. It has a distinctly different feel from the first three Vedas; there have long been differing opinions in India whether it should even be considered one of the Vedas. The verses and mantras of the Atharva Veda have a more obvious intent to manifest outward and *self-interested* results—from growing hair, to getting pregnant, to remaining sexually potent, to destroying a rival. The Atharva Veda is often thought to be a book of magic spells and incantations rather than a high-minded scripture, although much of the content is clearly spiritual in intent.

As you can see, even within the Vedas themselves the descending arc pattern of devolution is clearly evident. The Rig Veda, even today, is considered to express the highest consciousness of all the Vedas—while the Atharva Veda is often not considered to be in the same league, so to speak, as the other Vedas. We see an increasingly literal approach, from the symbolic and impersonal presented by the Rig Veda to the physical and ceremonial presented by the Yajur Veda. And finally we see the impersonal sublimity of the Rig Veda decline to a more personal and self-interested approach in the Atharva Veda.

Hidden Scientific Knowledge in the Vedas

Although our arguments for the great age, exalted purpose, and esoteric use of the Vedas may seem self-referential, and although hard facts may seem to support only a primitive animistic origin for the Vedas, we should also take into account the large body of astronomical, mathematical, and physical knowledge embedded in the Vedas, Brahmanas, Aranyakas, and Upanishads, knowledge popularly believed not to have been discovered in Europe until the Renaissance or later.

In her meticulously researched book, *Ancient Indian Insights and Modern Science*, physicist Dr. Kalpana M. Paranjape presents compelling arguments that the following scientific knowledge is found in the Vedas and attendant scriptures:

Physics and Astronomy

- The sun and planets are spherical.

- Each of the seven colors of the rainbow carries a different amount of energy.

- The sun is the source of all energy for life on earth.

- The earth rotates around the sun.

- The sun, earth, and other planets rotate on their own axes.

- The earth's rotation creates night and day.

- The earth's orbital path and axial tilt result in the seasons.

- The poles have six-month-long nights and days.

- The two tropics and the equator are separated by twenty-four degrees.

- The earth has a slightly elliptical orbit.

- The cause and timing of solar and lunar eclipses.

- Because of its orbit around the sun, the planet Venus is both the evening star and the morning star.

- The apparent movement of sunspots is due to the rotation of the sun.

- As seen from the earth, the full rotation of the sun takes twenty-seven days.

- The earth's orbit around the sun creates a plane, and on that plane are the twelve divisions of the zodiac.

- The precession of the equinoxes.

- The length of a solar year is 365.244 days.

- The moon's light is reflected from the sun.

- The sun's energy is generated by a continuous process at its core.

- The sun is gaseous.

- The earth's surface is 70% covered by water.

- The clouds consist of heat-produced water vapor, which in turn gives rise to rain.

- The stars are "innumerable."

- The stars exist in collections (*niharikas*), or galaxies, which rotate around their own center points.

- The earth and sun are part of a galaxy that rotates around a center point.

- The physical world is made up of atoms.

- The atoms have an internal structure resembling the solar system.

Mathematics

- The symbol and concept for zero

- The decimal system of notation

- The concept of infinity

- The concept of arithmetic progression

- The concept and value of pi

- The formula for calculating the area of a circle

- The concept of a number up to 10^{18}

- The theorem of diagonals (the Pythagorean Theorem)

- The means to determine square roots and cube roots

- The concept of negative numbers

- The concept of algebraic equations using letter symbols for unknown quantities

- The conception and expression of quadratic and indeterminate equations

- The geometry of the triangle, parallelogram, rectangle, and circle

- The geometry of the sphere, cone, and pyramid

Much of this knowledge — especially the astronomical — is derived from the Rig Veda; other concepts appear in the later Atharva Veda and Brahmanas. Even so, *none* of this knowledge is supposed to have been discovered until several thousand years later in Europe and the Middle East, beginning roughly with the Renaissance in the latter part of ascending Kali Yuga.

The scientific knowledge embedded in the Vedas is not expressed in the scientific terms we are familiar with today. For example, we know that the Vedas contained knowledge of the spherical shape of the sun because Mercury's journey around the sun is presented as a story of the interactions of sun and Mercury in personified forms.

Such descriptions are often dismissed as merely poetic, with the implication that the composer just *got lucky* when he expressed something in a way that could be interpreted as consonant with our modern knowledge. If so, the Vedic composers *got lucky* a lot!

It is true that our current rationalistic and empirical approach to gaining knowledge — theory, experimentation, and measurable, quantifiable results — is nowhere apparent in the Vedas. The Vedas are intuitively revealed experiences of reality — not the formalized, law-like abstractions from reality that make up the body of modern science — and consequently are considered a highly suspect source of facts by Western scientists.

Scientists, however, and indeed most of us, cannot perceive subtle layers of reality. Even those open to the possibility often share the general opinion that subtle layers of knowledge are revealed only dreamily, fleetingly, vaguely, fuzzily, or even symbolically — but definitely not literally or exactly.

This may not be the case, however.

Annie Besant and C. W. Leadbeater, prominent members of the Theosophical Society, from 1895 to 1933 conducted intuitive *investigations* into the nature of atoms. They compiled a large number of descriptions and drawings of what they observed in deep trances. Their descriptions were quite detailed and complex — in fact more complex than the known facts of the day.

Many years after the passing of Besant and Leadbeater, physicist Dr. Steven M. Phillips began to study their journals. He published his findings in 1980 in *Extra-Sensory Perception of Quarks*. A thorough examination of their psychic investigations led Phillips to conclude that Besant and Leadbeater had accurately described the number and nature of quarks—sub-atomic particles that make up the larger structures of the nucleus of the atom, such as protons and neutrons—*years ahead* of their discovery by modern physics.

The *rishis*, the composers of the Vedas, may not have set out to embed scientific knowledge in the mantras, but because they describe their direct and actual experience of our multi-layered reality—Spirit, thought, energy, and the physical world—their perceptions included such knowledge anyway.

We believe the Vedas reveal two significant characteristics of descending Treta Yuga. One, Treta Yuga man possessed an exalted and subtle understanding, far beyond our own. The Vedas reveal multi-layered, highly-nuanced and sophisticated shades of meaning, including detailed knowledge of the physical world, knowledge popularly believed to have only recently been discovered. The Vedas express knowledge and sophistication far beyond the merely primitive animism mainstream archeology and anthropology ascribe to them.

Two, the Vedas clearly reveal the pattern of *devolution* characteristic of the descending arc of the yuga cycle. The Rig Veda, composed at least as early as 7300 BC, is the oldest Veda and yet it is the acknowledged pinnacle. The other Vedas, and the complementary scriptures that came after it, though in our terms still highly advanced, nonetheless show, through the course of Treta Yuga, a steady drift toward more outward, ritualistic practice and self-interested use.

Chapter 14

Descending Treta Yuga—
The Conscious Matrix

Timeline

6,700 BC Beginning of the most recent descending Treta Yuga

6,400 BC End of the 300-year transition period (*sandhi*) from descending Satya Yuga

3,400 BC Beginning of 300-year transition period (*sandhi*) to descending Dwapara Yuga

3,100 BC End of the most recent descending Treta Yuga

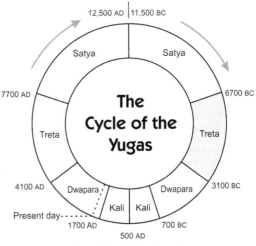

Duration of descending Treta Yuga:
3,600 years

In Sri Yukteswar's explanation of the yugas, descending Treta Yuga man saw himself existing within an interconnected matrix of thought. Many people, perhaps most people alive during that era, were able to directly perceive the interwoven thoughts and energies that made up the matrix. They saw that the matrix of thought guided the formation of everything else—thought became energy, and energy became matter.

They also perceived, according to Sri Yukteswar, that underlying the matrix of thought was *divine magnetism*. Paramhansa Yogananda referred to divine magnetism as the "power of all powers." The power of *divine magnetism* isn't, however, as we explored in Chapter 9, a blind force, as natural powers tend to be thought of today. Divine magnetism is itself *conscious* and *intelligent*.

Imagine yourself surrounded by and part of a conscious matrix of thought in which you can directly perceive the forming and unforming of the reality around you. Not only that, but imagine that by interacting with the different conscious aspects of the matrix, you can *personally* influence the forming and unforming of the reality around you. How then, would you describe your view of the world to another person?

It has often been said that the Eskimos, who live their lives north of the Arctic Circle and thus are constantly in the cold, have over twenty words to describe what most of us simply call "snow." The Eskimos, living surrounded by snow, find it necessary to communicate to one another small differences in types of snow conditions.

Treta Yuga man perceived himself to be surrounded by a conscious matrix of thoughts and energies, and thus found it necessary to communicate to one another subtle differences in what today most of us think of as simply God or Spirit. Just as the Eskimo has different names for snow, so Treta Yuga man naturally had different names and definitions for distinct aspects of the all encompassing conscious matrix, each with attendant powers and qualities.

The Eskimo has simply named types of snow, while Treta Yuga man was able also to communicate and interact *with* these different aspects of divine manifestation—and they with *him*. The many aspects of the conscious matrix with which Treta Yuga man could interact were each distinct, each intelligently conscious, each unborn yet undying, each powerful and self-aware—each, in the term we understand today, a god.

As quoted in the previous chapter, Sri Aurobindo described the different aspects of the conscious matrix as godheads:

> These godheads were at once masters of physical Nature ...
> the soul powers of the cosmos ... the children of the Infinite,
> and each of them, too, is in his origin and his last reality, the
> supreme Spirit putting in front one of his aspects.[1]

Divine Pantheons

Since the majority of people in descending Treta Yuga, according to the yuga tradition, shared an awareness of the conscious matrix, we would expect some evidence of this worldview to have survived. Evidence of this worldview has not only survived; it may be the single most common attribute of all ancient cultures — interconnected families of gods — known as pantheons.

Every major culture throughout the ancient world had a well-established pantheon of gods. The pantheon best known in the West is found in Greece: Zeus, Hera, Apollo, Athena, and many other gods dwelled on Mount Olympus and influenced the affairs of mortal men.

In Africa there are at least ten pantheons that appear to be related to one original pantheon. As different languages developed in Africa, the names and qualities ascribed to the various gods in their pantheons began to drift apart, but strong similarities continue to exist between them. In North America, we see a similar pattern among the numerous pantheons of the Native Americans. The more than three hundred tribes of North America all share a tradition of transcendent gods interwoven into their daily lives.

The Olmec of Mesoamerica had a pantheon that evolved into the Mayan and Aztec pantheons. The oldest (3000 BC) and least known culture in South America, the Norte Chico civilization, shows evidence of a pantheon of gods, including the striking figure of what has come to be called the Staff God, which appears on many of its ancient stone monuments. The indigenous people of Australia shared a pantheon of gods, as do the cultures of Polynesia and Micronesia.

The Chinese have an extensive and quite sophisticated pantheon of gods, ruled over by the Jade Emperor. The ancient Egyptians have perhaps the most elaborate pantheon, depicted in the numerous temples, thousands of sculptures, and extensive hieroglyphics they left behind.

As we explored in the last chapter, the Vedas describe a pantheon of gods that remains, even today, a significant part of worship and religious practice in India. Linguistic studies have revealed that Greek, Sumerian, Roman, Germanic, Norse, Celtic, and Slavic pantheons are all related to the Indian pantheon. They share many of the same gods, although the names for them have drifted linguistically since their shared beginning.

There are no ancient cultures that do not have a pantheon of gods. Moreover, there are distinct similarities amongst all the pantheons. Although the names, qualities, and powers differ, there are several core commonalities:

- The gods are immortal and transcendent.

- The gods differ among themselves, each having unique powers and knowledge that can be used to affect the physical world and the lives of men.

- The gods are consciously aware of the lives and thoughts of men.

- The gods can be communicated with by men.

Modern science's current materialistic bias prevents any interpretation of the gods that lends them any credibility or any actual reality. The prevailing interpretation is that such beliefs are the superstitious, but unfounded attempts of ignorant people to make sense of their world—to explain natural phenomena as the result of the capricious powers of unseen beings. If the pantheons of gods are the product of superstition, why would every culture in the world, independently, evolve the same kind of superstition? If there is absolutely no basis for such belief, why did it arise everywhere? And why so similarly? Why not one single god being responsible for everything? Why not some impersonal force? Why anything at all, if it is just made up?

The Western mind has been conditioned to believe that the gods of the ancient pantheons are either completely untrue (the scientific outlook), or false and idolatrous (the monotheistic outlook), but in the Eastern mind there is more room for appreciating that God the Spirit could manifest to man in more than one form. Most Eastern religious beliefs, whose origins are far older than those of Western monotheistic religions, include the core concept of an omnipresent divinity that is warp and weft of the fabric of creation and that *manifests* in distinct and visible forms. Western belief systems, on the other hand, relegate any divine presence to a distant realm beyond the gross physical world, where it can only be experienced after death.

The cycle of yugas suggests that the pantheons of gods found in cultures around the world may not be, as prevailing theory has it, the result of primitive ignorance, but the remnants of higher awareness—remnants from an age when man's life experience was inseparable from his awareness of the gods, with whom he could and did interact. One thing we do know: The pantheons of gods were the most common spiritual concept found in all ancient cultures.

Overcoming the Limitations of Time

One of the hallmarks of Treta Yuga man, according to Sri Yukteswar, is his ability to overcome the limitations of time. Evidence exists that, during descending Treta Yuga, man may have known ways to predict the future with great accuracy.

In India today there is an ancient tradition based on the *Bhrigu Samhita* or *Book of Bhrigu*. The *Book of Bhrigu* consists of hundreds of thousands, perhaps millions, of astrological *readings*. No one knows how many readings can be found in the *Book of Bhrigu* because the pages of the book don't exist in any one place. They are scattered all over India, in collections of loose pages, bound into bundles, which have been copied over and over and handed down from generation to generation in the ancient tradition of the *Bhrigu pundits*.

Tradition has it that the original Bhrigu readings were created in Treta Yuga, and that the Bhrigu who started the tradition was *rishi* Brighu, one of the composers of the Vedas. The existence of the tradition does not in itself prove that the *Book of Bhrigu* began so many millennia before—except for one astonishing fact—many Bhrigu readings accurately describe the lives of people living today, even though we know they were written down hundreds, or more likely thousands of years ago. Even more tellingly, the living Bhrigu pundits, who serve as custodians of the vast numbers of Bhrigu readings, have no idea how the readings were created. They merely read from them, copy them faithfully, and hand them down from one pundit to the next. No one living today knows how these readings were created.

In his book, *India's Ancient Book of Prophecy*, Swami Kriyananda, a leading American disciple of Paramhansa Yogananda, describes his experience of receiving a Bhrigu reading. In 1959, after many hours of slow going, Kriyananda arrived at a small village many miles from Patiala, India. The pundit did not know Kriyananda, and could not have known he was coming.

After ascertaining Kriyananda's time and place of birth, the Bhrigu pundit cast his horoscope. He then searched through many bundles, containing thousands of loose pages, until he located Kriyananda's page. He had cautioned Kriyananda that not everyone who came to him had a page to be found. However, he finally determined that he had found a page for Kriyananda by matching the horoscope found on the page to the horoscope he had just done for him. From the reading given him by the pundit, Kriyananda shares the following:

> My place of birth in this life was correctly given, though misspelled: Rumania was written, "Rumanake." The reading stated that my father named me "James" — my actual first name at baptism. The reading said that I have lived in America. It gave my monastic name, Kriyananda. A fact was brought out about my family that I myself did not know, but that I was able to verify some months later after my return to America. [That his mother had had a miscarriage.] This reading made a number of unexpected predictions, several of which have already since come true.[2]

Kriyananda went on to get a second reading from another Bhrigu pundit in another city. This reading began by saying that Kriyananda had already received another Bhrigu reading, "from me," and went on to provide additional accurate information. From this pundit, Kriyananda was able to borrow the actual page from which the pundit gave his reading. He took the page to the Archeological Department of India and spoke with the Director, Dr. A. Ghosh, who, after examining the document, told him that the paper and ink were at least 150 years old.

We find nothing in the newspaper's daily horoscope that gives any inkling that this kind of accurate foretelling is even remotely possible. Indeed, astrology in general is held in little regard in the West. It is more likely to be the punch line of a joke than to be taken seriously. Yet *The Book of Bhrigu* should give us pause.

In Yogananda's *Autobiography of a Yogi*, Sri Yukteswar is quoted as saying:

> Charlatans have brought the stellar science to its present state of disrepute. Astrology is too vast, both mathematically

and philosophically, to be rightly grasped except by men of profound understanding. If ignoramuses misread the heavens, and see there a scrawl instead of a script, that is to be expected in this imperfect world. One should not dismiss the wisdom with the 'wise.'[3]

We are conditioned to think of all things as being separate, material, and decidedly non-conscious. Treta Yuga man, on the other hand, knew himself to be an inextricable part of a decidedly conscious and fundamentally interconnected and non-material reality. In the same way that we are aware of the physical weather, Treta Yuga man was aware of the subtle weather of conscious forces flowing within and around him — whether these were the thoughts and energies of a nearby person, or the unique, magnetic influence of a distant planet or field of stars.

Today meteorologists apply scientific method to predicting the weather — from local conditions for the next day, to worldwide conditions for the next year. The natural forces that govern the weather behave in lawful and therefore predictable ways. However, there are so many variables that the science of predicting the weather requires complex models running on the most powerful computers. As the models are refined, the data measured becomes more complete, the measurements become more precise, and weather predictions are steadily improving. In time, we may be able to predict the weather far into the future, to determine the kind of growing season we can expect next year, or, perhaps, the best weekend for a picnic.

Astrology, similarly, is a predictive science based on the lawful, but to us hidden forces that make up the conscious matrix. Astrology has many predictive models, including the horoscope, which, in knowledgeable hands, can accurately predict future events in a person's life. Other models, apparently lost to us, such as those that enabled the creation of *The Book of Bhrigu*, allowed Treta Yuga man to accurately describe the lives of people who would be born thousands of years in the future.

As descending Treta Yuga came to a close, most people lost their direct and innate awareness of the subtle forces of the conscious matrix. They could no longer directly perceive the myriad astrological influences. They still understood, however, the importance of tracking these influences and predicting their effects on the lives of individuals and on the world.

It is not surprising then that, toward the end of Treta Yuga when man's innate perception of subtle forces was on the wane, we find many *physical* observatories for tracking the paths of the sun, moon, stars, and planets were created all over the world. Some of the earliest known observatories, such as the Goseck Circle in Germany, Nabta Playa in Egypt and Mnajdra in Malta were begun as early as 4500 BC. Between approximately 3400 BC and 2900 BC, the *sandhi* transition period from Treta Yuga to Dwapara Yuga, we find scores more observatories were built, including New Grange in Ireland, Stonehenge and Avebury in England, Carnac in France, Almendres Cromlech in Portugal, Kokino in Macedonia, Gilgal Refa'im in Syria, and early stages of the Great Pyramid in Egypt. There are many more we are not mentioning and that are often collectively referred to as the megalithic observatories since many of them were made with very large stones.

Modern archeology would have us believe that the rapid spread of observatories during this time period occurred because with the rise of agriculture farmers needed to know when to plant crops. But this simple agrarian reason does not explain the diversity and complexity of observations made possible by the megalithic observatories.

Built into the large man-made mound of New Grange observatory is a passage or tunnel that allows an observer to see Venus once every eight years, on the winter solstice, just before dawn, enabling observers to track the planet's forty-year cycle. Why track the forty-year cycle of Venus (five phases of eight years each) if all they needed to know was when to plant their crops?

Other megalithic observatories allowed people to calculate and therefore predict lunar and solar eclipses, to track the precession of the equinoxes, to mark the phases of Venus, to observe the orbits of Mercury, Venus, Jupiter, and Saturn, and to accurately determine the summer and winter solstices as well as the spring and fall equinoxes. Some of this information would have been useful to farmers; but the more complex calculations these observatories made possible are central to astrological rather than agricultural prediction.

The transition from Treta to Dwapara Yuga, when megalithic observatories were built, is also likely to have been the time when astrology became defined and its formulae articulated. As the direct perception of subtle conscious forces faded, other means to gauge subtle influences — such as the horoscope, a complex geometric and mathematical model incorporating planetary and stellar motions — would have begun to augment and eventually replace the innate awareness of Treta Yuga man.

The oldest surviving horoscope, dating to 410 BC, was found in Babylon. Additionally, there are Babylonian records indicating that astrology was practiced as far back as 1500 BC. However, references to the *nakshatras* in the Vedas, the lunar "houses" of the zodiac, lead many to conclude that the methods of astrology have their origin concurrently with the much older Vedas.

The current Eastern approach to astrology, often called Vedic astrology, is significantly more complex than Western astrology and has many formulae that no one today can explain — a phenomenon especially interesting in light of the cycle of the yugas. For example, a central predictive tool of Vedic astrology is the system of the *dashas*, periods of time that together add up to 120 years. No one today knows how these time spans are calculated, yet they can be used to explain and predict significant influences and events in a person's life with great accuracy.

The astonishing existence of the *Book of Bhrigu* suggests that the innate awareness of subtle forces and the advanced mental powers of Treta Yuga man led to the ability to create detailed descriptions of the lives of people as yet unborn — to the ability to predict the future. However, as Treta Yuga man's mental and perceptual abilities waned, he began to rely more on physical observatories and astrological formulae to predict the future. By the end of descending Dwapara Yuga and into Kali Yuga, even the intention behind the formulae became lost, and astrology fell into further decline.

Interestingly, many scientists predicted that the rise of science, beginning in the 1600s AD, would destroy any last credibility remaining to astrology. Yet today, in the beginning centuries of ascending Dwapara Yuga, the interest in and practice of astrology is expanding rapidly. Astrology, practiced as a formulaic science, may be an inherently Dwapara Yuga phenomenon.

Demigods

Treta Yuga corresponds to the Silver Age of the Greeks, who also used the name Age of the Demigods. They considered this era to be a time when men had great powers, when some men were considered to be the offspring of unions between gods and men, or to have been born with divine qualities.

The concept of an Age of Demigods was not limited to the Greeks. The Native American Hopi's Second World was populated by men and women possessing extraordinary powers. The Chinese legend of the Three August Ones ascribes great wisdom and power to three emperors who gave man the keys to moral living, agriculture, and medicine. The Three August Ones are said to have passed on to mankind the wisdom of the gods. Among the best-known demigods are Rama, whose life and exploits are told in India's *Ramayana*, and Gilgamesh, whose life and exploits are told on clay tablets of Sumerian cuneiform in the *Epic of Gilgamesh*.

Dating the origins of these epics is difficult. The only certainty is that they were put into *written* form sometime in descending Dwapara Yuga; but because they are generally thought to have existed as oral traditions long before they were written down, their likely origin was in descending Treta Yuga.

There are a number of common themes shared by the surviving Treta Yuga stories about demigods:

- Rama in the *Ramayana* and Gilgamesh in the *Epic of Gilgamesh* both go on epic journeys and encounter powerful demonic adversaries. The Three August Ones in similar fashion travel through China encountering and battling demonic adversaries.

- Rama, Gilgamesh, and the Three August Ones experience realms barred to other men: Rama in the court of the gods; Gilgamesh in the underworld; and the Three August Ones in frequent converse with the gods.

- Rama, Gilgamesh, and the Three August Ones all possess extraordinary powers, which they use scrupulously to protect mankind.

- Rama, Gilgamesh, and the Three August Ones directly relate their ancestry to the "first man":

  a) Rama is in direct lineage from *Manu*, India's first man, the "law giver" who is said to have passed on the wisdom of Satya Yuga.

  b) Gilgamesh is in the lineage of *Alulim*, the first Sumerian king: "After the kingship descended from heaven ..."

  c) The first of the Three August Ones is *FuXi*, himself the first man.

- Rama, Gilgamesh, and the Three August Ones are often described as "god-kings" and are portrayed as moral and benevolent rulers, loved by their subjects.

Those well-versed in ancient cultural traditions may notice that we have not so far mentioned other well-known heroes, such as Heracles (Hercules) and Odysseus of the Greek tradition, Cuchulain of the Celtic/Irish tradition, Siegfried of the Germanic tradition, and the five Pandavas of the Indian tradition, as told in the *Mahabharata*. The heroes in these tales do share similarities with Rama, Gilgamesh, and the Three August Ones. They are often portrayed as semi-divine and possessing great powers. It is, however, more difficult to reliably date them as far back as Treta Yuga, although some experts do so.

These heroes are in many cases associated (perhaps erroneously) with dateable historical figures whose lives fall into descending Dwapara Yuga or even into Kali Yuga. The lives of some of these heroes have been so distorted over time that their true and ancient origin is lost to us. As new research is conducted, some of these heroes may be dated earlier and, indeed, Rama, Gilgamesh, and the Three August Ones may be dated later. Our purpose here is not to determine the place of each hero in the time frame of ancient history, but to show that the concept of demigods has its earliest origin in Treta Yuga and that Rama, Gilgamesh, and the Three August Ones are among the best examples.

Why are demigods pertinent to our conception of descending Treta Yuga? In Treta Yuga, according to Sri Yukteswar, individuals were able to wield great power — as they developed the *self-mastery* to do so.

Treta Yuga man's mental abilities and innate attunement to divine magnetism, "the power of all powers," gave him a potential for accomplishment only slightly less miraculous than Satya Yuga man's.

However, unlike Satya Yuga man, Treta Yuga man's increased sense of self, as an individual separate from Spirit, rather than as an inextricable part of Spirit, inevitably led some to seek power for its own sake. No longer fully conscious of the unifying presence of Spirit, some individuals would have seen no reason to use their abilities for the greater good, while others would have sought power in accordance with dharma and service to mankind. Here may well be the origin of the tales of demigods and demons fighting one another for supremacy, tales found in cultural traditions worldwide.

What kind of powers might the demigods of Treta Yuga have possessed? Treta Yuga man's comprehension of divine magnetism, in combination with mental powers, mantras, will, concentration, and *self-mastery*, may have allowed him to do things that not even our technology allows us to do today.

Even now, there are an ever-increasing number of controlled experiments demonstrating man's ability to affect physical objects just by thinking about them. Uri Geller's "parlor trick" of bending a spoon with his mind has become a cliché, but PEAR (Princeton Engineering Anomalies Research) has shown conclusively that *everyone* can affect the outcome of otherwise random physical processes simply by mentally focusing on the objects in the experiment—some people are simply better at it than others.

Rama in the *Ramayana* and Gilgamesh in the *Epic of Gilgamesh* are able to control natural forces. Rama uses mantras to bring down lightning and to harness the wind to defeat his foes; other weapons he "supercharges" with mantras before using them against his enemies.

The meanings of specific words in ancient languages are often debated. For example, the Sanskrit root word "go" is generally translated as "cow." It appears so often in the Vedas that readers are forgiven for assuming the Vedic culture was largely about keeping cattle. However, some Sanskrit scholars declare that "go" means "the inner light"—the personal perception of subtle inner light. When the meaning "inner light" is applied to the word "go" in the Vedas, the Vedas are transformed into a clearly obvious description of spiritual practices—not the practice of raising cattle.

Similarly in the *Ramayana* and the *Epic of Gilgamesh*, words assumed to have such meanings as "bow," or "spear," or "sword" — simply because it is assumed they couldn't mean anything else — may have had more subtle meanings as well, or could be names for mental weapons or techniques for which we have no analog in our era. We may simply not be able to imagine what such weapons are or how they work.

In the *Ramayana*, Rama is pitted against Ravana, a demon-king residing in what is today the island country of Sri Lanka, off the southern tip of India. Near the end of the epic tale, Rama brings his army to Sri Lanka from the Indian mainland by building a bridge across the strait that separates India from Sri Lanka. In the *Ramayana*, the tale is told that by piling stones into the water to create a causeway Rama's army is able, in just a few days, to cross the strait.

This story is usually dismissed by mainstream historians as the cumulative exaggeration, over hundreds of years, of a small war between two tiny kingdoms, one on the Indian mainland, and one in Sri Lanka. Yet with the aid of satellite photography, an ancient causeway can be seen stretching just beneath the surface of the ocean waters between India and Sri Lanka (see *Figure 15*).

NASA/courtesy of nasaimages.org

Figure 15—Satellite photograph of "Rama's Bridge." Sri Lanka is in the middle left of the photo, India in the upper left. The middle section of the thin formation connecting the two land masses is currently under water.

Is "Rama's Bridge" simply a freak formation that by chance resembles the one in the *Ramayana*—or is this thirty-kilometer causeway what remains of the causeway Rama and his army crossed to defeat Ravana? Geologists cannot reach agreement on what natural forces might have formed Rama's Bridge. Currents depositing sand have been ruled out since seasonal shifts in ocean currents take away any sand deposited earlier in the yearly cycle. General uplift along with the Indian subcontinent has also been ruled out. One geologist, without offering any explanation, has said that the bridge looks as if it was created by a "local" uplift. Could Rama's powers have included attunement to the elemental forces that shape the earth?

The possibility that Rama created this land bridge is obviously highly speculative, but the exploits of demigods, preserved in oral traditions and myths from around the world, include moving mountains, parting seas, and using *mantric* weapons so powerful that they could destroy the earth. Explained away by mythologists and archeologists as the natural tendency of storytellers to exaggerate, these tales nonetheless come down to us from an age—Treta Yuga—described by Sri Yukteswar as a time when man had great powers.

Divine Kings

Rama, Gilgamesh, and the Three August Ones are also all believed to have been divine kings or emperors. A look back into the known history of Treta Yuga reveals that many ancient kings were considered to be semi-divine, or to possess divine attributes—a trend that continued well into descending Dwapara Yuga. The Chinese called it the Mandate of Heaven; they considered their emperors to be the Sons of Heaven. The Three August Ones were succeeded, according to Chinese tradition, by the Five Emperors, who were considered to be morally perfect sage-kings. The Sumerians maintained that, from 3300 BC all of their kings were semi-divine, to 2300 BC, 800 years into descending Dwapara Yuga. Egyptian kings, beginning with the First Dynasty of Menes in approximately 3100 BC, were considered to be Sons of Horus and were enjoined to use magic only for the benefit of the people.

The reigns of the Vedic kings, chronicled in Megasthenes' list, and frequently referred to in the *Ramayana* and the *Mahabharata*, stretch back to the beginning of Treta Yuga, the era of the much-revered Manu. The ancient Vedic kings were consistently depicted as courageously adhering to dharma. The Vedic Indians called such kings *rajarshi*, a word combining *raja* (royal) and *rishi* (enlightened sage). The *Ramayana* portrays the father of Sita, King Janaka, or Rajarshi Janaka, as a man renowned equally for his wise benevolence as a ruler and for his enlightened consciousness.

Mainstream historians and archeologists assume that the depiction of ancient kings as semi-divine was merely a means to claim legitimacy, and that belief in the concept was only made possible by the general ignorance of the time. Alternatively, the *actual* higher awareness of Treta Yuga man may well explain the origin of belief in the divine nature of kings.

In Treta Yuga the consciousness of every person *was made obvious by his abilities*. Those few remaining with the consciousness of Satya Yuga would have been able to work miracles at will. The preponderance of people with Treta Yuga consciousness would have been able to communicate telepathically, and many would have been able to display great powers. At the other end of the spectrum, those few with Dwapara Yuga and Kali Yuga consciousness would have been equally marked by their lack of ability to communicate telepathically and by their lack of powers. The stratification of Treta Yuga society would have been based on clear differences in natural ability.

In contemporary society, differences in consciousness are not so obvious. We all have the same basic *outward* capabilities. Our leaders, for example, may give lip service to high morals, but in the end not deliver. It is simply not possible to know with certainty whether or not they are genuine by observing any *outward capabilities*. The high-minded rhetoric, the sincere-seeming smile and declaration of values could in the end all be false fronts hiding self-interest and amorality.

The clear attributes of higher consciousness of Treta Yuga man would have enabled him clearly to see the best choice for ruler—the one most attuned to dharma and with the highest degree of *self-mastery*. Any lingering question of a particular person's qualification to rule could have been decided by those who had the highest, Satya Yuga consciousness, the spiritual leaders of society. In turn, *their* opinion would have been respected because of their obvious spiritual stature, verified by *their* miraculous powers.

The presence of higher consciousness in the ancient past would explain not only the tradition of divine kings but also the veneration ancient cultures had for past rulers and other important figures. Our forward-looking society, the product of an ascending consciousness, tends to dismiss everything that went before as inferior. Conversely, the Egyptians, Sumerians, ancient Chinese, and Vedic Indians, all products of a descending consciousness, revered their past—and clung to traditions long after they had stopped understanding them, or had forgotten their true purpose.

The oral traditions that come to us from Treta Yuga, such as the *Ramayana*, and the *Epic of Gilgamesh*, may have suffered many distortions by the time they were written down in descending Dwapara Yuga. But even so, if we set aside our preconceptions for a moment, and try to view these carefully preserved oral traditions as having originally been *accurate descriptions* of the consciousness, people, and events of Treta Yuga—and not simply the tall tales of storytellers—we may then more easily accept that Treta Yuga man was able to do things and perceive things well beyond our present comprehension.

The stories told in ancient epics of various cultural traditions, and especially in the Vedas, reveal to us a world in which people lived among the gods—and knew themselves to be god-like. According to Sri Yukteswar's explanation of the yugas, Treta Yuga man was innately and directly aware of the conscious matrix arising from the power of *divine magnetism*. The earth, natural forces, other people, the gods, their own thoughts, distant planets, even distant stars, were all living strands woven into the interconnected conscious matrix of which they perceived themselves to be an inextricable part.

Only when Treta Yuga man's innate awareness of the conscious matrix began to fade, and the powers and perceptions that accompanied this awareness began to wane, did he begin to turn to more material solutions to meet his needs. Ironically, it is this transition to greater material dependence that archeologists and historians point to as the *beginning* of civilization.

Chapter 15

Descending Treta Yuga —
Unexplained Knowledge

Timeline

6,700 BC Beginning of the most recent descending Treta Yuga

6,400 BC End of the 300-year transition period (*sandhi*) from descending Satya Yuga

3,400 BC Beginning of 300-year transition period (*sandhi*) to descending Dwapara Yuga

3,100 BC End of the most recent descending Treta Yuga

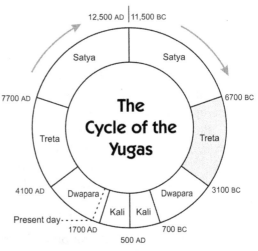

Duration of descending Treta Yuga:
3,600 years

The theory of linear evolution, in which each-new-bit-of-knowledge-has-to-be-derived-from-the-one-before, drives modern archeology. Archeologists love to come up with the *first* instance of—take your pick—writing, metallurgy, medicine, agriculture, architecture, pottery, etc., but always at the same time careful to make a connection to the previously accepted *first* instance in the chain of development.

Because of the each-new-bit-of-knowledge-has-to-be-derived-from-the-one-before approach, the experts are likely to dismiss out of hand anything anomalous, anything out of sequence with the prevailing chain of knowledge. An isolated bit of anomalous knowledge goes against deep-seated convictions about how knowledge develops: it must come at the end of a chain of development. Even solid evidence of pre-existing knowledge, if it falls outside the accepted chain of development, will rarely be taken seriously.

Such has been the fate of the Piri Re'is map.

The Piri Re'is Map

In his 1966 book, *Maps of the Ancient Sea Kings, Evidence of Advanced Civilization in the Ice Age*, Professor Charles Hapgood makes a compelling case that advanced knowledge of the geography of the world existed long, long before the sixteenth- and seventeenth-century European age of explorers.

Professor Hapgood's starting point is the Piri Re'is map. Discovered in 1929 in the old Imperial Palace in Constantinople, the map indicates its date of creation as 1513 AD. It also identifies itself as the property of Piri, an admiral (Re'is) of the Turkish navy—thus its common name, Piri Re'is.

To modern eyes the map looks old and inaccurate. In the first place, it does not use the Mercator projection style to which we have become accustomed. The Mercator projection style presents a flat representation of the spherical earth by making the lines of longitude (those running north and south) equally spaced, even at the North and South Poles where in reality the lines of longitude meet.

The Mercator projection style map is very familiar to us; we rarely see any other style (see *Figure 16*). But the Mercator projection style map is not without problems—the map makes landmasses in the far north or far south appear to be much larger than they actually are. Greenland appears to be much larger than Europe, when in fact it is only a fraction of the size. Antarctica appears to be enormous and vastly elongated and doesn't resemble its true size and shape at all. However, the Mercator projection does a good job of presenting the landmasses on either side of the equator, where the majority of people live.

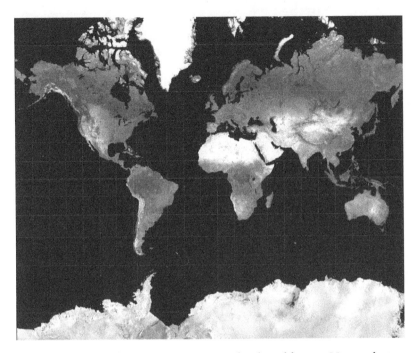

Figure 16 — The Mercator projection style of world map. Notice the immense distortion of Greenland at the top of the map and of Antarctica at the bottom.

The Piri Re'is map, on the other hand, uses an entirely different map-making style, one that today has fallen completely out of use. Whereas in the Mercator projection style, the lines of longitude are always vertical and north is always directly "up," the Piri Re'is map has different orientations for north depending on what part of the map you are viewing (see *Figure 17*).

The style is known as portolan; many maps contemporaneous with the Piri Re'is were drawn in this style. At first glance, because we mentally compare with the Mercator projection, the continents appear distorted. Professor Hapgood and a dedicated band of graduate students spent many years painstakingly "translating" the portolan style into the Mercator style. Once they unraveled the underlying approach to its construction, an approach that indicates that the mapmakers had known the principles of spherical trigonometry, they found the Piri Re'is map to be highly accurate.

Figure 17—A part of the Piri Re'is map showing parts of South America (left side) and Africa (right side). The red circles in mid-ocean provide different "Norths" depending on where you look on the map.
(Public domain, Bilkent University.)

In fact, it was more accurate than it could possibly have been.

The Piri Re'is map accurately shows parts of the coastline of Antarctica known as Queen Maud Land. Not only was Antarctica unknown in the 1500s when Piri Re'is lived, but also that section of the coastline, accurately drawn on the Piri Re'is map, is currently under ice, and has been for thousands of years. We know the Piri Re'is map is accurate because when compared to modern maps of Antarctica, maps made with the aid of seismic mapping techniques, it shows the same actual contours of the continent that are, today, hidden under hundreds, even thousands of feet of ice.

The Piri Re'is map also shows rivers and lakes in what is now the Sahara Desert of North Africa. These features were commonly dismissed as fanciful embellishments of an ignorant mapmaker, but Professor Hapgood wasn't so quick to dismiss them. The overall accuracy of the map had already greatly impressed him. In particular, the accurately drawn presence of Antarctica, on a map made more than one hundred years before Antarctica was "discovered," seemed to be more than simply a lucky guess. How could the map's accuracy be explained?

Most of the writing on the map refers to the map itself, but in one section Piri Re'is himself explains that his map is actually a copy of a much older map. In fact, Professor Hapgood and his team went on to discover that the Piri Re'is map is an amalgam of maps merged together and copied from copies of copies that appear to have originated sometime before the first or second millennium BC. Earlier than that the trail runs cold.

Undaunted by this highly unorthodox finding, Professor Hapgood took another approach to dating the origins of the Piri Re'is map. Instead of assuming that the mapmaker couldn't have known the contour of Antarctica in Queen Maud Land, and that the Sahara was a desert bereft of lakes and rivers, he asked the question, "When in the past would this section of Queen Maud Land have been free of ice and when in the past would the Sahara have had rivers and lakes?"

The answer to both is the same. From approximately 5000 to 3000 BC, the climatic period known as the Mousterian Sub-Pluvial or the Neolithic Pluvial would have created both a green Sahara and an ice-free Queen Maud Land. Modern satellite photos of the Sahara reveal the contours of ancient rivers and lakes that once existed where now the climate is hot and dry. We also know that during this era the ice briefly retreated from the coast of Antarctica in Queen Maud Land.

Hapgood's meticulous research indicates that not only were the principles of spherical trigonometry known long, long before their generally accepted date of formulation, but also that, to have known and mapped so precisely the longitudes of the world's land masses, ancient man must have traveled the globe freely and extensively.

Hapgood is not alone in coming to this conclusion. One can find intriguing evidence of racial, religious, and linguistic similarities between ancient China and ancient North America, and between ancient India and ancient South America and Mesoamerica. The similarities and connections are so strong that direct communication with and/or settlement of those areas by the ancient Chinese and Indians seem very likely.

Hendon M. Harris Jr.'s book, *The Asiatic Fathers of America*, makes a strong case that the descending Treta Yuga Chinese frequently traveled to North America. Harris derives his conclusions from close study of the *Fu Sang* maps, which have been part of Chinese lore for millennia. On close examination of the maps, Harris began to believe that the "Land of the Rising Sun" was not, after all, Japan, but the West Coast of America. Particular descriptions of prominent geographic features, especially a convincing description of the Grand Canyon, led Harris to a lifetime of diligent research, during which he matched location after location in North America to the *Fu Sang* maps.

It has long been agreed that the North American Indians are racially a match to the Chinese, but current theory has it that the indigenous Americans migrated over a frozen ice bridge from Asia to North America in the thirteenth millennium BC. Harris suggests that these distant ancestors to the Chinese, however and whenever they first populated North America, were repeatedly visited by their seafaring Chinese cousins: the result was a two-way exchange of culture. For example, he finds strong similarities between certain Hopi and Chinese myths.

Figure 18 — (left) Olmec head. (right) Detail showing columns of glyphs from second century AD La Mojarra Stela 1. The stela gives a Long Count date of 8.5.16.9.9, or 156 AD. Some columns are glyphs from the Epi-Olmec script. (Public domain, Maunus.)

The Olmec of Mesamerica, whose earliest origins are obscure, show cultural and racial connections to Vedic India and Africa. The Olmec are best known for the immense stone heads that they left behind in the jungle of the Yucatan Peninsula of Mexico. Seventeen of them have been found so far; the oldest has been dated to approximately 1350 BC. The heads each weigh as much as 25-tons and portray people who seem to have Negroid features and wear a distinctive helmet. The Olmec also left exquisite small carvings in jade, some of which reveal figures in classic hatha yoga postures, including an inverted pose and the scorpion pose.

The Olmec are thought to have been the first people to use what is now popularly known as the Mayan calendar. The Mayan calendar has a start date of 3114 BC, which coincides almost precisely with the 3100 BC beginning of descending Dwapara Yuga. Did the ancestors of the Olmec live in Mesoamerica at the start date of the Mayan calendar, or did they bring the calendar from ancient India?

Many scholars, beginning with the venerable Wilhelm von Humboldt (1767–1835), have commented on similarities between South American and Indian cultures. Humbolt, considered to be the father of linguistics, found numerous similarities between Quichua, the language family of the Andes, and Sanskrit:

Quichua	Sanskrit
akapana (clouds colored by sun)	aka (painting)
chani (price)	jani (produce)
chinkat (jaguar)	sinha (lion)
chirau (resplendent)	sura (to shine)
huakra (horn)	vakra (curved)
kakarpa (tent)	k'arpara (parasol)
mita (time)	mita (step passage of time)
muti (pounded corn)	mut (to pound)
nana (sister)	nanda (sister)
pakkni (to break)	pike (to break)
paksa (the moon)	paksa (the full moon)
pisi (small)	pis (to break into small pieces)
pitata (bedroom)	pita (house, cottage)
simpa (cord)	samb (to tie)
soro (spiritual liqour)	sura (spiritual liquor)
sokta (six)	s'as (six)

Dr. Robert von Heine-Geldern (1885–1968), noted ethnologist, archeologist, and historian of the ancient world, made a lifelong study of the ancient cultures of Southeast Asia, beginning in India and extending to Indonesia. Dr. von Heine-Geldern found that the Mayan and Southeast Asian cultures had very strong similarities. On the basis of ancient Indians' known use of ships to Indonesia, he saw no reason that they could not have crossed the ocean to Central America.

Western theories of the development of civilization focus on the Fertile Crescent, an area including the Tigris and Euphrates River Valleys, the Levant, and the Upper Nile. Western archeologists are wary, even grudging about including India or China in the same chronology of the development of civilization. Further, the idea that India and China had attained high degrees of development before the Fertile Crescent civilizations arose, let alone that these cultures were capable of world travel and the dissemination of their culture to North and South America, receives little acknowledgement in the West.

Cultural pride has led some scholars to proclaim, in the East as well as the West, that *their* ancient culture is the true beginning of civilization. Such claims have obscured the perception of what was likely one interconnected world culture in Treta Yuga from which *all* ancient civilizations descended. Rather than civilization developing from one tiny area around 3100 BC and *expanding* outward from there, instead, a number of closely related world cultures already existed, but began to *become isolated* and lose contact in 3100 BC, when mankind's innate ability to communicate telepathically over large distances had run its course.

Ancient maps and strong cultural and linguistic connections between Asia and North and South America present evidence unexplained by the current mainstream view. We believe that, as more information surfaces, a picture of a rich worldwide Treta Yuga culture will emerge.

Ancient Standards

More examples of unexplained knowledge exist in the intriguing evidence for ancient units of measurement based on the dimensions of the earth—geodetic standards, as they are called today—as well as for a surprisingly high degree of standardized use of such units.

The idea of basing a standard of length on the dimensions of the earth is believed to have been suggested first by a French priest, Gabriel Mouton, in 1670 AD. Mouton proposed as a standard the length of one minute of arc along a meridian. In June 1799 AD, France adopted the metric system. The meter was originally defined as one ten-millionth part of a meridianal quadrant of the earth, based on measurements of the arc of the meridian between Dunkirk and Barcelona.

Evidence suggests, however, that our metric system was by no means the first geodetic measurement system. The historian of metrology, Livio Catullo Stecchini, contributed a ninety-five-page appendix to Peter Tompkins' classic *Secrets of the Great Pyramid*. Stecchini discusses the geodesy of the ancient Egyptians in considerable detail; he shows that from pre-dynastic times (i.e. the end of descending Treta Yuga) they carefully sited cities, monuments, and important markers according to accurate lines of latitude and longitude.

Because the Nile's yearly flooding obliterated boundary markers, the Egyptians had to resurvey annually the entire river valley. There is no question that they were skilled at measuring surface distances and angles. Stecchini describes a pre-dynastic geodetic system that was superseded by a less precise system in the dynastic period. He shows that the pre-dynastic Egyptians were well aware that the distance corresponding to a degree of longitude changed with latitude. He asserts that even the oblate shape of the earth was taken into account. Stecchini concludes that the Egyptian geodetic system implies precise knowledge of the circumference of the earth.

Richard Thompson discusses ancient measures in his book *Mysteries of the Sacred Universe*: he relates the circumference of the earth to the Hindu *yojana*, *hasta*, and *krosha*, the Khmer *hat*, and the Chinese *li*. He concludes that those who defined the ancient units must have understood Earth's shape and size very well.

In 1955, Alexander Thom published "A Statistical Examination of the Megalithic Sites in Britain" in the *Journal of the Royal Statistical Society*. After carefully surveying over 250 megalithic sites in Britain and Scotland, including Avebury, Stonehenge, Hill O' Stanes, and the Ring of Brodgar, Professor Thom concludes that they were all constructed on the basis of a common unit of measure—what he calls the Megalithic Yard. Many of the megalithic structures of Britain and Scotland were begun about 3300 BC, close to the end of descending

Treta Yuga. The Megalithic Yard continued to be used as a building standard for over a thousand years into descending Dwapara Yuga.

We find another example of a level of standardization that is not explained by established theory in the Indus Valley Civilization (in present day Pakistan). The Indus Valley Civilization is best known for its two largest cities, Harappa and Mohenjo-daro. The ruins of these cities were rediscovered in 1842, but were not thoroughly excavated until the 1920s. The earliest layers of these two cities date to about 3300 BC, near the end of descending Treta Yuga.

What first struck many of the archeologists was the fact that the two cities were laid out in a rectilinear grid, with streets intersecting at right angles. Further excavation revealed that there were conduits for fresh water to enter the city and sewers to remove waste. Both cities possessed central areas with sizable public baths, government buildings, and large storage areas for grain.

Archeologists were further amazed that the oldest layers of the cities showed the highest level of organization and building quality. They found no evidence of experimentation. No earlier layer of cruder development. These cities sprang forth as though *designed*. The sense of planned building is reinforced by the most astonishing discovery of all. All of the Indus Valley Civilization — extending across 100,000 square miles and covering a time span, beginning in 3300 BC, of over a thousand years — used the same *standardized* size of mud brick. Their most basic building block was the same wherever the Indus Valley Civilization expanded. The bricks were of such high quality and so uniformly made that in the twentieth century Indus Valley Civilization ruins were dismantled and the bricks reused by the British for railroad bridges and embankments.

The existence of so many standardized and often geodetically derived ancient measures cannot be accidental. These measures provide strong evidence that ancient man knew the dimensions of the earth, and further indicate that he applied the knowledge systematically to surveying, building, and city planning.

The Neolithic Non-Revolution

According to mainstream archeological theory, the years from roughly 5000 to 3000 BC (corresponding to the middle to ending years of descending Treta Yuga), were the years that saw the key developments that led to the birth of civilization, the so-called "Neolithic Revolution." According to the theory, this period saw key discoveries in agriculture, animal domestication, and the use of the plough especially, as well as the establishment of increasing numbers of settlements—all of which are believed to have finally combined serendipitously and synergistically around 3300 BC in Sumeria to create the cradle for the birth of civilization.

This "cradle of civilization" view of human development is a purely evolutionary theory. The reasoning is that small pockets of Stone Age people (Neolithic means "New Stone Age") made specific discoveries and inventions that were then passed on to other small pockets, which in turn passed them on to others. The theory has it that new discoveries and inventions started in one location, were spread from there, were enhanced and improved as they spread, until a critical mass of new ideas and inventions came together in *one location* (the Tigris and Euphrates River Valleys): at this point mankind made a revolutionary leap into civilization—the *Neolithic Revolution*.

Linguist and archeologist Gordon Childe is credited with coining the term "*Neolithic Revolution*" in the 1920s. Though still widely accepted, this theory of the birth of civilization, like many archeological theories born in the first half of the twentieth century, is not holding up well in the light of new discoveries.

Far from having emerged just prior to their miraculous convergence in Sumeria around 3300 BC, all the key developments believed to have been responsible for the Neolithic Revolution are now known to have been around for *thousands* of years before Sumeria's rise. Nor were these developments spread by diffusion—one group teaching another, which in turn teaches another. Most of the key developments believed to be responsible for the birth of civilization not only existed long before Sumeria's rise, but existed *independently* all over the world.

Rye, emmer wheat, eikorn wheat, and barley, all cultivated grains, were grown in the area of the Tigris and Euphrates Rivers as early as 11,000 BC—8000 years before the rise of Sumeria. Millet and rice were being grown in China by 10,000 BC. Figs were being grown in the Jordan River Valley in 9000 BC. Pepo squash and maize were being grown in Mexico by 8000 BC and 7000 BC respectively. Moschata squash and arrowroot were being grown in South America by 8000 BC—peanuts, potatoes, and manioc only slightly later. Only recently, taro and banana were determined to have been grown in New Guinea by 8000 BC[1].

We can see from these recent finds that man knew how to cultivate a large variety of fruits and grains thousands of years before the emergence of what is considered civilization—and not just in the Near East. Man grew food all over the world. Yet the ability to grow food did not, as the theory of the Neolithic Revolution would have it, cause people to stop gathering wild foods. *The two methods existed side by side for millennia.*

Many of these new discoveries regarding ancient agriculture are the result of applying new methods of research and analysis to archeology, and these new methods have not yet been extensively used. Once the new methodology is widely applied by archeologists, evidence of even older and more widespread agriculture will likely be found.

New methods of research and analysis are also being applied to dating animal domestication. In addition to DNA analysis of large populations of domestic and wild animals (to ascertain when certain species were first domesticated), scientists are looking for patterns in the shape of animal bones (patterns that indicate human handling) and for milk fat in ancient pottery (which indicates systematic milking of domesticated animals).

New findings resulting from these new methods indicate that animal domestication occurred considerably earlier than previously believed. Fossil evidence of horses in close proximity to human settlements has been found in Afghanistan dating to 15,000 BC—at least 5000 years earlier than horses were previously thought to have been domesticated. Evidence of the domestication of goats in the Middle East can be found dating to 7000 BC.

Especially intriguing, because so completely contrary to prevailing theory, is a new study indicating that the pig may have been domesticated, independently, in at least seven locations around the world. Mainstream archeologists have assumed for years that the pig was domesticated in only one or two places in Asia and that the associated knowledge was spread from those sites. While at the University of Durham, Keith Dobney, who conducted an extensive study of the domestication of the pig, said, "our findings turn this theory on its head." Dobney's study indicates that domestication also occurred independently in Central Europe, Italy, Northern India, and the mainland and islands of Southeast Asia.[2]

The plough, once considered essential to the Neolithic Revolution, is now known to have been used as early as the 6000 BC in several areas in what is now modern Turkey, including Catal Huyuk. New discoveries are pushing the dating of pottery, similarly, farther and farther back in time. Evidence from finds in the Yuchanyan Cave in Hunan Province, China indicates that fired pottery, once believed to be a catalyst of the Neolithic Revolution, was made in China as early as 18,000 BC[3]. We also know that the Jomon people of Japan were making fired pottery by 12,000 BC.

Even if we give the theory of the Neolithic Revolution the benefit of the doubt, and assume that the revolution required not only the initial critical developments but also the immediate *proximity* of a significant number of these critical developments in order for the great leap of civilization, the theory still falls down. In the immediate area of the Tigris and Euphrates River Valleys we find evidence of cultivated grains as far back as 10,000 BC, domesticated goats and oxen from 7000 BC, and fired pottery and the plough from 6000 BC—all 3,000 to 7,000 years *before* the supposed Neolithic Revolution.

According to Childe's theory, the Neolithic Revolution was irresistible. Once man discovered the agrarian lifestyle, the obvious superiority of settling down in one place, growing food, and using animals for food and labor would have swept aside the inferior lifestyle of the so-called hunter-gatherers. Either man was incredibly stupid, since it took at least 3,000 to 7,000 years to see the benefits of civilization once he had the means to make it happen, or there is something wrong with the theory.

What is becoming clearer with each new discovery is that the people of descending Treta Yuga knew and used all the "discoveries" considered key to the "inevitable" start of civilization long before the rise of Sumeria in 3300 BC, and yet consistently chose instead to live lightly on the earth.

Why? We think the reason may be that the mental capabilities of Treta Yuga man made what is today considered civilization unnecessary and unattractive. Treta Yuga man saw the systematic physical exploitation of the earth for food and shelter as the lower, not the higher way of life. Treta Yuga man clearly knew how to grow food, domesticate animals, build settlements, make pottery—in addition, there is evidence of basic dentistry in Mehrgahr in 6000 BC, and a map of the world by 5000 BC. But Treta Yuga man simply didn't feel compelled to use his practical knowledge, as the theory of the Neolithic Revolution would have it, to create civilization as we define it. Instead he used this knowledge as he chose, where he chose, but otherwise continued to live lightly on the earth.

It is only as Treta Yuga man's mental abilities waned in the last centuries of descending Treta Yuga, when he could no longer rely on using his advanced abilities to provide his needs, that we see him turn to widespread agriculture and the city structure as an alternative. It isn't until the *sandhis*, or transition periods at the end of Treta Yuga and the beginning of Dwapara Yuga (3400 to 2900 BC) that the famous ancient cities sprang up around the world—Ur, Sumer, Harappa, Mohenjo-daro, Memphis, and South America's Caral.

As Treta Yuga ended, a new Dwapara Yuga pattern emerged.

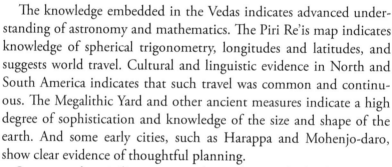

The knowledge embedded in the Vedas indicates advanced understanding of astronomy and mathematics. The Piri Re'is map indicates knowledge of spherical trigonometry, longitudes and latitudes, and suggests world travel. Cultural and linguistic evidence in North and South America indicates that such travel was common and continuous. The Megalithic Yard and other ancient measures indicate a high degree of sophistication and knowledge of the size and shape of the earth. And some early cities, such as Harappa and Mohenjo-daro, show clear evidence of thoughtful planning.

It appears that civilization, or at least what we think of as civilization, was born not from a serendipitous revolutionary leap forward, but from deliberate choice resulting from man's changing awareness and motivation as he descended into Dwapara Yuga.

Beginning with the *sandhi* or transition period from Treta Yuga to Dwapara Yuga in 3400 BC, man began to rely more on the material world to meet his needs—but he did so with much greater awareness and knowledge than the current linear theory of development can explain. Instead of Stone Age people with no mental development pulling themselves up from the mud, we see instead intelligent people accepting a more material lifestyle, and approaching it with system, order, and method—as is evident from their knowledge of math, physics, geodetic standards, geography, and especially, as we will see in upcoming chapters, energy.

Chapter 16

Descending Dwapara Yuga —
The Great Pyramid

Timeline

3,100 BC   Beginning of the most recent descending Dwapara Yuga

2,900 BC   End of the 200-year transition period (sandhi) from descending Treta Yuga

900 BC   Beginning of 200-year transition period (sandhi) to descending Kali Yuga

700 BC   End of the most recent descending Dwapara Yuga

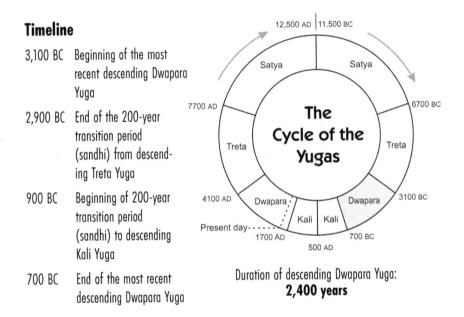

Duration of descending Dwapara Yuga:
2,400 years

No single artifact more clearly reveals the presence of advanced knowledge in the ancient past than the Great Pyramid of Giza. No single ancient artifact more clearly highlights the transition from descending Treta Yuga to descending Dwapara Yuga than the Great Pyramid of Giza. And no single ancient artifact turns the linear conception of human development on its head more thoroughly than the Great Pyramid of Giza.

Mainstream theory holds that the Egyptian civilization began slightly later than Sumeria's rise in 3300 BC. Egypt is commonly thought to have risen to prominence when Menes united Upper and Lower Egypt in 3100 BC. Prior to that, mainstream theory holds, many small and separate groups of people lived along the Nile, using Neolithic Stone Age tools, and surviving with rudimentary agricultural practices.

After Menes united Egypt, mainstream theory asks us to believe, people who had formerly eked out their precarious Stone Age lives along the Nile learned, in just a few centuries, how to build what was then and what remained for the next five millennia the most sophisticated structure in the world. And, after having built it, managed to achieve nothing like it ever again.

Mainstream archeologists treat the Great Pyramid, like the proverbial elephant in the room, as though it weren't there. Or, if they do acknowledge it, they minimize its importance — transform an elephant into a mouse.

The Great Pyramid has fascinated people for thousands of years, and has inspired hundreds, perhaps thousands, of books. Herodotus, in the fifth century BC, described it in his *Histories*. The Caliph Al-Ma'mum, in the ninth century AD, spent the better part of a year exploring the Great Pyramid. Nor has interest waned. A recent online search produced over *six million* matches for "The Great Pyramid."

It is surely the most measured structure on earth. Sir Flinders Petrie spent the best part of 1880 through 1882 meticulously and scrupulously measuring every line, plane, and surface of the Great Pyramid — measurements still regarded as reliable. Among many other extensive surveys, J. H. Cole's, conducted in 1925 for the British colonial government, is considered by many archeologists to be definitive.

Like climbing Mount Everest, scaling the heights of understanding the Great Pyramid appears to be an irresistible challenge. Sir Howard Vyse visited Egypt in the early 1800s and ended up so intrigued with the Great Pyramid that he remained there for decades. Today his methods of exploration are an archeologist's worst nightmare (he was enamored of using gunpowder to blast his way into suspected passages), but he is credited with establishing some of the first "scientific" theories about the Great Pyramid, many of which hold sway even today. His work and passion for his subject made him, in scholarly eyes, the first Egyptologist.

While Vyse may be first in the line of those who in modern times have devoted themselves to studying the Great Pyramid, the line is steadily growing longer. Peter Tompkins' seminal book *Secrets of the Great Pyramid* (1972) was among the first to present newer, alternative theories of the purpose and construction of the Great Pyramid. And today we have a new generation of archeologists and enthusiasts studying the Great Pyramid, such as Robert Schoch (*Pyramid Quest*), Robert Bauval (*The Orion Mystery* and *The Egypt Code*), John Anthony West (*Serpent in the Sky: The High Wisdom of Ancient Egypt*) and Graham Hancock (*Fingerprints of the Gods*).

One would think there could be nothing left to say on the subject. However, the more the Great Pyramid is measured and studied, the more discoveries are made, and the more questions arise. The standard theory—that it was built using only copper tools, wood, rope, and sweat, as a tomb for the Pharaoh Khufu—is still around, but it is less and less able to answer the questions that new evidence gives rise to.

New theories abound as to how and why it was built and what it was used for—from the mystical to the astronomical, from the alien to the practical. But one theme informs almost all the new theories—the Great Pyramid could not have been built by primitive people just out of the Stone Age. It is simply *too precisely* built to have been constructed with copper and stone chisels, and its design is simply *too sophisticated* to have been conceived from the knowledge ascribed to the people of that era.

Figure 19—The Great Pyramid of Giza. (Creative Commons, Nina Aldin Thune.)

Exquisite Form

What first intrigues people who study the Great Pyramid are its measurements. Also striking are its sheer size, exactness of orientation, and the level of craftsmanship and knowledge of mathematics revealed in its construction. Clearly, this is no ordinary structure.

The base of the Great Pyramid covers an area of over thirteen acres. It is composed of over 2.3 million limestone and granite blocks; some weigh as much as 100,000 pounds and were transported to the site from as far away as 500 miles. The Great Pyramid is 449 feet tall and remained the tallest building in the world until the thirteenth century AD when the spire of Lincoln Cathedral in England eclipsed it. Even so, the Great Pyramid is over half the height of the Empire State Building and remains, *5,000 years later*, the heaviest structure on earth.

The base of the Great Pyramid deviates from being perfectly level around its entire circumference by less than 7/8ths of an inch. The sides of the pyramid are aligned to within three minutes of an arc (1/20th of a degree) to the true cardinal directions—north, south, east, and west. Some speculate that it was originally aligned *exactly* to the cardinal directions, but is now slightly less so because of seismic shifts in the earth's crust.

The circumference of the Great Pyramid in relation to its height gives a ratio of 22/7—the value of pi. One can also calculate the value of phi (1.618)—better known as the "golden ratio"—from the dimensions of the pyramid. It is almost certain that the dimensions of the Great Pyramid were deliberately chosen to express these timeless ratios.

The exterior of the Great Pyramid today appears to be step-like from base to apex. However, the Great Pyramid was originally cased in limestone, which filled in the steps and created a perfectly flat contour. The joints between the limestone facing blocks (a few still remain) line up to within .02 inches; the line between blocks is barely perceptible. There is evidence that the granite and limestone casing stones were polished to a shine. The Pyramids of Giza all shared this style of facing. Gleaming in the desert sun, they would have been visible for miles.

Amazing measurements are also found in the interior of the Great Pyramid, notably in the Descending Passage, which extends from the exterior wall of the pyramid to a rough-hewn chamber in the bedrock below. The constructed part of the passage deviates from being perfectly straight by only 1/50th of an inch over 150 feet. The entire length of the passage, including the lower stretch that is carved out of bedrock, deviates by only 1/4th of an inch over 350 feet.

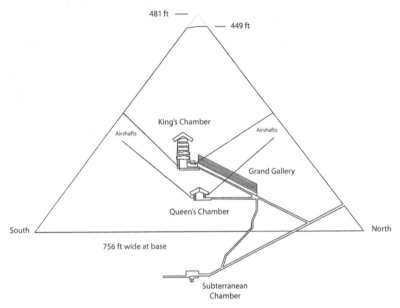

Figure 20—Interior structures of the Great Pyramid. Note the complexity of the ceiling above the King's Chamber.

After carefully studying the Great Pyramid with the eye of a professional machinist—the modern craft that is able to produce objects with the highest degree of accuracy and precision known today—Christopher Dunn, author of The Giza Power Plant, concluded, "The bald fact is that the Great Pyramid—by any standard old or new—*is the largest and most accurately constructed building in the world.*"[1]

The Great Pyramid, given its size and the inherent limits of physical materials, would have been a nearly *perfect form* when first completed. Mathematically, materially, and aesthetically, nothing like it has been built in the five millennia since its construction. Perhaps our ascending Dwapara Yuga culture will eventually build something matching its pure and exquisite form—but it hasn't done so yet.

Precision Construction

Any discussion of the Great Pyramid eventually gets around to how it was built. The standard theory is that 100,000 men labored for three months of each year for twenty years, using wooden rollers and levers, plaited flax rope, hardened copper chisels, and stone tools. This picture comes mostly from Herodotus' fifth century BC *Histories*, in which he recounts stories he heard while traveling in Egypt. His account *should* be received with skepticism since the Great Pyramid was already nearly 2,500 years old when he heard the stories. Surprisingly, however, the standard theory leans heavily on Herodotus' version.

However, the main reason that the standard theory persists is because most archeologists believe that wood, rope, stone, and hardened copper were all that could *possibly* have been available to use, therefore the ancient Egyptians simply must have figured out a way to use them to build the Great Pyramid. While the argument itself is somewhat circular, its proponents maintain that lacking proof of other means of construction, it is the only logical explanation. While this argument does have merit, it isn't very satisfying.

The standard theory has many flaws. One is simply scale. In Dr. Joseph Jochmans' book, *The Hall of Records: Hidden Secrets of the Pyramid and Sphinx*, he questions whether there would have been enough wood in all of Egypt and the Levant to provide the millions of wooden rollers and levers needed — this area was, after all, a desert in the era when it was built. The crushing weight of the limestone blocks would have splintered the wooden rollers rather quickly. If, on average, ten rollers were destroyed in the process of transporting one 20,000-pound stone block miles from quarry to pyramid and then up the pyramid, they would have needed 23,000,000 rollers. That is a lot of trees.

Plaited flax rope presents an equally difficult problem. Because the rope would wear out quickly, vast amounts of flax would be required to make the rope needed to bind and haul the 2.3 million blocks of the Great Pyramid. One speculation is that, to keep up with demand, *all* the croplands along the Nile would have to be devoted to growing flax.

Even if solutions to the problems presented by scale and lack of raw materials can be found in, for example, foreign trade, no one has provided a convincing explanation for how hardened copper tools could have been used to create the precision surfaces and joints found all over the Great Pyramid. Especially problematical is to explain how the ancient builders could have shaped granite—which is considerably harder than the hardened copper tools themselves.

In his book, *The Giza Power Plant*, Christopher Dunn describes using precision tools of the machinist's trade such as the *parallel*, a handheld plane machined to within 2/10,000ths of an inch of perfect flatness on one side, to measure and analyze the craftsmanship found in the Great Pyramid and other structures on the Giza Plateau. He placed the parallel against the outside and inside surfaces of the so-called sarcophagus found in the second pyramid. When he shone a flashlight from the opposite side of the parallel (toward his eyes) he could detect no light between the parallel and the side of the sarcophagus—none. No matter which way he turned the parallel, or where on the side he placed it, he could see no light between the parallel and the sarcophagus. His test showed that the sides of the sarcophagus had been polished to within10,000ths of an inch of perfect flatness!

Even using the best machine tools available today, achieving that degree of flatness is difficult. Using hand tools, it is simply impossible.

Dunn has gone on to find many examples in and around the Great Pyramid that show marks characteristic of such high-speed tools as drills, sonic drills, and lathes. Nor is he alone in his discoveries. Petrie noted during his survey in the 1800s that many items showed circular markings consistent with the use of drills or lathes.

Clearly, no one has found an ancient high-speed drill among the ruins of the Giza Plateau. But equally clearly, no one has come close to providing any other explanation for the high degree of machinist-level precision in evidence. Creating even *one* surface of a flatness measured in 10,000ths of an inch cannot have been an accident. It could only have been done deliberately.

Last, but no means least, is the problem of organization. How could a primitive society, believed by the standard theory to have only recently emerged from the Stone Age, be capable of the organization, planning, and building skills required to sustain such an effort for decades? An effort that resulted in the single most enduring, most precisely made structure in the world. Unless the ancient Egyptians were in fact far more advanced than the standard theory allows, the Great Pyramid would have to stand as the most colossal example of beginners luck in the world.

Ancient Grounds

The date of completion of the Great Pyramid, according to the standard theory, is approximately 2560 BC. The key fact to support this date is the presence of quarry marks, graffiti-like daubs of reddish paint found on a few stones high up inside the Great Pyramid above the King's Chamber, marks that are believed to associate the Great Pyramid with the Pharaoh Khufu. Khufu's dates are fairly well-established, and thus provide a time frame for the Great Pyramid as well.

There has, however, long been some resistance to this argument. A few quarry marks have seemed much too little evidence on which to base the entire decision. Until recently, though, there was really little else on which the decision could be based. But in the 1980s, Professor Wenke of the University of Washington led a team who performed carbon-14 dating on minute bits of charcoal found in the mortar that was used between some of the core, out of sight, stone blocks in the Great Pyramid.

Wenke's findings pushed back the dates for all of the Giza pyramids by an average of 374 years,[2] and so placed the Great Pyramid's completion around 2900 BC — roughly at the end of the *sandhi*, or transition period, at the beginning of descending Dwapara Yuga.

Determining the age of the Great Pyramid is complicated by evidence that it was built in stages. It has long been known that the Great Pyramid is built over a mound rising approximately one hundred feet above the level of the Giza Plateau. This has long puzzled Egyptologists. It would have been far easier to simply level the mound than to build over it.

Robert Bauval, author of *The Orion Mystery* and *The Egypt Code*, suggests that the mound may have been in use as an observatory before the Great Pyramid was built. Noting that the lower courses of the Great Pyramid employ a slightly different building style, he further suggests that the first phase of the Great Pyramid may have been to create an observation platform equal to the height of the mound. If true, the dates of this observation platform may fall in with those of the wave of megalithic observatories built between 3400 and 2900 BC.

It is also likely that the Giza Plateau was used for astronomical and sacred purposes long before the Great Pyramid was completed. Dr. Robert Schoch, Professor of Geology at Boston University, has recently completed an analysis of the weathering of the enclosure of the Great Sphinx, and of the adjoining Sphinx Temple and Valley Temple.[3] His conclusion: the oldest parts of these structures were built sometime between 7000 and 5000 BC—as long as 4,000 years before the Great Pyramid was completed.

Figure 21 — The Great Sphinx as we see it today. The Sphinx Temple is in the foreground.

Only the head of the Sphinx projects above the Giza Plateau. The body was carved out of the limestone bedrock by excavating a pit surrounding the monument that forms a three-sided enclosure. The West and South walls of the Sphinx enclosure show a pattern of erosion by running water. How could the Sphinx, residing in the desert conditions of Egypt, ever have been eroded by water?

Around 12,500 BC the Sahara entered a moist period (the Mousterian Pluvial), which persisted in alternation with some drier intervals until the end of the last wet period about 3000 BC. At this point the arid conditions we know today set in. To have been so deeply eroded by running water, the Sphinx enclosure would have to have been excavated, and the Sphinx sculpted, sometime well before the end of wet period. While acknowledging some uncertainties in the assumptions involved in the estimate, Schoch concludes that, to account for the depth of erosion in evidence on the sides and in the floor of the Great Sphinx enclosure, the oldest part of the enclosure would have to have been excavated between 7000 and 5000 BC.

Figure 22—West wall of the Sphinx enclosure showing the coved appearance with vertical runnels, characteristic of erosion by running water. Notice that a second wall below the first and immediately behind the rump of the Sphinx shows no water erosion.

The evidence of erosion indicates that the Giza plateau was in use well back into descending Treta Yuga. The evidence also supports Professor Wenke's carbon-14 based earlier dates for the Great Pyramid, and Bauval's theory that the pyramid was built in stages. The Great Pyramid may have achieved its final form around 2900 BC, perhaps earlier, but the site itself was likely to have been in use for many millennia beforehand.

Higher Purpose

Ask almost anyone and they will tell you the Great Pyramid was a tomb for a Pharaoh. It is quite understandable why so many people readily believe this to be its purpose. Egypt may be best known for the pyramids, but a close second is King Tut's and other royal tombs in the Valley of the Kings. However, the Great Pyramid was likely never a tomb, despite prevailing opinion and the standard theory.

What is not generally known is that the first tombs of the Valley of the Kings date to the sixteenth century BC, thirteen centuries *after* the Great Pyramid was built. In fact, most of the tombs, mortuary temples, and burial areas, such as the Theban Necropolis, began around 2000 BC with the advent of the Middle Kingdom. The practice of mummification using natron and the custom of burying riches with royalty for use in the afterlife were also mostly Middle Kingdom developments from almost a thousand years after the Great Pyramid was constructed.

No mummy or burial treasure was ever found in the Great Pyramid. The usual explanation — that tomb robbers must have removed the treasures and mummies long ago — does not hold up under closer examination. We have a reliable account of the first exploration of the upper chambers of the Great Pyramid. In the ninth century AD, Caliph Al-Ma'mum tunneled and blasted his way into the upper chambers. He and his workers remarked on the absence of any soot on the ceiling indicating the previous use of torches. The Caliph and his men searched thoroughly but found only the stone coffer in the King's Chamber.

Further, despite the overwhelming size and majestic presence of the Great Pyramid, qualities that would seem to make it suitable for a royal burial, the inner chambers are utilitarian. They don't have the beautiful bas-relief or painted hieroglyphics and scenes on the walls that we find in Middle Kingdom tombs and temples. Nor are the chambers and passages in the Great Pyramid well suited to laying out treasure.

The entry to the King's Chamber is so low that one has to crouch or crawl to enter. The so-called sarcophagus in the King's Chamber is too small for a person of average height to stretch out in, yet it is too large to have been brought in after the Great Pyramid was completed — it had to have been built into the chamber during construction. Perhaps most telling is the presence of airshafts that bring fresh air into the

King's Chamber. Not only would the deceased Pharaoh not need any air, the fresh air would speed decomposition, a rather counter-productive feature if the goal of the chamber was to preserve the Pharaoh for all eternity.

Further, the Great Pyramid, as previously described, was precisely and complexly built with features unnecessary for a tomb. For example the Grand Gallery, which provides access to the King's Chamber, is large and has a complicated ceiling and wall design. If the goal were merely to create a passage to the King's Chamber, the Grand Gallery could have been made much more simply.

The King's Chamber, by contrast, is plain. The walls and ceiling are smooth polished granite. Yet hidden above the chamber is an extremely complex ceiling — six levels constructed with the heaviest blocks of stone in the Great Pyramid (see *Figure 20*). The conventional explanation is that these extra ceilings create *relieving chambers* above the King's Chamber to handle the immense weight of the stone above it. But the ceiling of the Queen's Chamber, which is lower in the structure bears even more weight, and yet has only a simple peaked ceiling.

Such seemingly unnecessarily complex features as the Grand Gallery and the ceiling of the King's Chamber, as well as the overall and fantastic precision of the Great Pyramid, have led many people to search for other purposes behind the building of the Great Pyramid. Among the alternative theories are the pyramid as a great machine, as an astronomical observatory, as a kind of Rosetta Stone of higher knowledge, and as a channel for subtle energies.

There are also theories that ascribe mundane purposes to the Great Pyramid — a storehouse for grain and a fixed survey point to help reestablish borders after the annual Nile flood. However, they are not very convincing since it seems like a lot of effort to have gone to in order to store not very much grain, and there must have been other ways to provide a fixed point for resurveying the Nile Valley which did not require tens of thousands of men for decades to create.

Some theorists have seen the dimensions of the inner chambers and passages as indicators of the chronologies of history — a kind of history in stone. Charles Piazzi Smyth, in *Our Inheritance in the Great Pyramid* (1864), proposed practically every inch of the Great Pyramid was an encoding of the events of the Bible. Others, such as Robert Menzies and David Davidson, followed in his footsteps. One can't help thinking that for them, the Great Pyramid was like the proverbial Rorschach inkblot, in which they could see whatever their minds chose to see.

Other more plausible theories begin with the Great Pyramid's precise alignment to the cardinal directions, and with the astronomical sightings possible from the Descending Passage and the airshafts in the King's Chamber. Robert Bauval goes even further. In his groundbreaking book, *The Orion Mystery*, he makes the case that the Great Pyramid is part observatory and part of a star map laid out on the ground in grand scale.

Seen from above, the Great Pyramid and the second and third pyramids on the Giza Plateau mirror the alignment and brightness of the three stars that make up Orion's Belt. Currently, the alignment of the three stars of Orion's Belt and of the three Pyramids of Giza is very close, but not exactly the same. However, very interestingly, from the point of view of the cycle of the yugas, their alignment is closest to being exact in 11,500 BC, when Sri Yukteswar tells us mankind's development was at its peak.

Other theorists have seized on the mathematical relationships of the dimensions of the Great Pyramid, such as pi and phi, and teased out many more relationships, concluding that the Great Pyramid is a time capsule of knowledge left for us to rediscover.

A recent theory, engagingly and exactingly described in Christopher Dunn's *The Giza Power Plant*, makes a well-reasoned and well-researched case that the Great Pyramid's dimensions and weight would make it resonate with the seismic pulse of the earth.

The millions of tiny shifts in the earth's crust, mantle, and core are believed by some scientists to result in a constant pulse, with a long but measurable wavelength. Dunn believes that the Great Pyramid is the correct size to vibrate in harmony with the earth's pulse, just as a shorter piano string vibrates in harmony with a longer string even if the longer string is octaves lower. Dunn then makes a meticulous argument that the Grand Gallery and the King's Chamber could have been equipped in such a way as to "step up" the low frequencies of the earth's pulse into higher and higher, and more and more energetic, frequencies. Dunn theorizes that the "relieving chambers" above the King's Chamber are actually resonance chambers and that the granite beams that make up the six ceilings were carefully positioned and sized to vibrate intensely and create piezoelectric energy from their high quartz crystal content. Dunn believes that the Great Pyramid, as a last "step up," could have created high-energy microwaves.

Since, as the study of the yugas indicates, the Egyptians of this time understood the presence of energy underlying all matter, it follows that the Great Pyramid could have been built as a passive concentrator of energy. If the ancient Egyptians understood the laws of energy yet did not have an established tradition of mechanical technology (not needed in Treta Yuga), harnessing the earth's seismic power in this profoundly simple and ecologically harmonious manner may well have been the natural result.

None of the foregoing theories can or should be ruled out. Yet it is perhaps more likely, if the Great Pyramid is indeed a purpose-built device and not merely an extremely large burial mound, that its purpose would be more in line with the knowledge and mental capabilities of Treta Yuga. Just as, in our era, we typically apply our new knowledge of energy to old mechanical forms — the first automobile, for example, was a "horseless" carriage — it is likely that, upon entering Dwapara Yuga, the ancient Egyptians applied their "new" knowledge of energy to the "old" mental practices of Treta Yuga.

Anecdotal evidence strongly suggests that the Great Pyramid affects the conscious experience of those inside its various chambers. Perhaps the best-known account is from Paul Brunton's *A Search in Secret Egypt*. In the 1930s, while spending a night in the King's Chamber, Brunton had a profound and life-changing out-of-body experience. He recounts being told esoteric truths by his "guide" and, while his physical body lay unmoving, being shown undiscovered chambers in the Great Pyramid.

Napoleon Bonaparte visited the Great Pyramid and requested that he be left alone in the King's Chamber. His aides reported that he emerged some time later, white and shaken. When asked what had happened he wouldn't answer directly; he seemed to fear that no one would believe him. To this day, alas, we don't know what he experienced.

Elisabeth Haich, in her book *Initiation*, recounts a former life as an initiate in ancient Egypt; much of her account involves the Great Pyramid. She maintains that the Great Pyramid was used methodically as a spiritual catalyst. "Initiates" — those who had advanced far by their own efforts but who weren't quite capable of achieving a high state — were helped, by the pyramid's influence, to break through.

Haich recounts that initiates were carefully prepared for the experience. She describes at length the need for initiates to refine their bodies, especially their nervous systems, to be able to handle much higher frequencies of subtle energy. Even more important, the initiates needed to prepare their minds with disciplines of concentration and meditation so as not to be overwhelmed by the experience.

Just as the Vedas may have provided a way for descending Treta Yuga man to achieve the higher states of consciousness common to Satya Yuga, the Great Pyramid may have been a way for descending Dwapara Yuga man to achieve the higher states of consciousness common to Treta Yuga. The Great Pyramid may have been built to be an enormous passive lens to focus subtle energy, allowing the ancient Egyptians to nudge the consciousness of those who were suitably prepared into the higher states of awareness still remembered from Treta Yuga.

Haich explains further that the other two Pyramids of Giza were used for preliminary stages of spiritual development. She describes the entire Giza Plateau as a home both for those in training to receive initiation and for those who had received it. Haich maintains that the initiates were Egypt's most precious achievement, insuring that their culture was guided and aided by those who were truly wise.

As one can imagine, mainstream archeologists roll their eyes when they hear such theories. As rational empiricists they can only accept what can be measured and thereby (in their eyes) proven. But even by a rational empirical standard, the Great Pyramid's precision of construction, embedded mathematical formulae, and exact orientation, elevate it far above the capabilities and knowledge ascribed to the ancient Egyptians in the standard linear theory of human development. We are confident that in time researches into the Great Pyramid will play a significant role in revolutionizing archeological thought.

Chapter 17

Descending Dwapara Yuga —
Energy Awareness

Timeline

3,100 BC   Beginning of the most recent descending Dwapara Yuga

2,900 BC   End of the 200-year transition period (*sandhi*) from descending Treta Yuga

900 BC   Beginning of 200-year transition period (*sandhi*) to descending Kali Yuga

700 BC   End of the most recent descending Dwapara Yuga

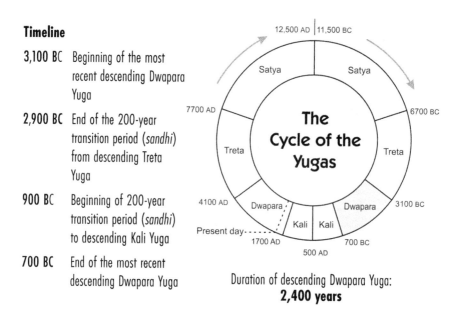

Duration of descending Dwapara Yuga:
2,400 years

The keynote of Dwapara Yuga is energy awareness. Dwapara Yuga is an era when mankind as a whole comprehends that energy underlies all matter. We would, therefore, expect to find evidence of energy awareness being put to use in descending Dwapara Yuga as clearly as we find it in ascending Dwapara Yuga. In fact, there is ample evidence of energy awareness being put to use in such ancient cultures as Egypt, China, and India during descending Dwapara Yuga—but the energy awareness was put to use, for the most part, in a very different way than we are familiar with today.

Today's energy awareness is expressed primarily through the development of technology. Our technology is in turn founded on laws of energy "discovered" and refined over the last three hundred years—electromagnetism, gravitation, and the strong and weak nuclear forces. The exploitation of these four types of energy is at the heart of modern technology.

Unlike our era, however, when we had to rediscover forgotten knowledge about the laws of energy, descending Dwapara Yuga man *inherited* the knowledge from his Treta Yuga predecessors. The concepts embedded in the Vedas alone indicate that mankind was aware of many fundamental principles of physics, mathematics, and astronomy. In such books as Professor Kalpana Paranjape's Ancient Indian *Insights and Modern Science*, Subhash Kak's *The Astronomical Code of the Rgveda*, Richard Thompson's *Vedic Cosmography and Astronomy*, and Brajendranath Seal's *The Positive Sciences of the Ancient Hindus*, the authors tellingly demonstrate that descending Treta Yuga man and, therefore, descending Dwapara Yuga man, knew energy was the underlying reality of matter—in a broad spectrum of knowledge, including atomic and subatomic realms; the nature of electromagnetism, gravity, even the strong and weak nuclear forces; the rotations, orbits, and motions of the earth, sun, planets, and stars; and the size and structure of the earth.

The people of Treta Yuga made very little direct use of this knowledge, however, since they were able to meet their needs and wants by using mental powers, but, as we showed in previous chapters, they did make *some* material use of the higher knowledge they possessed, for example, the Egyptian's ability in pre-dynastic times to conduct sophisticated surveys which reveals their knowledge of the size and shape of the earth. This knowledge is further revealed in the ancient maps, such as the Piri Re'is map and other portolan style maps, which had to have been derived by the use of spherical trigonometry. We can also see that the people of descending Treta Yuga had applied their knowledge of astronomy, including the knowledge of the precession of the equinox, to their construction of the Megalithic observatories, such as New Grange, Stonehenge, Nabta Playa and many others.

However, Treta Yuga man didn't need, or want, to *focus* on the application of energy. His mental powers made such focus unnecessary. Any process initiated by the power of thought automatically works its way to completion through energy and then into matter. Thought is the higher law, energy the lower. Thought controls energy. If he could control thought he didn't need to control energy as a separate process.

Once man entered descending Dwapara Yuga, however, and lost Treta Yuga's mental powers, he needed to exploit energy awareness more directly to meet his needs. We do know from the Great Pyramid's dimensions that descending Dwapara Yuga Egyptians made use of such knowledge inherited from Treta Yuga as the mathematical concepts of pi and phi, concepts that current theory holds were not "discovered" until millennia later. We can also infer from the precision of the Great Pyramid's construction, that the Egyptians of this era made other pragmatic use of their advanced knowledge. And, if either theory is true, either that the Great Pyramid captured seismic energy via "stepping up" the resonant frequency of the earth, or that the Great Pyramid was used to concentrate subtle energies for the advancement of spiritual initiates, then we can also conclude that they knew not only how to make things precisely, but how to make things which took advantage of the principles of energy.

However, the question poses itself, if Treta Yuga knowledge was passed on into Dwapara Yuga, why didn't Dwapara Yuga man do more with it? Where are the amazing technologies of descending Dwapara Yuga? This argument is often put forward as indirect proof that mankind couldn't have possessed such advanced knowledge in the ancient past.

To begin to answer this question, we need to recognize our own modern bias—the assumption that since our *ascending* Dwapara Yuga culture has developed extensive technological applications from our understanding of energy, therefore any culture possessing similar knowledge would have created similar technology.

There are several reasons why this might not be the case—from the purely pragmatic to the esoteric. One pragmatic reason comes from the enormous difference in population between descending Dwapara Yuga and our ascending Dwapara Yuga. The estimated population of the world at the commencement of *descending* Dwapara Yuga in 3100 BC was 25 million people. The estimated population of the world at the commencement of *ascending* Dwapara Yuga in 1700 AD was 750 million people—thirty times as many—and the disproportion only grew larger after 1700 AD.

The world population roughly doubled from 1700 to 1900 AD to 1.65 billion, roughly doubled again by 1960 to 3.1 billion, and roughly doubled yet again by 2000 to nearly 6 billion people. Compare that to the world population of 25 million people in 3100 BC, and we see there are nearly 250 *times as many* people alive today as there were then.

Six billion people comprise a lot of mouths to feed and bodies to clothe and shelter. Necessity has definitely displayed her maternal nature by responding to the enormous demands such a large population creates. In the very short period of time since the 1700 AD beginning of ascending Dwapara Yuga, invention after invention to provide food, clothing, shelter, improve lives, make money and, alas, fight wars, have spilled out into the world.

But would the same explosion of invention and technology have happened if the 1700 AD world population had only been 25 million? For one thing, our current infrastructure—electric generation, transportation, communication, manufacturing, and the acquisition of raw materials—even if greatly scaled down, would require millions more people to maintain than were alive at any point during descending Dwapara Yuga.

Our world's goods, services, and infrastructure are dependent upon very long, very complex chains of technology-enabled industries. Even such a simple product as a modern wooden pencil with an eraser actually requires a long chain of linked activities by tens of thousands of people– from creating the machines to cut and mill the wood, to mining, processing, and transporting the graphite, to creating the synthetic chemicals for making the eraser, to mining, processing, milling, and forming the little metal band that holds the eraser to the pencil.

Building a nuclear power plant, or developing a computer, requires vastly longer and more complex chains of technology-enabled industries supported by an infrastructure maintained by tens of millions of people. For example, in 1942, in order to produce enough uranium-235—just a few pounds—for the first atomic bombs, the tiny U.S. town of Oak Ridge, Tennessee was transformed into a government-run city of 75,000 people. Thousands of centrifuges were built to extract uranium-235 from the natural isotope uranium-238. After three years of constant labor by tens of thousands of workers, enough enriched uranium was produced for just two bombs.

The chains of linked activities that could be maintained by a population of only 25 million spread across the world would have been much, much shorter, and much, much simpler. Even if, possessed of advanced knowledge, the people of descending Dwapara Yuga could *envision* more technologically advanced artifacts, to support the complex mix of industries required to make them would have been impractical, perhaps impossible.

Instead of the great machines and vast infrastructure of today, the technologies developed in descending Dwapara Yuga were in proportion to what the population could support. What we see in ancient Dwapara Yuga is high knowledge and low complexity. The Great Pyramid, for example, demonstrates knowledge of mathematics, subtle energy, and the application of advanced techniques for precision construction, and yet is made from simple stone.

Artifacts from the early centuries of descending Dwapara Yuga, in particular, show a high quality of manufacture. Edward Malkowski's book, *When It Rained In Egypt*, describes the eerily lifelike crystal eyes of Egyptian statures of the era. The workmanship points to an understanding of optical principles, and to knowledge of grinding and polishing high-magnification lenses. Many misidentified crystal objects, long residing in museums from the Near East to the venerable British Museum, have recently been properly identified as magnifying lenses — several from the Old Kingdom era (2900–2500 BC) — determined by the research of Robert Temple and described in his book, *The Crystal Sun*.

The presence of high quality lenses and optical technology in Old Kingdom Egypt is further borne out by a recent discovery at Abydos of an ivory knife handle dated to approximately 3300 BC.[1] The knife handle is carved so finely that the work can be seen only with the aid of high magnification; the craftsman too would therefore have required high magnification, and very fine tools, to do the carving in the first place.

The Cairo Museum contains granite "bowls" from the era of the Great Pyramid. Christopher Dunn's *The Giza Power Plant* makes a case for the "bowls" as "resonators" placed in the Great Pyramid's Grand Gallery to concentrate seismic energy and convert it into other forms. With characteristic care and accuracy, Dunn measures and analyzes of the "bowls." He finds an amazing uniformity of thickness—and absolutely no explanation for how they could be made using simple tools. Dunn's opinion as a professional machinist is that the bowls could only have been made using high-speed lathes.

A copper-alloy necklace, found in Harappa (Indus Valley Civilization, ca. 2500 BC) is made from extremely fine wire. Such fineness can only be achieved by drawing the wire through a series of graduated perforations[2]—a methodology on par with present-day knowledge and craftsmanship (see *Figure 23*).

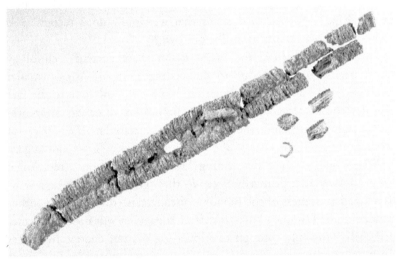

Figure 23—Harappan copper-alloy exceptionally fine wire necklace, 2500 BC. (Copyright Harappa Archaeological Research Project/Harappa.com. Courtesy Dept. of Archaeology and Museums, Govt. of Pakistan.)

Nor are finds of ancient high quality craftsmanship limited to Ancient India and Egypt. Peter Lu, a graduate student at Harvard University's Graduate School of Arts and Sciences, made a minute examination of several Chinese ceremonial stone axes dating from 4000 to 2500 BC.[3] Lu noticed that the polishing of the axes had resulted in a "mirror-like luster." Conventional wisdom has it that the ancient artisans used sand, which is primarily composed of quartz, to polish stone. Lu, however, using X-ray diffraction, electron microprobe analysis, and scanning electron microscopy, determined that the axe heads had been polished using a substance much harder than quartz, in fact as hard as diamond—and that furthermore, the ancient ceremonial axe heads had a polished surface superior to surfaces polished using modern techniques involving the use of diamond polishing compounds.

Descending Dwapara Yuga technology was simple by today's standards, but inexplicably more advanced than mainstream archeological theory can explain. Perhaps, had their population pressures been as great as ours are today, the people of descending Dwapara Yuga would have had more need for technological inventions. It also remains quite possible that there was more technological inventiveness than we know of in descending Dwapara Yuga, evidence for which is yet to be found or which has returned to dust, or that we simply don't recognize as technology because it is so unlike our own.

However, we believe the main reason more ancient technology hasn't been found isn't due to descending Dwapara Yuga's smaller population and lack of infrastructure, but is primarily due to the fact that descending Dwapara Yuga man's application of energy awareness took a significantly different turn than ours has to date. *Life force*, not atomic force, was the energy of choice in descending Dwapara Yuga.

When man entered descending Dwapara Yuga from Treta Yuga, his needs were met primarily *inwardly* through mental powers; a well-developed awareness of the life force already existed. We, on the other hand, entered Dwapara Yuga from Kali Yuga when our needs were met primarily *outwardly* through manipulating matter; energy awareness was nonexistent.

Descending Dwapara Yuga man adapted to the loss of his mental powers by using his already well-developed awareness of life force in an *inward* way similar to that of his Treta Yuga forebears. Ascending Dwapara Yuga man, on the other hand, adapted his newfound awareness of energy to manipulating matter more effectively in an outward way similar to his Kali Yuga forebears.

Thus our culture has gravitated to expressing its energy awareness through technology; descending Dwapara Yuga culture gravitated to expressing its energy awareness though the personal application of life force—what we think of today as *magic*. Magic, in all its forms and uses, is really nothing more than the methodical application of energy to affect the material world—but in the case of magic it is the application of inner, subtle energy, or *life force*, not electromagnetic or nuclear forces.

Magic

Magic was a way of life in descending Dwapara Yuga. We consistently find evidence, woven through the ancient cultures of Egypt, India, China and the Near East, of the everyday use of magic. The idea of priests blessing the fields to aid the crops seems quaint and superstitious to us today. But ancient texts indicate the magical blessings of the priests carried real power, and were as effective as the pesticides and fertilizers we use today. Magical charms and potions seem hopelessly backward to us today. But the subtle energies psychically trained healers impregnated them with were as effective in healing as modern drugs are for us today. The idea of the Ark of the Covenant being used as a weapon is the stuff of Indiana Jones fantasy today. But powerful individuals were able to focus their energy through such physical objects such as spears, swords, and bows to transform them into devastating weapons.

Magic wasn't just a collection of practices. Magic was a worldview. Descending Dwapara Yuga man not only understood that the physical world was sustained by energy, he *experienced* energy directly. The practice of magic was the practical expression of that experiential awareness.

We are conditioned to believe that magic is a con job, trickery, or illusion—or even evil. Our negative conditioning reflects magic's fall into disrepute during Kali Yuga, long after its widespread and dominant use in descending Dwapara Yuga. Once descending Dwapara Yuga's energy awareness vanished, Kali Yuga "magicians" resorted to illusions and tricks. Also during Kali Yuga, magic and magical practices were condemned by the rising monotheistic and highly exclusive religions of Christianity and Islam. Magic was branded as idolatrous, evil, and demonic because magic's uses were woven together with the worship of pre-Christian and pre-Islamic gods.

Our negative perception of magic is further compounded by the real presence of a dark side—comparable to modern technology's dark side: biological weapons, poison gas, "suitcase" nuclear bombs. Magic's dark side included ways to harm or kill other people, and the deliberate unleashing of negative energies for personal gain or power. But we should remember that magic, like technology, is only a means to affect the material world. How magic, like technology, has been used

to affect the material world comes down to the motivations of its practitioners and is not inherent in the magic itself.

Unlike Treta Yuga's mental powers, Dwapara Yuga magic required a
material methodology to be effective. Magical instruments were needed: the staff or rod, which eventually became known as the "magic
wand"; the location, such as temple sites with elaborate geometric lay-
outs and symbols; physical objects to focus upon, which eventually
came to be known as "charms"; complex rituals, involving fire, water,
air, and earth; and, of course, the formulae of chanted sounds and
mantras, which eventually came to be known as "spells."

The methodical use of life force, in combination with these specialized material aids, is, in a real sense, the dominant "technology" of
descending Dwapara Yuga. Nor was the practice of magic mysterious
or shrouded in secrecy, as it became in Kali Yuga. Magic was ordinary,
everyday. The methodical use of life force was as ubiquitous as material
technology is for us today. For example, medical practices, recognizable to us even today, were widespread in ancient Egypt, India, and
China—yet much that we consider magic is woven inextricably into
these medical practices.

The Edwin Smith Papyrus, which dates to sixteenth century BC
Egypt, but is believed to have been based on material from a thousand
years earlier, is a description of trauma treatment—especially surgery.
It includes physical examination, treatment, and prognosis. Practices
include suturing, preventing and curing infection with honey and moldy
bread, stemming bleeding, and immobilizing the body for head and
spinal cord injuries. The Edwin Smith Papyrus also reveals a great deal
of anatomical knowledge, including descriptions of the meninges and
external surface of the brain, cerebrospinal fluid, and intracranial pulsa-
tions. The heart, blood vessels, liver, spleen, kidneys, and ureter were
described in some detail. Yet for every practice recognizable to modern medicine, the Edwin Smith Papyrus additionally specifies spells,
potions, charms, and prayers to the gods as aids to the healing process.

Ayurveda, India's ancient system of medicine and health, has its origin in the Atharva Veda. The dating of the Atharva Veda is difficult,
tied as it is to the dating of the other Vedas. But it is safe to say that it
was composed either shortly before, or sometime during, descending
Dwapara Yuga. The *Sushruta Samhita*, a compendium of *Ayurvedic*

practices, contains descriptions of 1,120 illnesses, 700 medicinal plants, 64 mineral preparations, and 57 preparations made from animal sources. Among the 1,120 illnesses described are angina pectoris, diabetes, and hypertension; surgeries described include plastic surgery, cataract surgery, treatment of fractures, and cesarean sections. And, like the practices described in the Edwin Smith Papyrus, woven throughout the *Sushruta Samhita* are mantras, meditations, prayers, rituals, and astrological aids to the healing process.

Based on the discovery of stone acupuncture needles, acupuncture in China is believed to have been practiced by at least 3000 BC. Acupuncture is part of what is known as Traditional Chinese Medicine (TCM), and includes Chi Gong, the meditative practice of directing the life force (Chi) within the body, Tai Chi Chuan, a system of slow and deliberate movements focused on the Chi to promote health and longevity, and Chiatsu (also spelled Shiatsu) massage which, like acupuncture, works with opening channels and promoting the flow of life force throughout the body. And again, as is true with ancient Egyptian medicine and Ayurveda, woven through TCM are myriad practices for attuning oneself to subtle forces that promote health.

Nor can we any longer view the subtle or "magical" side of these practices as merely superstition. The Chinese practice of acupuncture and some of the subtle practices of Ayurveda have undergone a renaissance over the last century, and have gained wide acceptance in the West. Our modern scientific understanding is still catching up with how they work, but there appears no longer any doubt that they do work. TCM and Ayurveda both present a view of health based on the free flow of life force. Now that people in our modern society are becoming more aware of the subtle energies flowing through their bodies, these ancient systems are being embraced once again.

The use of magic in the ancient world was by no means confined to healing. In hundreds of Egyptian documents, including the *Egyptian Book of the Dead* and *The Pyramid Texts* can be found descriptions of the divine potency from which magic arose (identified particularly with the goddess *Heka*), specific rituals for specific needs (known as *Seshaw*), sacred texts that recorded the rituals (known as *Rw*), and medicinal prescriptions (known as *Pekhret*). The use of magic as detailed in these documents covered the full gamut of human activities—the pursuit of love, wealth, family, safety, health, and well-being. Egyptian life was steeped in the use of magic.

Magi, a priestly title etymologically linked to the word magic, comes from the tradition of Zoroastrianism. Among several candidates for the historical Zoroaster—the name "Zoroaster" was probably a title—the earliest appears to date to the fourth millennium BC[4]. Zoroastrianism was centered in what is now Iran, but its influence was probably much wider. The tenets and practices of Zoroastrianism share many similarities with the Vedic practices of ancient India, including the concept of *dharma* (called *asha* in Zoroastrianism) and most pertinently, in regard to magic, the use of chants—or as they later came to be known, incantations—for various purposes both spiritual and mundane. Such practices express the magic-based worldview of descending Dwapara Yuga.

Similarly, the Atharva Veda, the last of the four Vedas, presents subtle solutions for all aspects of life. There are spells for warding off female rivals and spells for overcoming baldness. There are rituals and mantras for making weapons more powerful and rituals and mantras for ensuring bounteous crops. There are spells for the first tooth of a baby and spells to regain a kingship.

The Atharva Veda and the Egyptian Rw provided detailed descriptions for the use of magic. They were "technical manuals" on how to direct subtle forces to achieve desired outcomes. Some practices required priests specially trained in their use, but most of the rituals were for ordinary people to use in the ordinary course of their lives.

Today, magic is largely considered to be superstitious belief, with no actual efficacy. But numerous accounts from antiquity indicate that magic worked well and was used widely. In the Hebraic tradition, Moses and Aaron came before the Pharaoh to try to convince him that he should give the Israelites their freedom. During the audience, Aaron turned his staff into a snake. Pharaoh's magicians also turned their staffs into snakes, but Aaron's snake defeated theirs. What is interesting in this story is the acceptance that these powers existed—that Pharaoh's magicians *could* actually turn their staffs into snakes. Moses and Aaron did not try to unmask the Pharaoh's magicians as frauds. Instead they tried to convince Pharaoh that the magic Aaron performed was more powerful than the magic *his* magicians could perform.

Magic was also quite practical. The illustration below (see *Figure 24*)—dating from descending Dwapara Yuga—shows an Egyptian who has hired boatmen to ferry his cattle across the crocodile-infested Nile. One of the boatmen is making a gesture to cast a protective spell over the smiling animals—while the crocodile rests contentedly on the riverbed.

Scene from Fifth Dynasty Mastaba of Ti at Sakkara.

Figure 24—An Egyptian boatman uses magic to protect cattle crossing the Nile. (Image in public domain, as per Greg Reeder, 8/26/10.)

We know from various records that magic was methodically applied to healing, building wealth, daily life, and warfare. So it is not a great stretch to imagine that magic may be the answer to some of the unsolved mysteries of descending Dwapara Yuga.

Of enduring fascination is how ancient man managed to move and accurately place enormous blocks of stone. The lintels of Stonehenge, each weighing up to 50 tons (100,000 pounds), are placed over two standing stones that rise to 20 feet in the air. The granite blocks in the ceiling of the King's Chamber each weigh as much as 80 tons (160,000 pounds) and were brought from 500 miles away. The Easter Island statues, the largest of which weighs almost 90 tons (180,000 pounds), were brought from *inside* a volcanic crater several miles away.

To give these weights some perspective, a passenger car weighs up to two tons (4,000 pounds). A fully loaded truck and trailer can be up to 80 feet long and can weigh up to 40 tons (80,000 pounds). Empty railroad freight cars weigh approximately 30 tons—fully loaded they can weigh up to 140 tons (280,000 pounds). Large construction cranes or tower cranes, which you may see next to high-rise buildings under construction, typically have between 100 and 200 tons' lifting capacity. The strongest tower crane made today can lift 265 tons (530,000 pounds).

How descending Dwapara Yuga man moved the lintels of Stonehenge, the King's Chamber stones, and the Easter Island statues has attracted nearly endless speculation; the mainstream consensus is that the work was probably done with wooden rollers, levers, and ropes—an argument that has gained credibility on the basis of experimental approximations of the process. But these stones aren't even close to the biggest stone blocks ancient man is known to have moved.

It was not unusual for ancient man to move stone blocks weighing 300 or 400 tons (800,000 pounds). The largest ever found are the three stones of the Baalbek Trilithon, which form part of a massive retaining wall and platform for an ancient temple complex in what is now Lebanon. Heliopolis, a temple complex devoted to Jupiter, sat atop the Baalbeck platform around 350 BC; however archeologists agree that the temple platform, of which the Trilithon is a part, was built far earlier, sometime in descending Dwapara Yuga.

The three stones of the Baalbek Trilithon average 750 tons (1,500,000 pounds) each. Still in the quarry, mostly cut and dressed, is a fourth stone block weighing almost 1,000 tons (nearly 2,000,000 pounds) (see *Figure 25*). Not only are these stone blocks astonishingly large, but they were also transported over a mile from the quarry to the temple site.

Not only were these stones almost inconceivably massive, it should be noted that unlike the lintel stones of Stonehenge and the ceiling stones in the King's Chamber of the Great Pyramid, that needed to span a certain distance and therefore needed to be of a certain size, *there is no reason for the Baalbek Trilithon stone blocks to be so large.* The retaining wall of the temple platform at Baalbek contains other large blocks that weigh 300 to 400 tons, but most of the stone blocks used to make the retaining wall are much smaller.

Why then did they use such monumentally large stone blocks? According to current theory (assuming for the moment the theory is possible) thousands of people would have labored many weeks to move even one 750-ton stone block into place. Smaller stones occupying the same space could have been moved into place much more easily and quickly. Why use three single blocks each weighing over 1.5 million pounds?

*Figure 25—The unused stone still in the quarry near Baalbek.
Est. weight 1,000 tons. (Ralph Ellis; http://en.wikipedia.org/wiki/
File:Baalbek-stoneofpregnantwoman.jpg.)*

Perhaps the answer is simply *because they could*—and could do so without the massive physical effort currently believed necessary.

Looked at from a scientific point of view, descending Dwapara Yuga man's attunement to subtle energy, and his well-developed and methodical practice of magic, must have given him the ability to change the properties of matter, or to generate fields of energy that could affect matter. He did not generate these fields by drawing power through physical machines, as in creating a magnetic field by running electricity through wire, but by drawing subtle power through his body and/or through other physical objects.

Today we have immensely heavy maglev (magnetically levitating) trains that "float" on magnetic fields. You may have seen an object "floating" inside large electro-magnets—perhaps some poor frog, lazily spinning in the intense magnetic field. Perhaps in descending Dwapara Yuga there were specialist "movers," magicians whose training was in aiding the construction of ancient structures by levitating immense stones, so that others could push or pull them into the desired position.

Admittedly, this scenario is speculation, but it is informed speculation. Remember, the notion that thousands of people managed to drag a block of stone weighing 1.5 million pounds over a mile, using only ropes and wooden rollers, is also speculation. There is no record of how the work was actually done. Deliberately quarrying stones so large that moving them would absorb every able-bodied person for miles around and many weeks of labor—such a project seems pretty stupid, especially if, as in the case of the Baalbek Trilithon, stones of such massive dimensions were not a structural requirement.

Another enduring mystery that might have a magical explanation are the Nazca Lines, located in Peru's Nazca plateau. Hundreds of these "lines" run across the high Nazca plateau. These lines are actually shallow trenches exposing the lighter colored limestone beneath the surface. The "lines" form pictures of various animals, such as the hummingbird pictured below, and geometric shapes. Other lines run straight for miles—very straight—even over small rises and gullies.

The mystery is that one can only recognize the shapes from hundreds of feet in the air. Seen from ground level, the trenches appear to be randomly placed and directed. But viewed from a plane or helicopter the lines become "drawings"—many of animals—birds, monkeys, spiders (see *Figure 26*).

The Nazca Lines, like all stone structures, are very difficult to date using present scientific methods. There are signs of human habitation near the lines, but no way to determine whether the inhabitants were the builders. Conjectures about the time of excavation range from as late as 1500 AD to as early as 2500 BC.

Explanations for how ancient man viewed the lines vary enormously. Some maintain that the lines were shamanistic, had their own power and purpose, and weren't meant to be seen. Perhaps the most famous theory is that they were made by ancient astronauts or alien visitors to be seen from spacecraft. Another possible viewpoint, more in keeping with Sri Yukteswar's explanation of the yugas, is that descending Dwapara Yuga man's use of magic allowed him to levitate—perhaps even to levitate some kind of platform from which to enjoy the view.

We are, of course, speculating. Yet the Nazca Lines clearly need to be viewed from a great height. There are no nearby hills from which they can be seen. After all, the question of their significance did not emerge in our era until they were observed from airplanes!

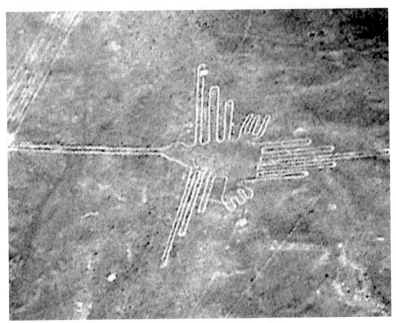

Figure 26—Stylized hummingbird seen from hundreds of feet above the Nazca plain in Peru. (Photo by Martin St-Amant, Creative Commons.)

In our Dwapara Yuga future, man may yet turn more to the inward use of life force; he may yet accomplish what would today seem "magical." As we described in earlier chapters on ascending Dwapara Yuga, we are even now seeing a steady increase in the awareness and use of life force. The feats of athletes and martial artists grow steadily more astounding, healing through stimulation of the *life force* is gaining more and more adherents, and telekinesis, though still a rarity, is also becoming better understood and practiced, as is amply demonstrated in PEAR's experiments.

However, such inward use of life force was the starting point for descending Dwapara Yuga man. In the early centuries of descending Dwapara Yuga, magic would have been in common use. It was a way of life. Descending Dwapara Yuga man would have given the use of magic no more notice than we give technology when we step into a car and drive, or watch a live newscast from the other side of the earth. Magic was simply how things were done.

Descending Dwapara Yuga was profoundly shaped by the individual's use of subtle powers. The material technology that did exist, although sometimes revealing advanced knowledge, was for the most part simple. Technology, in applications from medicine to warfare, was mixed with magic, and, indeed, took second place to magic.

Today, using technology based on the insight that all matter is condensed energy, we are able to convert matter to energy and, in certain instances, energy to matter. The inherent mutability of matter that these feats reveal was exploited *intuitively and magically* in descending Dwapara Yuga, rather than *scientifically and technologically* as they are today. But the same laws of energy, laws that underlie all matter, govern both approaches.

Chapter 18

Descending Dwapara Yuga —
Trends

Timeline

3,100 BC Beginning of the most recent descending Dwapara Yuga

2,900 BC End of the 200-year transition period (*sandhi*) from descending Treta Yuga

900 BC Beginning of 200-year transition period (*sandhi*) to descending Kali Yuga

700 BC End of the most recent descending Dwapara Yuga

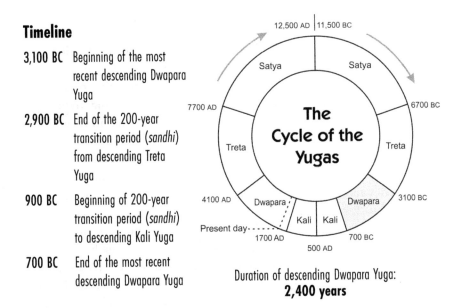

Duration of descending Dwapara Yuga:
2,400 years

Dwapara Yuga is characterized not only by energy awareness, but also by *self-interest*. In Chapter 3, we described some of the most influential trends that have occurred in our era with the emergence of *self-interest*. One in particular stands out—the rise of commerce. Perhaps no other single activity has shaped the twentieth and now twenty-first century more significantly. Our world has become one interconnected economy, and commerce has become a primary driver of the development of our technology and culture.

Going hand in hand with the emergence of commerce is the emergence of cities. Based on recently published worldwide figures, for the first time in recorded history more people live in cities than in the country—and the trend is only accelerating. Quite simply, cities currently provide the most energized and fluid environment for Dwapara Yuga man's *self-interest* to go to work. It should come as no surprise then that at the beginning of *descending* Dwapara Yuga, when man's motivation became more self-interested, there was a similar burst of growth in both commerce and cities.

The Rise of Cities and Commerce

What archeologists think of as the beginning of civilization (the rise of Sumeria, the Indus Valley Civilization, and Egypt in the period between 3300 and 2900 BC), was in fact the beginning of complex cities. As we explored in the final chapter on descending Treta Yuga, the concept of the Neolithic Revolution, when mankind is supposed to have made a great leap forward because of the confluence of such developments as agriculture, animal domestication, pottery, and the plough, appears not to hold together. Most, if not all, of the key discoveries and developments had already been present for millennia.

Why then the abrupt shift to city living, stratified societies, overproduction of food and other goods for the purpose of trade or export? Archeologists take the view that man was finally *able* to do these things—that he was using recent inventions to new advantage. Our study of the yugas tell us that man suddenly *wanted* to do these things—that he was using inventions known for millennia in new ways to suit his new motivation.

A number of cities, large settlements actually, existed prior to the beginning of descending Dwapara Yuga, but an entirely new breed of city sprang up with the advent of Dwapara Yuga. These were larger and more complex—and built around commerce. Many had shared granaries, artisans' districts, and market places, and were typically built on trade routes along rivers and coasts.

We see the first significant division of labor and societal stratification in these cities as well. Artisan, scribe, and trader became increasingly common occupations. And there was, of course, the tax collector.

Governments began levying taxes on commerce, as they had already levied taxes on agriculture.

Sumeria and the city of Eridu are generally credited with being the first of the trend. Eridu is believed to have risen along the banks of the Euphrates River around 3300 BC. The famous city of Ur and dozens of others sprang up in the Tigris and Euphrates Valleys over the next 300–400 years, and Babylon was not far behind.

The rise of Indus Valley Civilization, whose principal cities include Harappa and Mohenjo-daro, also began about 3300 BC; as in Sumeria, dozens more cities soon sprang up along the Indus River, quickly establishing a trading region of over 100,000 square miles.

After Menes, the first ruler of the First Dynasty of Egypt, united Upper and Lower Egypt in 3100 BC, cities such as Memphis and Abydos quickly grew along the Nile. The first cities of the Minoan civilization of Crete began sometime around 3200 BC. The ancient city of Troy on the coast of the Anatolian Peninsula began in approximately 3000 BC.

Nor was the sudden growth of cities confined to the Near East and Indus Valley. Some of the first recognized cities of China, such as Ningbo and Chang'an, came to prominence in the period from 3000 to 2000 BC. We even find the trend across the ocean in South America. The city of Caral, on the Pacific coast of what is now Peru, began about 3000 BC. Caral was the principal among many other trading cities of the Norte Chico civilization.

Commerce shaped the societal development and structure of these ancient cities. Harappa, Mohenjo-daro, and other Indus Valley Civilization cities had a common building style. Along the main streets, hundreds of buildings, especially those nearest the city centers, had living quarters built over shops. One of the most distinctive types of artifact found in the Indus Valley Civilization is the personal seal. Tens of thousands of different cylindrical seals have been found in Harappa and Mohenjo-daro alone. The seals were rolled over clay or wax to make a distinct impression for marking and sealing the goods on which the seal was affixed. At its peak, in roughly 2600 BC, the Indus Valley Civilization had spread to Northern India, Afghanistan, and Iran and covered over a million square miles. Judging by the sheer quantity of seals found in Harappa and Mohenjo-daro, trade was not limited to a few merchants or the rulers. The large number of seals suggests that what we might think of as the average citizen could, and did, engage in trade.

Commerce also drove the early development of writing. The Sumerian writing system, generally known as cuneiform and believed to be the first form of writing, evolved from a system of clay tokens originally used to represent trade goods. Cuneiform's first uses were largely accounting and record keeping. Only later did it develop into a general purpose writing system. The Indus script, or Harappan script, as it is also called, is actually a collection of the symbols taken from the thousands of commercial seals already mentioned. Many of the earliest examples of "documents," clay tablets from Sumeria and hieroglyphs from Egypt, are commercial records—warehouse lists and lists of transactions. The earliest scribes, people whose specialized occupation was writing, were occupied almost exclusively in recording taxes, maintaining inventory lists, and accounting for commercial transactions.

By the middle of descending Dwapara Yuga, around 2000 BC, trade was commonplace from the Far East to the Near East. There is evidence that many kinds of food, livestock, oils, timber, textiles, dyes, silk, spices, gold, silver, copper, tin, ivory, ebony, and gems were traded freely across an area of millions and millions of square miles, encompassing thousands of cities from China to Egypt. Cities rose to power and prominence on their commercial success. By 1700 BC, Babylon was the largest city in the world, and, eclipsing the once wealthy Ur, dominated trade in the Euphrates River valley.

Trade, and the accumulation of wealth, continued to dominate activity throughout descending Dwapara Yuga, but toward the waning centuries, worldwide trade began to diminish due to war. In descending Kali Yuga, the Greeks and Romans traded only with Egypt, Persia, and the rest of the Roman Empire. By the Dark Ages, approximately 500 AD to 1000 AD, civilization was at its lowest ebb and traffic along traditional trade routes had trickled to a halt. The Silk Road to China was rarely traveled. Spices were virtually unknown in Europe. Awareness of other cultures became dim, spawning fanciful tales of giants and monsters living in other parts of the world. It wasn't until the fourteenth century AD and the era of Marco Polo that such trade routes as the by then fabled Silk Road began to reopen. The Age of the Explorers began in the fifteenth and sixteenth centuries; knowledge of the wider world returned. By then, the brisk trade of three thousand years before had been long forgotten.

We can easily see why archeologists and historians consider the birth of civilization to have come in the early centuries of Dwapara

Yuga. That is when people started behaving as we do now! — keeping written records, having specialized occupations, working hard to get ahead, seeking material wealth. Sound familiar?

Quality of Life

Our age is so accustomed to the steadily improving quality of life of the last several centuries. Most people assume that the farther back in time one goes, the more squalid and primitive the life of the average person would have been. Such an assumption is accurate as far back as the Dark Ages. In the Dark Ages life expectancy was very short, living conditions were extremely poor, medicine was barely practiced, and human rights were non-existent.

But if we go even further back in time to descending Dwapara Yuga, living conditions were surprisingly good. Ancient Egypt had courts of law, individual land ownership, legal contracts, medical treatises and physicians, cosmetics, board games, and children's toys. There is little evidence of the modern conveniences that we currently consider indispensible to a comfortable life, but the average descending Dwapara Yuga man appears to have enjoyed plenty to eat, good health, physical safety, personal possessions, the opportunity for wealth, and the enjoyment of personal freedom.

Pictured below are examples of frescoes found among the ruins of the Minoan civilization, which began in approximately 3000 BC (see *Figure 27*). The Minoan culture was centered on the island of Crete in the Mediterranean, but spread to many nearby islands, such as Santorini, the scene of the catastrophic volcanic explosion believed to have ended their civilization in 1500 BC.

The women and scenes depicted in these frescoes express beauty, ease, refinement, and contentment — not qualities most people associate with life in the ancient past. Acrotiri, a Minoan site on the ill-fated island of Santorini, had water closets (a type of indoor toilet) and hot and cold running water — the hot water provided by a nearby geothermal source. We can appreciate from the frescoes that the Minoans had a well-developed sense of beauty, could produce sophisticated clothing and jewelry, were no strangers to makeup, and that the profession of the hair dresser is very ancient.

Although the hieroglyphic style renders the human form very stiffly, the scene of Queen Nefertari (thirteenth century BC) playing the board game Senet suggests she didn't live as stiffly as she was painted (see *Figure 28*). Museums contain many other board games from Mesopotamia; chess is believed to have originated in India during descending Dwapara Yuga.

It is popularly assumed that the average person in descending Dwapara Yuga was subject to a lord or ruler as he was in the feudal system of medieval Europe. Records of life in Egypt indicate that this may not have been the case. Legal records indicate a system of individual ownership of the fields along the Nile. Then as today, taxes were levied on farmers and merchants. Individuals had redress in a court system that based its decisions on precedents and existing laws.

Figure 28 — (left) Queen Nefertari playing Senet (Public domain, Yorck Project); (right) a Senet board. (Photo, taken at the Brooklyn Museum, courtesy of Deror Avi.)

Indentured servitude existed in Egypt, but was voluntary. Indentured servants could own property and enter into contracts on their own; their children did not automatically become slaves. Many very powerful people were indentured servants.

We described in the previous chapter the methodical practice of medicine in ancient Egypt, India, and China. Popularized horrors of ancient medicine such as blood-letting or giving patients concoctions of ground gems were actually practices of Kali Yuga. Dwapara Yuga medicine showed awareness of the laws of health; medical practices appear to have been both advanced and subtle.

Hollywood — not scholarship — is responsible for popular images of vicious overseers wielding whips to drive hapless thousands of slaves to build the Great Pyramid. The fragments of documents, the art work and artifacts that we have from descending Dwapara Yuga paint a very different picture. Society was ordered and civil. Individuals had rights that were respected and defended. Commerce and the pursuit of wealth were the primary drivers of behavior. Health, well-being, and pleasure were quite attainable.

Spoken Language

Recent scholarship has traced the first instance of the widely spread story of the "Confusion of Tongues"—usually associated with the Tower of Babel—to the reign of Peleg in Mesopotamia around 3000 BC. Mankind's relatively sudden need to rely on speech, after so many millennia of telepathic communication, would naturally have led to stories about the transition. Within a span of five centuries (the combination of the two transition periods (*sandhis*), from Treta Yuga to Dwapara Yuga—3400 to 2900 BC), mankind went from a single universal mental language of thoughts, images, and symbols, to many separate spoken languages.

Basics of human language such as syntax, structure, and vocabulary would have to have developed quickly. Geographically distant groups of people who previously shared the ability to communicate telepathically *and* over long distances, would have been cut off one from another. Finding themselves suddenly isolated, they would likely have developed independent approaches to spoken language.

This picture of the rapid development of language is, in fact, borne out in the study of historical linguistics. Languages contain their history in their spelling, vocabulary, and usage. Linguists have identified only a small number of proto-languages (seminal languages), from which all the languages we know today have descended, including Proto-Indo-European (India, Near East, and Europe), Proto-Sino-Tibetan (China, Mongolia, Tibet), and Proto-Arabic (Arabia, Egypt, North Africa). All known languages descend from a small number of these proto-languages and trace their development to an earliest vocabulary and structure—and to nearly the same time period—middle to late descending Treta Yuga.

If the mainstream theory of linear development were true, we would not expect all the world's languages to have evolved from so few seminal languages in such a short period of time. If, as the linear theory of human development would have us believe, mankind was dispersed across the world in tens of thousands of small groups of hunter-gatherers for at least 60,000 years prior to the birth of civilization, then the roots of our languages should be untraceable, let alone traceable to a double handful of proto-languages. If the linear theory were true, then languages should be fuzzy, complicated agglomerations of syntax and vocabulary contributed to by the thousands of small hunter-gatherer bands, each of which had evolved its speech independently; current languages should be more like English, which has borrowed grammar, syntax, and vocabulary from thousands of sources.

Yet such is not the case.

The double handful of proto-languages, from which all other languages descended, all seem to have been fairly coherent and well-formed by sometime during descending Treta Yuga or the beginning of descending Dwapara Yuga. The linguistic evidence is consistent with highly intelligent people recognizing the need for spoken languages and developing them deliberately, methodically, and relatively quickly.

As mentioned in a preceding chapter, the grammar and syntax of Sanskrit appear deliberately constructed to enable subtle nuanced communication of spiritual subjects. Up to the end of descending Treta Yuga Sanskrit remained a sacred language used only for chanting. But with the waning of Treta Yuga man's telepathic capability, Sanskrit was pressed into service as an all-purpose language. Sanskrit rapidly devolved into many hundreds of languages and dialects and reached the largest number of variations in Kali Yuga. During Kali Yuga, India alone had over 600 languages and dialects, at least 400 of which had descended from Sanskrit.

In our era the trend is reversing. As we progress into ascending Dwapara Yuga, many dialects, and even complete languages, are dying out. Lamented by some, this trend nonetheless seems inexorable, an expression of exponentially increasing worldwide communication. Linguists predict that at our present rate of change, a hundred years from now may see only a handful of spoken languages — a reversal of the trend of descending Dwapara Yuga, and a foreshadowing of a time when mankind once again speaks one shared, telepathic language.

It is interesting to note that linguists have long wondered why spoken language was so slow to develop even though individual and group interaction had been commonplace for a very long time beforehand. It is difficult to reconcile the existence of sophisticated artifacts from the fourth to tenth millennia BC—sacred sites, settlements with thousands of people, advanced cave paintings, elaborately made statues, and beautiful carvings of gods and goddesses—with a very crude level of communication. As in our examination of the theory of the Neolithic Revolution, we have to conclude either that man was incredibly stupid, or that there is something wrong with the current theory of the development of language. Spoken languages proliferated rapidly at the beginning of descending Dwapara Yuga—not because man suddenly *figured out* how to communicate, but because man suddenly *needed* to communicate via the spoken language.

Overcoming the Limitations of Space

In our ascending Dwapara Yuga era we are overcoming the limitations of space by instantaneous communication, increasingly rapid transportation, perhaps one day even instantaneous travel.

Just as descending Dwapara Yuga man channeled his energy awareness in a different, more *inward* way than ours—magic rather than technology—so too he took a more inward approach to overcoming the limitations of space. Through our ascending Dwapara Yuga technology, we have overcome the limitations of space that are created by *distance*. The people of descending Dwapara Yuga, on the other hand, overcame the limitations of space that are created by space itself—the *barrier* between the physical world and the energy world.

Modern physics continues to wrestle with the yet unsolved problem of how the physical universe suddenly sprang into being. What is the source of the almost inconceivable amount of energy that condensed into the physical matter of the universe? It is all very well to say that the starting point was the big bang, but what fueled the big bang?

More recently, physics is wrestling with the conundrum that there simply isn't enough matter in the universe to account for very basic behaviors of the universe on an astronomical scale. For example, the known laws of gravitation, applied to the visible matter in the universe, should long ago have resulted in a significant slowing of the expansion of the universe, perhaps even a contraction. But the universe has continued its rapid expansion.

The two leading explanations for the universe's continued rapid expansion are the theories of dark matter and dark energy. They are called "dark" because they are theorized to be undetectable by any known means. They are there, but we can't measure them. Current theories posit that dark matter and dark energy account for 96% of the universe's gravitational effect—21% dark matter and 75% dark energy. Dark energy is theorized to be a force with properties fundamentally different from those of any known type of energy. Most significantly, dark energy repulses rather than attracts—thus *pushing* the stars apart.

Think about that for a moment. Physicists cannot account for 96% of the matter and energy that makes up the universe and that determines its gravitational behavior—and 75% of the universe is comprised of a mysterious energy, one that behaves unlike any known force and that is causing our universe to expand rapidly.

Also on the frontier of physics is string theory, which suggests that all matter may arise from a substrate of energy—strings and rings of energy vibrating at a wavelength too short to be detectable by any *physical* instrument.

Modern physics may be on the brink of deducing an energy universe that sustains and interpenetrates the physical. Ancient teachings in India, China, and the Near East, described such a realm long, long ago. What is more, they described space as a *perceptual barrier, a veil* that separates the physical universe from the energy universe. As long as we rely on sensory perception alone, we cannot know anything beyond space's limitations; but awareness of subtle energy, of life force, can allow us to pierce the veil of space.

The ancient teachings of the East do not stop at merely positing the realm of energy. They describe it as an astral heaven—subtle, often beautiful, and infinitely mutable—and a destination on the soul's long journey—in fact, a recurring destination on the soul's long journey.

Christianity and Islam, whose tenets and dogmas were formed during Kali Yuga, stand in contrast to nearly every other, much older religious tradition in one key area—reincarnation. The religious beliefs of nearly half the world's population include the concept that we live and die many times in a long process of spiritual development and final redemption.

Concomitant with the belief in reincarnation we often find the belief that it is possible to communicate with those who have passed on. In the West, bringing up this subject is likely to make people back away from you rather quickly! Nonetheless, we have solid evidence that the people of descending Dwapara Yuga not only believed in reincarnation, but also developed systematic and successful ways to communicate with their ancestors and other departed souls.

In China, archeologists have unearthed over 20,000 "oracle bones," used during the Shang Dynasty (eighteenth to twelfth century BC) to communicate with ancestors. Significant matters were weighed and decided upon based on communication with the departed through the oracle bones. In China during this period, communication between the earthbound and those that had gone on before was believed to be a perfectly normal part of everyday life.

Contemporaneous with the use of oracle bones was the Chinese practice of the *shi*, or *personator*. An ancestral spirit would enter the *shi* (someone trained as a medium) and would eat and drink with the family while telling them of his new life on the other side. Even today reverence for ancestors runs strong in Chinese culture. Many families maintain an altar to their ancestors, and make offerings to them in such celebrations as the annual *Ghost Festival*.

Egypt, as many scholars observe, was preoccupied with the afterlife. By the Middle Kingdom (approximately 2000 to 1600 BC), Egyptian burial customs had become extremely elaborate—and not only for those of wealth and standing. The process of mummification, the pictures and symbols placed on the walls of tombs and on the inside of sarcophagi, and elaborate magic rituals performed for the dead, as expressed in such texts as the *Egyptian Book of the Dead*—all derive from the immediacy of their awareness of the energy realms, or astral heavens, to which they believed they would go after death.

Nor was the awareness limited to the living. An Egyptian papyrus tells the story of Ramses III (1194–1163 BC), who was a victim of a harem conspiracy. *After his death Ramses initiated a lawsuit!* Through an oracle he communicated orders for the court to convene an inquiry into the crime. He testified as to the specific individuals involved and detailed their deeds. The court duly convicted and sentenced the conspirators.

Even today, the succession of Lamas in Tibetan Buddhism is based on finding children who display knowledge of the life and personal effects of previous lamas. Indian news frequently carries stories of children remembering previous lives. In one story, a child of three or four described a life he had led in a nearby village. He described the home he had lived in and, most tellingly, the secret place where he had hidden his money. His parents took him to the village, and to the astonishment of all, the child found a cleverly hidden cache of money.

Quite recently, Andrea and Bruce Leininger's *Soul Survivor: The Reincarnation of a World War II Fighter Pilot* caused a sensation in America. The book convincingly tells the story of their young American child's memories of a previous life as a WWII fighter pilot. His memories are not vague. He remembers the name of the ship he served on, the type of plane he flew, and the specific circumstances of his death. All of his specific memories have been corroborated.

The people of Dwapara Yuga not only pierced the veil of space to communicate with their ancestors, but their innate awareness of the energy realm was fundamental to their ability to work magic. Awareness of one's life force (the microcosm) is just one side of the coin. The other side of the coin is awareness of the energy which sustains the physical universe (the macrocosm).

Furthermore, the practice of magic in descending Dwapara Yuga was closely connected to the worship of the gods—who also exist in the energy realm.

The rituals of magic drew on the powers of the gods. As we explored in chapters on descending Treta Yuga, the gods are facets of God the Spirit. The gods have no reality separate from God the Spirit, but are nonetheless unique expressions, possessing distinct elemental qualities and consciousness. In descending Treta Yuga, man's level of awareness was so high that he was, in a sense, equal with the gods. By descending Dwapara Yuga, man could still sense the presence of the gods, but had become more a supplicant than an equal.

Even so, using the aids of magic, particularly mantas and chants, with the focus and concentration brought about by ritual, Dwapara Yuga man could attune himself to the power of the gods and could then channel that power into magical uses. The most adept became elite priests and magicians. Yet even the average person, by virtue of attunement to subtle energy, could work magic with the help of attunement with the gods.

Thus ancient man overcame the limitations of space by piercing the veil between matter and energy to communicate with souls who had gone on before and by drawing on the subtle energies of the gods to aid in the use of magic. The practice of magic was itself an overcoming of the limitations of space, since magic is able to affect people and things instantly, regardless of distance.

There is an oft-quoted saying that any technology we don't understand is indistinguishable from magic. The saying often comes with stories of African natives thinking that cameras have magically captured their spirit. Yet we know the camera operates in lawful ways. We can perhaps turn this saying on its head by saying that any magic we don't understand may be indistinguishable from technology. It is simply foreign to our understanding and experience, yet operates in lawful ways.

Steady Loss of Knowledge and Energy Awareness

Just as there was a deterioration of awareness and ability from the beginning of descending Treta Yuga to its end, there was a similar deterioration of awareness and ability from the beginning of descending Dwapara Yuga to its end.

Over the 2400-year span of descending Dwapara Yuga, the quality of structures and artifacts clearly declined. The extensive archeological study of the last 150 to 200 years in Egypt clearly makes the decline especially apparent. Egyptologists often comment that the quality of the structures and artifacts of the Pre-Dynastic and Old Kingdom periods (approximately 3200 to 2500 BC) is much higher than that of the Middle and New Kingdom periods (approximately 2000 to 1000 BC).

The Great Pyramid is an obvious example. More than 100 other pyramids were built after it, but none match the quality of the Great Pyramid and the other Pyramids of Giza. Most people don't even know these later pyramids existed, mostly because there is often little left to be seen. Below (see *Figure 29*) is an example of a pyramid from 400–500 years after the pyramids of Giza (built for Sahure, Fifth Dynasty), and another example from 500 years after the first (built for Amenemhet I, Twelfth Dynasty).

The quality of the pyramids built after the Pyramids of Giza falls far short of the standard established at Giza. They are now mostly reduced to rubble. Built on poor foundations, weakened by building shortcuts and inferior quality limestone, the remnants, like the pyramid of Amenemhet I pictured below, are today nearly unrecognizable as pyramids. More than 100 locations have been identified as pyramid sites — all that remains of most are indistinct mounds.

Similarly, the high quality of the artifacts of the early centuries of descending Dwapara Yuga was never equaled later in the yuga. As already mentioned in the previous chapter, many Egyptian statues from the early centuries of descending Dwapara Yuga had eerily lifelike crystal eyes. By the Middle Kingdom era (2000 to 1600 BC), this practice had died out and the eyes on statues were painted.

Figure 29 — (left) Sahure's pyramid, of the Fifth Dynasty, built approximately 2500 BC; (right) the Amenemhet I pyramid, of the Twelfth Dynasty, built approximately 1970 BC. (Both photos courtesy of Jon Bodsworth.)

The Indus Valley Civilization follows the same pattern. Around 1900 BC, the heartland of the Indus Valley Civilization was abandoned because of the drying up of the Saraswati River. Even then, only halfway through descending Dwapara Yuga, the construction techniques had degenerated.

When Harappa and Mohenjo-daro were first built, in approximately 3300 BC, the cities showed a marked sophistication — rectilinear street plans, standardized bricks, running water, planned sewerage, well-organized central areas including public baths, government buildings, and plazas. By 2000 BC, other Indus Valley Civilization cities were built with far less organization and quality.

The most pronounced evidence of decline is to be found in spiritual awareness and in the way magic was used. In the opening centuries of descending Dwapara Yuga, magic mantras and rituals were practical extensions of the worship of the gods, and the worship of the gods, in its highest expression, was a means to commune with God the Spirit, from which the gods arose. We could say that the power to use magic was a byproduct of early Dwapara Yuga man's sensitive attunement to the gods.

Over the ensuing centuries of descending Dwapara Yuga, man's self-interest began to cloud his awareness of his divine nature. The use of magic became the primary purpose of his worship of the gods. Until, by the waning centuries of descending Dwapara Yuga, magic was used to *command* the gods. In *A History of Magic and Experimental Science*, author Lynn Thorndike writes, "In the later religion of the Egyptians ... [they] believed that they could terrify and coerce the very gods ... compelling them to appear ... or to admit the human soul to an equality with themselves."[1]

Man's increasing focus on self-interest resulted in the use of magic to coerce, harm, or even kill others. Not all denizens of the energy realm are benign. Malign spirits were summoned from the energy realm to aid in working harmful magic. This practice became part of what is known as known as black magic. The rituals of black magic included summoning malignant spirits, sacrificing animals in order to gain power, and using objects with dark associations (such as human bones) as a focus for magic. Egypt, in particular, fell into the use of black magic—a misuse of magical powers that is widely believed to have led, at the end of descending Dwapara Yuga, to Egypt's utter ruin.

The worship of the gods became also increasingly outward and complex. The number of gods proliferated in Egypt, India, and China toward the end of descending Dwapara Yuga. Egypt built many hundreds of temples to specific gods or goddesses. Each god or goddess had its own priesthood. Each priesthood developed increasingly detailed ritual.

In India, we see this trend also reflected in the proliferation of scriptures. By the end of descending Dwapara Yuga, the four Vedas had been embellished by hundreds of Upanishads and thousands of Puranas, as well as by an enormous body of other scriptures. These spiritual texts were philosophical as well as liturgical. The Puranas, especially, told story after story of the relationships of gods, demigods, and men—few of these stories had originally been in the Vedas. The canon of Vedic literature became immense.

China, too, toward the end of descending Dwapara Yuga, experienced an increasingly complex expression of the worship of the gods. In the transition (c.1600 BC) from the Xia Dynasty to the Shang Dynasty, we see that royal and priestly positions had become hereditary. Priests were no longer chosen by merit, but by birth—a trend also found in Egypt, India, and the Near East. *Outward form* had become more important than *inward attunement*.

We can see that magic's steady degeneration was accompanied by the steady decline in man's awareness of his own divine nature. The quest for personal power and personal pleasure, whether sought through magic, warfare, or commerce, dominated the last centuries of descending Dwapara Yuga—a time not unlike our own—if we think of technology as our age's equivalent to magic.

The story of Moses (from approximately 1200 BC), returning from Mt. Sinai with the Ten Commandments only to find his people dancing and reveling, worshipping the golden calf, symbolizes the state of the world in the last centuries of descending Dwapara Yuga. The golden calf represents the degraded worship of the gods and the coercive use of magic, while the revelry represents the turning away from subtle and personal spiritual awareness to embrace material pleasure.

Descending Dwapara Yuga shares many familiar trends with our ascending Dwapara Yuga. It's hard not to think that the wealthy trade barons of today would be perfectly comfortable among the wealthy trade barons of ancient Babylon. The motivations were the same, as were the rules—buy low, sell high. Nor would it be hard for the average person of today to adapt to everyday life in descending Dwapara Yuga—accumulating wealth, staying healthy, raising families, and enjoying the pleasures of life—once that average person became accustomed to the use of magic and the lack of modern conveniences!

Even less accepted in the West, but commonplace in the East, is belief in reincarnation. Western attitudes, however, are changing rapidly. The first 300 years of Dwapara Yuga (1700 AD to the present) have seen an upsurge of interest in psychic phenomena in the West. Some of the first séances in the West were popularized in the 1700s by George Lyttelton, author of *Dialogues of the Dead*. Both the Theosophical Movement and Spiritualism began in the mid-1800s. Western interest in Eastern religions—an interest that included reincarnation and psychic awareness—began with such early Indologists as Max Müller, in the middle to late 1800s.

In the twentieth century, interest in the psychic and spiritual realms has exploded. Yoga, which includes the ancient practice of physical stretches to promote subtle energy awareness, is a household word throughout the world. People turn to psychic readers with increasing regularity for insight on everything from health to love to wealth to spiritual matters. In time, as was apparently the norm in descending Dwapara Yuga, more people may become psychically aware, and may even come to accept the reality of subtle communication with those in other realms. In the U.S., according to recent surveys by the Harris Poll, 27% of the population now believes in reincarnation; the percentage has nearly doubled in only fifty years.

Although technology clearly is ascending Dwapara Yuga's most prominent feature in our time, we may see in the centuries ahead that our cultures, like those of descending Dwapara Yuga, turn to more inward methods of using energy awareness. Alternative healing practices are an early indicator of a trend we are likely to see in a variety of human endeavors. The tremendous powers of Treta Yuga and Satya Yuga man should give us the perspective that we are capable of far more than we now know. In time, our mighty technology may seem puny in comparison to what man can do unaided.

Chapter 19

Descending Dwapara Yuga —
Decline & Transition

Timeline

3,100 BC Beginning of the most recent descending Dwapara Yuga

2,900 BC End of the 200-year transition period (*sandhi*) from descending Treta Yuga

900 BC Beginning of 200-year transition period (*sandhi*) to descending Kali Yuga

700 BC End of the most recent descending Dwapara Yuga

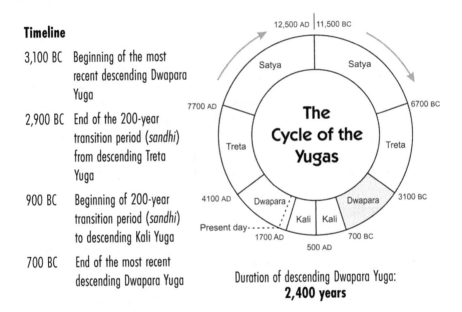

Duration of descending Dwapara Yuga:
2,400 years

Two overarching trends shape Dwapara Yuga—*energy awareness* and *self-interest*. By the ending centuries of descending Dwapara Yuga, energy awareness was decreasing and self-interest was increasing. The combination of these two trends, one waning and the other waxing, brought on the collapse of descending Dwapara Yuga cultures around the world.

The End of Magic

Descending Dwapara Yuga cultures were shaped by magic—a combination of the personal awareness of the realm of energy, attunement to the gods, and the development of individual powers derived from the use of life force. Jeremy Naydler has devoted many years to the study of the ancient Egyptian's cultural and spiritual life. Among his books are *Temple of the Cosmos* and *Shamanic Wisdom in the Pyramid Texts*. In his collected essays, *The Future of the Ancient World*, he writes, "[The ancient's] was a consciousness intent upon maintaining the presence of the gods in their experiential world ...."[1] Magic was everywhere evident.

However, as descending Dwapara Yuga drew towards its end, personal awareness of subtle energy became less and less common, and, as a result, the practice of magic gradually lost its effectiveness. Many scholars have seen the waning centuries of descending Dwapara Yuga as a time when man experienced a fundamental shift in outlook. Although he does not subscribe to the concept of descending Dwapara Yuga, British historian J. A. G. Roberts, author of *China: Prehistory to the Nineteenth Century*, writes that the fall the Shang Dynasty and the beginning of the Zhou Dynasty in 1046 BC was more than a political change: "[I]t was the end of an era. The age of magic and the belief in Shangdi, the ruler of the spirits and the ancestor of the Shang, was overturned."[2]

Imagine, if you will, that your modern conveniences gradually become less and less functional. Sometimes when you flip the switch the light comes on normally, sometimes only dimly, and finally not at all. Sometimes your car starts, and finally it doesn't. Sometimes you hear someone on your phone, and finally you hear no one. Sometimes your medicines work, and finally they don't. Were this to happen, we would be forced to abandon our entire infrastructure, our entire scientific worldview, and to start over.

We're not making a prediction, but are, rather, looking at our dependence on technology as a way to illustrate descending Dwapara Yuga man's dependence on the everyday, practical use of magic. Magic was both infrastructure and worldview. We have less energy-dependent, mechanical technologies to fall back on. Descending Dwapara Yuga man, however, once he had lost touch with energy awareness, had little to fall back on. Because his way of life was so focused on the inward application of energy awareness, he had developed little material technology. His millennia-old way of life was coming to an end, and he was ill-equipped to respond.

The problem was compounded by the fact that while magic was dying, *self-interest* was intensifying. In the early centuries of descending Dwapara Yuga, a relatively enlightened self-interest manifested as interest in trade and commerce, and a still benign, but more self-centered use of individual powers than we saw in descending Treta Yuga. During the course of descending Dwapara Yuga, however, *self-interest* became steadily more pronounced: more and more emphasis on the accumulation of wealth and on the pleasures of the material life; the increasing use of magic for personal gain and personal power—ultimately magic left moral behavior behind to become black magic. The clearest sign of the intensification of *self-interest* in the waning centuries of descending Dwapara Yuga was the dramatic increase in armed conflict and the resulting worldwide destruction.

The Bronze Age Collapse

War was not unknown even in the early and middle centuries of descending Dwapara Yuga. Some of the first defensive walls were built around the city of Uruk in Sumeria circa 3000 BC. Many Indus Valley cities were walled around 2500 BC as were Babylon and several Egyptian cities along the Nile. Many Shang Dynasty cities in China similarly were walled by 1600 BC. The horse-drawn war chariot came into its heyday by 2000 BC and was in use from China to Egypt. Bronze armor and weaponry were well-developed, as were the means to manufacture them.

Nonetheless, war was very limited in the early and middle centuries of descending Dwapara Yuga. Archeological evidence of cities destroyed by war, mass graves of war dead, or other indications of highly destructive wars is rare, some experts say nonexistent, until late in descending Dwapara Yuga.

In the *last* centuries of descending Dwapara Yuga, on the other hand, war reached new levels of aggression and destructiveness. Beginning in approximately 1200 BC, the archeological record suddenly shows hundreds of cities completely destroyed by war. Along with the evidence of widespread destruction we also find the first evidence of the use of iron.

The development of iron was a direct result of an ancient arms race. Iron implements require much greater effort and more involved methods to create than does bronze. Descending Dwapara Yuga man made the extra effort for one overriding reason — iron weapons were superior to bronze weapons. The ancient arms race, catalyzed by the collapse of the old magical way of life and by the self-interested and uncontrolled pursuit of material power and security, created so much chaos and disruption that the empires of descending Dwapara Yuga began to fall one after the other. Historians even have a name for this period — the *Bronze Age collapse.*

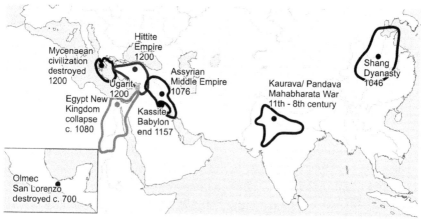

Figure 30 — Empires and kingdoms that collapsed near the close of descending Dwapara Yuga. Boundaries are based on Haywood's Historical Atlas of the Ancient World.

No civilization, culture, empire, or kingdom was untouched during this calamitous period (see *Figure 30*). Some civilizations, such as China and India, survived but fractured into many small kingdoms and dynasties. Other empires, such as Egypt, were diminished and became subject to others. Many cultures and kingdoms, such as the Hittites, Kassites, and Olmec, simply disappeared.

After more or less inheriting the culture and territory of the calamitously destroyed Minoan civilization, by 1450 BC, the prosperous Greek city of Mycenae, had gained domination over the Aegean Sea area. According to Homer, the capital city of the Mycenaean civilization was established by Agamemnon, the monarch whose armies destroyed Troy. The civilization flourished for at least 300 years, until about 1200 BC, when it was burned and destroyed.

At its peak (around 1300 BC), the Hittite empire stretched from central Anatolia (modern Turkey) to the Levant (the land bordering the eastern edge of the Mediterranean). It became the most powerful state in the Middle East. Only a century later, the Hittite empire collapsed. The collapse was caused partly by internal political chaos and partly by invasions by the Phrygians, a people of mysterious origins who migrated into Anatolia from Thrace (modern Bulgaria), and by the Sea People, who also invaded Egypt, Syria, Palestine, and Cyprus. The Hittite capital, Hattusas, was burned to the ground and never rebuilt. Although Hittite culture persisted at a low level in some small city-states, it was destroyed forever by the Assyrians in the eighth century BC.

The "Sea People," who helped bring down the Hittite and Egyptian empires, are a mystery. No one knows with any certainty who they were or where they came from. They appear to have been extremely aggressive sea-going tribes who raised havoc throughout the eastern Mediterranean.

As Egypt entered the twelfth century BC, the empire began to be severely disrupted by invasions of the Sea People and raids by the Libyans, and by internal political and economic chaos. In 1176, Ramses III recorded a battle with the invading Sea People, and soon after, the Egyptian world empire collapsed. For the next three thousand years, Egypt would be almost continuously under the control of foreign powers.

Over time the Kassites infiltrated and eventually took over Babylonia. Because the Kassites adapted so completely to local Babylonian traditions and honored the established Sumerian and Akkadian cultures, their 400-year rule was never felt to be a foreign domination. During the latter part of their rule, religion and literature thrived. But by the end of the thirteenth century BC, Kassite power had begun to decline. It disintegrated further under attacks from neighboring Assyria and Elam, and ended for good in 1157 BC.

Ugarit, an international trading center on the coast of Syria, maintained itself as a neutral independent state and flourished from the second millennium BC. The city became rich with art and libraries, and was home to wealthy merchants from all around the eastern Mediterranean and the Middle East. To deal with the bewildering variety of then-current forms of writing, the scribes of Ugarit devised the Semitic alphabet, which became the basis for all subsequent alphabetic scripts. The city was destroyed shortly after 1200 BC, its demise attributed to earthquakes, famines, and the mysterious Sea People.

The powerful Middle Assyrian Empire, which at its height stretched from the Persian Gulf to the upper Euphrates, was brought down in 1076 BC by invasions of the Aramaeans, a Semitic tribe from northern Syria. There followed a dark age that lasted until about 900 BC.

The beginning of the Shang Dynasty in China, the first dynasty for which significant archaeological and historical records have been found, is traditionally dated at 1766 BC. The Shang period is notable for the development of bronze casting and for the creation of the Chinese pictographic writing system. In 1046 BC, King Xin, the last Shang ruler, was overthrown by a combination of local rebels and King Wu of the Zhou state to the west. King Wu is traditionally credited with establishing the Zhou Dynasty.

The Zhou Dynasty in turn, though technically lasting until the third century BC, went through major upheavals in the eighth and ninth centuries BC and fractured into many smaller kingdoms. The Zhou Dynasty that continued until the third century BC controlled only a fraction of the kingdom it wrested from the Shang.

India's Indus Valley Civilization by 1900 BC had spread to its greatest extent, encompassing all of what are today Pakistan, part of Iran and Afghanistan, and all of Northern India. At its peak the Indus Valley Civilization was dealt a major blow by drought and the resultant disappearance of the Saraswati River, which once flowed from the Himalayas through the heart of the civilization. Many of the major cities, such as Harappa and Mohenjo-daro, were eventually abandoned.

As a result of the drought, by 1350 BC the influence of the Indus Valley Civilization waned and died to the west (in Afghanistan and Iran); the still vital remnants of the civilization remained to the east in the Ganges plain of Northern India. However, by 700 BC, what remained of the Indus Valley Civilization in Northern India had splintered into sixteen different kingdoms, known as the *Maha Janapandas.*

The era from the tenth to the eighth century BC led eventually to the formation of the kingdoms of the *Maha Janapandas* and is the most likely historical setting for the *Mahabharata*, one of India's great epics. The *Mahabharata* contains India's most famous scripture, the Bhagavad Gita. In addition to the cultural and spiritual treasures contained in the *Mahabharata* is a central, political theme. From the beginning of the epic the question is asked, who should rule, the one with a hereditary claim or the one who has merit? The *self-interest* of one character, Duryodhana, who insists on heredity rather than merit as the basis for his claim to the kingdom, plunges the entire kingdom into war. The battle of Kurukshetra and the death of thousands of warriors and soldiers are seen by the characters in the epic as the end of a more enlightened and less self-interested age — and the beginning of a dark future for mankind.

The trend of Bronze Age collapse can be found in the Americas as well. Reliable dates from this era are hard to come by in Mesoamerica and South America, simply because there has been far less archeological study in these regions than in Asia and the Near East. But we do know that, in what is now Peru, the Norte Chico civilization, whose principal city was Caral, flourished from 3000 BC to at least 1800 BC. After that, nothing much is known — until, by 900 BC, the Chavin culture had risen and the Norte Chico civilization had disappeared.

What we know of the Mesoamerican Olmec civilization is also scant. The Olmec are best known for the gigantic stone heads they left behind in what is now south-central Mexico. Archeological dating indicates that the Olmec were present in Mesoamerica in the thirteenth century BC. We don't know precisely when the Olmec culture ended; but we do know that it was in decline by 900 BC, and by 400 BC had been completely supplanted by Teotihuacan's civilization and eventually by the Mayans and Aztecs.

What we see, then, in the latter part of descending Dwapara Yuga — especially the period from 1200 to 700 BC — is that every world civilization went through major disruption, dislocation, and often violent destruction. What existed in 700 BC were the splintered and fractured remnants of once larger empires; many other empires had simply disappeared. The Hittite, Assyrian, Babylonian, Kassite, Mycenaean, Phrygian, Aramaean, Harappan, Olmec, Norte Chico, and many other civilizations, empires, and cultures no longer existed.

As a result, confusion reigned for several hundred years, from approximately 1000 to 600 BC. Historians often refer to this period as the *Ancient Dark Age*. Dominant political and cultural patterns that had been destroyed in the *Bronze Age collapse* failed to reform until the beginning of descending Kali Yuga.

It appears as if man did not know how to cope with his changed world. It is as if man, having lost touch with his familiar, magical world, rapidly tried to control as much of the material world as he could. Self-interest became fixated on material gain. Thus ensued a sort of worldwide land grab — and in the process, great destruction.

It is not hard to see that we find ourselves in a similarly perilous transition (see *Figure 31*). Like the last five centuries of descending Dwapara Yuga, the first three centuries of our era have witnessed nation-states coming and going with dizzying speed. The political maps of Europe, Africa, the Middle East, and Central Asia have changed beyond recognition in the three centuries since 1700 AD.

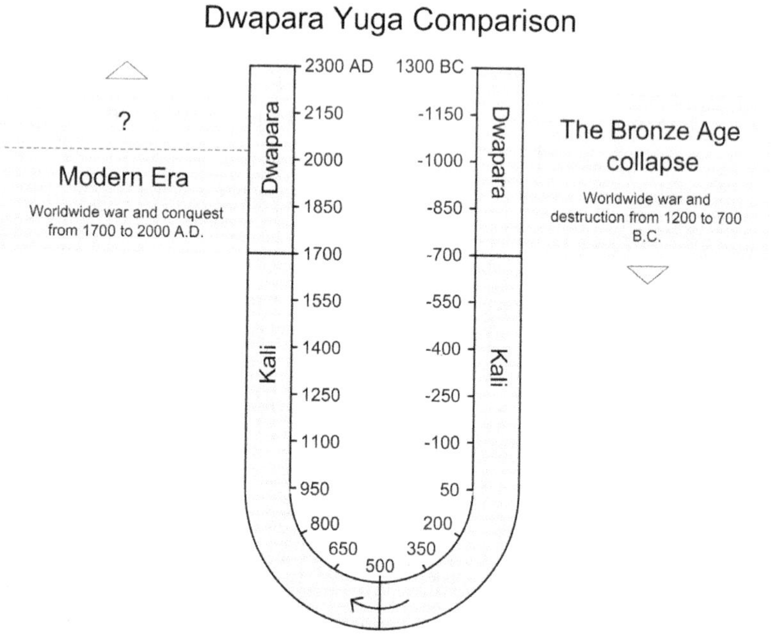

Dwapara Yuga Comparison

Figure 31 — Similarities between our modern era and the Bronze Age collapse

European colonial empires have come and gone, European national boundaries have expanded and shrunk with the seesawing of their military and economic fortunes. The Soviet Union formed and fell, African and Near Eastern borders were redrawn with bewildering frequency, and two World Wars have left the world deeply changed — and shaken.

Driven by war, conquest, and conflict, disrupted (in our case) by newfound energy awareness and its resulting capabilities, and threatened by shifting balances of power, our modern world seems frequently to teeter on the brink of self-destruction. New political and cultural forms have yet to fully establish themselves — they are vying for dominance in our future with such established forms as nation-states answerable to no other; inflexible, exclusive religious and cultural traditions; and massive, controlling, bureaucratic government.

Our era has the advantage of positive momentum — the trend is toward consolidation and growth, rather than toward dissolution and decline. Although optimism fades occasionally, the general tenor of our times is that we can and will improve on all fronts — and that peaceful coexistence is possible. But the formula *self-interest* x *energy awareness* suggests that our path to peaceful coexistence may be rocky. Our world is all too tense for comfort.

Yet our modern era is also a time of awakening to a higher, more spiritual awareness. The ability to destroy the world, and the ability to better know the inner self are ironic companions on our journey into energy awareness. Ours is an era full of both peril and promise.

Transition to Kali Yuga

By the end of *The Bronze Age Collapse*, mankind began the transition to Kali Yuga's matter-centered awareness. Descending Dwapara Yuga entered its 200-year *sandhi*, or transition period, in 900 BC. Descending Kali Yuga's 100-year *sandhi* began in 700 BC and ended in 600 BC. During the 300 years of the combined transition periods, and for a few centuries into descending Kali Yuga, mankind enjoyed an awakening, a flowering of ideals, which parallels our own recent *Age of Enlightenment*, and a reawakening of interest in humanistic principles and the spiritual teaching of the East (see *Figure 32*).

During the transition, Krishna (ninth century BC), Buddha (sixth century BC), and Lao Tzu (sixth century BC) offered mankind new spiritual perspectives. Philosophers, from China to Greece, presented an enlightened, humanistic worldview. The old magical way of looking at the world and the worship of the gods were reevaluated and reinterpreted into a more rational and human-centered worldview.

Dwapara Yuga/Kali Yuga Transition

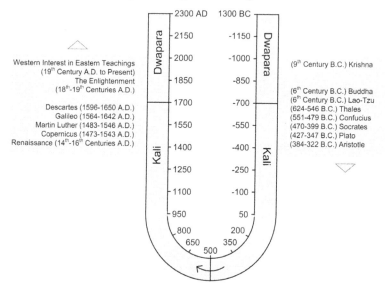

Figure 32—Similarities in interest in humanism and Eastern teachings in our modern era, and the end of descending Dwapara Yuga and the beginning of descending Kali Yuga

By the end of descending Dwapara Yuga, the worship of the gods had become intricately complex. The pantheons of Egypt and China had grown to hundreds of gods. India, too, suffered from a similar divine inflation. Each god engendered unique liturgies, rituals, and ways of proper worship. Vedic India is known to have practiced extremely complex rituals, some lasting for weeks and involving scores of Brahmin priests, with seemingly endless offerings and mantras, carefully timed to exact moments of each day, performed in meticulously prescribed settings and orientations. It would seem that the less awareness the people actually had of the gods, the more they tried to make up for it with ritual.

The loss of true awareness of the gods was compounded, at the end of descending Dwapara Yuga, by an almost complete *outward* dependence on the gods. The worship of the gods had devolved almost entirely into a means to satisfy personal and material needs and desires. The temples were treated like vending machines — put your ritual offering in the slot and out should come the object of your desire. The gods were asked to provide man with *anything* he desired, even if the desire was to harm or kill other people. By his extreme self-interest descending Dwapara Yuga man lost his moral bearings. Everything, good and bad, was sought from the gods.

During the transition from descending Dwapara Yuga to descending Kali Yuga the pendulum swung the other way. Man, once more, became the determiner of his own destiny. Man's innate divinity, his capacity for reason and self-reliance, were once again central, counterbalancing the previous over-dependency on the gods.

In the *sandhi* of descending Dwapara Yuga, an age dominated by ritualistic worship of the gods, Krishna emphasized the importance of each person's personal relationship with the Divine, from which all the gods arise. Krishna presented the teachings of *yoga*, techniques that could lead the individual to union with God. The Bhagavad Gita records Krishna's words on yoga: "Those who worship the gods, go to the gods. But those whose worship Me, come to Me."

Buddha (sixth century BC), recognizing the futility of rejuvenating the proliferating rituals of Vedic India, also placed man at the center of his own destiny. Buddha taught people, essentially, to forget the gods, to concentrate rather on what can be known — that man suffers, and that only through taking personal responsibility for living and behaving rightly, can man escape his suffering. Buddha was not denying the Divine, but bringing man to see individual effort as more important than reliance on the gods.

Lao Tzu (sixth century BC) brought a similar message to China. The essence of his philosophy was that man suffered when he fell out of harmony with the Tao, the unseen power at the root of all manifestation. Like Buddha's and Krishna's, Lao Tzu's philosophy enjoined people to use their own free will to live in harmony with the Tao.

The flowering of Greek humanistic philosophy began with Thales in roughly 625 BC and came to its fullest expression in Plato around 350 BC. The premise was that man's inherent faculty for *reason* was sufficient to ferret out the Truth—a welcome change from the (by then) empty rituals to the gods.

During this same time period, Confucius, and later his student Mencius, developed the philosophic system that became known as Confucianism—the emphasis was on using reason and moral ideals to find one's place in the societal web. Confucianism was a philosophical and social expression of Lao Tzu's teaching of finding harmony with the Tao.

In different ways, the Greek and Chinese philosophers, and the spiritual teachers Krishna, Buddha, and Lao Tzu, all tried to reawaken in man the knowledge of his own divinity, and his role in determining his own destiny. But the reawakening didn't last. It could not survive Kali Yuga's relentlessly material consciousness. Buddhism all but died out in India during Kali Yuga, and only just survived in monasteries in China and Tibet. The spiritual philosophy of Lao Tzu was eclipsed by the social philosophy of Confucius, which in turn devolved into a hereditary class system for generations of Chinese. Knowledge of Greek philosophy nearly died out. Had not the Arabs and the Irish maintained copies of the old texts, Greek philosophy would not have survived.

Nor were the teachings of great philosophers and spiritual leaders the only casualties of Kali Yuga's merciless decline. As we explored in Chapter 2, science, math, and engineering, based on logic and reason rather than on the intuitive approach of Treta and Dwapara Yuga, briefly flowered in Greece and Rome in the early centuries of descending Dwapara Yuga, but died out once more by the third century AD. The early attempts at democracy in Greece were too feeble to withstand the rule of might. And the brief era of such enlightened and reformist rulers as Ashoka the Great of India and Solon of Athens lasted only a fitful few centuries.

Kali Yuga's dark influence finally erased even the *knowledge* of the past and plunged mankind into a kind of collective amnesia. The destruction of all the books in China, ordered by the Emperor Chin in the third century BC, meant the loss of enormously significant knowledge of early Chinese history and way of life. Similarly, the burning of the Library of Alexandria in the third century and again in the fourth century AD is reputed to have destroyed between half a million and a million scrolls.

By 500 AD, man had once again reached the nadir of his development.

~~~~~~~~~~

And thus man came full circle through the cycle of the yugas — and once again began to ascend toward his full potential. Today, we find ourselves once more in Dwapara Yuga. Our energy awareness has transformed our way of life. Yet, as we know from watching the news, the uneasy state of the world is eerily similar to the decline and destruction at the end of descending Dwapara Yuga.

We can see nations using military might, and individuals and corporations using economic power — vying for world dominance. Yet we can also see the emergence of a new spiritual awareness arising from our newfound awareness of subtle inner energy. Now is the time, lest we be overwhelmed by destruction and greed, for those with an attunement to those subtle, inner realities to spread the balm of peace and serenity. Although the general trend of ascending Dwapara Yuga is determined by powerful forces, the specific unfolding of this age is ours to influence. Our enlightened future is certain, but our path to it is not.

Chapter 20

Previous Yuga Cycles

Homo sapiens, according to prevailing archeological and paleon-tological thought, evolved at most 200,000 years ago. The standard theory has it that the ancestors of today's modern humans lived marginal lives in small bands of hunters and gatherers for well over 100,000 years. Twenty to thirty thousand years ago, they began to develop improved stone tools and weapons, which allowed them to hunt more effectively and to develop semi-permanent settlements. Around eight thousand years ago they began to develop civilization.

The cyclic nature of the yugas, in marked contrast to the standard linear theory of human development, suggests that mankind has not only been through one cycle of the yugas, but has been through many *previous* yuga cycles as well. In fact, Paramhansa Yogananda said that *civilized* man has existed on earth for over 50 million years—a time frame that would include hundreds of 24,000-year yuga cycles and the rise and fall of thousands of civilizations.

How Old Is Man?

The first objection to a 50-million-year time frame for civilized man is the apparent evidence of far more recent evolutionary stages of man. Mankind is said to have evolved from ape-like *australopithecus* to man-like Neanderthal in a little over three million years.

This may not be true for several reasons. It is important to keep in mind that the oldest fossil found does not mean that no older fossil will ever *be* found. Just recently, paleontologists found "Ardi," a hominid fossil from 4.4 million years ago. Although Ardi might be on an evolutionary branch different from man's, the find nonetheless holds out the possibility of even earlier fossil evidence of man still to be found.

It is also important to keep in mind that paleontology's assertion that the earlier stages of man's evolution were unintelligent is based on one part evidence and ninety-nine parts theory. The ninety-nine parts theory is the Darwinian, evolutionary view that holds sway today. The Darwinian view is that the earlier the fossil, the more primitive and less intelligent the creature must have been. The logic of the theory is applied without deviation to all hominid fossils.

The Darwinian view was recently thrown a significant curve, however, with the 2003 discovery of Hobbit Man, or *homo floresiensis*, on the island of Flores in Indonesia. Hobbit Man fossils indicate that he lived from around 90,000 years ago to as recently as 13,000 years ago. He was a tool user, and so, by Darwinian definition, intelligent.

As the name implies, Hobbit Man is very small. What threw the paleontological community into a (for paleontologists) roaring debate, was the fact that he was not a diminutive *homo sapiens*, or small version of modern man, as was the expectation. Hobbit Man simply does not fit into any convenient categorization. In fact, Hobbit Man shares many morphological similarities (in physical form) with the fossil remains of *australopithecus afarens*, most often called "Lucy," which predated him by over three million years.

This begs the question, if Hobbit Man was intelligent, despite his small brain size, and shared with Lucy a morphology different from that of modern humans, why couldn't Lucy and Lucy's ancestors also have been intelligent? The answer is that there is no reason why she couldn't — except that the Darwinian view precludes it. Take away the Darwinian view and there is no inherent, demonstrable facts to prove Lucy less intelligent than modern man.

Because brain size is usually put forward as an indication of intelligence, and because Lucy had a smaller brain than modern man, she is assumed to be less intelligent as well. But there is no proven correlation between the brain sizes of those of genius and those of low intelligence. If mental capacity were only a matter of brain size, then Cro-Magnon Man, who existed ten to thirty thousand years ago and had a brain 25% larger than ours, should, according to the Darwinian view, have passed on his superior genes to all of us alive today. If intelligence were only a matter of brain size, then we should probably be consulting the blue whale on a number of issues. If children, with their far smaller brains, can be prodigies, then Lucy could have been intelligent.

Lastly, it is important to keep in mind how little evidence exists upon which current paleontological theory is based. The accepted view of the development of man during the period from Lucy (about 3.2 million years ago) to *homo habilis* (about 1.6 million years ago) is based on *fifteen partial skeletons*—some so partial that they are limited to a few bones that no one can be entirely sure belonged to the same individual.

Paleontologists have built up, from this extremely scant evidence, pictures of what they suppose these individuals looked like—always hairy and vacant-eyed—together with descriptions of how they behaved, how they walked, what they ate, how they took care of their young, what their motivations were, and what they may have felt. Not surprisingly, all this conjecture fits neatly into the Darwinian view.

Political polling has familiarized us with the notion of *margin of error*. The margin of error for a poll group of over *one thousand* people—on one specific question—is still 3%. The multiple conclusions, which paleontologists base on only one, partial fossil sample, on the other hand, have a margin for error approaching 100%! That is to say, their conclusions could just as easily be wrong as right.

From the late 1800s until the mid-1900s, comparisons of Neanderthal fossils to "modern man" were made largely by examining the morphology (physical shape) of the bones. Paleontologists, interpreting their finds as examples of a recent evolutionary stage of modern man's development, found physical characteristics in the bones that supported the image of the grunting, hunched-over, long-armed, sloped-forehead caveman. This picture of Neanderthal man conformed to the prevailing thought of the time—but simply is not true.

Modern forensic examination and genetic studies paint a very different picture. All the morphological characteristics found in Neanderthal fossils, those used to support the idea of an ape-like man, are, in fact, found in modern humans as well. It turns out that present-day examples of the heavy brows and stronger bones, the main differences attributed to Neanderthal man, can be found in most modern day populations. In other words, Neanderthal man really didn't look that different from some modern men.

The revised picture of Neanderthal man includes pinkish skin (not hairy), upright posture, with height and body proportions similar to modern man's, and strongly developed foreheads, as opposed to the sloping gorilla-like forehead of popular imagination. The recent discovery of a Neanderthal hyoid bone (the larynx, or voice box), also indicates that Neanderthal man would have had the same capacity for speech of modern man.

Much of the changed view of Neanderthal man can be attributed to genetic research. The Max Planck Institute for Social Anthropology and the Lawrence Berkeley National Laboratory are working to completely sequence Neanderthal DNA in order to compare it with the DNA of modern man. Early results indicate greater than expected similarity between Neanderthal and modern man. Several studies indicate that Neanderthal man shares up to 99.9% of modern man's genes. In fact, many of the geneticists working on Neanderthal DNA have come to believe that Neanderthal man is actually the same species as modern man.

Also emerging from the study of Neanderthal DNA is evidence that Neanderthal man is at least 1.1 million years old. From analysis of DNA, geneticists can estimate backward to form a timeline of evolutionary change — a history of ancestors. The oldest Neanderthal DNA is 500,000 years old, but contains evidence of a 1.1-million-year history.

There *is* overwhelming fossil evidence that clearly indicates that all species have gone through evolutionary changes, man included. Far from overwhelming, however, and far from clear is evidence for *when* intelligent man first appeared on earth. Evolving body shapes alone (morphology) cannot give us that answer. "Lucy" could have been highly intelligent and highly advanced spiritually — only the Darwinian view precludes scientific consideration of this possibility.

As we will explore in the next few pages, the earth is very hard on ancient evidence of any kind. The likelihood of finding a 50-million-year-old human-like skeleton is remote — but nonetheless possible. In the early 1900s the oldest known human-like fossils were believed to be about 200,000 years old. Now the oldest known human-like fossils are believed to be 3.2 million years old. Is 50 million years old really so far out of the question?

Earth's Destructive Power

At this point you may be asking, "If intelligent man has existed for millions of years and has passed through hundreds of yuga cycles, then where is all the evidence? Where are all the ancient ruins and other artifacts of man's distant past?"

The first answer is that it is more amazing than not that *anything* survives from even five thousand years ago, let alone five million years ago, given the destructive forces constantly at work on the earth. The second answer is that despite earth's destructive power, there is more truly ancient evidence of intelligent man than most people realize. Before we tell you about some of these finds, let's look at the forces arrayed against the survival of ancient artifacts.

Relentless natural forces are arrayed against the survival of ancient artifacts. Seemingly mighty structures can disappear in a surprisingly short time. In *The World Without Us*, Alan Weisman describes the likely stages of decay of the city of New York if suddenly abandoned. He based his book on interviews with scientists and with those who actually maintain the city.

In the first stage of decay, paper and wood would degrade the fastest, leaving behind no trace of their original form or intent. Most would disappear within years; some would last decades; in rare cases, centuries. Water, mold, insects, and bacteria would make quick work of most paper or wood structures and artifacts.

Metals would go next. A car left out-of-doors could dissolve into rust, or corrode, and blow away on the wind in as little as a hundred years—body, chassis, engine, and all. The fabrics and synthetic materials in the rest of the car would gradually crack and flake, eventually becoming dust. Oddly enough, the last to disappear would be the tires, but even they will succumb in a few hundred years.

The buildings would be next. Once the lightning rods had rusted away, lightning would inevitably start fires. Anything untouched by fire would be subject to slower but still-relentless forces. Rain, sunlight, and natural contraction and expansion would gradually weaken any remaining seals around doors and windows and so allow water and wind into buildings. Once the barriers to the elements were breached, water could enter freely and begin its work of demolition.

The developments that allow us to build skyscrapers to astonishing heights, reinforced concrete and metal girders, are also their Achilles heel. Once water corroded the metals in the "reinforced" walls and floors, they would easily collapse in strong winds. Foundations too, once kept free of underground water by continuous pumping, would quickly become saturated, and the buildings increasingly unstable. New York's subway system, for example, would flood within hours of pump failure. Within weeks or months, all basements and subbasements in Manhattan would be immersed.

Once the buildings had collapsed, the power of plants would go to work. Over time, roots and seeds would enter tiny cracks and, with astonishing power, break concrete and natural stone into tiny bits. As the iron reinforcing bars in the concrete corroded, channels would be left for more water and plants to enter deep into the concrete. In a cold climate such as New York's, ice would fracture the concrete from inside the same channels. Mr. Weisman predicts that in only a thousand years, the entire city of New York would be reduced to unrecognizable humps and hills densely covered with trees and plants.

One of the last materials to disintegrate would be plastic. We do not know the precise lifespan of plastic, but we do know that plastic is subject to natural forces—particularly sunlight. Left in direct sunlight for a few years, even thick blocks of plastic will degrade and flake away, dispersing as dust on the wind. The plastics and other manmade artifacts that escaped the first wave of destruction would eventually end up in the ground, buried and partly protected from such natural forces as wind and ice. But nothing can protect plastic from bacteria.

Bacteria is the most prevalent form of life on earth. All the continents, even Antarctica, have innumerable bacterial species living in soil, plants, and animals. The seas are filled with bacteria, some living thousands of feet below the surface. They can live in extreme conditions, even in Yellowstone National Park geyser pools, some just under the boiling point. The bacteria from the top twenty feet of earth's soil would easily outweigh the combined total of all other life on earth.

Bacteria's ubiquity is significant because bacteria eat anything and everything. Bacteria not only thrive on organic substances, but have also adapted to minerals, acid solutions, streams of chemicals in undersea volcanic vents, and yes, plastic. Recent experiments conducted by a sixteen-year-old, Daniel Burd of Canada, won him a science prize and a lot of attention for isolating bacteria that had adapted to consume some types of plastic[1]. In another development, scientists have adapted bacteria to consume nuclear waste![2]

There are also other natural forces at work whose effects are not always slow and minute, but vast and cataclysmic. Earthquakes, volcanic eruptions, asteroid impacts, tidal waves, glaciers and changing ocean levels are all capable of widespread and, sometimes, sudden destruction.

We are still in an ice age, even though the last ice age is popularly thought to have ended about 13,000 years ago. The current ice age technically began 2.6 million years ago, when ice remained near the poles year round. Throughout the 2.6 million years of the current ice age, the amount of permanent ice on the earth has alternately advanced out from the poles and retreated back toward the poles—in a rhythm of what are called *glacial maximums* and *glacial minimums*. Thirteen thousand years ago, therefore, was not the end of an ice age, but marked the end of a glacial maximum, and the beginning of a glacial minimum.

During the most recent glacial maximum, permanent ice completely covered what is today Great Britain, Canada, Norway, Sweden, and Finland. Ice pushed as far south as Germany, northern France, and a large part of Russia. In the United States, the Great Lake states were under ice. The Great Lakes are in fact the melt water left behind by the glacier's retreat, which began about 15,000 years ago.

Glaciers covered the Himalayas and the Tibetan Plateau, the European Alps, and extended well down into North America's Rocky Mountains. Ice similarly extended northward from the South Pole into Africa, South America, and Australia. Some earlier glacial maximums extended even farther toward the equator and covered nearly all of Europe, North America, and Russia, as well as large parts of Africa, Australia, and South America.

Glaciers obliterate everything in their path. Their crushing weight, their gradual but inexorable motion, can reshape mountains—in the process they can grind away so much rock that the elevation drops by thousands of feet. During glacial minimums, such as ours, the more northern and southern latitudes have temperate, and from our standpoint, desirable climates; the equatorial regions have hotter and less desirable climates. It is likely that during glacial minimums human populations preferred to live closer to the poles, where the climate was more moderate. It is precisely these areas that become heavily glaciated during glacial maximums; the encroaching ice would utterly destroy anything left behind by man.

Supervolcanoes are so large that only recently have geologists become aware of their existence. The usual volcano leaves behind a characteristic cone-shaped mountain. Supervolcanoes, by contrast, leave behind an enormous crater—sometimes fifty miles or more across. Yellowstone National Park in Wyoming, with its thermal springs and geysers, is in fact the heart of a semi-active volcano. The last eruption was approximately 160,000 years ago, and another larger one 640,000 years ago. They covered most of the Western United States with a thick coating of ash, and altered weather patterns around the world.

Seventy-five thousand years ago, the Toba supervolcano in Indonesia erupted and spewed so much gas and dust into the atmosphere that life on earth was seriously threatened by the ensuing lack of sunlight. Ash from the eruption has been found thousands of miles away. Scientists have theorized that the amount of ash ejected—a calculation based on the known distance the ash spread—would have blotted out the sun for years before it settled out of the atmosphere.

If glaciers and volcanoes aren't devastating enough, we have asteroid impacts. As just one example, a group calling themselves the Holocene Impact Working Group (HIWG) believe they have found evidence of a major asteroid impact in the Indian Ocean. Immense ocean floor sediment deposits can be found in characteristic curved patterns, called chevrons, left by a massive tidal wave that struck the southern end of Madagascar, off the east coast of Africa. These deposits cover an area the size of Manhattan, and point like a weather vane to the middle of the Indian Ocean. HIWG's research has led to the conclusion that the impact occurred approximately 4,800 years ago, and may be the event responsible for many of the flood stories found around the world.

As the glaciers have retreated over the past 13,000 years, the melt water has gradually raised the ocean level over 200 feet. Tectonic forces have, over the same span of time, raised some continental areas and lowered others. Underwater archeology has only recently discovered Greek coastal cities and temples inundated during the last 2,500 years by the rising sea. As more sites are found submerged off the coast of Greece, India, and elsewhere, the clear implication is of thousands of cities destroyed by rising ocean levels.

If natural forces, slow and inexorable, or rapid and cataclysmic, do not destroy past evidence of mankind, then mankind itself probably takes care of most of the rest. From an archeological perspective, normal human life, modern as well as ancient—including throwing out the trash, remodeling a home, or demolishing and rebuilding—destroys the record of the past.

If the Giza Pyramids weren't so massive, they would probably have been carried off, block by block, to build something else. Today the Great Pyramids of Giza appear step-like. When they were built, however, the sides were smooth, the steps filled in with triangular blocks of white limestone. This outer limestone covering was carried off and used to build the signature white buildings of "Old" Cairo.

Different Cycles, Different Development

Another factor that may influence the evidence we are able to find from the past is that the *particular ways* in which mankind developed may have varied considerably from cycle to cycle. The only constant we can expect from cycle to cycle is the increase and decrease of *dharma* in a 24,000-year cycle. How *specific* civilizations developed would have been subject to many changing influences.

These influences—all of which could affect how a specific yuga cycle unfolded—include physical conditions, such as long-term climate patterns, ice ages, and desertification; catastrophic events, such as glaciations, asteroid impacts, and volcanic eruptions; perhaps even long-term evolutionary changes, such as adaptations to our senses or physical characteristics.

Population, especially, might vary considerably from cycle to cycle. As already mentioned, Mt. Toba erupted approximately 75,000 years ago with such force that billions of tons of ash were flung into the atmosphere. Scientists believe there was so much ash in the atmosphere that nearly *all* sunlight striking the earth's atmosphere was reflected away, and as a result, nearly all plant and animal life died off in the ensuing *years* of near darkness. Geneticists estimate, based on studies of present and ancient DNA, that the world's population was reduced to mere *thousands* after Mt. Toba's eruption.

The present yuga cycle stands in marked contrast to the Mt. Toba era— the last ten or eleven thousand years of benign conditions (the Holocene Epoch), together with the last three to four thousand years of steady weather patterns, free from global catastrophe, have produced an environment conducive to population growth. As a result, our population has risen to *billions*.

This vast population is the major determinant of the scope of our Dwapara industry and technology. The larger the population, the more complex the systems needed to support it. Water systems are a key example. Los Angeles, California gets water from over *600 miles* away, from the Sacramento River in the northern part of California. To pump *millions* of gallons a day from the Sacramento River and over a range of hills requires the largest water pumps ever built, and *megawatts* of electricity to run the pumps. With its much smaller population of less than a hundred years ago, Los Angeles could supply its water needs from nearby sources.

Dramatically increased population, however, led not only to Los Angeles' immense water project, but also to thousands of miles of canals, hundreds of reservoirs, massive water filtration systems, and sewage treatment plants the size of small villages. The history of any major industry—transportation, communication, mining, manufacturing, agriculture, energy production—demonstrates that, as population increases, industrial complexity increases exponentially.

Our choices of technology are not necessarily inevitable either. People in previous cycles might have pioneered different ways of solving the same problems. The electric car, for example, had a firm foothold at the beginning of the twentieth century. In the early 1900s the largest automaker in the United States was the Electric Vehicle Company. Had the electric car become dominant, our civilization's dependence on oil might never have happened. But, at a critical time, oil was easily available in Pennsylvania, close to the inventors of the internal combustion engine.

Nuclear power and nuclear technology may also be simply *accidents* of our particular cycle—specifically, the timing of the second world war. The war, and the population pressures in the background, led to an intense and costly effort to create the atomic bomb, and then to extend the knowledge gained to harnessing controlled nuclear reactions for power generation. In a past or future cycle, the path of development might as easily be non-nuclear.

People in previous cycles may have made such fundamentally different choices in the course of their development that we would not recognize the evidence of their technology even if it were all around us. Perhaps certain species of trees, common to us today, were in a previous cycle genetically adapted to provide man a form of usable energy. Such an idea may not be as speculative as it now seems. Even now, scientists are conducting well-funded research into adapting bacteria to create electrical storage devices; other scientists are using genetic manipulation to grow organic cells that can function as living computers. Once Dwapara Yuga man has developed for a few hundred more years, he may recognize evidence of ancient civilizations we can't understand at present.

The Surviving Evidence

The earth is constantly changing and recycling. The record of the past is easily crushed, burned, pulverized, consumed, dissolved, washed away, carried away, submerged, buried, or turned to dust, by slow and inexorable forces such as corrosion and bacteria, or by rapid and cataclysmic events such as volcanoes and continents in upheaval, or by man's natural penchant to reuse.

Small amounts of physical evidence from the very distant past have nonetheless survived. Because these bits of evidence, in their great age, don't fit the prevailing archeological model, they are ignored or downplayed, and so remain popularly unknown.

The paintings in the Lascaux Caves in France, mentioned in Chapter 11, are dated to approximately 13,000 BC. However, equally sophisticated paintings (see *Figure 33*), using perspective and polychrome techniques, and dating back more than 20,000 years before Lascaux, have been found in caves in Chauvet (France) and Altamira (Spain).

Also approximately 35,000 years old is the exquisite Venus of Brassempouy (see *Figure 33*). Since very old artifacts are conventionally considered to have a religious significance, this graceful carving has been stereotyped as a "Venus," or goddess figure. If we set aside the conventional view, the carving could equally well be seen as simply a lovely young woman.

Even earlier is the sculpture of a snake, discovered in a cave in the Tsodilo Hills of Botswana, Africa. The snake is so well carved that, despite its great age—estimates range from 70,000 to 90,000 years old—one can still make out what appear to be scales on the skin.

As recently as 2008, tools found in Ethiopia in the 1970s and presumed to be 175,000 years old, were retested using the new argon-argon technique—based on comparing different argon isotopes in the volcanic ash that surrounded the tools—and were determined to be 276,000 years old.[3]

Figure 33—(left) Horses from the Chauvet Cave in France, circa 35,000 years old; (right) the Venus of Brassempouy, also circa 35,000 years old. (Venus of Brassempouy photo courtesy of PHGCOM.)

In August of 1870, a well-drilling project in Lawn Ridge, Illinois brought up a coin-like object from a depth of thirty-five meters. The object was round, made of copper, of a uniform thickness and appeared to have cut edges. Both sides of the object were decorated with unfamiliar human figures and an indecipherable script or hiero-glyphs. Professor Alexander Winchell, at the time the State Geologist for Michigan, and a prominent coin expert, William Ewing DuBois, both examined the object and determined it to have no known origin and to be unlike any historically known coins or similar objects. Professor Winchell presented it to the Geological Section of the American Association in Buffalo, New York in 1876. The stratum in which the coin was found indicates that it was 200,000 to 400,000 years old.[4]

In 1969, in Oklahoma City, workmen cutting into a rock shelf found an inlaid tile floor three feet below the surface. Durwood Pate, an Oklahoma City geologist, examined the floor closely and concluded that it had to have been manmade. The stones were laid out in parallel lines that intersected to form diamond shapes. The rough underside and smooth surface of the stones indicated the wear normal for a floor. When Pate made a further examination, he discovered mortar between the tiles. The best estimate dates the floor at 200,000 years old.[5]

Pieces of ocher, an intensely staining natural clay, still used today for tinting paints, have been found at a 300,000-year-old site (Terra Amata) in France, and at a 250,000-year-old site near Bečov, in the Czech Republic. Ocher was mined in the Hunsgi Cave in South India as early as 300,000 years ago and in the Wonderwerk Cave in South Africa as early as 400,000 years ago.

In 1865, in the Abbey Mine in Treasure City, Nevada, miners found a two-inch-long cavity in a piece of feldspar that clearly showed the thread pattern of a screw that once was present but had corroded away. The feldspar deposit is estimated to be 21 million years old.[6]

An article written by Michael A. Cremo describes his meeting with a former Russian naval officer named Alexander Rudenko. Rudenko discovered, on a Baltic Sea beach in the Kalinin region of Russia, a piece of amber (preserved tree sap). Amber itself is common in the area. This particular piece of amber was remarkable for enclosing a tiny piece of woven fabric — the amber, and presumably the fabric inside, had to be at least 25 million years old.[7]

Other evidence includes screw threads in ancient rocks, metal artifacts encased in coal, and manmade floors and walls found in strata laid down millions of years ago — even a convincing description of the discovery of modern human-like fossils in strata as old as 50 million years in a gold mine under Table Mountain in Tuolumne County, California.[8]

Alas, most of these discoveries have disappeared, or are owned by collectors who won't allow them to be examined — and worst of all, these discoveries were removed from their place of discovery before verifiable scientific tests and measurements could be made. The discoveries are, therefore, and with some justification, regarded as unreliable by the archeological community. Nonetheless, the quantity of evidence currently known promises more discoveries to come—discoveries we hope will be handled according to existing scientific standards.

The obliterating power of natural forces, in combination with mankind's collective amnesia as it goes through Kali Yuga, effectively eliminate all but tantalizing glimpses of the eras before our current cycle.

Yet even glimpses should make us reconsider the standard theory. If modern man existed only in the last 200,000 years, who was mining ocher in India 400,000 years ago? Who fashioned those tools in Ethiopia 276,000 years ago? Who dressed and laid the stone floor in Oklahoma City 200,000 years ago? What culture produced a metal screw that corroded away in a feldspar deposit formed 21 million years ago? Who wove the fabric that survived as a tiny fragment in a piece of amber at least 25 million years old?

We also have to ask, what else may be found? What evidence of advanced civilizations, evidence we are not yet advanced enough to recognize, will be revealed "hiding in plain sight"?

PART FIVE

Conclusion

Chapter 21

The Tipping Point

The evidence appears overwhelmingly to support the Darwinian (linear) view of human development—from *australopithecus afarens* ("Lucy") to *homo cardriverus* ("Lucy Smith"). Even well-established theories, however, can be overturned surprisingly quickly.

Today prevailing thought in geology rests on the central theory of plate tectonics, or continental drift as it is often called, which is now considered to be the fundamental cause of many geologic phenomena such as mountain formation, volcanoes and earthquakes. The concept of continental drift was first seriously presented by Alfred Wegener in his 1915 book, *The Origin of Continents and Oceans*. But it wasn't until more than 30 years later that the concept of continental drift finally reached its tipping point. A 1947 study revealed that the seafloor is not composed of the same material as the continents. It was determined that the seafloor is much thinner and more malleable than the material which makes up the continents, and therefore continents might actually be able to "drift" over it. This one discovery tipped the balance of thought toward the concept of continental drift.

Once the theory of continental drift passed the tipping point of acceptance in the 1950s, geologists made discovery after discovery that corroborated the theory. Geologists were able to identify the boundaries of the various continental and seafloor plates around the world. The mid-Atlantic and mid-Pacific ocean ridges were examined and it was found that the sea floor is actually spreading, due to steady undersea volcanic eruptions, revealing the previously unknown force that moves the continents.

In the 1950s and 1960s, dramatically increased university and government funding became available for exploring the theory of plate tectonics. Geologists now think not only that the continents are moving, but that their movements can be tracked to two separate epochs during which all the continents formed one contiguous whole—a *supercontinent*—and then broke up and drifted apart once again into the many continents we know today.

In the early 1940s, no reputable geologist believed an entire continent *could* "drift." A mere fifteen years later, no reputable geologist believed a continent *didn't* "drift."

Most significant from our point of view, once the concept of continental drift reached its tipping point, scientists began to re-examine known facts. Mysteries became solved, not only by the discovery of new facts, but by fitting what was already known into a new framework of thought. They knew, for example, that volcanoes and earthquakes tended to occur along coastlines, but not why. With the acceptance of the concept of continental drift, science suddenly found the explanation not only for coastal volcanoes and earthquakes, but for a wide range of what had been only partially understood phenomena.

We believe a similar tipping point is coming in the fields of archeology and prehistory. There is a growing body of evidence that doesn't fit with prevailing thought, and that can no longer be easily dismissed as poor science—the product of undisciplined research methods. The emerging evidence is in fact often the result of the increasingly common trend of applying the latest scientific techniques from other disciplines to research and discovery in archeology and paleontology.

Much Remains to be Discovered

Most people tend to think that, by now, the ancient record of man's past has been well explored. This is *very, very* far from the truth. Unlike physics, chemistry, materials science, or computer science—which drive the development of modern technology—archeology and paleontology do not get the "big money." The Large Hadron Collider (LHC), recently built in Switzerland to research particle physics, cost over *nine billion dollars* to design and construct. More money may have been spent on the LHC—a single project—than on all the archeological and paleontological exploration, excavation, research, and analysis *ever conducted*.

You could say that archeology and paleontology are poor relations in the family of science. They have no practical application (i.e. do not make money), and as a result, receive little funding. Career professionals in these fields are usually modestly paid university professors; research funding comes from limited university and museum budgets or national grants; and actual excavation relies on a lot of volunteer effort.

Sophisticated archeological and paleontological research is painstaking and time-consuming. Even small digs (measured in meters, not kilometers) can take years, even decades, to be fully explored. Because of archeology's time-intensive nature, the lack of funding, and the immense size of our world, only a tiny fraction of one percent of the earth's surface has been professionally examined.

Sarah Parcak, an archeologist with the University of Alabama, is a specialist in identifying potential archeological sites by analyzing satellite imagery. In 2003 and 2004, she identified and confirmed eighty-three sites in the Nile Delta and Middle Egypt which had never been seen before. The Nile River Valley is archeologically the most intensively studied area in the world. Yet even along the Nile, Parchac was quoted in a recent article on CNN Online, she estimated that only "1/100th of 1% of all sites" have been found.[1]

Underwater archeology, like the use of satellites, is also giving us a new appreciation for what remains to be found. In 2002, using sonar, scientists discovered a submerged city in the Bay of Cambay on the west coast of India. Most of the exploration has been conducted by bottom scanning sonar. The picture painted by sonar is of a city five miles long by two miles wide — quite large by ancient standards. The city was well built and shares the rectilinear layout of Indus Valley Civilization cities such as Harappa. Carbon dating of a piece of wood dredged up from the site suggests an inhabited city as early as 7500 BC, making it thousands of years older than any other settlement of similar size.

Even more recently, attention has been drawn to El Mirador in the Yucatan area of Guatemala, a site that may prove to be the largest ancient city so far discovered in Mesoamerica. El Mirador was first discovered in 1926, but was far from thoroughly examined until 2003, when Dr. Richard Hansen of Idaho State University initiated a major investigation. His teams have concluded that El Mirador was inhab-ited in the sixth century BC by up to 100,000 people. The city also contains the largest pyramid in the Americas—in volume, though not in height, larger even than the Great Pyramid of Giza.

El Mirador is just one of thousands of known Mesoamerican sites that have received serious attention. The others remain unexplored due to lack of funding and difficult conditions.

Known, but unexplored archeological sites are not unusual. They may even be the norm. Many known sites have received little or no attention. One of the most notable is in China—a pyramid-shaped hill even larger than El Mirador. The hill is believed to contain the burial place of Emperor Chin (from whom China gets its name). Legend has it that the tomb contains elaborate artifacts, including a lake of mercury. The hill remains untouched.

While we are respectful of the effort and scholarship that has gone into mainstream archeology and paleontology, we also respect-fully decline to think that there is an airtight case for the prevailing thought—far from it. We believe much remains to be discovered. And we believe there remains much room for disagreement about evidence uncovered to date.

A Tipping Point for Science?

Mainstream acceptance of the yuga cycle will require a tipping point not just in archeology and paleontology, but also in the acceptance of non-material reality. Current science is founded on material empiri-cism; by its very nature, it cannot consider true anything that cannot be measured by material means.

There is a joke told of a man arriving in heaven and being escort-ed around by a heavenly guide. After seeing many wonders, the man notices a very high wall stretching away for some distance in both directions. The new arrival exclaims, "What is that wall doing here?" His guide quickly answers, "Ssshhh! Those are the Catholics. They don't think anyone else is here!"

Currently, modern science behaves like the Catholics in the story. Walled in by its insistence on making measurements based on *objec-tive*, material criteria, science cannot acknowledge the validity of what it considers subjective human experience. Not all scientists take this narrow view in their personal lives; the *scientific method*, however, which is predicated on objective (i.e. non-human) measurement, has no alternative.

The findings of PEAR (Princeton Engineering Anomalies Research), which indicate that people can have a telekinetic effect on matter, appear not to have made a dent in the wall of scientific skepticism. Because PEAR has not been able to *measure* any force causing what is obviously occurring, science cannot take seriously these telekinetic effects.

It may be, however, that material science's influence on informed opinion is beginning to diminish. Science's rise in prominence and acceptance was due, no doubt, to its practical, knowable results. Hard to argue with. But science, as currently practiced, may have reached the apex of its arc. People are increasingly realizing that science doesn't have all the answers, and none of the answers to the most important questions — how to find happiness, meaning, love, and fulfillment.

As a result, more people are turning their attention within, to direct personal experience, to find the answers to these age-old and still-vital questions. As their attention turns within, they are discovering subtle realities that no machine can measure. Our life force and deeper, spiritual reality are beyond material measurement — at least as scientific measurement is conducted today — but are not beyond personal experience.

Our Enlightened Future

The enlightened past gives us a glimpse of our enlightened future. The Great Pyramid, the Vedas, the ancient myths of Paradise on earth — each, in its own way, tells what our future holds.

Mankind has much more potential than is generally realized — as does each of us. A study of the yugas gives us a glimpse not only of *mankind's* future, but of our own personal future as well. Sri Yukteswar tells us in *The Holy Science* that, as each individual journeys to enlightenment, he will pass though and comprehend the levels of awareness of the four yugas — awareness of matter in Kali, of life force in Dwapara, divine magnetism in Treta, and Spirit in Satya.

Our examination of the past has revealed many ways man has understood and expressed the knowledge and awareness of each yuga.

We hope that, as you explored the ancient past and the potential future with us, you have come to appreciate that all forms of spiritual expression have their origins in man's own, inherently spiritual nature. From the first stirrings of intuitive awareness of energy to the liberating experience of Self-realization, man is only rediscovering his essential nature.

We do not need to wait for the slow unfolding of the yugas to find Self-realization. In the personal future of each one of us, enlightenment awaits. It is ours to claim. Self-realization is within reach of anyone, in any age.

Appendix

Sri Yukteswar's "Dual"

On first reading *The Holy Science*, many readers are intrigued by the "dual," as described by Sri Yukteswar, which plays an integral role in the cycle of the yugas. In this appendix, we have provided two potential explanations for what the dual may actually be—one from the standpoint of modern physics-based Western astronomy, the other from the perspective of ancient Eastern astronomy that is represented by geometrical relationships. Either explanation is only speculation on our part since neither explanation admits of certain proof at this time. Nonetheless, we think you will find these explanations interesting, if not decisive.

(Note: the following explanations can get fairly technical. We have tried to be as clear as possible and avoid too much jargon, but you may find it difficult to follow some of the points if you do not have a basic understanding of astronomy. To make it any clearer, however, we would have to write another book!)

First you may find it interesting to read Sri Yukteswar's description of the mechanism that brings about the cycle of the yugas. It is very brief. Here are his words from *The Holy Science* as published in India in 1920:

> We learn from the oriental astronomy that moons revolve round their planets and planets turning on their axes revolve with their moons round the sun, and the sun again with its planets and moons taking some star for its duel [sic]

revolve round each other in about 24000 years of our earth which causes the backward movement of the equinoxal [sic] points round the Zodiac. The sun also has another motion by which it revolves round a grand centre called Bishnunavi which is the seat of the creative power Brahma the universal magnetism. It informs us further that this Brahma the universal magnetism regulates Dharma the mental virtues of the internal world. When the sun during its revolution round its dual comes to the place nearest to this grand centre the seat of Brahma — this takes place when the autumnal equinox comes to the first point of Aries — this Dharma the mental virtue becomes so much developed that man can easily comprehend all even the spirit beyond this visible world. And after 12000 years when the sun goes to the place farthest from this grand centre — which takes place when the autumnal Equinox is on the first point of Libra — this Dharma the mental virtue comes to such a reduced state that man cannot grasp anything beyond the gross material creation.[1]

The State of Astronomy in 1894

In 1894, when *The Holy Science* was written, the concept of the cosmos in Western astronomy was very different than the cosmos we know today. Our Milky Way Galaxy was the entire known universe and very little was understood of its structure. By 1920 astronomers were debating about the size of our Galaxy and the nature of celestial objects then known as "white nebulae." The scientific community was divided over the question of whether these nebulae were incredibly distant island universes or nearby objects. The matter was settled in 1924 when Edwin Hubble determined the size and scale of the Andromeda Galaxy. Shortly thereafter Jan Oort determined that our galactic system is rotating about a center in the direction of Sagittarius.

It is important to remember that Sri Yukteswar's *grand center* ("The sun also has another motion by which it revolves round a grand centre called *Bishnunavi* which is the seat of the creative power *Brahma* the universal magnetism."), which may well be our galactic center, could not have been based on Western astronomical findings at the time when *The Holy Science* was written. Sri Yukteswar may have intuited the nature of our galaxy, if indeed the grand center does correspond to the galactic center, and thus have anticipated discoveries well ahead of his time. Or, as we'll explore later, Sri Yukteswar may have based his description of the causes of the yuga cycle on another, very ancient system of "oriental astronomy."

Western Astronomy and the "Dual"

Sri Yukteswar writes:

> "the sun again with its planets and moons taking some star
> for its duel [sic] revolve round each other in about 24,000
> years of our earth...."

Perhaps the most obvious conclusion which one can draw from this description is that Sri Yukteswar is describing our sun as part of a binary stellar system. Astronomers have long considered this a possibility since it became apparent in the 1950s that the majority of stars in the universe are members of multiple star systems. The 24,000 year period, described by Sri Yukteswar, indicates that a companion star to the sun should be close enough to be easily spotted—unless it were a dark object such as a failed star not quite massive enough to ignite. Such a star, called a *brown dwarf*, could have gone undetected given its extremely faint heat signature. However, with the aid of better survey telescopes, some space-based, which are constantly being developed, if such an object (a brown dwarf) is out there, it will likely be found soon.

One reason to search for evidence of a large object outside the known solar system is to explain such things as the periodic extinctions of life on the Earth. Some postulate that these may be due to an influx of comets perturbed by an undiscovered large distant planet. The orbits of comets have been studied to find evidence of such an object, but the results so far have not been conclusive. Victor Clube and Bill Napier have shown that certain calamitous historical events and shifts in attitudes about comets correlate with bombardment by cometary debris. Some of the periods of cometary influx identified by

Clube and Napier coincide with the times of change of yugas, so there
may well be some connection.

Understanding the Precession of the Equinoxes

The completion of the phrase regarding the dual we discussed above
is shown below with an additional section highlighted:

> "the sun again with its planets and moons taking some star
> for its duel [sic] revolve round each other in about 24000
> years of our earth **which causes the backward movement
> of the equinoxal [sic] points round the Zodiac.**"

This "backward movement" is the well-known *precession of the equinoxes*; the slow westward rotation of the intersection of the plane of the
earth's orbit with the plane of the earth's equator. An imaginary great circle in the sky represents the earth's equator, another imaginary line called
the *ecliptic* traces the annual apparent path of the sun around the zodiac
representing the plane of the earth's orbit in space. The equatorial plane
is inclined 23½° to the ecliptic. The polar axis of the earth very slowly
sweeps out a cone in space centered on the perpendicular to the plane
of the earth's orbit (see *Figure 34*) This motion causes (in a geometrical
sense) the intersection of the equator and the ecliptic to move westward
one degree every 71 years—this is the *precession of the equinoxes*.

On March 21 and September 21, give or take a day, the sun crosses
these intersection points, marking the beginning of northern hemisphere and southern hemisphere spring respectively. If we could see
the stellar background of the sun on these days, we might notice that
each year the sun is a tiny bit farther west of its previous year's position
on the equinox.

What then *physically* causes this conical motion of the earth's axis of
rotation? Sri Yukteswar tells us that it is the result of the sun and the
star that the sun took for its dual rotating around each other. Here we
run into a direct conflict with scientific orthodoxy. Any basic astronomy textbook will inform you that it is the gravitational pull of primarily the moon, but partly also the sun, on the equatorial bulge of the
Earth that causes the precession of the equinoxes. The Sun and Moon
pull on the earth's bulge as though trying to correct its 23½° tilt to the

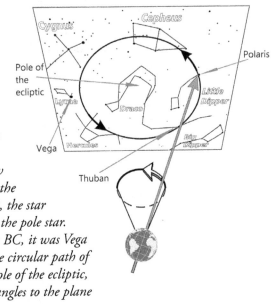

*Figure 34 — The change
in the pole star associated
with the precession of
the equinoxes. Whichever
star, if any, is in line
with the polar axis of
the earth is the pole star
of the age. As the earth's
axis precesses, the direction
of the pole moves around
a circle in the sky. Just now
it points to Polaris, but to the
ancient Egyptians c. 2450, the star
Thuban (α Draconis) was the pole star.
In the twelfth millennium BC, it was Vega
(α Lyrae). The center of the circular path of
the pole in the sky is the pole of the ecliptic,
i.e. the direction at right angles to the plane
of the earth's orbit.*

ecliptic plane. The textbook will tell you that this situation is physically analogous, though opposite in direction, to the familiar wobbling effect of gravity on a tilted spinning top or gyroscope. Astronomers have built a highly refined model based on this idea which goes all the way back to Isaac Newton. They see no reason to question its fundamental assumptions.[2]

On the other hand, Walter Cruttenden, author of *Lost Star of Myth and Time*, suggests that if the sun does have a companion, the orbital rotation of the solar system would *itself* cause what we observe as the precession of the equinox, and that there is no need to evoke the influence of the sun and moon on the equatorial bulge to account for all of the observed precession. He calls attention to various phenomena internal to the solar system, including certain timings of the moon and annual meteor showers that behave as he would expect if this were the case and not as the orthodox model would lead one to expect.

He correctly points out that there are plenty of anomalies in physics and astronomy that could spark fundamental shifts in our understanding, perhaps leading to a verification of Sri Yukteswar's model of the cause of the precession of the equinoxes. Walter Cruttenden has been very persistent in encouraging scientists to reexamine some of their assumptions around the precession of the equinoxes and the possibility of a binary companion to the sun. He organizes an annual Conference on Precession and Ancient Knowledge (CPAK) to air viewpoints on alternative history and alternative science that bear a relationship to the yuga cycles.[3]

Until more evidence is found, however, either direct or indirect, we can only speculate on the "dual" being a binary companion to the sun. At some point in the future some combination of new celestial observations and new physics theories could provide an astronomically clear explanation of Sri Yukteswar's description of the way in which stellar motions underlie the cycle of yugas.

Oriental Astronomy and the Dual

Meanwhile there is another way to explain Sri Yukteswar's description of the cycle of the yugas that draws as much on astrology, or "oriental astronomy," as it does on astronomy. Sri Yukteswar was an astrologer of great renown. It would not be surprising to find that he used the same understanding of astronomy current in India at the time of his writing *The Holy Science* for both his astrology and for his description in *The Holy Science*.

A close reading of the quotation from *The Holy Science* that began this appendix reveals that Sri Yukteswar is attributing his explanation to the teachings of "oriental astronomy." He begins the quoted passage with, "We learn from the oriental astronomy that ..." Two sentences later he reiterates the point, with "It informs us further ..." The word "oriental" in Sri Yukteswar's day simply meant "Eastern" (relative to Europe), so we can take it to mean a traditional Indian astronomy passed down perhaps from Vedic times.

The Śatapatha Brahmana is an ancient Vedic text composed sometime during the descending Dwapara Yuga that is considered by some to be second in importance only to the Rig Veda. It appears to be a source, of at least part, of what Sri Yukteswar means by the teachings of oriental astronomy. As we enter the ascending Dwapara Yuga, Sri Yukteswar is reintroducing knowledge from the previous Dwapara Yuga.

In her 1996 book, *Ancient Indian Insights and Modern Science*, Kalpana Paranjape of the Bhandarkar Oriental Research Institute, relates a description of the universe according to the Śatapatha Brahmana as interpreted by the highly regarded scholar Pt. Motilal Sharma of Jaipur.[4] Translating Pt. Motilal Sharma's Hindi text, she writes:

> Whole universe orbits around Svayambhu which is steady. Its field of influence is called paramakasa, which covers all the space in the universe. *Paramesthi* (galaxies) moves around Svayambhu and its field of influence is called mahasamudra. Its orbital path is called rajovrtta. The sun moves around paramesthi in 25 thousand years on an orbital path called ayanavrtta. Its field of influence is called Samvatsara. The earth moves around the sun in one year on an orbital path called krantivrtta and its field of influence is called ilanda. The moon orbits round the earth in one month on an orbital path called daksavrtta. The sun and the earth also move around themselves about their respective axes.

This description matches up with Sri Yukteswar's very well if we identify Paramesthi with the dual of the sun, and Svayambhu with the grand center. Although Pt. Motilal Sharma identifies Paramesthi with the *galaxy*, if we examine the word carefully we will see that it admits of a different interpretation. The sun's 25,000-year path about *paramesthi* is called *ayanavrtta*. The word *ayana* refers to precession, so ayanavrtta is the westward motion of the equinoctial point around the ecliptic. *Param-* means highest or superior, while *-sthi* means a place or location. To an astronomer, the highest point above the ecliptic is the ecliptic pole. On a suitably oriented star map, the ecliptic pole is the center of the circle representing the ecliptic, just as the celestial pole marked by Polaris is the center of the circle representing the equator and as the zenith is the center of the circle of the horizon or the highest point above the horizon. In the Purana literature of India, the *height* of a planet above the ecliptic is known to mean the *angular* height.[5] So the *highest* or superior point relative to the ecliptic must be the ecliptic pole. On the chart below (see *Figure 35*) *Paramesthi* (the ecliptic pole) is shown as the center of the circle of *ayanavrtta* (the ecliptic) just as it would be on a star map.

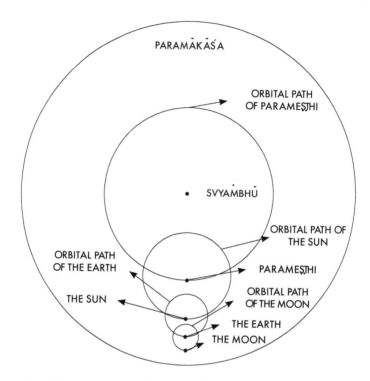

Figure 35 — *The universe according to the Śatapatha Brahmana. (Reproduced from K.M. Paranjape Ancient Indian Insights and Modern Science by permission.)*

In the language of modern astronomy it is the relative location (direction in space) of the pole of the ecliptic and the pole of the equator that determines the location of the vernal and autumnal equinoxes. The change in the location of the crossing points of the ecliptic and the equator, i.e. *the precession of the equinoxes*, is caused (geometrically speaking) by the slow rotation of the two poles about each other. The pole of the ecliptic makes a small circle in the sky with a period of roughly 40,000 years, while the pole of the equator (the rotation axis of the earth) makes a wide circle with a period of about 25,700 years.

By identifying Sri Yukteswar's "dual" with the Parmesthi of the Śatapatha Brahmana, and Parmesthi with modern astronomy's pole of the ecliptic all three descriptions of precession — that of Sri Yukteswar, Śatapatha Brahmana and modern astronomy — are reconciled.

If you have read *The Holy Science* quotation carefully, you should be objecting: "But he says the sun and the planets and their moons move, not just the earth." This is easily understood from the standpoint of the ancient almanac maker who serves the practice of astrology. As Sri Yukteswar was more of an astrologer than an astronomer, this is an appropriate perspective. For astrological purposes it is the location of a celestial body along the ecliptic that is of primary concern, and to account for the precession of the equinoxes the almanac maker would simply add a little correction to the positions he computed for all the planets together.

The "Dual" Revisited

Now we have created another mystery: why would Sri Yukteswar have used the word "dual" instead of the more conventional term "pole"? The word "dual" as a noun is not to be found in any dictionary of the English language, but it does have a specialized meaning in mathematics.[6] The dual of a theorem in plane geometry is obtained by exchanging the roles of points and lines. For example, the theorem that two points are connected by only one straight line has as its dual the theorem that two straight lines cross at only one point. In solid geometry a cube having 6 faces and 8 corners has as its dual, by the exchange of faces and corners, an octahedron which has 8 faces and 6 corners. (Lines joining the center points of each adjacent face of the cube create the octahedron.) The application of this mathematical principle of duality to a specialty of mathematics called *projective geometry* is particularly relevant since astronomical calculations can be based on the projection of the celestial sphere on a plane surface. In that case it is correct terminology to consider that the *dual* of a great circle (such as the ecliptic on the celestial sphere) is the pair of points at right angles to the plane of that circle — in other words, the *poles*.

It would have been perfectly accurate for Sri Yukteswar to identify the direction of the axis of the rotation that gives rise to the precession of the equinoxes in this way. This principle of duality was first enunciated in 1826. Sri Yukteswar wrote *The Holy Science* 68 years later than this, so there was plenty of time for this idea to get into the textbooks of his day. He is said to have audited university courses, and we can imagine that given his interest in astronomy and astrology he would have been aware of geometric concepts in some depth.

In 1971 the mathematician Olive Whicher published *Projective Geometry: Creative Polarities in Space and Time*. She writes about the relations between points and lines at length in terms of duals, but when she comes to discuss the relation between points and planes, she chooses to substitute the term *pole* for *dual* to avoid confusion, further confirming that the terms are interchangeable.[7]

A look at the history of this concept opens up more possibilities for understanding why Sri Yukteswar would have chosen such an obscure terminology. At about the time the French mathematician René Descartes (1596–1650) was developing *analytical* geometry, the sort now taught in schools, his friend, another French mathematician Girard Desargues (1591–1661), was developing *projective synthetic* geometry. Projective geometry is considered by some to be the most pure and general expression of geometry from which the more familiar geometries can be derived, but it has been generally ignored.

It was a popular topic in mathematics in the early nineteenth century, but fell out of fashion toward the end of the century. There has been renewed interest lately as it has application in computer graphics.

It is interesting to note that *analysis* is more characteristic of the thinking in Kali Yuga as it deals with physical measures, while *synthesis* is more in line with the thinking of Dwapara Yuga, being more concerned with relationships independently of scale or measure. In fact, Olive Whicher's book is totally lacking in abstract mathematical notation—the concepts are communicated in words and pictorial examples only. The related buzzwords today include *holistic* and *holographic*. This leads us to another aspect of *dual* that might have justified Sri Yukteswar's use of the term. The Austrian philosopher and mystic Rudolf Steiner (1861–1925) was very much inspired by projective geometry. Mathematician Olive Whicher quotes Rudolf Steiner in her book:

> It was through synthetic geometry mainly that I brought myself to the point of consciousness concerning the process of clairvoyance.... through it one can become clear about the process of spiritual perception.... He who approaches mathematics in the right spirit will find that it can be

regarded as a model, a pattern of the way in which super-sensible perception may be achieved. For mathematics is simply the first stage of supersensible perception.[8]

Steiner's concept, mathematically developed further by Olive Whicher and George Adams, proposed an etheric or "counterspace" in which the points and planes of our normal physical space are interchanged in their function. It would be from this space, the *dual* of the space of our normal perceptions, that extrasensory perceptions arise, transcending the limitations of distance and time. This would be a space properly described as "center everywhere, circumference nowhere."

A recent article in the prestigious journal *Science* employed the term in much the same way.[9] It discusses a development in string theory mathematics called holographic correspondence in which string theory of 10 or 11 dimensions can be equated to a theory of the 4-dimensional space-time world of our experience. The one formulation, being the dual of the other allows computations that would be impossible in one description to be performed practically in its dual description.

Could it be that Sri Yukteswar employed what appears to us as an obscure term specifically in order to direct our thinking toward a more expansive concept of space and time appropriate to Dwapara Yuga?

Conclusion

Whether the star that the sun chose for its dual turns out to be a physical object with which our solar system is doing a cosmic dance, or simply a colorful way of referring to the pole of the ecliptic, or something else we haven't even dreamed of, we are left with the mystery of how changes in our cosmic environment could influence our consciousness in such a systematic way as to further our spiritual evolution over the many centuries of the precessional cycle. Clues from the past are showing us the significance of modern research results, while advances in science are helping us recognize the truths hiding in ancient texts. But if we ignore the likelihood that the ancients actually understood better than we do, then we will lose even the benefit of guidance those clues can give us. We hope that the bits and pieces we have assembled here will contribute in some way to a deeper understanding of the subject.

Notes

Chapter 1—The Cycle of the Yugas

1. Sri Yukteswar 1920, *vii–ix*.
2. Ibid, *vii–ix*.
3. Ibid, *vii–ix*.
4. Ibid, *vi*.
5. Ibid, *vi*.
6. Ibid, *vi*.
7. Ibid, *vi*.
8. Ibid, *vi*.
9. Guthrie 1957, 71.

Chapter 2—The Kali Yugas

1. This list was compiled primarily from Jalandris' *Remnants of the Lost: Three Billion Years of Man's Unknown History*, pp. 5–7. Portions were also taken from Luciano Canfora's *The Vanished Library: A Wonder of the Ancient World*.
2. Sri Yukteswar 1920, *xiv*.

Chapter 3—Ascending Dwapara Yuga—The Energy Age

1. Sri Yukteswar 1920, *xiv*.
2. Yogananda 1946/2004, 167.
3. Yeo et al. 2005, 3235.
4. Yogananda 1946/2004, 154.

Chapter 4—Ascending Dwapara Yuga—Currents

1. Sri Yukteswar 1920, *xiv*.
2. Bierce's 1911 classic is available in many print and internet editions, including Project Gutenberg: www.gutenberg.org/ebooks/972.
3. Yogananda 1986, 59–71.

Chapter 6—Ascending Dwapara Yuga—The Future

1. Walters 1992, 25.

2. Swanson 2003, 31.
3. Ibid, 32.

Chapter 7—Ascending Treta Yuga—The Age of Thought

1. Sri Yukteswar 1920, *xix*.
2. Yogananda 1946/2004, 168.
3. Talbot 1991, 96–97.
4. Yogananda 1946/2004, 401.
5. Ibid, 344.
6. Sri Yukteswar 1920, *ix*.
7. Yogananda 2008, 90.
8. Yogananda 1946/2004, 168.

Chapter 8—Ascending Treta Yuga—Trends

1. Sri Yukteswar 1920, *ix*.
2. Yogananda 2008, 90.

Chapter 9—Ascending Satya Yuga

1. Sri Yukteswar 1920, *ix*.
2. Yogananda 1946/2004, 148.
3. Ibid, 143–44.
4. Ibid, 117.
5. Ibid, 147.
6. Ibid, 201.

Chapter 10—Descending Satya Yuga—Three Misconceptions

1. Piperno et al. 2004, 670–73.
2. Crabtree and Campana and Ryan 1989, 25.
3. Settegast 1990, 1–2.
4. Biesalski 2002, 1270–78.
5. Reprinted with the permission of The Free Press, a Division of Simon & Schuster, Inc., from THE LOST CIVILIZATIONS OF THE STONE AGE by Richard Rudgley. Copyright © 1999 by Richard Rudgley. All rights reserved.
6. Archeo News 2006.
7. Heinberg 1989, *xxvii*.

Chapter 11—Descending Satya Yuga—Paradise

1. Heinberg 1989, 17.
2. Campbell et al. 1988.

Chapter 13—Descending Treta Yuga—The Vedas

1. Coppa et al. 2006, 755–56.
2. Balakrishna 2006.
3. Aurobindo 1920.

Chapter 14—Descending Treta Yuga—The Conscious Matrix

1. Aurobindo 1920.
2. Kriyananda 1967, 12–15.
3. Yogananda 1946/2004, 162–63.

Chapter 15—Descending Treta Yuga—Unexplained Knowledge

1. Balter 2007, 1830–35
2. Larson et al. 2005, 1618.
3. Palmer 2009.

Chapter 16—Descending Dwapara Yuga—The Great Pyramid

1. Dunn 1998, 66.
2. Koch 1999.
3. Schoch and Stille 1997.

Chapter 17—Descending Dwapara Yuga—Energy Awareness

1. Temple 2009.
2. http://www.harappa.com/indus3/218.html
3. Cowen 2005.
4. Settegast 1990, 211–15.

Chapter 18—Descending Dwapara Yuga—Trends

1. Thorndike 1923, 7.

Chapter 19—Descending Dwapara Yuga—Decline & Transition

1. Naydler 2009, 202.
2. Roberts 2000, 13.

Chapter 20—Previous Yuga Cycles

1. Keim 2008.
2. Black 2010.
3. Ravilious 2008.
4. Cremo and Thompson 1993, 801.
5. The Above Network 2005.
6. Noorbergen 1977, 42.
7. Cremo 2008, 19.
8. Cremo and Thompson 1993, 94–100.

Chapter 21—The Tipping Point

1. Tankersley 2008.

Appendix

1. Sri Yukteswar 1920, *vi–vii*.
2. Etz 1999.
3. See www.cpakonline.com
4. Paranjape 1996, 36.
5. Thompson 2000, 223.
6. The word also has a specialized meaning in linguistics where it refers to numbers, as in singular, dual, and plural.
7. Whicher 1971, 220.
8. Ibid, 22. Quoted from Rudolf Steiner: Die Bedeutung der Anthroposopie im Geistesleben der Gegenwart (6 lectures 1922), Dodrnach 1957.
9. Hartnoll 2008, 1639–40.

—

Bibliography

"Ancient Tile Floor Found in Oklahoma." The Above Network, June 27, 2005. http://www.abovetopsecret.com/forum/thread149991/pg1 (accessed August, 2008).

Aurobindo, Sri. "An Essay on the Vedas." 1920. http://www.hinduwebsite.com/divinelife/auro/auro_veda.asp (accessed June, 2009).

Balakrishna, S. "Atri's Solar Eclipse." *Vedic Astronomy*, 2006. http://www.vedicastronomy.net/deltat.htm (accessed June, 2009).

Balter, Michael. "Seeking Agriculture's Ancient Roots." *Science* 316, no. 5833 (June 29, 2007): 1830–35.

Bauval, Robert. *The Egypt Code*. London: Century, 2006.

Bauval, Robert, and Adrian Gilbert. *The Orion Mystery: Unlocking the Secrets of the Pyramids*. New York: Crown, 1994.

Bierce, Ambrose. *The Devil's Dictionary*. New York: Dover, 1911/1958.

Biesalski, H. K. "Meat Consumption: Evolution and Progress: Meeting held on 18th Oct. 2000, Hamburg, Germany." *European Journal of Clinical Nutrition* 56, no. 12 (December 2002): 1270–78.

Black, Gemma. "'Uranium-eating' bacteria to clean-up radioactive sites." Cosmos Online, March 30, 2010. http://www.cosmosmagazine.com/news/3372/uranium-eating-bacteria-clean-radioactive-sites (April, 2010).

Brier, Bob, and Jean-Pierre Houdin. *The Secret of the Great Pyramid: How One Man's Obsession Led to the Solution of Ancient Egypt's Greatest Mystery*. New York: HarperCollins, 2008.

Brunton, Paul. *A Search in Secret Egypt*. Burdett, NY: Larson Publications (for the Paul Brunton Philosophic Foundation), 2007.

Campbell, Joseph, Bill D. Moyers, Catherine Tatge, and David Grubin. *Joseph Campbell and the Power of Myth with Bill Moyers*. New York: Mystic Fire Video in association with Parabola magazine, 1988.

Canfora, Luciano. *The Vanished Library: A Wonder of the Ancient World*. Berkeley, CA: University of California Press, 1990.

Clube, S. V. M., and Napier, William M. *The Cosmic Winter*. Oxford, UK: Basil Blackwell, 1990.

Coe, Michael D. *The Olmec World: Ritual and Rulership*. Princeton, NJ: Princeton University, 1996.

Coppa, A., L. Bondioli, A. Cucina, D. W. Frayer, C. Jarrige, J. F. Jarrige, G. Quivron, M. Rossi, M. Vidale, and R. Macchiarelli. "Palaeontology: Early Neolithic tradition of dentistry." *Nature* 440 (April 6, 2006): 755–56.

Cowen, Robert C. "The high tech of prehistory." The Christian Science Monitor, March 3, 2005. http://www.csmonitor.com/2005/0303/p16s01-stss.html (accessed October, 2009).

Crabtree, Pam J., Douglas V. Campana, and Kathleen Ryan. 1989. *Early Animal Domestication and its Cultural Context*. Philadelphia: MASCA, the University Museum of Archaeology and Anthropology, University of Pennsylvania, 1989.

Cremo, Michael A. "Forbidden Archeologist." *Atlantis Rising* 72 (November/December 2008): 19–21.

Cremo, Michael A., and Richard L. Thompson. *Forbidden Archeology: The Hidden History of the Human Race*. San Diego: Bhaktivedanta Institute, 1993.

Cruttenden, Walter. *Lost Star of Myth and Time*. Pittsburgh, PA: St. Lynn's Press, 2005.

de Santillana, Giorgio, and Hertha von Dechend. *Hamlet's Mill: An Essay on Myth and the Frame of Time*. Boston: Gambit, 1969.

Dunn, Christopher. T*he Giza Power Plant: Technologies of Ancient Egypt*. Santa Fe, NM: Bear and Co., 1998.

Etz, Donald V. "This Restless Globe." Astronomical Society of the Pacific, 1999. http://www.astrosociety.org/education/publications/tnl/45/globe1.html (accessed September 6, 2003).

Frawley, David. *Gods, Sages and Kings: Vedic Secrets of Ancient Civilization*. Salt Lake City, UT: Passage Press, 1991.

Gallwey, W. Timothy. *The Inner Game of Tennis*. New York: Random House, 1974.

Gardner, Howard. *Frames of Mind: The Theory of Multiple Intelligences*. New York: Basic Books, 1983.

Guthrie, William Keith Chambers. *In the Beginning: Some Greek Views on the Origins of Life and the Early State of Man*. London: Methuen, 1957.

Haich, Elisabeth. *Initiation*. Santa Fe, NM: Aurora Press, 2000.

Hancock, Graham. *Fingerprints of the Gods*. New York: Crown Publishers, 1995.

Hapgood, Charles H. *Maps of the Ancient Sea Kings: Evidence of Advanced Civilization in the Ice Age*. Philadelphia, PA: Chilton Books, 1966.

Harris, Hendon M. *The Asiatic Fathers of America*. Taitung, Taiwan: Harris, 1973.

Hartnoll, Sean. "Stringing Together a Solid State." *Science* 322 (December 12, 2008): 1639–40.

Haywood, John. *Historical Atlas of the Ancient World*. New York: Metro Books, 2002.

Heinberg, Richard. *Memories and Visions of Paradise: Exploring the Universal Myth of a Lost Golden Age*. Los Angeles: J. P. Tarcher, 1989.

Jalandris. *The Hall of Records: Hidden Secrets of the Pyramid and Sphinx*. San Francisco: Holistic Life Travels, 1980.

Jalandris. *Remnants of the Lost: Three Billion Years of Man's Unknown History*. San Francisco: Holistic Life Travels, 1981.

Kak, Subhash. *The Astronomical Code of the Rgveda*. New Delhi: Aditya Prakashan, 1994.

Keim, Brandon. "Teen Decomposes Plastic Bag in Three Months." Wired Online, May 23, 2008. http://www.wired.com/wiredscience/2008/05/teen-decomposes/ (accessed October, 2009).

Koch, David H., Pyramids Radiocarbon Project. "Dating the Pyramids." *Archaeology*, vol. 52 (September/October 1999).

Kriyananda, Swami. *India's Ancient Book of Prophecy*. Nevada City, CA: Ananda Publications, 1967.

Larson, Greger, Keith Dobney, Umberto Albarella, Meiying Fang, Elizabeth Matisoo-Smith, Judith Robins, Stewart Lowden, et al. "Worldwide Phylogeography of Wild Boar Reveals Multiple Centers of Pig Domestication." *Science* 307, no. 5715 (March 11, 2005): 1618.

Leininger, Bruce, Andrea Leininger, and Ken Gross. *Soul Survivor: The Reincarnation of a World War II Fighter Pilot*. New York: Grand Central Publishing, 2009.

Malkowski, Edward F. *When It Rained in Egypt: Breaking Into a New History*. Champaign, IL: Bits of Sunshine Publishing Co., 2004.

Malthus, Thomas R. *An Essay on the Principle of Population*. London: Electric Book Co., 1798/2001.

Merriam, John C. *Papers of John C. Merriam*. 1899. N.p.; n.d.

Naydler, Jeremy. *The Future of the Ancient World: Essays on the History of Consciousness*. Rochester, VT: Inner Traditions, 2009.

Noorbergen, Rene. *Secrets of the Lost Races: New Discoveries of Advanced Technology in Ancient Civilizations*. Indianapolis: The Bobbs-Merrill Co., 1977.

Pales, Léon, and Marie Tassin de Saint Péreuse. *Les Gravures de La Marche*. Bordeaux: Imprimeries Delmas, 1969.

Palmer, Jason. "'Oldest pottery' found in China." BBC News, June 1, 2009. http://news.bbc.co.uk/2/hi/sci/tech/8077168.stm (accessed November, 2009).

Paranjape, Kalpana M. *Ancient Indian Insights and Modern Science*. Bhandarkar Oriental Series, no. 29. Pune, India: Bhandarkar Oriental Research Institute, 1996.

Phillips, Stephen M. *Extra-Sensory Perception of Quarks*. Madras, India: Theosophical Publishing House, 1980.

Piperno, Delores R., et al. "Processing of Wild Cereal Grains in the Upper Palaeolithic Revealed by Starch Grain Analysis." *Nature* 430 (July 22, 2004): 670–73.

Ravilious, Kate. "Humans 80,000 Years Older Than Previously Thought?" National Geographic News, December 3, 2008. http://news.nationalgeographic.com/news/2008/12/081203-homo-sapien-missions.html (accessed November, 2009).

Roberts, J. A. G. *China: Prehistory to the Nineteenth Century: An Illustrated History*. Stroud: Sutton, 2000.

Rudgley, Richard. *The Lost Civilizations of the Stone Age*. New York: Free Press, 1999.

Schoch, Robert M., and Alexander Stille. "Dating the Sphinx." *New Yorker*, vol. 73 (April 14, 1997).

Schoch, Robert M., and Robert Aquinas McNally. *Pyramid Quest: Secrets of the Great Pyramid and the Dawn of Civilization.* New York: Jeremy P. Tarcher/Penguin, 2005.

Schreiber, Flora Rheta. *Sybil.* Chicago: Henry Regnery, 1973.

Schumacher, E. F. *Small is Beautiful: Economics As If People Mattered.* New York: Harper and Row, 1973.

Seal, Brajendranath. *The Positive Sciences of the Ancient Hindus.* London, New York [etc.]: Longmans, Green and Co, 1915.

Settegast, Mary. *Plato Prehistorian: 10,000 to 5,000 BC: Myth, Religion, Archaeology.* Hudson, NY: Lindisfarne Press, 1990.

Sidharth, B. G. *The Celestial Key to the Vedas: Discovering the Origins of the World's Oldest Civilization.* Rochester, VT: Inner Traditions, 1999.

Smyth, Charles Piazzi. *Our Inheritance in the Great Pyramid.* London: W. Isbister, 1874/1880.

"Snake carving in Botswana may be first sign of worship." Archaeo News, December 3, 2006. http://www.stonepages.com/news/archives/002172.html (accessed October, 2008).

Swanson, Claude. *The Synchronized Universe: New Science of the Paranormal.* Tucson, AZ: Poseidia Press, 2003.

Talbot, Michael. *The Holographic Universe.* New York: HarperCollins, 1991.

Tammet, Daniel. *Born On a Blue Day: Inside the Extraordinary Mind of an Autistic Savant: A Memoir.* New York: Free Press, 2007.

Tankersley, Cameron. "Satellites unearthing ancient Egyptian ruins." CNN Online, December 23, 2008. http://www.cnn.com/2008/TECH/science/12/23/satellites.archaeology.egypt/index.html (accessed November, 2009).

Temple, Robert K. G. *The Crystal Sun: Rediscovering a Lost Technology of the Ancient World.* London: Century, 2000.

———. "Forbidden Technology." 2009. http://www.robert-temple.com/articles/crystalSunFreemansonryToday.html (accessed October 6, 2009).

Thigpen, Corbett H., and Hervey M. Cleckley. *The Three Faces of Eve.* New York: McGraw-Hill, 1957.

Thom, A. "A Statistical Examination of the Megalithic Sites in Britain." *Journal of the Royal Statistical Society*, Series A (General) 118, part 3 (1955): 275–95.

Thompson, Richard L. *Mysteries of the Sacred Universe: The Cosmology of the Bhagavata Purana.* Alachua, FL: Govardhan Hill Publishers, 2000.

———. *Vedic Cosmography and Astronomy.* Los Angeles: Bhaktivedanta Book Trust, 1989.

Thorndike, Lynn. *A History of Magic and Experimental Science, Vol. 1.* New York: Columbia University Press, 1923.

Tilak, Bal Gangadhar. *The Orion: Or, Researches Into the Antiquity of the Vedas.* Poona, India: Ashtekar and Co., 1916.

Tompkins, Peter, and Livio Catullo Stecchini. *Secrets of the Great Pyramid.* New York: Harper and Row, 1971.

Walters, J. Donald. *Education for Life.* Commerce, CA: Ananda Publications, 1986.

———. *Money Magnetism: How to Attract What You Need When You Need It.* Commerce, CA: Crystal Clarity Publishers, 1992.

Waters, Frank, and Oswald White Bear Fredericks. *Book of the Hopi.* New York: Viking Press, 1963.

Watson, Lyall. *Supernature.* Garden City, NY: Anchor Press, 1973.

Wegener, Alfred. *The Origin of Continents and Oceans.* Translated by John George Anthony Skerl. London: Methuen and Co, 1924.

Weisman, Alan. *The World Without Us.* New York: Thomas Dunne Books/St. Martin's Press, 2007.

West, John Anthony. *Serpent in the Sky: The High Wisdom of Ancient Egypt.* New York: Harper and Row, 1979.

Whicher, Olive. *Projective Geometry: Creative Polarities in Space and Time.* London: Rudolf Steiner Press, 1971.

Yeo, Ye, *et al.* "Quantum Teleportation Via a Two-Qubit Heisenberg XY Chain—Effects of Anisotropy and Magnetic Field." *Journal of Physics A: Mathematical and General* 38, no. 14 (April 8, 2005): 3235–43.

Yogananda, Paramhansa. *Autobiography of a Yogi.* Commerce, CA: Crystal Clarity Publishers, 1946/2004.

————. *How To Be a Success*. Commerce, CA: Crystal Clarity Publishers, 2008.

Yogananda. *The Divine Romance*. Los Angeles: Self-Realization Fellowship, 1986.

Yukteswar, Swami Sri. *The Holy Science* (Kaivalya Darsanam). Kidderpore, India: Atul Chandra Chowdhary, Kidderpore Press, 1920.

Diagrams, Illustrations, and Images

Index

About the Authors

Joseph Selbie

Joseph studied ancient Western cultures at the University of Colorado and ancient Eastern cultures at UC Berkeley. He has had a keen interest in ancient history since grade school. He has taught and lectured on the principles of Eastern philosophy for over thirty years. Joseph lives with his wife at Ananda Village, a spiritual community in Northern California. His website is www.theyugas.com.

David Steinmetz

David's background includes 40 years of scientific work, including astronomy at the University of Arizona and optics at Xerox Palo Alto Research Center. Currently, he teaches about the yugas, ancient world cultures, astronomy, and physics at the Ananda College of Living Wisdom. He has been writing and lec-turing on the topic of the yugas for more than a decade. David lives with his wife at Ananda Village, a spiritual community in Northern California.

Swami Sri Yukteswar and Paramhansa Yogananda

About Swami Sri Yukteswar and Paramhansa Yogananda

Swami Sri Yukteswar (1855–1936) was a Hindu monk, an enlightened teacher and astronomer, and a man of profound wisdom. The guru of Paramhansa Yogananda, Sri Yukteswar's life story is chronicled in Yogananda's classic *Autobiography of a Yogi*—one of the most beautiful and glowing tributes to a spiritual mentor in the history of literature.Sri Yukteswar was the chief disciple of the great yoga master of Benares, Lahiri Mahasaya, who in turn was a disciple of the deathless Himalayan master, Mahavatar Babaji.In 1894, under the guidance of Babaji, Sri Yukteswar wrote *The Holy Science*, a deep and powerful book that, in a quiet and almost casual way, presents revolutionary teachings—including a precedence-shattering re-interpretation of the Hindu yuga cycle (ages of man). Sri Yukteswar gave instruction to his students in his hermitages in Serampore and Puri, India. Months after his passing, he rematerialized his physical form to speak with his disciple, Yogananda. The details of that extraordinary event and conversation are told in the chapter of Yogananda's autobiography titled "The Resurrection of Sri Yukteswar."

Paramhansa Yogananda was born in India in 1893, and was trained from his early years to bring India's ancient science of Self-realization to the West. In 1920 he moved to the United States to begin what was to develop into a worldwide work touching millions of lives. Americans were hungry for India's spiritual teachings, and for the liberating techniques of yoga. Yogananda's message to the West highlighted the unity of all religions, and the importance of love for God combined with scientific techniques of meditation. In 1946 he published what has become a spiritual classic and one of the best-loved books of the 20th century, *Autobiography of a Yogi*. In addition, Yogananda established headquarters for a worldwide work, wrote a number of books and study courses, gave lectures to thousands in most major cities across the United States, wrote music and poetry, and trained disciples. He was invited to the White House by Calvin Coolidge, and he initiated Mahatma Gandhi into Kriya Yoga, his most advanced technique of meditation.

Further Explorations

Autobiography of a Yogi

Paramhansa Yogananda

Autobiography of a Yogi is one of the world's most acclaimed spiritual classics, with millions of copies sold. Named one of the Best 100 Spiritual Books of the twentieth century, this book helped launch and continues to inspire a spiritual awakening throughout the Western world.

Yogananda was the first yoga master of India whose mission brought him to live and teach in the West. His firsthand account of his life experiences in India includes childhood revelations, stories of his visits to saints and masters, and long-secret teachings of yoga and self-realization that he first made available to the Western reader.

This reprint of the original 1946 edition is free from textual changes made after Yogananda's passing in 1952. This updated edition includes bonus materials: the last chapter that Yogananda wrote in 1951, also without posthumous changes, the eulogy Yogananda wrote for Gandhi, and a new foreword and afterword by Swami Kriyananda, one of Yogananda's close, direct disciples.

Also available in Spanish and Hindi from Crystal Clarity Publishers.

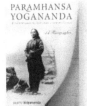

Paramhansa Yogananda
A Biography with Personal Reflections and Reminiscences
Swami Kriyananda

Paramhansa Yogananda's life was filled with astonishing accomplishments. And yet in his classic autobiography, he wrote more about the saints he'd met than about his own spiritual attainments. Yogananda's direct disciple, Swami Kriyananda, relates the untold story of this great master and world teacher: his teenage miracles, his challenges in coming to America, his national lecture campaigns, his struggles to fulfill his world-changing mission amid incomprehension and painful betrayals, and his ultimate triumphant achievement.

Kriyananda's subtle grasp of his guru's inner nature and outward mission reveals Yogananda's many-sided greatness. Includes many never-before-published anecdotes and an insider's view of the Master's last years.

Metaphysical Meditations
Paramhansa Yogananda

Metaphysical Meditations (1952 edition reprint) is a classic collection of meditation techniques, visualizations, affirmations, and prayers from the great yoga master, Paramhansa Yogananda. The meditations given are of three types: those spoken to the individual consciousness, prayers or demands addressed to God, and affirmations that bring us closer to the Divine.

Select a passage that meets your specific need and speak each word slowly and purposefully until you become absorbed in its inner meaning. At the bedside, by the meditation seat, or while traveling—one can choose no better companion than *Metaphysical Meditations*.

Scientific Healing Affirmations
Paramhansa Yogananda

This reprint of the original 1924 classic by Paramhansa Yogananda is a pioneering work in the fields of self-healing and self-transformation. He explains that words are crystallized thoughts and have life-changing power when spoken with conviction, concentration, willpower, and feeling. Yogananda offers far more than mere suggestions for achieving positive attitudes. He shows how to impregnate words with spiritual force to shift habitual thought patterns of the mind and create a new personal reality.

CRYSTAL CLARITY PUBLISHERS

If you enjoyed this title, Crystal Clarity Publishers invites you to deepen your spiritual life through many additional resources based on the teachings of Paramhansa Yogananda. We offer books, e-books, audiobooks, yoga and meditation videos, and a wide variety of inspirational and relaxation music composed by Swami Kriyananda.

See a listing of books, visit our secure website for a complete online catalog, or place an order for our products

crystalclarity.com
11123 Goodrich Blvd., Commerce, CA 90022
800.424.1055 | clarity@crystalclarity.com

ANANDA WORLDWIDE

Crystal Clarity Publishers is the publishing house of Ananda, a worldwide spiritual movement founded by Swami Kriyananda, a direct disciple of Paramhansa Yogananda. Ananda offers resources and support for your spiritual journey through meditation instruction, webinars, online virtual community, email, and chat.

Ananda has more than 150 centers and meditation groups in over 45 countries, offering group guided meditations, classes and teacher training in meditation and yoga, and many other resources.

In addition, Ananda has developed eight residential communities in the US, Europe, and India. Spiritual communities are places where people live together in a spirit of cooperation and friendship, dedicated to a common goal. Spirituality is practiced in all areas of daily life: at school, at work, or in the home. Many Ananda communities offer internships during which one can stay and experience spiritual community firsthand.

For more information about Ananda communities or meditation groups near you, please visit **ananda.org** or call 530.478.7560.

The Expanding Light Retreat

The Expanding Light is the largest retreat center in the world to share exclusively the teachings of Paramhansa Yogananda. Situated in the Ananda Village community near Nevada City, California, the center offers the opportunity to experience spiritual life in a contemporary ashram setting. The varied, year-round schedule of classes and programs on yoga, meditation, and spiritual practice includes Karma Yoga, personal retreat, spiritual travel, and online learning. Large groups are welcome.

The Ananda School of Yoga & Meditation offers certified yoga, yoga therapist, spiritual counselor, and meditation teacher trainings.

The teaching staff has years of experience practicing Kriya Yoga meditation and all aspects of Paramhansa Yogananda's teachings. You may come for a relaxed personal renewal, participating in ongoing activities as much or as little as you wish. The serene mountain setting, supportive staff, and delicious vegetarian meals provide an ideal environment for a truly meaningful stay, be it a brief respite or an extended spiritual vacation.

For more information, please visit **expandinglight.org** or call 800.346.5350.

Ananda Meditation Retreat

Set amidst seventy-two acres of beautiful meditation gardens and wild forest in Northern California's Sierra foothills, the Ananda Meditation Retreat is an ideal setting for a rejuvenating, inner experience.

The Meditation Retreat has been a place of deep meditation and sincere devotion for over fifty years. Long before that, the Native American Maidu tribe held this to be sacred land. The beauty and presence of the Divine are tangibly felt by all who visit here.

Studies show that being in nature and using techniques such as forest bathing can significantly reduce stress and blood pressure while strengthening your immune system, concentration, and level of happiness. The Meditation Retreat is the perfect place for quiet immersion in nature.

Plan a personal retreat, enjoy one of the guided retreats, or choose from a variety of programs led by the caring and joyful staff.

For more information or to place your reservation, please call 530.478.7557 visit **meditationretreat.org**, or email **meditationretreat@ananda.org**.